SHAPING A MONASTIC IDENTITY

A VOLUME IN THE SERIES

Conjunctions of Religion and Power in the Medieval Past

EDITED BY BARBARA H. ROSENWEIN

A full list of titles in the series appears at the end of the book.

SHAPING A MONASTIC IDENTITY

Liturgy & History at the Imperial Abbey of Farfa, 1000–1125

SUSAN BOYNTON

Cornell University Press ITHACA & LONDON

Publication of this book was made possible, in part, with the generous support of the Dragan Plamenac Publication Endowment Fund of the American Musicological Society.

First published 2006 by Cornell University Press

Printed in the United States of America

Library of Congress Cataloging-in-Publication Data

Boynton, Susan, 1966–
    Shaping a monastic identity : liturgy and history at the imperial Abbey of Farfa, 1000–1125 / Susan Boynton.
        p. cm. — (Conjunctions of religion and power in the medieval past)
    Includes bibliographical references and index.
    ISBN-13: 978-0-8014-4381-7 (cloth : alk. paper)
    ISBN-10: 0-8014-4381-4 (cloth : alk. paper)
    1. Abbey of Farfa—History.   2. Benedictines—Italy—Farfa—Liturgy—History.   3. Monasticism and religious orders—Italy—Farfa—History—Middle Ages, 600–1500.   4. Church music—Italy—Farfa.   5. Farfa (Italy)—Church history.   I. Title.   II. Series: Conjunctions of religion & power in the medieval past.
    BX2624.F3B69 2006
    271'.1045624—dc22

                                                                2005017718

Cloth printing   10 9 8 7 6 5 4 3 2 1

CONTENTS

TABLES, MAP, FIGURES, AND EXAMPLES

ACKNOWLEDGMENTS

The research for this book was supported by a National Endowment for the Humanities Postdoctoral Rome Prize Fellowship at the American Academy in Rome (1998–99) and an Italian Fulbright Travel Award. The writing was completed during a junior faculty leave granted by Columbia University in 2003–4 and a stay at the American Academy in Rome as a visiting scholar in 2003. I am extremely grateful for insightful comments on the entire manuscript by Barbara Rosenwein, Brenda Bolton, Louis Hamilton, an anonymous reader for Cornell University Press, Jennifer Harris, and Andrea Kirsh. For access to the collections at Farfa and for many kindnesses over the years, I am grateful to the archivist at Farfa, Lucia de Miglio, and the director of the library, Massimo Lapponi, as well as to Claudio Piccione, Patrizia Lombardozzi, and Gianni D'Andrea. Charles McClendon has encouraged me from the outset of the project and has repeatedly offered invaluable advice and essential comments. Isabelle Cochelin guided me through the history of Cluny and its customaries, turned her sharp eye on manuscripts in Rome, and shared a memorable trip to Farfa in a truck generously loaned by Lisa Fentress, who has been an invaluable source of information and a role model for interdisciplinary research. Dominique Iogna-Prat has supported my work both by offering valuable commentary and by inviting me to speak at Cluny in 1999 on the relationship between Cluny and Farfa, and to co-organize, with Isabelle Cochelin, a conference on the Cluniac customaries at the Centre d'études médiévales in Auxerre in 2002. Kristina Krüger shared unpublished studies and answered many questions. Lori Kruckenberg offered essential comments and bibliographic suggestions. I am grateful to Jan Ziolkowski and Eckehard Simon for the opportunity to speak to the Harvard Medieval Seminar, and to Nils Holger Petersen for several invitations to the University of Copenhagen's Center for the Study of the Cultural Heritage of Medieval Rituals. Paola Supino Martini provided paleographical help and Fulbright sponsorship in Rome in 1998–99; I regret that her untimely death prevented me from showing her the final results of my work.

Jane Huber expertly produced the musical examples. Maryam Moshaver edited the final version of the book with extraordinary insight and enthusiasm. Robert Somerville gave me crucial bibliographic references and explained their context. Constancio del Alamo and Elizabeth Valdez del Alamo generously provided bibliographic references and helped me gain access to libraries in Spain. Ange Romeo-Hall saw the book through production with inexhaustible patience. Stuart and Alice Boynton provided professional editing and enthusiasm; Robert Boynton and Barbara Boynton also offered encouragement throughout. For his innumerable contributions to the completion of this project I am indebted above all to Jens Ulff-Møller, photographer, scanner, translator, and chauffeur extraordinaire.

AASS   *Acta sanctorum quotquot toto orbe coluntur.* Ed. Joannes Bollandus and others. 69 vols. Antwerp: Victor Palme, 1643–1940.

AH   *Analecta hymnica medii aeui.* Ed. Guido Maria Dreves and others. 55 vols. Leipzig: O. R. Reisland, 1886–1922.

BAV   Biblioteca Apostolica Vaticana, Vatican City.

BHL   *Bibliotheca hagiographica Latina.* Ed. Society of Bollandists. 2 vols. and supplement. Brussels: Société des Bollandistes, 1898–1901.

BV   Biblioteca Vallicelliana, Rome.

BN   Biblioteca Nacional, Madrid.

BN   Biblioteca Nazionale, Rome.

BNF   Bibliothèque Nationale de France, Paris.

CAO   *Corpus antiphonalium officii.* Ed. Réné-Jean Hesbert. 6 vols. Rome: Herder, 1968–79.

CCM   *Corpus consuetudinum monasticarum.* Siegburg: Franz Schmitt, 1963–.

CCCM   *Corpus Christianorum, continuatio mediaeualis.* Turnhout: Brepols, 1971–.

CCSL   *Corpus Christianorum, series Latina.* Turnhout: Brepols, 1954–.

CLCLT   *Cetedoc Library of Christian Latin Texts.* Release 3 (*CLCLT*-3). 3 CDs. Turnhout: Brepols, 2003.

CF   Gregory of Catino. *Il Chronicon Farfense di Gregorio di Catino.* Ed. Ugo Balzani. 2 vols. Fonti per la Storia d'Italia, 33–34. Rome: Istituto Storico Italiano, 1903.

CO   *Corpus orationum.* Ed. Eugene Moeller and Jean-Marie Clément, completed by Bertrand Coppieters 't Wallant. 13 vols. *CCSL* 160. Turnhout: Brepols, 1993–2003.

CSEL   *Corpus scriptorium ecclesiasticorum Latinorum.* 95 vols. Vienna: Tempsky, 1866–.

GS   *Le sacramentaire grégorien.* Ed. Jean Deshusses. 3rd rev. ed. 3 vols. Fribourg: Editions universitaires, 1979–92.

LT   *Liber tramitis aeui Odilonis abbatis* Ed. Peter Dinter. *CCM* 10. Siegburg: Franz Schmitt, 1980.

MGH   *Monumenta Germaniae Historica.* Berlin: Weidmann, 1877–.

PL   *Patrologiae cursus completus, series Latina.* Ed. Jacques-Paul Migne. 221 vols. Paris: Migne, 1844–66.

RF   Gregory of Catino. *Il Regesto di Farfa compilato da Gregorio di Catino.* Ed. Ignazio Giorgi and Ugo Balzani. 5 vols. Rome: Società Romana di Storia Patria, 1883–1914.

SHAPING A MONASTIC IDENTITY

t he medieval abbey of Farfa, situated high in the Sabine hills off the via Salaria about thirty miles north of Rome, forms the center of a quiet village surrounded by vineyards, olive groves, and verdant farmland. Although the Benedictine community that resides there today is small, in the central Middle Ages Farfa was one of the most powerful monastic institutions in central Italy. An imperial abbey independent of the popes and local bishops, it possessed extensive landholdings and a strategic position overlooking the valleys on the way to Rome.[1] The abbey enjoyed an unusually privileged position from its founding in 705 until 1122, when it began to come under increasing papal control as a result of the Concordat of Worms. Historians have attributed Farfa's exceptional importance to the political diligence of its abbots. These enterprising men pursued astute strategies of land management and repeatedly solicited confirmations of the monastery's property and privileges from the Lombard, Frankish, Carolingian, Ottonian, and Salian rulers to whom the abbey was successively subject. In the eleventh and early twelfth centuries, heightened prosperity, assisted by imperial patronage and the stability brought about by several lengthy abbacies, fostered a significant renewal in the arts and letters. The subject of this book is this period of Farfa's history as viewed through the meticulous records of its properties, the narratives of its political affiliations and internal intrigues, the evidence preserved in its material culture and architecture, and, especially, the abbey's music and liturgy as reflected in the manuscripts produced there. These records of musical and liturgical performance shed light not only on the community's daily and yearly ritual cycles but also on its networks of power and its modes of expressing and consolidating its multiple identities.

Architecture, wall painting, and book production in the eleventh and early twelfth centuries reflect the broad geographic range of the abbey's associations and patronage. After the Cluniac reform at the beginning of the eleventh cen-

---

1. Farfa is located in the Diocese of the Sabina, whose history is not well documented before the eleventh century; see Gams, *Series episcoporum*, 12; Leggio, "L'abbazia di Farfa," 164–65. For general histories of Farfa see Schuster, *L'imperiale abbazia di Farfa;* and Stroll, *The Medieval Abbey;* the latter focuses primarily on the political history of the abbey in the eleventh and twelfth centuries.

tury, subsequent decades saw the construction of the Romanesque abbey church (consecrated by Pope Nicholas II in 1060) and the erection of the bell tower. Decorated with vivid frescoes on its interior walls, the tower is an early central-Italian example of a structural type seen in the north of Italy and in the monasteries of the Ottonian Empire.[2] Manuscripts copied in the monastic scriptorium show the fusion of a central Italian visual vocabulary and a distinctive style of script with influences from both southern Italy and the Germanic lands to the north.[3] Important evidence of the cultural and political relationships between Farfa and other monastic institutions can be found in books produced at Farfa, such as the *Liber tramitis,* the first extensive document describing life at the abbey of Cluny, with which Farfa retained a close connection.[4] Networks of power and relationships of patronage are reflected in the *Register, Chronicle,* and other works compiled over decades by the monk Gregory of Catino (ca. 1060–1135), Farfa's prolific and long-lived historian.[5]

The creation and performance of liturgical music and texts also offer significant insights into the history of the monastery and the ideologies of its community.[6] Although historians, paleographers, art historians, and archeologists have long studied Farfa's cultural and historical legacy, few have made connections among the various forms of historical evidence available at Farfa. Privileging property and politics, studies of the abbey's history often omit the liturgy altogether;[7] yet inscribed in the daily performance of the liturgy lies a

2. For the architecture of the abbey church and references to publications resulting from the excavations at Farfa in 1978–85, see McClendon, *The Imperial Abbey;* and Gilkes and Mitchell, "The Early Medieval Church." Forthcoming in the final excavation report is McClendon's response to the study by Gilkes and Mitchell.

3. On connections between patronage and the arts at Farfa, see chap. 4.

4. On the *Liber tramitis,* see chap. 3.

5. Gregory's most important works are the Farfa *Register* (*Il Regesto di Farfa,* ed. Giorgi and Balzani) and the Farfa *Chronicle* (*Il Chronicon Farfense,* ed. Balzani), hereafter cited respectively as *RF* and *CF.* On his writings, see chap. 1.

6. The manuscripts produced and used at Farfa in the ninth through twelfth centuries and the works of Gregory of Catino constitute the principal sources employed in this book. For short descriptions of the liturgical manuscripts from Farfa used in this book, as well as bibliographical references, see appendix 1. Paleographical analyses of manuscripts produced at Farfa from the ninth century through the early twelfth century can be found in Supino Martini, *Roma.*

7. See Clark, "Monastic Economies?"; Drew, "Land Tenure and Social Status"; Ring, "The Lands of Farfa"; and Stroll, *The Medieval Abbey* (see also Boynton, Review of Mary Stroll).

perspective on monastic identity that is inaccessible to purely historical, political, and archeological narratives. Recent studies that attribute a political dimension to the Farfa liturgy tend to interpret the liturgy as a tool for displaying and maintaining power and thus overlook its central importance as a cultural practice. Although these studies reaffirm the importance of the liturgy as a source of information about Farfa's patronage, politics, and relations with other monasteries, they focus primarily on hagiographic texts, not on the full range of available evidence.[8] The liturgical manuscripts from Farfa, particularly their musical contents, are central materials in the abbey's cultural history.[9] Drawing on the music as well as the texts, this book reveals new connections between Farfa's liturgy, as preserved in its service books, and its history, as transmitted by narrative and archival sources. My central argument is that the manifold forms of corporate identity that existed within the monastic community at Farfa in the eleventh and twelfth centuries can be adequately perceived only by taking into consideration the centrality of liturgical performance in reflecting and shaping these identities. To understand the liturgy not just as product but also as practice and performance is to apprehend its full range of functions: praise, prayer, teaching, exegesis, expression of spiritual self-identification and affiliation, and much more besides.

The term *liturgy* here designates repeated sacred actions that have symbolic meaning, are performed primarily by the monks in the church and other spaces of the monastery, and have predetermined forms and structures which can be reconstructed, at least in part, with recourse to service books from the appropriate time and place. This definition distinguishes liturgy as a particular subset of the much broader and less clearly defined phenomenon of ritual.[10] Understood as practice, liturgy can be described as a living nexus, an "arena of intense communication of cultural values and the negotiation of power within social formations at given historical moments."[11] Life in a me-

8. See Longo, "Agiografia e identità monastica" and "Dialettiche agiografiche"; and Susi, "Strategie agiografiche altomedievali."

9. To date the only published studies by musicologists are Boe, "Music Notation"; and Boynton, "Eleventh-Century Continental Hymnaries," "Frammenti medievali," and "Liturgy and History." Schuster's 1909–10 studies of the liturgical books have never been superseded, but they deal with the texts alone. See Schuster, "De fastorum agiographico ordine," "Martyrologium Pharphense," and "Spigolature farfensi."

10. On definitions of ritual, see Bell, *Ritual: Perspectives and Dimensions* and *Ritual Theory.* For a critique of historians' use of narrative accounts of ritual, see Buc, *The Dangers of Ritual.*

11. Flanigan, Ashley, and Sheingorn, "Liturgy as Social Performance," 714.

dieval Benedictine monastery such as Farfa centered on the performance of the liturgy, which occupied the majority of the monks' waking hours. The services celebrated daily included (but were not limited to) the eight hours of the divine office as well as two masses, one sung by the community alone early in the morning and another High Mass later in the day at which outsiders could be present.[12] In the course of these ceremonies and other occasional ones the community sang together for several hours a day. Indeed, most liturgical texts were sung or chanted, resulting in a vivid soundscape of varied musical styles.

The liturgy at Farfa, like that of all medieval ecclesiastical institutions, included certain elements typical of its geographic area, some aspects particular to the abbey's own customs, and other components that were more universal. Local traditions were of profound importance in the medieval liturgy. Although one can discern characteristic features of regions defined by linguistic or political boundaries or ecclesiastical jurisdictions such as dioceses, each institution (collegiate church, parish church, cathedral, or monastery) had a distinctive profile that resulted from its own particular ceremonial traditions. Among the variable factors were the degree of solemnity accorded to feasts; the saints venerated in the calendar; the selection and ordering of certain chants, readings, and prayers; the repertories of sung poetry for the Mass and office (sequences, tropes, and hymns); and the itinerary of processions. Even minor details of text or melody could act as markers of traditions specific to an institution, differentiating one church from another even when both were located in the same city. It is no exaggeration to say that, for ecclesiastical institutions, liturgy and ritual formed the foundation of corporate identity.

Medieval commentators on the liturgy tell us that the act of singing itself was understood to create as much meaning as the words or accompanying gestures of worship.[13] The symbolic and salvific power of the monks' psalmody had inestimable significance in a culture that held up perpetual psalmody as an ideal—however remote—of monastic observance.[14] The model of ceaseless monastic singing was invoked in the earliest preserved document associated with Farfa, the privilege granted by Pope John VII in 705, which stated

12. Thorough accounts of the medieval monastic liturgy of the hours are *The Divine Office in the Latin Middle Ages;* and Tolhurst, *Introduction to the English Monastic Breviaries.*

13. See Ekenberg, *Cur Cantatur?* and Fassler, *Gothic Song* and "The Meaning of Entrance."

14. On the symbolism of the *laus perennis,* see Rosenwein, "Perennial Prayer at Agaune."

that the benefit of papal favor should be manifested by the observance of the monks, who should "persist day and night in the singing of hymns, psalms, and spiritual songs."[15] Similarly, in the tenth through twelfth centuries, donation charters from Farfa allude to the community's psalmody, which was thought to save the souls of benefactors.[16] This perceived spiritual power, a hallmark of medieval monasticism, helps us to understand the connections between the abbey and the communities around it.

In the discursive space of the medieval liturgy, the sacred was inseparable from the political, and the boundaries between insider and outsider were porous. As Barbara Rosenwein has shown in a study of Cluniac liturgy, a range of secular and sacred meanings informed ritual performance by monks who appeared cut off from the world even as their daily worship resonated with the concerns of their families of origin.[17] The focus of the present study on liturgical performance by the community at Farfa does not entirely ignore the lay benefactors who, although usually physically absent, were implicitly present through ritual commemoration. Indeed, one of the important functions of the medieval monastic liturgy was the remembering of friends and benefactors.[18]

The monks themselves embodied the connection between the monastery and the outside world. In the eleventh and twelfth centuries, many donors came from the same extended families as the monks, who were mainly from the region surrounding Farfa. Links between those within the abbey and their lay counterparts led not infrequently to tensions that could explode into open conflict. At stake in the clashes between Farfa and its adversaries were the most essential components of the monastery's identity: its property, its independence, and ultimately its patronage. These central concerns of the community are articulated throughout its early history and recounted in the *Chronicle* and the cartularies compiled by Gregory of Catino, in a career that spanned four decades, from 1092 to 1132.

According to Gregory, Farfa was founded in late antiquity when Lawrence, a Syrian ascetic, arrived in the Sabina accompanied by his sister Susanna. Lawrence became bishop of the Sabina but renounced the episcopate to live at

---

15. *RF* 2:24: "Iccirco uestra religio hanc apostolici privilegii tuitionem indeptam, fructuosum atque laudabile concessum beneficium demonstret. Ante omnia in psalmis et ymnis, et canticis spiritualibus, diebus ac noctibus permanentes" and see Rosenwein, *Negotiating Space,* 108.

16. On these documents, see chap. 4.

17. Rosenwein, "Feudal War and Monastic Peace."

18. Some of the many studies on this subject are Iogna-Prat, "The Dead"; McLaughlin, *Consorting with Saints;* and *Memoria,* ed. Schmid and Wollasch.

Farfa, where he built a church in honor of the Virgin Mary, John the Baptist, and John the Evangelist.[19] Gregory is almost the only source of information on the foundation of Farfa, and further facts about the historical identity of Lawrence remain elusive.[20] Abandoned during the Lombard invasions of the sixth and seventh centuries, the abbey was refounded at the beginning of the eighth century by Thomas of Maurienne, a priest from the Savoy. Beginning with this second foundation, the history of the abbey is more extensively documented. In 705 Faroald II, the Lombard duke of Spoleto, obtained from Pope John VII a privilege that acknowledged the patronage of the Lombard dukes but reserved for the popes the right to consecrate the abbots of Farfa.[21] This arrangement would change later in the century under Carolingian patronage of the abbey.

By the second half of the eighth century, the abbey had accumulated considerable landholdings through donations from the dukes of Spoleto and other members of the Lombard nobility. It now stood at the intersection of territories claimed or coveted by the papacy, the Duchy of Spoleto, and the Lombard and Frankish kingdoms.[22] A series of Frankish abbots strengthened the monastery's ties to the emerging Carolingian empire. Farfa was implicitly joined to the Frankish kingdom in 774, when Charlemagne declared himself king of the Lombards after defeating the Lombard king Desiderius at Pavia. Turning to Farfa's new royal patron in 775, Abbot Probatus requested from Charlemagne a confirmation of the abbey's special status. With this diploma, Farfa became the first monastery in Italy to which Charlemagne granted exemption from the local bishop's control and guaranteed free election of its abbots (subject to confirmation by the king).[23]

---

19. *CF* 1:125. The association of Eastern hermits with the origins of the abbey is supported by the existence, near Farfa, of a mountaintop hermitage inhabited in the sixth century; see Branciani, "Il monte S. Martino in Sabina," 55, 58–74, 91; and Leggio, "L'abbazia di Farfa," 171.

20. Leggio ("L'abbazia di Farfa," 69) proposes an identification of Lawrence as a bishop of the Sabina who was documented in 554. It is possible that the figure of Lawrence conflated two different saints, one of whom was an early bishop of Spoleto; see Gordini, "Lorenzo Illuminatore" and "Lorenzo, vescovo di Spoleto."

21. *RF* 2:23–25; *CF* 1:136; Jaffé, *Regesta*, 246; Kehr, *Italia pontificia* 1:59. See Rosenwein, *Negotiating Space*, 108.

22. On donations to Farfa in the eighth century, see Costambeys, "Piety, Property, and Power"; Felten, "Zur Geschichte der Klöster Farfa und S. Vincenzo," 3–23, 38–57; and Pohl-Resel, "Legal Practice and Ethnic Identity."

23. *Pippini, Carlomanni, Caroli Magni diplomata*, 141–42 (no. 98; May 24, 775); *RF*

Charlemagne's second diploma for Farfa, enacted five days later, stated that the abbey's immunity (*emunitas*) applied to all its holdings.[24] In this period, exemption from episcopal control and immunity from taxation or intervention by local royal agents were closely intertwined; both might be implied by the use of the word *immunity* in a charter.[25] These were the same rights given to the immune and exempt royal monasteries situated in the Frankish kingdom, such as the abbeys of Lérins, Agaune, and Luxeuil, all named explicitly in Charlemagne's first privilege. His second privilege of 775 likens Farfa's immunity to those of other monasteries within the Frankish kingdom and refers to Farfa itself as "within our kingdom, God willing" (*infra regna, deo propitio, nostra*).[26] Charlemagne showed further support for Farfa in a diploma of 776, which confirmed all the possessions that previous rulers had given the abbey.[27] In 781 he formally granted the Sabina to Pope Hadrian but never withdrew the privileges he had granted Farfa in 775; furthermore, he again affirmed his protection of the abbey in 803.[28] In practice, then, the pope had no jurisdiction over the abbey and its lands, as Thomas Noble has pointed out.[29] Decades later

---

2:108–9. The privilege of John VII (*RF* 2:24) had referred to the local bishop as the person most likely to confirm Farfa's newly elected abbots, dedicate its churches, and ordain its monks.

24. *Pippini, Carlomanni, Caroli Magni diplomata*, 142–43 (no. 99; May 29, 775); *RF* 2:107–8.

25. Rosenwein, *Negotiating Space*, 4. I am grateful to Barbara Rosenwein for pointing out this double meaning.

26. Noble (*The Republic of St. Peter*, 158) states that the phrase "just as the other monasteries that are seen to have been built in our kingdom" ("sicut et caetera monasteria, quae infra regna nostra constructa esse uidetur") must imply that Farfa was not in Charlemagne's kingdom, but that the phrase "monasterii sancte marie, infra regna, deo propitio, nostra" in the same diploma (*Pippini, Carlomanni, Caroli Magni diplomata*, 143; May 29, 775) suggests that Farfa's presence in the Lombard duchy of Spoleto, newly under Frankish rule, by extension placed it in the Frankish kingdom. Felten ("Farfa und S. Vincenzo," 15) interprets this phrase as evidence that Charlemagne did not intend to treat the duchy of Spoleto as belonging to the papal patrimony.

27. Noble, *The Republic of St. Peter*, 157–59; *Pippini, Carlomanni, Caroli Magni diplomata*, 156–57 (no. 111; June 9, 776); and *RF* 2:112–13. Charlemagne issued two further diplomas referring to specific property that had been donated by Hildebrand, the Lombard duke of Spoleto; see *Pippini, Carlomanni, Caroli Magni diplomata*, 198–99, 217–18 (nos. 146 and 160; August 18, 782 and March 28, 788); and *RF* 2:117–18, 124.

28. *Pippini, Carlomanni, Caroli Magni diplomata*, 267–68 (no. 199; June 13, 803); and *RF* 2:143–44.

29. Noble, *The Republic of St. Peter*, 158–59.

Emperor Lothar I explicitly exempted Farfa from papal control when he renewed the privileges of his predecessors in 840.[30] Clearly, the Carolingians, and later the Ottonians and Salians, viewed Farfa as part of the empire despite the abbey's location near Rome. The political ramifications of this status shaped the history of the abbey throughout the central Middle Ages.

In the ninth century, through the prestige of Carolingian patronage and the stewardship of effective abbots, Farfa became increasingly powerful. Its status was expressed by an opulent complex of monastic buildings that included guest quarters for the emperor and his entourage.[31] Imperial patronage also had other implications for the life of the community. In principle Farfa would have been expected to follow the Benedictine Rule after the 817 Council of Aachen, which promulgated observance of the rule in the Frankish kingdoms.[32] The Benedictine Rule is a set of regulations for life in a monastery; it became the most widely diffused text of this kind beginning in the ninth century.[33] The rule provides instructions for how monks are to be fed and clothed; it also describes the various administrative duties carried out by appointed members of the community. But we do not know when Farfa adopted the rule,[34]

30. *Lotharii I et Lotharii II diplomata*, 146–53 (no. 51; Dec. 15, 840); *RF* 2:233–38. This document describes the *tuitio* and *defensio* of Farfa by the Frankish kings, who continued the protection offered by the Lombards. It dwells at length on discussions between Abbot Ingoald of Farfa and papal legates regarding the abbey's relationship to the Roman church, stating that the pope acknowledged he had no jurisdiction there except the right to consecrate the abbot. This emphasis on Farfa's freedom from papal jurisdiction is absent, less than twenty years later, from the privilege of Louis II; see *Ludovici II diplomata*, 116–21 (December 1, 857 or 859); *RF* 3:1.

31. The buildings were described by Abbot Hugh in his *Destructio* and have partially been brought to light by excavations; see McClendon, *Imperial Abbey*, 64–75.

32. Diplomas for Farfa of Emperors Louis the Pious and Lothar refer to the observance of the Benedictine Rule (*CF* 1:176, 188, 206), perhaps prescriptively rather than descriptively. Although Charlemagne's first diploma for Farfa called for abbatial elections "according to the Rule of Benedict," during the early Middle Ages it was common for monasteries to draw on a combination of rules. The other Carolingian royal abbeys mentioned in the diploma of Charlemagne followed various rules, including those of Basil, Benedict, and Columban.

33. For a text of the rule with English translation and commentary, see *RB 1980*.

34. The privilege of John VII states only that the monks lived "according to the monastic discipline and rule handed down by the fathers" (*RF* 2:24: "iuxta monachicam disciplinam et regulam a patribus traditam"). Costambeys ("The Monastic Environment," 133–34) suggests that Farfa followed the Benedictine Rule as early as the eighth century, perhaps because an early account of the abbacy of the Anglo-Saxon Wicbert states that

and in any case the execution of the council's decisions varied from place to place, as did the text of the rule and its application in practice.[35]

Farfa's first golden age came to an end in 898 when, after seven years of resisting Arab raids, the monks fled north to dependencies in the Marches and the abbey was destroyed in their absence. After their return in the tenth century, internal divisions troubled the community. Abbot Ratfred was poisoned in 936 by his rival Campo. Attempts by Prince Alberic of Rome to install reformers at the abbey in 936 met with resistance, and in 947 he forcibly installed as abbot a candidate of his own choice, Dagobert, who also was poisoned in 952. The subsequent abbot, Adam of Lucca (953–63), apparently had little experience of the religious life or of land management.[36] However, with the rise of the Ottonians, Farfa once again enjoyed imperial protection; Otto I confirmed the abbey's properties in 967 and intervened on its behalf in disputes, while Otto II appointed an Ottonian churchman, Adam of Casauria, as abbot.[37] After the prosperous abbacy of John (966–97), the prior who replaced him died after only six months and was succeeded by Hugh, a young monk from Farfa's priory at Antrodoco.[38]

It is the consensus of historians that the able stewardship of Hugh was a central factor in Farfa's rise to power after decades of decline, but this view has inevitably been shaped by Hugh's own interpretations of events.[39] Dwelling on the shortcomings of his predecessors and expressing hope for the spiritual

------

he violated the Rule of Benedict (*CF* 1:19). This text, however, was written no earlier than the middle of the ninth century (see chap. 1 in the present volume).

35. See Leyser, *Authority and Asceticism,* chap. 5; and Zelzer, "Von Benedikt zu Hildemar," esp. 129. I thank the anonymous reader for Cornell University Press for these references.

36. For succinct summaries of this period in the abbey's history, see Schuster, *Imperiale abbazia,* 100–1; and Supino Martini, *Roma,* 244–45. In this book the dates indicated for popes, abbots, and rulers are the dates of their reigns.

37. *RF* 3:108–18; Seibert, "Eines grossen Vaters Glückloser Sohn?" 315 n. 105; and Uhlirz, "Die italienische Kirchenpolitik der Ottonen."

38. Hugh's abbacy was divided into three periods: 998–1009, 1014–27, and 1036–38, with two different abbots, both named Guido, reigning in 1009–31 and 1027–35 (see appendix 2: table A.1). The complex chronology of the abbots in this period is explained in the footnotes to *CF* 1:106–7.

39. The *Destructio* is a chronicle of Farfa's history in the late ninth and tenth centuries; the *Relatio constitutionis* recounts Hugh's reform of the abbey. Written in the early eleventh century, these texts are edited in *CF* 1:27–58. The *Relatio* is discussed further in chap. 3.

renewal of the community, Hugh wrote in part to justify his reform of Farfa, which followed a period of instability and contestation. In 997 Hugh had purchased his position as abbot of Farfa from Pope Gregory V, thereby provoking the ire of Otto III, who expected to appoint the abbots of the imperial monastery. It is not clear why Gregory V—the first German pope and a cousin of Otto III—usurped the emperor's prerogative in this manner, for the two men usually worked together. Early in 998 Otto III annulled the election and installed his own candidate. Then, yielding to pleas from the monks, Otto finally confirmed Hugh as abbot of Farfa.[40] Otto then established an electoral procedure whereby the abbot, after being elected by the monks, would be presented to the emperor for confirmation before consecration by the pope.[41] Soon afterward Otto issued a second diploma, which confirmed the abbey's possessions and privileges.[42] Hugh then undertook to reform the community, establishing a Cluniac constitution with the help of Abbot Odilo of Cluny and William of Volpiano.[43] Hugh thereby initiated a loose affiliation with the abbey of Cluny, which later manifested itself in the *Liber tramitis,* produced at Farfa in the mid-eleventh century.[44]

With the support of Otto III, Abbot Hugh pursued an ambitious and mostly successful strategy of land acquisition and consolidation, making significant progress in restoring holdings lost in previous decades.[45] The early

40. Seibert ("Herrscher und Mönchtum," 255–56) has suggested that Otto's quick change of mind may have been influenced by Odilo of Cluny.

41. *Ottonis III diplomata,* 696 (no. 276; Feb. 22, 998); *RF* 3:122–24, 4:102. On this episode, see most recently Seibert, "Herrscher und Mönchtum," 254–55.

42. *Ottonis III* diplomata, 697–99 (no. 277; March 14, 998); *RF* 3:135–37.

43. Odilo of Cluny (961–1049) was an abbot of Cluny who came from an aristocratic family in the Auvergne; for recent discussions of his life and career, see *Odilon de Mercoeur.* William of Volpiano (962–1031) was a northern Italian monk who reformed and served as abbot of several monasteries in the late tenth and early eleventh centuries, including Saint-Bénigne in Dijon, Fécamp, Jumièges, Saint-Germain-des-Prés, and then founded the abbey of Fruttuaria on his own property in Italy. See Bulst, *Untersuchungen;* and Glaber, *Historiarum libri quinque,* lxx–lxxxii.

44. For the impact of the relationship between Farfa and Cluny on Farfa's liturgy, see chap. 3.

45. Otto III intervened in property disputes on behalf of Hugh, enabling the abbot to defend Farfa's claims on lands in Rome: one claim disputed by the priests of Saint Eustachio in 998, the other a claim against the abbey of Saints Cosmas and Damian in Mica Aurea (San Cosimato) in 999. See Warner, "Ideals and Action in the Reign of Otto III," 11–12.

eleventh century marked the height of central Italian *incastellamento* (encastlement), a complex of interlocking historical trends characterized by the building of fortified structures (including castles and walls around towns) by lay or ecclesiastical lords.[46] By concentrating the population in villages, these local authorities then controlled exploitation of the surrounding land and required the inhabitants to offer military service when needed.[47] Thus the proliferation of villages both enhanced economic growth and strengthened Farfa's defensive network. In addition to receiving donations of land, Farfa acquired old rural churches through purchase, exchange, or long-term lease; the abbots then founded or refounded fortified villages (*castra*) on the lands they had acquired (see map).[48] By the middle of the eleventh century, Farfa and a few lay families dominated much of the region. After 1050 the abbots of Farfa acquired private castral churches and their domains from lay owners through donations and purchases. Lay donors became vassals of Farfa by donating their freeholds to the abbey, which then invested the donors with the land as fiefs. The abbey maintained jurisdiction over the churches within these lands by excluding them from the new fiefs, thereby becoming both temporal and ecclesiastical ruler.[49] Land transactions were closely linked to monastic liturgical commemoration, and gifts of land to Farfa were accompanied by requests for the monks' prayers. Threats to Farfa's landholdings, which occurred frequently throughout the tenth and eleventh centuries, could be countered not only with military actions carried out by residents of the abbey's villages, but also by the *clamor,* a ritual cursing of enemies performed by the monastic community.

Building on the achievements of Abbot Hugh, Abbot Berard I (1047–89) successfully consolidated the abbey's holdings, acquiring eighty rural churches as well as small monasteries and priories. After the troubled abbacies of Rainald, Berard II, and Oddo, Berard III (1099–1119) brought to fruition the

---

46. On *incastellamento* in central Italy generally, see Wickham, *Il problema dell'incastellamento;* for a more recent, comparative view, see Wickham, "A che serve l'incastellamento?" The seminal study for the region of Lazio is Toubert, *Structures* 1:303–447. See also the critique of Toubert in Hoffmann, "Der Kirchenstaat im hohen Mittelalter." Wickham (*Il problema dell'incastellamento,* 11, 57–58, 65–66) notes that the process of centralization (*accentramento*), defined as the concentration of population and building of habitations around fortified castles, is not identical to the building of fortifications (*incastellamento*), but that in the Sabina they were closely linked.

47. I am grateful to Louis Hamilton for many discussions of *incastellamento.*

48. Toubert, *Structures* 2:885–86.

49. Ibid., 2:888.

The *Castra* of the Abbey of Farfa in Lazio (after Toubert, *Structures*)

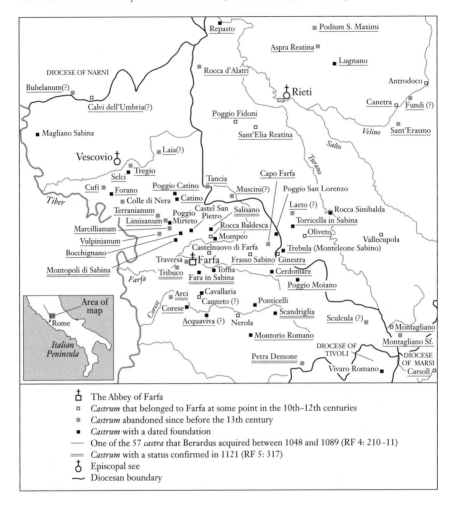

legacy of Berard I.[50] By 1118, when the privilege of Emperor Henry V confirmed Farfa's possessions, the holdings encompassed much of central Italy, including land, fortified villages, churches, and dependent monasteries and priories, as well as land and water routes throughout the Sabina and in Umbria, Abruzzo, and the Marches, the regions bordering Lazio to the north and northeast.[51]

50. The names Beraldus and Berardus are essentially variants of each other. They are cross-referenced throughout Savio, *Monumenta onomastica romana medii aevi* 1:708–79, 5:232. For convenience, I refer to Beraldus (as he is called in documents) as Berald III.

51. Toubert, *Structures* 2:904; *RF* 5:302.

Although Farfa was always first and foremost an imperial abbey, it also benefited from the favor and protection of the popes, a relationship established in 705 by the privilege of John VII. In 1049 Leo IX granted a privilege of exemption conceding to Abbot Berard I the right to choose a bishop to consecrate the altars in the abbey church.[52] In 1060 Abbot Berard I invited Nicholas II to rededicate the two altars in the newly rebuilt east end of the abbey church.[53] On several occasions during the same year, Nicholas's actions toward Farfa manifested both his protection of the imperial monastery and the papacy's expanding role outside Rome. Nicholas ruled in Farfa's favor in a dispute over property between the abbey and the local Crescenzio and Ottaviani families, investing Abbot Berard I with the disputed property.[54] After dedicating the altars at Farfa, Nicholas confirmed the abbey's possessions and privileges and pronounced an anathema on its enemies.[55] Nicholas sent three legates to Farfa to proclaim the anathema at Mass on September 14, the feast of the Exaltation of the Cross, in the presence of all the priors of Farfa's dependencies and possessions in the Marches, as well as powerful local laymen.[56] In retrospect, these gestures seem all the more significant because they occurred during the minority of Emperor Henry IV, when there was no strong imperial presence to counterbalance the influence of the pope. Later in the century, however, Farfa's relations with the popes cooled as its abbots upheld loyalty to the emperors at all costs.

Farfa's status in relation to the papacy and the empire began to change after the Concordat of Worms, which was concluded between Pope Calixtus II and Henry V in 1122. The concordat decreed that papal consecration of bishops and abbots within the empire (but outside Germany) would precede imperial investiture.[57] Since Farfa and its lands fit this description, its abbots were now to be consecrated by the pope before their investiture by the emperor. This

52. *RF* 5:284. An undated privilege of Pope Gregory VI (1045–46) is now considered a forgery; see Hoffmann, "Der Kirchenstaat im hohen Mittelalter," 22 n. 51; *Paptsurkunden 896–1046*, ed. Zimmermann 2:1171–72, no. 624. I am most grateful to Robert Somerville for his help with this text.

53. *RF* 5:291; Jaffé, *Regesta*, 563; and Kehr, *Italia pontificia* 1:67.

54. For a recent discussion of the relations between Nicholas II and Abbot Berard I, see Stroll, *Medieval Abbey*, 48–56.

55. *RF* 5:292–93.

56. *RF* 5:293–96. On the ritual context of this anathema, see chap. 3.

57. The texts of the concordat are published in *MGH Leges* 4, *Constitutiones* 1, ed. Weiland, 159–61 (nos. 107–8); see also the commentary in Minninger, *Von Clermont zum Wormser Konkordat*, 189–209.

reversed the procedure that had been in place at Farfa since the reign of Otto III, according to which abbots elected by the community had been approved by the emperor *before* papal consecration. After a brief return to imperial patronage under Frederick Barbarossa and Henry VI at the end of the twelfth century, Farfa came increasingly under the control of the papacy, particularly during the pontificates of Innocent III (1198–1216), Honorius III (1216–27), and Urban IV (1261–64). Beginning in 1399, Farfa was ruled by commendatory abbots, who held the office as a benefice from the pope and drew on the abbey's revenues without residing there. In 1477 the congregation of Subiaco established a community of German monks at the abbey in order to reform it. Another wave of reform occurred when Farfa joined the congregation of Montecassino in 1567, against the will of the German monks, and brought in monks from the abbey of San Paolo fuori le Mura in Rome.[58] In 1836 Farfa became subject to the bishops of the Sabina, and one of them suppressed the abbey in 1860, bringing monastic life there to an end until the twentieth century.[59] It was through the intervention of Ildefonso Schuster, historian of Farfa and abbot of San Paolo fuori le Mura, that Farfa was joined to San Paolo in 1919, which led to the reestablishment of a monastic community at Farfa in 1921.[60] Schuster not only ensured the survival of monastic life at Farfa but also produced an important body of scholarship on its buildings and archives.

In this book I draw on the manuscripts from Farfa to expand our understanding of the multifaceted monastic identity revealed in its history-writing, literature, art, and, above all, liturgical compositions. Chapter 1 situates the historical works of Gregory of Catino in the broader context of cultural production at the abbey in the eleventh and twelfth centuries. It addresses the reworking of preexisting materials in several genres—including poetry, music, and narrative—in the context of institutional memory and the liturgical commemoration of saints. Chapter 2 takes up the hermeneutic character of the monastic liturgy, here understood as encompassing a broad variety of forms, and highlights several elements particular to Farfa. The relationship between Farfa and Cluny and its impact on liturgical practices is explored in chapter 3. Chapter 4 addresses the influence of imperial and southern Italian patrons on liturgical manuscripts and the visual arts at Farfa. Patronage and its evident

58. See Tappi-Cesarini, "Note sul reclutamento."

59. On Farfa after the early twelfth century, see Schuster, *Imperiale abbazia,* 347–93; and McClendon, *Imperial Abbey,* 14–17.

60. Schuster, *Imperiale abbazia,* 392; and Crippa, "Schuster e Farfa: Motivi di una predilezione," 78.

importance to the monks of Farfa, especially to Gregory of Catino, is a continuous strand throughout the book. Chapter 5 shows further connections between the abbey's politics and its liturgy, especially in compositions for the saints created in the particular historical context of the saints' cults at Farfa. In the Farfa *Register*'s narrative of the internal and external strife that divided the abbey in the 1120s, the introduction of a new style of music attested to by a manuscript from the abbey emblematizes the changes that were transforming the community and its place in the world. The fact that liturgical chant is described as a central facet of these transformations underscores the important role of the liturgy in shaping monastic identity at Farfa.

textual production at Farfa in the eleventh and twelfth centuries exemplifies a broad trend in western Europe toward the concretization of memory and oral traditions in writing.[1] In monasteries, this tendency was manifested in the preservation of documents and the creation of what Patrick Geary has called "archival memory,"[2] which engendered a proliferation of books with memorial and archival functions, such as cartularies, chronicles, customaries, and liturgical manuscripts.[3] The most important figure in the preservation and consolidation of Farfa's institutional memory was the monk Gregory of Catino. Gregory's works form part of a larger construction and transformation of memory at Farfa that is inseparable from the musical, liturgical, and hagiographic aspects of monastic textual production. Indeed, the music and texts created at Farfa reveal different facets of a single process: the reshaping of valued materials to produce new forms. Illustrating the modalities by which novel genres emerge from preexisting traditions, the examples discussed in this chapter bring out the connections between writing the history of Farfa and telling the stories of its most venerated saints through liturgical performance. It is this intermingling of liturgy and history that was of paramount importance in shaping the works of Gregory of Catino, whose writings exhibit a perception of the past profoundly influenced by the nature of liturgical time. The medieval liturgy fused separate temporal strata in a dense synchronic experience: the persons and events being commemorated, as well as the symbolism commentators associated with them, merged with the actions and words of performers in the real time of the present. This multilayered perception of time shaped Gregory's thinking and was manifested in the way he associated texts and events through their connections to the church year.

Consolidation and creation are linked metaphors for Gregory's recording

---

1. See Clanchy, *From Memory to Written Record;* and Geary, *Phantoms of Remembrance.*

2. For Geary's definition of "archival memory" see *Phantoms of Remembrance,* 81–114. On collective memory see particularly Remensnyder, *Remembering Kings Past;* and Fentress and Wickham, *Social Memory.*

3. On the archival function of musical notation in one type of liturgical manuscript of the eleventh century, see Boynton, "Orality, Literacy."

and cataloguing of the abbey's patrimony and for methods of liturgical composition involving the reuse of preexisting material. All are examples of adapting existing materials to the needs or tastes of the present. Like ancient *spolia* reused in medieval buildings, traditions from the past take on additional or altered functions and meanings when incorporated into a new work. In positing analogies between Gregory's creation of the archival and narrative memory of the monastery on the one hand, and the modalities of the transformation and reinterpretation of liturgical materials on the other, I follow the example of recent approaches that have expanded the study of memory in the Middle Ages to encompass both the memorializing of the past in the writing of history and the commemorative functions of the liturgy and of visual culture.[4] Although not at the center of this scholarly trend, music may offer the best example of the complexity and importance of medieval memory systems. The creation, transmission, and performance of music relied primarily on oral tradition and memorization.[5] Moreover, certain musical repertories have been aptly characterized as veritable arts of memory because they are organized around a web of interconnected references (both musical and textual) that have mnemonic functions.[6] In the broader context of memory as commemoration, music concretized the multilayered structure of the medieval liturgy.

In this chapter I begin by analyzing Gregory of Catino's writings of the late eleventh and twelfth centuries as a creative reshaping of Farfa's history and archival memory. Turning to his account of the founding of Farfa by Lawrence of Syria, I show that the structure of the liturgy influenced the way in which Gregory links the foundation to Lawrence's feast and to commemoration of the dedication of the altars in the abbey church. One of Gregory's sources for the second foundation of Farfa by Thomas of Maurienne further illustrates

4. On memory in the Middle Ages see Carruthers, *The Book of Memory* and *The Craft of Thought;* Geary, *Phantoms of Remembrance;* and Yates, *The Art of Memory*, 50–104. A recent project on the memory of origins in medieval institutions is presented in synthetic form by Caby, "La mémoire." On the medieval liturgy as the enactment of memory through ritual commemoration, see particularly *Memoria*, ed. Schmid and Wollasch; and McLaughlin, *Consorting with Saints*. Recent important studies of monumental memory include Valdez del Alamo and Pendergast, *Memory and the Medieval Tomb;* and Remensnyder, "Legendary Treasure at Conques."

5. Some studies by musicologists that address memory for music are Jeffery, *Re-envisioning Past Musical Cultures;* Levy, *Gregorian Chant and the Carolingians;* and Treitler, "The 'Unwritten,'" 145–49.

6. See, for instance, Boynton, "Orality, Literacy"; Busse Berger, "Mnemotechnics and Notre Dame Polyphony"; and Fassler, *Gothic Song.*

the close relationship between liturgy and the writing of history. In the final section of the chapter I demonstrate that the kinds of textual layering, reworking of preexisting materials, and flexibility of genre seen in the works of Gregory also shaped the composition of two unusual pieces of music written down at Farfa in the eleventh century.

The Works of Gregory of Catino

No student of Farfa can escape the voice of Gregory of Catino. By organizing and copying the abbey's archival documents, this monk created a vast textual legacy, recreating and reinterpreting the abbey's history even as he recorded it.[7] Because of Farfa's prominent position in the region, Gregory's works are also among the most important sources for the history of central Italy from the eighth through the eleventh century.[8] Probably the most prolific monastic archivist-chronicler of the eleventh and twelfth centuries, Gregory was born around 1060 to the aristocratic family of Catino, a village near Farfa, and was given to the monastery as an oblate at an early age.[9] Considering his lifelong devotion to the preservation of Farfa's documents, it is likely that Gregory was not only Farfa's archivist but also its librarian.[10] The latter

7. The most recent survey of Gregory's works, with references to previous bibliography, is Longo, "Gregorio da Catino." Supino Martini ("La produzione libraria," 595–601) offers a penetrating analysis of Gregory's character and literary background.

8. Gregory's methods and reliability have at times been questioned; see the summary of the debate in Costambeys, "Piety, Property, and Power," 32–36, 38–40. Among the studies of Gregory's methods are Kurze, "Zur Kopiertätigkeit Gregors von Catino"; and Zielinski, "Gregor von Catino und das Regestum Farfense" and *Studien zu den spoletinischen Privaturkunden*, 23–112.

9. On Gregory's family see *CF* 1:xxii–xxiii; *CF* 2:152; and *RF* 4:343. Between the ninth and twelfth centuries, most monks entered Benedictine monasteries as child oblates. The oblation (from *oblatio*, offering) of a child constituted an irreversible donation to the church. On the early history of this practice, see de Jong, *In Samuel's Image*.

10. The historical sources from Farfa cannot confirm this assertion. The *Chronicle* mentions neither cantor nor *armarius*, and the subscriptions of documents copied in the *Register* rarely specify the higher monastic offices other than abbot and prior; other subscribers are called *monachus, puer,* or *conuersus,* and the monks are sometimes also identified by ecclesiastical office (priest, deacon, subdeacon, or acolyte). Further information about Gregory's position in the community may have been included in the necrology (which apparently has not survived but might resurface when the abbey archive is catalogued). The little available data about Gregory's adult life is summarized in *CF* 1:xxxv–xxxvi, where Balzani states that Gregory apparently did not attain any office in the

role would have placed him in charge not only of the abbey's archives and books but of the liturgy as well. By the end of the eleventh century, the duties of monastic librarians had expanded considerably, and from the originally separate positions of *armarius* (librarian) and cantor (choirmaster) there had emerged a single monastic official, variously called *armarius* or cantor, who managed the library and also oversaw liturgical performance.[11] Although historians have usually overlooked the liturgical resonances in Gregory's writings, the liturgy was an important influence on his vision of Farfa's history.

Gregory's first major project was the Farfa *Register*, which he began to compile in 1092 and continued until the end of 1099 or sometime in 1100, when poor vision compelled him to consign the continuation of the project to his nephew Todino, also a monk of Farfa.[12] The *Register* is a cartulary, a collection of archival documents copied into a book in a particular order. Monastic cartularies were essentially an innovation of the eleventh and twelfth centuries. The utility of a cartulary resides primarily in its book form, which significantly facilitated access to the contents of the documents copied within it. The original documents were written on unwieldy single sheets of parchment and were often difficult to read as a consequence of damage or decay, or difficult to decipher because of the archaic scribal conventions used by notaries of the past.[13] Before the practice of compiling cartularies, consulting a charter entailed first locating it in a monastic archive and then deciphering an unfamil-

---

monastery—a statement that, because of the nature of the evidence, can be neither proved nor disproved.

11. Fassler, "The Office of the Cantor," 43–50.

12. BAV Vat. lat. 8487; for paleographic analysis with references to further bibliography, see Supino Martini, *Roma*, 270–76. The date of 1092 is based on the statement by John the Grammarian in his verse preface to the *Register*, affirming that Gregory was just over thirty years old when he began work (*RF* 2:24); see Kölzer, "*Codex libertatis*," 613–14. As Paola Supino Martini has demonstrated by means of a paleographic analysis of the autograph manuscript, Gregory worked on the *Register* at least through the end of 1099 and continued to copy parts of it for some time after he had officially turned the project over to Todino. According to Supino Martini (*Roma*, 273–74), even though the text in which Gregory records his having entrusted the *Register* to Todino appears on fol. 449r (*RF* 5:161), Gregory's hand appears intermittently in the subsequent twenty folios of the manuscript. Only beginning with fol. 469r does Todino's hand appear consistently without any contribution from Gregory.

13. Gregory himself makes reference to these considerations in his prologue to the *Register* (*RF* 2:7).

iar handwriting system; a cartulary enabled readers to peruse more recent transcriptions of the documents organized in a logical order. In addition to the usefulness of its contents, however, a cartulary had symbolic value as a repository of memory that fixed in writing the community's image of itself.[14] Thus a cartulary acted as both a guide to a monastery's possessions and a means of organizing its history.[15]

The Farfa *Register* contains copies of thousands of charters recording Farfa's possessions, organized in chronological order. It is one of the two earliest Italian monastic cartularies, the other being that of Subiaco.[16] Farfa's *Register* has been called a "revolutionary reference tool" not only because of its system of organization but also because of the care with which Gregory made the documents readable, both by separating words from each other and regularizing the spelling of many texts.[17] Between 1103 and 1107, Gregory created a second cartulary, the *Liber largitorius,* containing the rental contracts for the abbey's land.[18] The two cartularies were complemented by the *Liber floriger* (1130–32), an alphabetical-topographical index to the documents in the *Register,* which Gregory compiled near the end of his life.[19]

Gregory's other major work was the Farfa *Chronicle,* written between 1107 and 1119. The *Chronicle* represented an innovative form of history writing in which partial transcriptions of the archival documents are surrounded and occasionally glossed by Gregory's own narrative.[20] To some extent, narrative

14. Kölzer, "*Codex libertatis,*" 633–44.

15. On cartularies as a genre, see *Les cartulaires;* Bouchard, "Monastic Cartularies"; Chastang, *Lire, écrire, transcrire;* and Geary, *Phantoms of Remembrance,* 81–133.

16. On the registers of Farfa and Subiaco, see Kölzer, "*Codex libertatis,*" 622.

17. On word separation in the *Register* see Saenger, "The Separation of Words in Italy," 28. On Gregory's linguistic alterations and orthographic normalizations of Lombard charters to update their form and bring them into line with the Latinity of the late eleventh century, see Selig, "Un exemple de normalisation," 327–33. The original documents that Gregory transcribed are lost, but Selig compares his transcriptions in the *Register* to extant charters copied in the same period as Gregory's originals.

18. Rome, BN Farfa 2; for the edition, see *Liber largitorius.* On the manuscript, see Supino Martini, *Roma,* 276–80.

19. Rome, BN Farfa 2; see also Supino Martini, *Roma,* 282–84.

20. Rome, BN Farfa 1; and Supino Martini, *Roma,* 280–82. For a recent discussion of the chronicles of twelfth-century Italy, see Feller, *Les Abruzzes médiévales,* 47–62. Gregory's was the first chronicle in Italy to employ the hybrid form of a chronicle with transcriptions of documents from the cartulary. One of the works inspired by the Farfa *Chronicle* is the late twelfth-century cartulary-chronicle of the abbey of San Clemente at

had already played a part in the *Register,* in which passages of prose framed groups of documents. Gregory introduces the documents from each abbot's reign with a brief narrative account, and another such text recounts the sometimes very eventful transitions from one abbacy to the next. In the *Chronicle,* however, it is Gregory's point of view that becomes the structural foundation. Here he self-consciously reconstructs the past, using transcriptions of charters to corroborate his own account of events.[21] His writing blends the traditions of the community with a distinctive, sometimes cantankerous individual voice, as he constructs the history of Farfa by the very same act in which he records it.

What led Gregory to spend his adult life producing redactions of Farfa's archival memory? His prologue to the *Chronicle* makes it clear that in its memorial function it is intended to guide the decisions of the abbots. By selecting and abbreviating the documents and framing them with a synthesis of events—a process he compares to the purification of precious metals and of wine—he sought to make it more accessible and more central to the historical awareness of Farfa's abbots:

> And if one reflects rather often on the writings of the holy fathers of old sent to us, always of great utility, a clearer meaning is found in them. For the more we search in them, the more we may find, as if separated out, the quintessence of grain and the best unmixed essence of wine. On account of which we, too, have attempted to create this very brief work from the previous great work of charters, and the following briefer little book. And in this we have imitated the habits of skilled goldsmiths, who busy themselves purifying gold or silver many times in the fire, so that they may then execute a most splendid work. For just as wines that, when the sediments have been removed, pour forth smoother unmixed wine, and contained in a different, clearer vessel, offer a nectarlike sweetness to the drinkers, thus we have sought to shorten this third book of charters, and we have labored to transfer purer water from the more abundant spring into a smaller place, so that this book can also be read and reread rather frequently without weariness. May it be able to offer great care and very useful caution to its users, and may it administer the knowledge of all the possessions of this

---

Casauria; the main text is the cartulary, while the chronicle is written in the margins. See Feller, "Le cartulaire-chronique de San Clemente a Casauria." For a facsimile edition, see *Liber instrumentorum.*

21. Toubert, *Structures* 1:78, 84–86.

monastery to present and future governors, without the fastidiousness of a large history, and of great utility, when some effort is applied. For in this will be found the most ancient and new and truest liberty of this monastery: its own laws, its highest defense, and the proper guardianship by its users. For [the book] reports with a concise and truthful pen the individual acquisitions, the evil prodigalities, and the detestable dispersions of every abbot, and the injust invasions and impious destructions of all men.[22]

The key term here is *libertas,* meaning Farfa's independence from bishop and pope. As in the *Register,* the *Liber largitorius,* and the *Liber floriger,* Gregory stresses the antiquity of the abbey's *libertas,* first established in 705 by the privilege conceded to Thomas of Maurienne by Pope John VII, which the *Chronicle* refers to as a *privilegium totius libertatis* (privilege of complete liberty).[23] In the preface to the *Register,* Gregory calls the cartulary itself a *codex libertatis* (book of liberty),[24] which would ordinarily mean that it was a reaffirmation of the abbey's material possessions and a guarantee of its freedom from local—in this case papal—jurisdiction. Indeed, together with the *Collectio canonum,* a collection of excerpts from canon law that Gregory com-

---

22. *CF* 1:112–13: "Scriptura quoque sanctorum patrum nobis emissa priscorum si sepius ruminetur, magnę semper utilitatis, clariorque sensus in eis invenitur. Quanto enim plus eas investigamus, tanto magis velut discretam frumenti medullam vinique optimam in eis meracam reperiemus. Quapropter et nos de priori cartarum magno, et sequenti breviori libello, hoc tertium studuimus opus efficere brevissimum. In quo etiam aurificum peritorum mores imitati sumus, qui aurum vel argentum igni multoties satagunt purgare, ut opus splendidissimum exinde valeant perpetrare. Enimvero tamquam vina quę, fęcibus ablatis, mera suavioria fundunt, et in altero nitidiori vase recondita potantibus nectaream dulcedinem reddunt, ita hunc cartularum tertium librum studuimus breviare, et de ampliori fonte in breviori locello aquam laboravimus puriorem transferre, ut lectus et relectus sine tedio hic liber et frequentius, magnam sollertiam utillimamque cautelam prębere valeat eo utentibus, et notitiam bonorum omnium huius monasterii administret, pręsentibus posterisque rectoribus fastidio magnę remoto rei, studioque adhibito perfectę utilitatis. In hoc enim invenientur antiquissima novaque et verissima huius monasterii libertas, propria iura, defensio summa, custodia utentibus recta. Refert enim brachico veracique stilo cuiuscumque abbatis singulas acquisitiones, iniquas largitiones, detestabiles dispersiones, etiam quorumcumque hominum iniustas invasiones et impias diremptiones." Translations are mine unless otherwise indicated.

23. *CF* 1:127.

24. Although the literal translation puts "liberty" in the singular, the term refers collectively to the totality of Farfa's liberties.

piled to introduce the cartulary, the *Register* would seem to express antipapal bias.[25]

A canonical collection from around 1100 might be expected to contain texts reflecting the ascendancy of the papacy and the subjects promoted by the Gregorian reform such as the place of the pope in the church and the morals and behavior of the clergy. These themes are essentially absent from the *Collectio canonum*.[26] To explain the seemingly anachronistic character of the collection, Theo Kölzer has argued that it represents a specifically monastic type of canonical collection intended for internal use by the community. According to Kölzer, the fact that half the excerpts in the collection relate to church property reflects the *Register's* focus on Farfa's lands; it does not represent the monastery's response to the reform papacy or the investiture controversy. In this view, the *Register* was not necessarily a symbol of immunity from papal interference but rather a general reaffirmation of the abbey's material possessions.[27] But the historical context of the *Register* and *Collectio canonum* suggests otherwise. The years in which Gregory compiled these collections saw numerous threats to and encroachments upon Farfa's *libertas* by the antipope Clement III, as well as by the bishop of the Sabina, lay landowners, and even its own abbots. Hence both the *Register* and the *Collectio canonum* must be considered in the context of Farfa's political situation in the 1090s.

Gregory presents this period—beginning in 1089 with the aftermath of Abbot Berard I's death and ending with the election of Abbot Berard III in 1099—as one of uncertainty and factionalization. The problems arose in connection with the elections of abbots, during which tensions among the monks and a lack of leadership left the monastery vulnerable to takeovers. Observers both inside and outside the community were well aware that the vacuum of power that existed during the time between an abbot's death and the emperor's confirmation of his successor represented an opportunity for usurpation. But de-

---

25. Gregory compiled the *Collectio canonum* from 1099 to 1103; see Kéry, *Canonical Collections of the Early Middle Ages*, 264–65. The text was edited by Kölzer, *Collectio canonum*, and earlier by Pedeaux, "The Canonical Collection of the Farfa *Register*," 139–370. Although the text is often referred to as the *Collectio Farfensis*, as in Kéry's book, I use the designation *Collectio canonum*, which is also the short title of the edition by Kölzer. I am grateful to Robert Somerville for his help with this subject.

26. The first proponent of this interpretation was Fournier, "La collezione canonica," 299–301.

27. Kölzer, *Collectio canonum*, 6, 18, 75; Kölzer, "*Codex libertatis*," 643–47, and "Mönchtum und Kirchenrecht."

spite Berard I's threat of excommunication for anyone who might seek to perturb or subvert an abbatial election,[28] in the late eleventh and twelfth centuries there were many such attempts, some more successful than others.

Gregory's conservative and partisan perspective on this decade informed the *Register* and *Chronicle* alike. In the *Chronicle* and in narrative sections of the *Register,* Gregory describes the abbots with vivid immediacy, both recording the history of Farfa and shaping it to reflect his own interpretation of events. Nor was Gregory impervious to the favors of his patrons, for we must not forget that Berard III himself commissioned the *Liber largitorius* and the *Chronicle.* Thus his election in 1099 appears, in Gregory's account, all the more auspicious for following what is represented as a decade of disastrous misrule. In the prologues to these works, Gregory exhorts Berard III to help with the expenses incurred by his work and not follow the niggardly example of his predecessors.[29]

Compiling the *Register,* on the other hand, was Gregory's own idea; according to its preface, he embarked upon the project after first obtaining the assent of Abbot Berard II and senior monks of the monastery.[30] But approval was slow in coming. Berard II agreed to Gregory's proposal only "after considerable time"[31] and seems to have provided little or no financial assistance for the project thereafter, leaving Gregory to seek assistance from outside sources. The verse prologue to the *Register* by John the Grammarian states that a priest named Peter covered the initial costs of the parchment.[32] Embittered by the lack of support for his endeavors, Gregory bemoaned the stinginess of Berard II and depicted him in the *Register* as malicious, greedy, destructive, contentious, and conspiratorial.[33] Gregory's accounts of Berard's installation as abbot, his decadence, and his eventual demise form narrative bookends for the transcriptions of charters from his abbacy.[34] Because the most vitriolic

28. *RF* 5:236; and *CF* 2:200.

29. *Liber largitorius* 1:7; and *CF* 1:114–15.

30. *RF* 2:6.

31. *RF* 5:155; and *CF* 2:214 (*post aliquantum tempus*).

32. *RF* 2:24.

33. Mara ("Berardo," 765–77) points out that Gregory was evidently biased against Berard II: the documents in the Farfa *Register* suggest that the abbot was not as profligate and negligent as Gregory makes him out to be.

34. The election of Berard II is separated in the *Register* from Gregory's harshest condemnation of this abbot (*RF* 5:155–56, 159) by a long series of transcribed charters (*RF* 5:124–54).

passages come at the end of this section in the *Register*, they may have been copied after the abbot's death on March 25, 1099. Another possibility is that Berard's purported lack of interest in the project led Gregory to believe that his damning words would never reach the eyes of the abbot.

As Gregory relates the events of 1089–1099, dissent ensued among the monks immediately after the death of Berard I in 1089, when one faction within the monastic community, under the influence of Regizo, bishop of the Sabina, began to advocate the bishop's candidacy for the freshly vacant abbacy.[35] By night, Gregory writes, before the mandated three-day period had elapsed and even before Berard I had been buried, the community hastily concurred in the election of the monk Rainald, whom Gregory described as "fully imbued with monastic observance" but inexperienced in worldly affairs.[36] The abbey's liberty was under siege not only by internal political pressure exerted by the bishop of the Sabina but also by the antipope Clement III, who, Gregory states, unleashed unnamed conspirators in a plot to invade the abbey and change the outcome of the election. Despite internal divisions and infiltration by powerful outside forces, Gregory writes, the community upheld its tradition of free elections, standing firm in its choice of Rainald. But Rainald failed to meet the expectations of the community, which reproached him for his abusive behavior, his neglect of the monastery, and his tendency to acquiesce to manipulation by lay landowners.[37] The monks wrote to Henry IV requesting his intervention, promising in exchange to celebrate thirty masses annually in his honor on the anniversary of his death. Lack of funds, however, compelled the monks to delay their embassy to the emperor. Meanwhile, a Florentine monk named Berard, who lived at a priory of Farfa in the Marches and was thought to be a relation of Abbot Berard I, was secretly urged by a group of monks at Farfa to approach the emperor on his own account. This Berard convinced Henry to invest him with the abbacy. Under the name of Berard II, the newly appointed abbot made his way back to Farfa in the company of imperial legates. The hapless Rainald, upon hearing of Berard II's triumphal ap-

35. *RF* 5:122; and *CF* 2:205–8.

36. *RF* 5:121. In the *Chronicle* (*CF* 2:205–6) Gregory points out that the election violated canon law because the monks did not wait for the full three days after the death of Berard I.

37. Though he records the story of Rainald's brief rise to power, Gregory apparently did not consider Rainald's abbacy legitimate, for it does not appear in the catalogue of the abbots of Farfa in the *Liber largitorius* (Rome, BN Farfa 2, fol. 21), where the names of the three Berards follow upon one another (see *CF* 1:99).

proach, quickly fled the abbey.[38] Thus the community faced an uneasy transition from the ineffectual and hastily elected Rainald to the unelected Berard II, who, the monks now feared, would rule them like a tyrant.

Once Berard's election became official, his behavior quickly confirmed some of the monks' worst fears. Among his first actions as abbot, according to Gregory, were the rejection and abuse of those who had supported his rise to power. Many suffered sudden death without confession—struck down, in Gregory's view, by God himself. The narrative account in the *Register* relates Berard's sloth, gluttony, and unbridled cruelty. His servant, Gregory writes, was so terrorized by Berard's tyrannical demands and excessive abuse that he was forced to flee. Gregory paints a vivid picture of the moral corruption that tainted Berard's dealings. His favorites were spared disgrace for their crimes in return for oaths of loyalty. In handling disputes, he provoked further contention rather than settling conflicts between the monks. Gregory further charges him with altering the abbey's ancient customs, breaking his promises, and requiring the monks to wear wretched clothing while he himself dressed in luxurious garments. Perhaps most egregious for our chronicler, Berard II attempted to force foreign customs upon the community, stole from and depopulated the abbey's villages, and lost or neglected many of its domains, overriding both the anathemas and agreements of previous abbots, which had maintained the integrity of Farfa's holdings. And finally, adding financial loss to this lengthy catalogue of mismanagement, in 1097 Berard II directed a considerable proportion of the abbey's wealth into an ill-fated building campaign with the aim of constructing a new church atop nearby Monte Acuziano.[39]

According to Gregory, the final confirmation of the character and ultimate fate of Berard II came in the form of a terrible scene witnessed one night by some of the monks. The abbot was seen eating a tender and innocent child who had been boiled and roasted; as he devoured the tender limbs of the child piece by piece, the brothers fled outside from sheer fright. Gregory's description of the vision is ambiguous, for although he calls it both a vision and a dream (*uisio* and *uisio somnii*), he implies that the monks were physically present at the scene, referring to "certain [monks] standing there before him" (*quidam ante illum assistentes*), as if the shocking event had actually taken place. Moreover, Gregory's account presents the vision as experienced collec-

<hr />

38. *RF* 5:123; and *CF* 2:209.

39. The construction was never finished, and part of it still stands today on the slopes of Monte Acuziano. See *RF* 5:156–58; Bougard, Hubert, and Noyé, "Les techniques de construction en Sabine," 744; and Branciani, "Il monte S. Martino in Sabina," 74–79.

tively rather than individually. When the group of horrified monks returned to the scene a short while later, they saw Berard greedily chewing bread dipped in the brains of the child. The next day in chapter someone related the shared vision without mentioning the abbot's name. Berard, evidently unaware that he was the protagonist, interpreted the vision for the community as a sign of his condemnation of the act, and indeed the entire monastery's curse upon the perpetrator of such a crime. According to Gregory, the monks were amazed that Berard had unwittingly made this prophecy regarding himself.[40] Finally, in 1099, a group of monks devastated by Berard's neglect of the abbey set off to seek the aid of the emperor. But before their return, Berard died without taking last Communion. Gregory records that each time the host was placed in the abbot's mouth he was unable to swallow it, propelling it out with his saliva.[41]

By interpolating this colorful account of Berard II's abbacy among the archival documents copied in the *Register*, Gregory appropriated authority for his narrative. Describing the terrible vision as experienced collectively by the monks serves to authenticate the account as evidence, transforming even the sight of an abbot feasting on a roasted child into a kind of official record.[42] Such images may have functioned in the community's imagination as meaningful portents. Another example of a child's being cooked appears in the eleventh-century *Histories* of Radulfus Glaber (ca. 958–ca. 1046), a monk of the abbey of Saint-Germain in Auxerre. Glaber recounts that in the years soon after the turn of the millennium, as bishops in Italy and Gaul discussed liturgical practices in their synods, some suggested that the feast of the Annunciation (March 25), which often fell during Lent, could be celebrated instead on December 18, as was the custom in the Iberian peninsula. Without recording the decision of the synod, Glaber reports an event he witnessed later at the Burgundian abbey of Cluny, when some Spanish monks in residence there obtained permission to celebrate the Annunciation on December 18. This exception gave rise to a terrible vision:

> When they had celebrated this [feast], segregated from the rest of the community, two of the eldest monks of the house dreamt that night that they saw one of the Spaniards, armed with a cooking-fork, seize a young boy from upon the altar and put him in a frying-pan full of hot coals. The young

40. *RF* 5:155–56.

41. *RF* 5:159.

42. The narrative of Berard's abbacy in the *Chronicle* repeats much of the text from the *Register* but omits the monks' terrible vision and the fact that the abbot had died without Communion (*CF* 2:214–20).

boy cried out: "Father, Father, they are taking away what you have given." There is no more to be said: amongst us the ancient custom was very properly confirmed.[43]

To Glaber, this vision shared by two witnesses seemed to confirm the Frankish monks' traditional date for the Annunciation by condemning the foreign monks' practice as heterodox. In the same way that Glaber describes the testimony of the two monks at Cluny, Gregory presents the collective vision in which the monks saw Berard II devouring the child as confirmation and condemnation of the abbot's character. Thus Gregory's authorial voice becomes the voice of the judgment of history—its authority all the more unimpeachable because it rises from amid the documents transcribed in the Farfa *Register*.

Gregory's account of Farfa's next profligate abbot, Oddo (March 25–May 19,1099), again emphasizes the misguided and ineffective stewardship that left the abbey vulnerable to depredations by lay landowners. In a passage that appears in the *Register* between the transcription of the oath sworn by the new abbot to preserve the monastery's property, and the narrative of Oddo's downfall, Gregory describes Oddo as follows:

> A Lombard by birth who had lived in the community for a long time, Oddo was astute, cautious in negotiation, learned in the study of letters, quick, compassionate, nimble, affectionate, jovial, gracious, and appropriately amiable. Nevertheless, he was seen to be a greedy acquisitor of objects, a tireless and assiduous writer, a relentless worker, and more than moderately eager for distinction.[44]

Soon after Oddo's election, according to Gregory, some of the monks frightened Oddo into making a pact of protection (*pactum firmitatis*) with some local landowners, identified in the *Register* only as "count R. and his father-in-law." In exchange for the landowners' promise to safeguard the abbey, Oddo gave them money as a guarantee for the agreement, as well as numerous ornaments from the abbey church, including even the main altarcloth of the high altar. This transaction, Gregory states, was carried out secretly and in defiance of Oddo's oath—which he had just sworn before the entire community—to

43. Glaber, *Historiarum libri quinque,* 114–15 (I have modified France's translation).

44. *RF* 5:159: "langobardum quidem genere, sed nobiscum conuersatum ex plurimo tempore. Erat denique astutus et cautus in agendis negotiis, siue doctus prudentissime in litterarum studiis, nimiumque promptus, omnibus sociis compaties, abilis, affectuosus, hilaris, gratulosus et decenter amabilis. Verumtamen rerum uidebatur acquisitor cupidus, infatigabilis scriptor et assidus, laborator improbus, et honoris non modice auidus."

protect the abbey's property and independence. By effectively ceding control over Farfa to local laypeople, Oddo subverted the abbey's imperial patronage. Pawning the altarcloth powerfully symbolized this renunciation of the abbey's liberty. The context makes it clear that the altarcloth was charged with meaning for the monks of Farfa. When Abbot Berard I lay on his deathbed, it was this very cloth that was brought to chapter for all the monks to touch as they solemnly swore neither to accept nor to confirm any abbot who had not been elected canonically by the whole community and accepted by the emperor.[45] As we have seen, the elections of both Rainald and Berard II had violated this oath. Moreover, the altarcloth was probably one of those given to the abbey by Henry IV or the Empress Agnes.[46] Hence Oddo's action signaled disrespect for the abbey's imperial traditions, as the patrons were metaphorically present on the altar by association with textiles they might have worn themselves.[47] As Gregory's account of the episode makes all too clear, placing the altarcloth in the custody of local landowners was equally symbolic: it was tantamount to entrusting the abbey itself to the control of outsiders. This act of recklessness was symptomatic of the abbot's negligent attitude toward the institution in his care.

Gregory recounts that, upon discovering the abbot's deed, the monks lamented that their monastery had been subjugated to the counts. Those who had counseled Oddo heard of the community's reaction and convinced him to bring an army of the monastery's knights and peasants to intimidate the monks into confirming his election. Silenced but still resistant, some of the monks decided to seek help from the emperor. First they traveled to Farfa's priory of Offida (in the Marches) to invite one of the monks, Berard, to join them in their petition to the emperor. While they were away, however, Oddo died; upon hearing the news the monks returned to Farfa, and the entire community elected Berard as the next abbot, Berard III.[48]

In Gregory's retelling of this episode in the *Chronicle,* the spectacular manner in which he describes Oddo's demise makes it doubly clear that the abbot's lamentable fate was sealed because he could not make reparation for his transgression. Gregory's account of the abbot's downfall begins with a description of the remarkable transformation of Oddo's demeanor from his previous ease and grace:

45. *CF* 2:206.

46. *CF* 2:292: "uestes quattuor altaris principalis: primam ei dedit domnus Heinricus imperator, secundam dedit predicta regina." On imperial donations to the abbey, see chap. 4.

47. I am grateful to Louis Hamilton for suggesting this interpretation.

48. *CF* 2:226; and *RF* 5:160–61.

Whereupon it should be remembered and noted that the same Oddo, who previously during his abbacy we saw to be, as we related above, very prudent, very shrewd, and also very facile, afterward we observed him to be fearful, trembling, and inexperienced, and as if senseless, and deeply irrational in all matters. And finally, after he pawned the altarcloth of the altar of blessed Mary and whatever other ornaments of this church [he could], when reminded [of it] by someone speaking with him, he instead kept it to himself, excused himself, and professed to be unaware of the deed. But while he was putting off making amends for his deed, he was awaited for two days by the mother of the Lord. Then finally he became ill and began to weaken; his feebleness worsening, he sought extreme unction. When his request was announced in chapter, the prior, Romanus, who was in charge at that time, sent word to him, saying: "Since you have pillaged our lady Mary, therefore seek to make reparations, without which, however, we will neither perform the unction for you, nor, if you die, shall we bury you in the cemetery of the monks, but rather in the dung-pit." Upon hearing this, Oddo lamented and wailed greatly, and now, as if diminished in mind because he could not make up for his deed, he secretly asked to have unction performed by a certain canon, and to do penance without the brothers' knowledge. But while waiting for these things [to be done], for three nights he was struck very harshly in the face as if by an exalted woman with three very pointed rods. And the first night, he related this to the servant watching over him and implored him to come to his assistance. But on the second night the same guardian, ever watchful, heard him in the same vision, between lashings tearfully imploring the one who was striking him, and saying, "My lady, mercy." And when he woke up, the servant asked him why he cried out in his dreams. Then he showed the same servant the strokes of the wounds inflicted on the back of his body, and he confided that a certain lady was striking him rather sharply with three rods, saying to him, "Why have you pillaged me?" and he responding, "My lady, I did not do it." And she: "Who therefore dared to carry this out?" [To which] he replied, "The devil suggested it by means of heretics." After relating these things he then fell silent but lost the power of speech after two days. He was first administered the sacrament of the Lord, but, unanointed by the rite of unction, he died almost at the ninth hour on the vigil of the Ascension, when he was the fortieth abbot of this holy monastery, and he was buried on the following day, that is, on the feast of the Ascension itself.[49]

49. CF 224–25: "hinc referendum notandumque est, quod eundem domnum Odd-

The haughty lady is unmistakably the Virgin Mary; punishing the wayward abbot with a bundle of three rods that suggests an allusion to the Trinity, she administers corporal punishment resembling that traditionally meted out by the prior to misbehaving monks. Although Gregory describes the apparition of the wrathful Virgin as a feverish vision, he implies that her ire was all too real to the ailing abbot. Her stern character and aggrieved demeanor suggest that she represented the patron of Farfa. Perhaps a personification of the high altar itself and by extension, of the abbey, she ordered Oddo to account for the treasures he had so foolishly forfeited. The personification of the abbey as Mary is a common theme in documents from Farfa. Charters in the *Register* regularly speak of donations to the church as donations to the Virgin herself, and the privilege of Pope Leo IX (1051) addressed her directly:

> Keep what you keep; with the benediction of your son, possess what you possess. Certainly you are blessed among all women. Let no one take away

onem ante abbatiam, ut supra retulimus, prudentissimum sollertissimumque ac lo-quacissimum nec non et promptissimum vidimus, postea vero pavidum et tremebundum ignarumque et quasi amentem atque insensatum pene in cunctis perspeximus. Denique postquam altaris vestem beatę Marię et quęlibet ecclesię huius ornamenta oppignerare fecit, a quodam sibi faulante admonitus, immo cohercitus, excusavit se et non se esse con-scium illius facti professus est, sed cum emendare differret, biduo a Domini Genitrice ex-pectatus est, tunc demum diutissime ęgrotare et languescere cępit. Ingraviscente autem languore petiit unctionem, quod cum in capitulo referretur, Romanus prior qui tunc pręrat mandavit ei dicens: 'Quia expoliasti dominam nostram Mariam, ideo emendare stude. Sin autem, nec tibi unctionem facimus, nec, si obieris, in fratrum cimiterio, sed magis in sterquilinio te sepeliemus,' quibus auditis, maxime doluit et ingenuit, et iam quasi mente minoratus, quia factum emendare non poterat, petebat a quodam canonico clanculo perungi, et confratribus ignorantibus pęnitentiari. Sed hęc pręstolando, tribus noctibus durissime in visu quasi a sublimi femina tribus acerrimis virgis est cesus. Et prima quidem nocte, custodienti se famulo retulit hęc, et depręcatus est illum, ut sibi sub-veniret. Altera vero nocte idem custos pervigil audivit eum in ipsa visione inter flagella deprecantem lacrimabiliter eam quę se cedebat, atque dicentem: 'Mea domina, merce-dem.' Et cum evigilasset, interrogavit eum famulus cur in somnis vociferasset. Tunc ille ostendit eidem famulo illisiones vulnerum inflictas in corporis dorso, et confessus est quod quędam pręcelsissima femina tribus virgis acrius cedebat eum dicens: 'Quare expo-liasti me?' et ille dicebat: 'Mea domina, non feci ego.' Et illa: 'Quis ergo operari ausus est hoc?' at ille: 'Diabolus suggessit hęreticis.' His autem recitatis tunc quidem siluit, sed post biduum perdidit colloquium. Verumtamen prius communicatus est Domino sacra-mento. Sed unctionis inunctus misterio, obiit quasi non hora in dominicę Ascensionis vigilia, cum esset quadragesimus in huius sacri cęnobii electionis abbatia, sepultusque est altero die, idest in eiusdem solemnitate Ascensionis.

from you what is yours. Let no one be allowed to offend you in your possessions. . . . For if anyone should knowingly offend the holy mother of the Lord, he may not at all have the goodwill of her only-born son, indeed of her first-born son, our savior.[50]

As Kölzer has pointed out, Gregory's account of the Virgin Mary's appearance to Oddo was an admonition to all those who might play fast and loose with Farfa's property, thus functioning as a didactic illustration of the *Collectio canonum* Gregory had included in the *Register*.[51] One of the excerpts in the first book of the *Collectio canonum* states that those who knowingly sell church furnishings are to be punished with excommunication, concluding that "also held subject to this sentence of punishment will be those who have consciously taken for their own use ecclesiastical ornaments, altarcloths (*uela*) or any other furnishings, even utensils, or have believed they could sell or give them to others."[52] Oddo's downfall may be connected to the origins of the canon collection; according to Kölzer, Gregory began compiling it on May 23, 1099, only days after Oddo's death on May 18, the day of the vigil of the Ascension.[53] Thus the chapter on punishment for theft of ecclesiastical property should be seen in the context of Oddo's act, which may even have been one of the factors motivating Gregory's focus on canons regarding property.[54] The link suggested by Kölzer between Oddo and the *Collectio canonum* is characteristic of Gregory's approach to the recording and interpretation of events. As in the abbacy of Berard II, illness, death without unction, and supernatural visions were the punishments visited upon those who abused abbatial power. The *Collectio canonum*, compiled after Oddo's death in 1099 and included in the *Register*, therefore forms another thread connecting Gregory's accounts of the abbacies of Berard II and Oddo in the *Register* and *Chronicle*.

50. *RF* 5:280: "Tene quae tenes, cum benedictione filii tui posside quae possides. Benedicta quidem es inter omnes mulieres. Tua tibi nullus auferat. In bonis tuis te offendere nulli unquam liceat. . . . Si quis enim piam matrem domini scienter offenderit, bonam uoluntatem filii eius unigeniti immo et primogeniti saluatoris nostri habere omnino non poterit."

51. Kölzer, "*Codex libertatis*," 615.

52. Kölzer, *Collectio canonum*, 146 (I.26): "Sub hac quoque damnationis sententia et illi obnoxii tenebuntur qui ęcclesiastica ornamenta, uela uel quęlibet alia indumenta uel etiam utensilia sciendo in suos usus transtulerint uel aliis uendenda uel donanda crediderint." The text is *Concilii Bracarensis III, cap. II;* see *Canones apostolorum et conciliorum,* ed. Bruns, 2:99; and *Concilios visigóticos e hispano-romanos,* ed. Vives, 374.

53. Kölzer, *Collectio canonum*, 29.

54. Ibid., 74, 91.

Continued concern for the documentation of Farfa's property led Gregory, at the age of seventy, to compile his final work, the *Liber floriger*. Written in the tumultuous period from 1130 to 1132, this project was Gregory's last and, as events would have it, futile attempt to assert Farfa's independence after the abbey had passed into papal control as a result of the Concordat of Worms (1122). The *Liber floriger* comprises a historical introduction, excerpts from papal and imperial documents confirming the abbey's possessions, a collection of twenty-three canons excerpted from the *Collectio canonum*, and a four-part alphabetical list of the churches and other properties that had already been listed in the *Register* or in the *Liber largitorius*.[55] Laurent Feller has noted the "anti-historical" quality of the *Liber floriger*, which includes properties (such as a ninth-century list of slaves) that were no longer in existence. As an ideal rather than a real inventory, the *Liber floriger* seems to reflect a "desire to deny that time could have destroyed something that the monastery possessed."[56]

In a lengthy prologue, Gregory describes this product of his old age as shorter but more useful[57]—even more truthful—than his three earlier works. Of course, the notion of truth here must be understood in the context of Gregory's agency in shaping Farfa's history and his claims of authority for his version of the abbey's memory. He compares the ensemble of his four books to the four Gospels:

> And since in the others I recall having promised to have added nothing false, nothing mendacious, and nothing to be condemned in the transferring of things or to have changed anything except for the parts that were altogether too corrupt. . . . Certainly now in this fourth volume I promise to observe it more and more so that, in the manner of the four volumes of the Gospels, these four books do not diverge from the truth, nor should they be seen to disagree. For if in the other books, when I was young, I transmitted the truth, now that I am experienced I must prepare myself all the more with heart and mind to conserve that same thing, since all falsehood comes from the devil.[58]

---

55. For the contents of the manuscript, see Gregory of Catino, "*Liber floriger*," xv–xvi.

56. Feller, *Les Abruzzes médiévales*, 52.

57. Kölzer ("*Codex libertatis*," 640) points out that Gregory considered the *Liber floriger* the most important of his books because, as an index, it enables the reader to identify a possession of the abbey quickly and then locate the relevant documents in the *Register*.

58. Gregory of Catino, *Liber floriger*, 3–4: "Et quoniam in aliis me recolo spopondisse

Gregory's repeated protestations of truthfulness are particularly interesting in light of the significant revisions he made to the *Liber floriger*'s account of Farfa's first founder, Lawrence of Syria. Gregory's previous works show how difficult to trace were the most basic facts of Lawrence's life. With no early hagiographic or other textual tradition, the earliest origins of the monastery were wrapped in "the mystical veil of legend," as Ugo Balzani aptly put it.[59] In both the *Register* and the *Chronicle*, Gregory had readily acknowledged his inability to determine the year in which Lawrence founded Farfa, invoking circumstances such as the destruction of the monastery by the Lombards soon afterwards.[60] In the prologue to the *Liber floriger,* however, he adduces new information on the life of Lawrence:

> In this book we have introduced something more truly investigated here than in the other books about the time of most blessed Lawrence our father, and we have demonstrated the most complete liberty of this monastery as legally granted by the popes and by the most Christian and catholic emperors and kings, and always guarded and defended in times past and vindicated in many agreements.[61]

By juxtaposing the reference to Lawrence with the description of the *Liber floriger* as the ultimate vindication of Farfa's freedom and privileges, Gregory seemed implicitly to link the two. In the *Chronicle*, Gregory had already connected Lawrence's foundation of Farfa to his own assemblage of documentation in the *Register* by using the same expression to point out that both feats were achieved "not at public expense," meaning that neither Lawrence nor Gregory was beholden to those in power in his endeavors on behalf of Farfa.[62]

---

nil falsum, nil mendacium, nichilque damnandum in rerum translatione addidisse vel mutasse exceptis partibus pernimium corruptis. . . . Verum nunc in hoc quarto volumine magis magisque id observare me promitto, ut, more quattuor Evangeliorum voluminum, hi libri quattuor in nullo a veritate devient nec discordari videantur. Si enim in aliis libris, cum iuvenis essem, transtuli veritatem, multo amplius nunc, iam vẹteranus, idipsum me conservare corde et animo me constituere debeo, quia omne mendacium ex diabolo est."

59. See Gregory's preface to the *Chronicle* (*CF* 1:vii).

60. *RF* 2:4; and *CF* 1:127–28.

61. Gregory of Catino, *Liber floriger,* 4: "In quo etiam libello aliquid de beatissimi Laurentii patris nostri tempore verius hic indagatum quam in aliis libris inseruimus, et huius monasterii plenissimam libertatem a summis pontificibus et christianissimis catholicisque imperatoribus et regibus legaliter concessam et semper in preteritis temporibus custoditam et defensatam et in multis placitis evindicatam ostendimus."

62. In the *Register* Gregory stated that Lawrence "did not construct the monastery on

Thus Gregory presents his labors as another foundation of the monastery, this time a metaphorical one by which he preserved Farfa's historical memory.

Insisting yet again upon the veracity of his account, in the prologue to the *Liber floriger* Gregory proposes to report his findings "in a truthful manner" (*stilo veraci*), but goes on to relate a modified version of the foundation narrative which scholars today consider pure invention, not least because of its chronological inconsistencies.[63] This revised account makes Lawrence one of the twelve Syrians who traveled to Rome during the reign of Emperor Julian the Apostate (361–63) to venerate the church of Peter and Paul and then to visit Pope Urban I (222–230), who ordained Lawrence deacon.[64] Whereas the Farfa *Chronicle* mentions Lawrence's pilgrimage to Rome only in passing,[65] by recounting the ordination of Lawrence as deacon by Pope Urban in the *Liber floriger* Gregory connects the abbey's earliest origins to the papacy. After Julian's persecutions, the Syrians left Rome for various destinations; Lawrence went to the Sabina, where he became bishop and then renounced the episcopate to become a hermit.[66] Clearly, the mismatched regnal dates of the emperor and pope undermine the narrative's verisimilitude, and this account of Lawrence's activities before he arrived in the Sabina differs significantly from the earlier versions of his life in the *Register* and *Chronicle*. The reasons for the changes may lie in the contemporary political situation. Gregory compiled the *Liber floriger* in 1130–32, during the papal schism in which Pope Innocent II opposed the antipope Anaclet II. Abbot Adenulf of Farfa supported Innocent II, but it was Anaclet who controlled Rome and the Sabina. Anaclet invaded Farfa's lands, and Abbot Adenulf was forced to join Innocent II in exile. In 1132

---

public property" ("non de publico construxit monasterium"; *RF* 2:4). In the *Chronicle* he refers to the compilation of the *Register* as "carried out by the labors of my hands, and from whatever things could be acquired from outsiders, but not from the public authorities [i.e., not at the expense of the monastic community]" ("manuum mearum laboribus et a quibuscumque acquisitis extraneis, non tamen publicis"; *CF* 1:115). He then echoes his statement in the *Register* that the monastery was not constructed on public land (*CF* 1:127). The parallel was pointed out by Supino Martini ("La produzione libraria," 599–600).

63. See Maggi Bei, "Per un'analisi," 317–48.

64. "Passio XII fratrum qui e Syria venerunt," *AASS Iulii,* 9–15; see Paoli, *Agiografia e strategie politico-religiose,* 48. According to Paoli, by casting Lawrence as one of the twelve Syrians, Gregory manifested a tendency, widespread at the time in both Umbria and the Sabina, to identify popular local saints as belonging to the holy twelve.

65. *CF* 1:121.

66. Gregory of Catino, *Liber floriger,* 5–8.

Innocent named Adenulf cardinal deacon of one of the most important churches in Rome, Santa Maria in Cosmedin.[67] The modified biography of Lawrence in the *Liber floriger* suggests that Gregory intended to link Farfa's history more closely to the papacy than he had before, possibly in the context of the close cooperation between Adenulf and Innocent II.

Gregory's writings manifest an inventive reshaping and consolidation of Farfa's archival memory. Although working primarily as a scribe and compiler, he was also a historical witness whose voice blended with that of the documents he transcribed. In the prologue to the *Liber floriger* he becomes the interpreter of the abbey's history, which he presents as an exemplary instance of divine law, claiming for himself the authority of a canonical source. Gregory's four decades of scribal and authorial activity trace his trajectory from a historian striving to preserve and transmit his sources to an interpreter of the past appropriating the authority of his evidence for rhetorical ends. Like other medieval chroniclers, Gregory creates symmetry through recurrent motifs and patterns; his accounts of the abbacies of Berard II and Oddo share a common sequence of events: fatal errors of judgment followed by terrifying visions and inauspicious death. Gregory shaped the memory of his monastery by revealing through narrative what he considered to be the implicit significance of the documents in the abbey archives.

Memories of Foundation and Dedication

Although the foundation narrative in the *Liber floriger* constitutes a response to the abbey's new subjection to the papacy, the account of the foundation Gregory had written twenty years earlier in the *Chronicle* was closely bound to the liturgy celebrated on the feast of the founder, Lawrence of Syria (July 8). The foundation narrative in the *Chronicle* shows how Gregory made connections between the past and the present through liturgical chants and readings. The structure of the liturgy itself suggests ways in which it may have informed Gregory's thinking: it links widely separated events through juxtaposing texts, constructing a perception of time as multilayered simultaneity rather than linear progression. The symbolic layering of temporalities in the liturgy, like the multileveled exegesis of the Bible, endows people, objects, and actions with different yet interconnected meanings which are perceived simultaneously.[68] It is this multilayered sense of time that shaped Gregory's account of the foundation of Farfa.

67. See Maggi Bei, "Per un'analisi," 322–7; and Stroll, *Medieval Abbey,* 250–51.

68. The hermeneutic dimensions of the medieval liturgy are discussed further in chap. 2.

Although Lawrence's foundation of the abbey and the 1060 dedication of the altars in the abbey church were widely separated in chronological time, for Gregory of Catino these events were profoundly linked in liturgical time through the chants and texts of the Mass and the office. His account of Lawrence's arrival in the Sabina explicitly evokes liturgical commemoration with the phrase "our father Lawrence, the first builder of this holy monastery, whose annual solemnities we celebrate today with veneration."[69] This temporal reference to the celebration of Lawrence's feast "today" blurs the distinction between the distant past recounted in the *Chronicle* and the present experience of liturgical time and commemoration. It is likely that the *Chronicle*'s account of Lawrence's foundation of the abbey was performed annually on the day of his feast; similarly, the narrative of Farfa's refoundation around 700 by Thomas of Maurienne was read at Matins on Thomas's feast day. At the opening of the *Chronicle,* after the preface, Gregory extols the edifying effects of hearing exemplary narratives: "When the times of the holy fathers and the deeds of men are piously reread, and are religiously made known to the ears of the listeners, the prudent are edified and the wise, imitating those deeds in their own doings, are rendered more cautious, and they prosper happily in all things."[70] Here Gregory implicitly acknowledges the memorial function of his own writing, reminding the reader once again that the *Chronicle* was intended to familiarize the abbots of Farfa with the history of the monastery so as to guide their decisions and stewardship of the patrimony.

After relating how Lawrence became the bishop of the Sabina and then renounced the episcopate to choose the monastic life, Gregory cites the beginning of Matthew 7:17: "'A good tree brings forth good fruit,' and just as those coming in sheep's clothing are recognized everywhere by their fruits, thus our father most blessed Lawrence is present now and forever; it can be recognized that the fruit he offered to the almighty God after he put on the monastic garment was the better one."[71] This statement introduces the narration of

---

69. *CF* 1:121: "Pater noster Laurentius, huius sacri cenobii edificator primus, cuius hodie sollemnia annua veneratione recolimus."

70. *CF* 1:119: "Sanctorum tempora patrum sive gesta virorum cum pie releguntur, et audientium religiose auribus notificantur, prudentes ędificantur et in suis sapientes negotiis illa imitando, cautiores efficiuntur, et feliciter in omnibus prosperantur."

71. *CF* 1:125: "'Bona arbor bonos fructus facit,' et sicut venientes in vestimentis ovium cognoscentur utique ab eorum fructibus, sic pręsens pater noster beatissimus Laurentius nunc et in perpetuum cognosci potest quod fructum postquam monachico habitu indutus est, omnipotenti Domino optulit meliorem."

Lawrence's exploits in the Sabina, where, after expelling a poisonous dragon, he founded the monastery on Monte Acuziano. The good fruit symbolizes Lawrence's saintly actions. The image of the fruit-bearing tree, although it is not present in the Gospel reading for Lawrence's feast, is the theme of a sermon for the feast that appears in the autograph manuscript of the *Chronicle* between the prologue and the main text.[72] This sermon opens with a citation of the concordant passage on the good and evil trees in Luke 6:43–48:

> For there is no good tree that brings forth evil fruit: nor a corrupt tree that produces good fruit. For every tree is known by its fruit. . . . Every one that comes to me, and hears my words, and does them, I will show you what he is like. He is like a man building a house, who dug deep, and laid the foundation upon a rock. And when a flood came, the stream beat vehemently upon that house, and it could not shake it; for it was founded on a rock.

The sermon compares the fruit of good and bad trees to the words of good and bad people; heeding the word of God is likened to building a house on a solid foundation. The journey of Lawrence and his sister Susanna from Syria to Rome is interpreted as a progression to spiritual "higher places" (*loca excelsiora*), and the sermon concludes with an exhortation to imitate the example of Lawrence so as to attain salvation.[73] Although one cannot prove that Gregory's reference to the fruit-bearing tree in the *Chronicle* was inspired by this liturgical text, both the *Chronicle* and the sermon associate the image of the good fruit with the celebration of Lawrence's feast.

Even if he were not alluding to the sermon, Gregory would have known that Luke 6:43–48 was the Gospel reading at Mass on the annual commemoration of the dedication of a church.[74] This text was read both in the sermon for the feast of Lawrence and on the feast of the dedication. The two events are close together in the church calendar: Lawrence's feast fell on July 8, only two days after the dedication of the altars in the abbey church on July 6. Further expanding the temporal framework, the image of the good tree was also em-

72. Rome, BN Farfa 1, fols. 17r–18v. For a paleographical analysis of the manuscript, see Supino Martini, *Roma*, 280–81. Paoli (*Agiografia*, 44) attributes the sermon to Hugh of Farfa. The Gospel reading for the feast of Lawrence, from Mark, is indicated in a liturgical Gospel book copied at Farfa in the third quarter of the eleventh century: Madrid, BN Vitr. 20-6, fol. 74v. (On this manuscript, see chap. 4.)

73. *CF* I:103–6. The sermon cites only the first sentence, continuing "et reliqua" to suggest that the rest of the passage was read.

74. Klauser, *Das Römische Capitulare Evangeliorum*, 44, 91, 128, 170. Madrid, Biblioteca Nacional, Vitr. 20–6, fol. 96r.

ployed in the liturgy on the eighth Sunday after Pentecost (which usually fell in July), when the Gospel read at Mass was Matthew 7:17–18.[75] At Matins earlier on the same day, the ninth through twelfth lessons came from a patristic homily on this Gospel, focusing on the moral sense of the fruit-bearing tree as the orthodox expression of faith by the virtuous.[76] Matthew 7:18 also supplied the text of an antiphon commonly sung the following Sunday with the New Testament canticle at Vespers or Lauds.[77] Thus, at Farfa, four feast days sharing the theme of the fruit-bearing tree fell within a short space of each other in the month of July. Every July 6, the anniversary of the consecration of the altars, the Gospel at Mass compared the monastery to a tree bearing good fruit and to a house built on a solid foundation. Just two days later, on July 8, the Gospel and sermon celebrated Lawrence as a tree bearing good fruit. And the theme was evoked yet again within a few weeks, on the eighth Sunday after Pentecost. Related by their common allusion to the good fruit, the feast of Lawrence and the feast of the dedication jointly commemorated the founding of Farfa by Lawrence in time immemorial. From Lawrence, the good tree, proceeded the good fruit of the community and the monastic life. This link must have been of great significance to the monks of Farfa, for even after the reconsecration of the church on August 8, 1402, a fifteenth-century manuscript indicates July 6 as the date of the dedication in its liturgical calendar.[78] In the *Chronicle,* allusions to the celebration of Lawrence's feast and to the image of the good fruit evoke connections between the commemoration of Lawrence and that of the dedication. To perpetuate the memory of the first founder for his future readers, then, Gregory links these two moments in the history of his monastery through liturgical resonances.

Farfa's second founding by Thomas of Maurienne in the early eighth cen-

75. Madrid, Biblioteca Nacional, Vitr. 20–6, fol. 60v.

76. Pseudo-Origen, *Homilia 5 in Matthaeum* 7, 15–21, in *PL Supplementum* 4 (Paris: Garnier, 1968), 872–78. The homily appears in an office lectionary copied at Farfa in the second half of the twelfth century (Farfa, Archivio dell'Abbazia AF 278, fols. 44v–45v).

77. *CAO* 3:355, no. 3928: "A good tree cannot bear bad fruit, nor can a bad tree bear good fruit" ("Non potest arbor bona fructus malos facere, neque arbor mala fructus bonos facere"). This antiphon can also be sung on the tenth Sunday after Pentecost. For the liturgical assignments of this antiphon and the almost identical no. 3929 in numerous manuscripts, see the Cantus database, http://publish.uwo.ca/~cantus/, accessed June 25, 2003.

78. Schuster, "De fastorum," 24 n. 58; and Schuster, *Imperiale abbazia,* 348. The consecration is added to the calendar on July 6 in a fifteenth-century lectionary (Rome, BN Farfa 30, fol. 4r).

tury was also commemorated in the liturgy. The earliest extant textual source on the second foundation is a prose narrative divided into twelve lessons for Thomas's feast day (December 10) in an office lectionary copied at Farfa in the late eleventh century.[79] On Sundays and feasts, monastic Matins had twelve readings or lessons (*lectiones*) divided into groups of four; with chants, these four readings composed a subdivision of the service known as a nocturn.[80] The first four lessons were usually biblical, those of the second nocturn were patristic or hagiographic in origin, and those in the third nocturn were taken from the homilies of a church father or pope. On a saint's feast day, the lessons could consist entirely of hagiography; this is the case of the Farfa office for Thomas of Maurienne. The first eleven lessons recount the second founding of Farfa by Thomas in the early eighth century; the twelfth lesson chronicles the abbacies of his successors until the mid-ninth century.

This text has been the subject of much speculation by historians. After consulting the office lectionary at Farfa in 1853, Ludwig Bethmann concluded that the Matins lessons comprised the text that Abbot Hugh of Farfa had referred to as the *Libellus constructionis* (*Little Book of the Construction*). Bethmann published the office lessons in 1854, along with excerpts from other Farfa manuscripts.[81] Twenty-six years later, Ignazio Giorgi revised Bethmann's conclusions, establishing the foundation for the current consensus that the Matins lessons were excerpted from a much more extensive *Constructio*.[82] According to Giorgi's theory, the differences in length among the lessons indicate that the form of the text was changed when it was excerpted in the office lectionary.[83] Following Bethmann and Giorgi, Ugo Balzani published the Matins lessons from the lectionary under the title *Constructio Farfensis*.[84] However, the only clues to the contents of the lost *Constructio* are passing allusions in the writ-

79. Rome, BN Farfa 32. An office lectionary is a liturgical book containing the biblical and patristic readings for Matins. On this genre of manuscript see Palazzo, *Le moyen age,* 171–72; on the lessons of Matins see Martimort, *Les lectures liturgiques et leurs livres,* 71–102.

80. In cathedrals, collegiate churches, and parish churches, Matins on Sundays and feast days had only nine lessons.

81. "Historiae Farfenses colligit L. C. Bethmann," in *MGH Scriptores* 11 (Hannover: Hahn, 1854), 519–90.

82. To distinguish between the text in the lectionary and the lost narrative mentioned by medieval writers at Farfa, I will refer to the former as the Matins lessons, reserving the title *Constructio* for the lost text.

83. Giorgi, "Il *Regesto* di Farfa," 433–40.

84. *CF* 1:3–23.

ings of Hugh of Farfa and Gregory of Catino. The early part of the *Chronicle* contains several passages that match the account of the first thirteen abbots of Farfa found in the Matins lessons,[85] but Gregory apparently knew a version of the *Constructio* that was longer than the one preserved in the office lectionary. It had a prologue that both recounted the monastery's founding by Lawrence and told of its destruction during the invasions of the sixth century.[86]

The Matins lessons present the abbey's early history from a perspective that effectively serves the political aims of Gregory's *Chronicle*, and it seems possible that this text represents Gregory's reworking of an earlier source to support his historiographic and political agenda. Thus the liturgical text in the office lectionary, often considered the only extant vestige of the *Constructio*, could be in part a (re)construction of Farfa's history by Gregory himself.[87] My theory that Gregory himself altered the text of the Matins lessons does not preclude the existence of a ninth-century *Constructio*. In any case, the lessons are better understood as a creative rewriting of tradition in the ideological context of late-eleventh century Farfa, as Umberto Longo has proposed, than as an incomplete copy of the lost *Constructio*.[88] The liturgical function of the Matins lessons enhances rather than limits their effectiveness as a reading of history—a point that would not have been lost on Gregory of Catino. The annual cycle of the liturgy was central to his construction of Farfa's history.

New Songs from Old

The layering and interweaving of source with interpretation that informs the works of Gregory of Catino also manifests itself in several musical compositions created at Farfa during the eleventh century. Like Gregory's foundation narratives, these pieces recast existing texts in new forms to commemorate saints important to the monastic community. Just as the liturgical undertones and reminiscences in Gregory's *Chronicle* add meaning to his accounts of Lawrence of Syria and Thomas of Maurienne, music for the liturgy enriches

85. The series of abbots after Thomas, as recounted in the *Constructio*, is quoted verbatim in the following passages of the *Chronicle: CF* 1:147, line 15–148, line 13; 151, line 16–152, line 5; 155, lines 19–22; 163, line 33–164, line 2; 165, lines 20–23; 166, lines 11–16; 170, lines 3–9; 178, lines 11–17; 198, lines 1–13; and 208, lines 3–8.

86. Gregory states that "we read in the *proemium* of that authentic *Constructio*" (*CF* 1:128), and later states (*CF* 1:131–32) that the abbey's early history can be read in "the book of that same *Constructio*" (*legitur in eiusdem libro constructionis*) and its preface (*legitur in constructionis proemio*).

87. In chap. 5, I elaborate on the context that supports this argument.

88. Longo, "Agiografia e identità monastica," 340–41.

what we know from historical sources about the veneration of Benedict at Farfa.

The earliest preserved musical work from Farfa is a notated version of a poem in honor of Benedict by the northern Italian cleric Paul the Deacon (ca. 720–ca. 799), who spent many years at the court of Benevento and then at the abbey of Montecassino. Paul's *History of the Lombards* chronicles the Lombard people from their origins to 744; it is among the most important historical works from the early Middle Ages and was widely diffused in the centuries following its composition.[89] Saint Benedict makes only a brief appearance, as the subject of chapter 26 in the first book of Paul's *History*. Recounting the invasions of Italy by the Goths during the sixth century, Paul mentions Benedict's founding of abbeys at Subiaco and Montecassino and he alludes in passing to the account of Benedict's life in the *Dialogues* of Gregory the Great. After relating an episode in the life of Benedict not mentioned by Gregory, he returns to what he calls the "regular order" of his narrative of the Lombards, suggesting that the brief chapter on Benedict was a digression from the principal subject of the text. In many manuscript copies of the *History*, this chapter includes two poems in honor of Benedict, the first one beginning "Ordiar unde tuos sacer o Benedicte triumphos" [Where shall I begin your victories, O holy Benedict?].[90] At Farfa in the late ninth century, this poem was copied in a booklet, or *libellus*, and inserted into a manuscript of Gregory the Great's *Dialogues*, at the end of its second book.[91] The account of Benedict's life and miracles in book 2 of the *Dialogues* made it of great interest to monastic readers in the

89. McKitterick ("Paolo Diacono") has recently challenged the long-held assumption that Paul the Deacon wrote the *Historia Langobardorum* while a monk at Montecassino, arguing instead that Paul may have produced it in northern Italy. Costambeys ("The Monastic Environment") reaffirms the traditional interpretation that the emphasis on Montecassino and its founder in the *Historia Langobardorum* is part of Paul's interest in Benedict and Benedictine monasticism.

90. Paul the Deacon, *Historia Langobardorum*, ed. Bethmann and Waitz, 64–67. Neff (*Die Gedichte des Paulus Diaconus*, 27–34) prints a longer version and argues (25–26) that the text as it appears in the *Historia Langobardorum* represents the second redaction of the poem. The poem is found in numerous but not all manuscripts of the *Historia*; the current scholarly consensus is that Paul composed it before he wrote the *History* and added it to a later redaction of the text.

91. Rome, BV C.9, fols. 182–185. The *libellus* is a gathering composed of two nested bifolia. The dimensions and ruling of these leaves contrast with the rest of the book, but the script is contemporaneous. For a paleographical description of the manuscript, see Supino Martini, *Roma*, 241–42.

Middle Ages. The insertion of Paul's poem at this point in the manuscript was particularly appropriate because of a reference, in Paul's prose introduction to the poem, to the second book of the *Dialogues:* "As is known, blessed Pope Gregory composed his life in a pleasing manner in his *Dialogues.* And I, in proportion to the poverty of my talent, so that in honor of such a great father I might divide up his miracles one by one, I wove with elegiac meter in this manner: Where shall I begin your triumphs, o holy Benedict?"[92]

In the Farfa manuscript, however, Paul's poem is prefaced by a new first line in dactylic hexameter: "O uenerande amice dei Benedicte amator" [O venerable friend and lover of God, Benedict]. This added line is apparently unique to the Farfa manuscript.[93] The original poem is in epanalectic elegiac distichs, formed from pairs of hexameter and pentameter verses in which the first part of the hexameter line is repeated in the second part of the pentameter line. The narration of miracles performed by Benedict begins after the tenth line of the original poem, with one episode related in each distich, as described by Paul in the prose introduction to the poem. Although the added verse at the beginning of the poem creates two successive lines of hexameter, the structure of the elegiac distichs soon becomes clear:

O uenerande amice dei benedicte amator,	O venerable friend, lover of God, Benedict,
Ordiar unde tuos, sacer o benedicte, triumphos?	Where shall I begin your victories, o holy Benedict?
Virtutum cumulos ordiar unde tuos?	Where shall I begin your myriad virtues?
Euge beate pater, meritum qui nomine prodis, fulgida lux secli, euge beate pater.	Well done, blessed father, you who make your merit known by your name, [you] shining light of the world, well done, blessed father.
Nursia plaude satis tanto sublimis alumpno;	Sublime Nursia, applaud so great a pupil;

92. *Historia Langobardorum,* ed. Bethmann and Waitz, 64; and *Die Gedichte,* ed. Neff, 25: "Cuius uitam sicut notum est beatus papa gregorius in suis dialogis suaui sermone composuit. Ego quoque pro paruitate ingenii mei ad honorem tanti patris singula eius miracula per singula distingam, elegiaco metro hoc modo contexui: Ordiar unde tuos, sacer o benedicte triumphos."

93. The critical editions do not list the added verse among the variants, perhaps because the editions did not employ a siglum for the Farfa manuscript, as indicated by Stella, "La poesia di Paolo Diacono," 572–74.

Astra ferens mundo, Nursia plaude   Bearing the heavens to earth,
    satis.[94]   Nursia, applaud.

In the early eleventh century, musical notation was added to the entire poem, using the approximative graphic system of melodic representation known as neumes[95] (see fig. 1.1). The style of these neumes is typical of central Italy and particularly of the area around Rome in the first half of the eleventh century. They indicate neither pitches nor precise intervals but are intended rather to show the general contour of the melody and to indicate how to fit notes and phrases to the syllables of the text.[96] Neumes provided an archival record of a chant's shape which could refresh the cantor's memory during teaching and rehearsal. In this period, chant books were used primarily as a reference for the cantor during rehearsal and study rather than in performance; monks learned melodies not from a written record but by ear; they did not possess their own books for singing in choir. Upon joining a monastic community, monks had to memorize the psalms, hymns, and canticles that constituted the principal material of the eight daily offices. In preparation for a service, singers would rehearse their chants in front of the cantor, who could correct their errors from memory or from the books at his disposal.[97] It is typical of early eleventh-century notation that the neumes added to *O uenerande amice* resemble shorthand rather than a complete musical score.[98] Even though the neumes do not offer enough information to reconstruct the melody, they do show that each syllable of text is sung to a single note. It is also clear from

94. Rome, BV C.9, fol. 182r.

95. I have not yet found any other manuscript of this poem containing musical notation. The contour of the melody seems to reflect the meter of the poem.

96. Individual notes of the melody are represented by long diagonal or vertical strokes (*virgae*) and smaller, thicker rectangular shapes (*puncta*). Virgae usually indicate a higher relative pitch than puncta. The vocal nuances produced by the pronunciation of liquid consonants (*n, m, r, l*) are indicated by the small shapes, resembling a reversed letter *n*, that are appended to some of the virgae. This style of neumes, found in central Italy and elsewhere during the eleventh century, is typical of the earliest layer of notation in manuscripts from Farfa. On this type of notation, see Boe, "Music Notation"; and Ferretti, "Manoscritti in notazione neumatica koiné" and "Molti dialetti."

97. See Boynton, "Training for the Liturgy"; and Fassler, "The Office of the Cantor."

98. I italicize *O uenerande amice* when referring to the entire poem, placing citations of individual lines in quotation marks. *O uenerande amice* is the title used here for the version of the poem in Rome, BV C.9, while *Ordiar unde tuos* designates the poem as found (without the added first hexameter line) in other manuscripts of the *Historia Langobardorum*.

observing the contour of the neumes that the first hexameter line has its own melody which is distinct from the rest of the composition. With the second line of text begins another melody, this one repeated in every distich, with occasional slight variations discernible in the forms of the neumes. One important function of the notation is to indicate these subtle variations in the melody. The scribe might not have taken the trouble to add neumes to every verse if the tune were to be repeated identically throughout.[99]

The notation of *O uenerande amice* at Farfa fits into a broader trend in the central Middle Ages of adding neumes to a wide variety of Latin poetry, both ancient and medieval.[100] Although the specific forms and functions of these neumations varied widely, the basic intention of such annotation was to communicate an interpretation of the verse, either by translating an existing musical tradition into visual symbols or by representing a reader's understanding of it. The syllabic setting and repeated melody of *O uenerande amice* creates a musical declamation of the poem that heightens the experience of the elegiac meter and epanalectic verse structure for listeners and performers. Setting each distich to the same musical phrase emphasizes the role of those two verses as a textual and formal unit.[101] Similarly, setting apart the first line with its own unique melody heightens the musical and structural contrast with the couplets that follow. Only with the addition of music does the first verse noticeably unbalance the symmetry of the poetic structure. Thus the neumes constitute not only a declamation but also a reading or glossing of the poem, adding a new dimension to the textual narrative of Saint Benedict's miracles and effectively transforming it into a song.

With the addition of neumes, *O uenerande amice* raises the interrelated questions of genre and function. Musical notation implies at least the possibility of performance, and performance presupposes an occasion and purpose for singing the poem. As a narrative of Benedict's miracles, *O uenerande amice* would have been appropriate for performance on the saint's feast day, but in order to ascertain its function more specifically, and ultimately discover the meaning of the song for its users, it is necessary to understand what sort of

99. See Boynton, "Orality, Literacy."

100. On the notation of the early-medieval Latin *versus* see particularly Barrett, "Music and Writing"; on neumes added to ancient Latin poetry in medieval manuscripts, see Bobeth, "*Cantare Virgilium*" and *"Antike Verse"*; Wälli, *Melodien aus mittelalterlichen Horaz-Handschriften;* and Ziolkowski, "*Nota Bene,*" *Nota Bene,* and "Women's Lament."

101. I am grateful to Lori Kruckenberg for pointing out the significance of the syllabic setting.

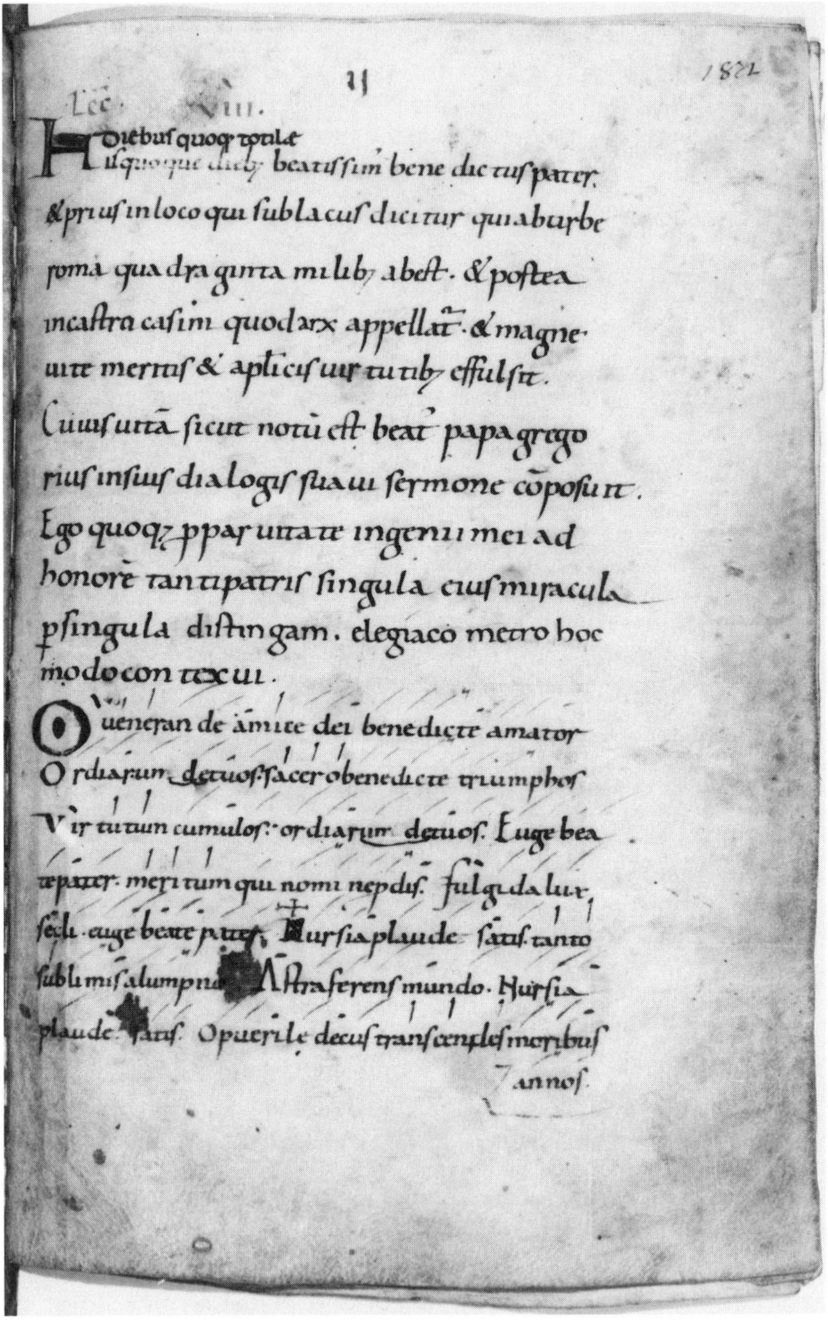

FIGURE 1.1. O uenerande amice Dei, *Rome, BV C.9, fol. 182r–v.* By permission of the Ministero per i Beni e le Attività culturali, Biblioteca Vallicelliana, Roma.

†

Exuperansque senes. opuerile decus. flos paradise tuus.
despexit florida mundi. Spreuit opus rome flos paradi
se tuus. Uas pedagoga tulit directo pectore tristi. Letare
formatur uas pedagoga tulit. Urbe uocamen habens.
ꝺ rone cautibus abdit. fert pietatis opem urbe
uocamen habens. Laudibus antra sonant. mortalibus
abdita cuneus. Cognita xpe tibi laudibus antra
sonant. frigora flabit niues. pfers tribus impiger
annis. Tempnis amore di. frigora flabit niueq. fraus
ueneranda placet. pietatis furta probantur. Q ii siccr.
altus erat fraus ueneranda placet. Signat adesse dapes
agapes sed luridus obstat. Hil minus al masi desfignat
adesse dapes. Orgia rite colit. xpo quia comoda auren.
Abstemiu pascens orgia rite colit. Pabula grata ferunt.
a uidi ad spe lea subulci. Pectorib. letis pabula grata
ferunt. Ignis abigne perit. Lacerant dū uiscera senucf
Car ne uf ethereus ignes abigne perit. Pestis iniqua
latens. pcul depre hensa sagaci. Hon tulit arma ꝯu

musical genre it represents. The text as written by Paul the Deacon can be compared to the lengthy hexameter poems of the eighth and ninth centuries often composed for liturgical use, such as those emanating from the abbey of Saint Gall.[102] The addition of the new first verse to Paul's poem blurs that affinity but creates a connection to another medieval musical genre: the sequence. A form of sung poetry performed during the Mass, the sequence originated in the ninth century in Francia. Some of the earliest sequences begin and end with a single verse; the rest of the composition is formed of paired verses, each sung to its own predominantly syllabic melody.[103] From a textual standpoint, *O uenerande amice,* with its isolated hexameter followed by elegiac distichs, recalls to some extent the form of an early sequence. Musically, however, because each distich has the same melody, the connection is less evident.

Nonetheless, *O uenerande amice* can be compared to some early sequences from Italy that do not feature consistent patterns of parallelism in the distichs, but instead employ one melody that is repeated more or less consistently to successive verses of the text, as in *O uenerande amice.* In the aggregate, such compositions suggest a distinctive approach to the genre of the sequence that seems particularly pronounced in the Italian repertory. The sequence *Alma fulgens crux praeclara,* transmitted only in Italian manuscripts, employs one basic melodic pattern that is varied throughout.[104] Even more similar to the structure of *O uenerande amice* is one version of the southern Italian sequence *Lux de luce* that begins with a hexameter line sung to its own melody and continues with verses sung to variants of a different melody.[105] This version of *Lux de luce* survives in four eleventh- and twelfth-century manuscripts from Benevento as well as in a late eleventh-century one from Rome, and could have been known to the Farfa monk who notated *O uenerande amice.*[106] Comparing *O uenerande amice* to the rare form of the Italian sequence represented by *Lux de luce* yields a loose but inconclusive analogy: though a superficial formal resemblance between the two is undeniable, it does not provide a framework for understanding the unique form that Paul the Deacon's poem acquired at Farfa.

102. Stotz, *Ardua spes mundi.*

103. For recent surveys of the sequence, with previous bibliography, see especially Hiley, *Western Plainchant,* 172–95; and Kruckenberg, "Sequenz."

104. See Brunner, *The Sequences of Verona,* 185–88. I am grateful to Lori Kruckenberg for this reference.

105. See Levy, "*Lux de luce.*" *Lux de luce* is entirely in hexameters, while *O uenerande amice* is in elegiac distichs except for the first line in hexameter.

106. Levy, "*Lux de luce,*" 43–44.

Besides the added first line and the neumes, further annotations to the manuscript created an accumulation of layers that gradually transformed the meaning and performance context of Paul's poem. Some time after the text was notated, a cross was added at the end of every pair of distichs. (One of these crosses appears in figure 1.1 over the *N* of *Nursia,* in the middle of the fifth line with neumes.) The crosses might have been intended to divide the poem into strophes of four lines, making its form like that of a hymn of the divine office.[107] Mario di Nonno, however, has suggested that the crosses instruct the singer to repeat the first verse as a refrain between pairs of distichs, as would be the case in the performance of a processional hymn.[108] The crosses may not reflect the performance practice that was intended by the notator, but rather an articulation of the text preferred by a later user of the manuscript.

This interpretation of the genre of *O uenerande amice* as a processional hymn is the most plausible explanation of its liturgical function, but the manuscript context of the song suggests yet other settings for its performance. Once incorporated into the manuscript of the *Dialogues,* the poem became an integral part of its received text. The heading "book 2" (*liber ii*) was added to the upper margins of the manuscript (with *liber* on the verso and *ii* on the recto), suggesting that a medieval librarian at Farfa perceived *O uenerande amice* as part of the second book of the *Dialogues.* What was the practical function of this combination? The placement of *O uenerande amice* after the second book of the *Dialogues* suggests that the poem could have been performed as a musical interlude after the prose of Gregory the Great was recited as a patristic reading in the refectory, at the collation, or at the night office of

107. Smolak ("Poetologisches zu den Benedikthymnen," 510) has pointed out that the distichs could be interpreted as hymn strophes. His observation is based on the edited text of the poem. Medieval Latin office hymns are composed of strophes, usually of four lines; each strophe is sung to the same melody. For a general introduction to the genre, see Boynton, "Hymn."

108. Di Nonno ("Contributo alla tradizione di Prisciano," 127) bases this suggestion on comparison with another isolated hexameter, "O uenerande amice Dei Nycholae amator," which is the first line of a hymn in epanalectic elegiacs (like *Ordiar unde tuos*) that was added in the thirteenth century after the *vita* of Saint Nicholas in BAV Vat. lat. 1190 (fol. 5r–v). In this case, however, the desired performance of the poem is more clearly indicated in the manuscript: part of the incipit (*O uen-*) is repeated in the margin after the first two distichs. The text is edited in *AH* 43:261–62. On processional hymns see Hiley, *Western Plainchant,* 146–48.

Matins.[109] The phrase "eighth lesson" (*Lectio octaua*), added in the eleventh century at the top of the first page of the *libellus,* identifies the prose introduction to the poem as the eighth lesson of Matins.[110] The eighth lesson was the final reading in the second nocturn, which on feasts of saints was reserved for hagiographic readings.[111] Although the manuscript of the *Dialogues* into which the *libellus* was inserted was not originally a liturgical work, the monks of Farfa evidently adapted it for liturgical use by adding cues to indicate the division of the text into lessons. The account of Saint Benedict's life in the second book of the *Dialogues* was a natural choice for performance on the saint's feast day.[112] The syllabic style, poetic structure, and extensive length of *O uenerande amice* make it an unlikely candidate for performance as the eighth responsory of Matins; the song was more probably sung as a processional hymn on the feast of Benedict.

Whatever the precise liturgical function of *O uenerande amice,* it is clear that a musician at Farfa had gone to great pains to record the melody for the entire poem at a time when musical notation was a rare skill practiced only by specialists. This gesture shows the importance of performance, as well as of writing, in the commemoration of the venerated founder of Western monasticism. Benedict was also the author of the rule revived at Farfa by Abbot Hugh in the early eleventh century; perhaps the special attention given to the song for Benedict reflects renewed interest in that saint as a consequence of Hugh's reform and the accompanying observance of the Benedictine Rule. The notation fits into a series of scribal interventions that created the Benedict song as

109. A later example of the poem's reception into the *Dialogues* is illustrated by a twelfth-century central Italian manuscript that contains *Ordiar unde tuos* at the end of book 2 (BAV Pal. lat. 265, fols. 34r–35v).

110. The rubric, abbreviated as *Lec. VIII^a*, is difficult to date with precision, but the symbol for abbreviation and superscript *a* resemble those found in eleventh-century manuscripts from Farfa.

111. On the hagiographic lessons for the second nocturn of Matins, see Heffernan, "The Liturgy and the Literature of Saints' Lives," 91–95.

112. Although the two office lectionaries from Farfa lack the section that would have contained the feast of Benedict, the feast is found in numerous other books, including the lectionaries from Cluny; see Etaix, "Le lectionnaire de l'office," 115, no. 40. The adaptation of the second book of the *Dialogues* as a liturgical reading appears in two other manuscripts from central Italy: two eleventh-century legendaries (Rome, Biblioteca Casanatense 713 and 718) and a twelfth-century copy of the *Dialogues* (BAV Pal. lat. 265). In the latter, the prose section preceding the poems contains the annotation *Lectio octaua* (fol. 33r) as in Rome, BV C.9.

it appears in the Farfa manuscript: the interpolation of the new first verse; the copying and insertion of the *libellus* into the manuscript of the *Dialogues;* and the addition of neumes to the poem, of the crosses between pairs of distichs, and of the running header that incorporates the song into the second book of the *Dialogues.* By creating new contexts for *O uenerande amice* over time, these layers of annotations resemble the gradual accumulation of meaning in the works of Gregory of Catino. Thus the changes made to the manuscript reflect successive reinterpretations of the poem on the part of those entrusted with conserving it in the monastic library, even as Gregory's writings reshaped the history of Farfa in the act of transmitting it. In the musical notation of the poem, as in Gregory's remaking of Farfa's documents, a new significance emerges from the transformation of Paul the Deacon's text. Musical performance situates the song in the annual cycle of liturgical time. In performance, *O uenerande amice* emerges from the accumulated annotations that reveal its liturgical function within the commemoration of Saint Benedict.

The textual layering seen in *O uenerande amice* can be compared to the process of elaboration in another song from eleventh-century Farfa, *Radix Iesse,* which builds on a preexisting hymn through the musical and textual practices of elaboration and interpolation known as troping (see ex. 1.1).[113] Liturgical tropes are additions or interpolations to a preexisting chant; they represent a wide variety of forms, styles, and theological content.[114] Troping engenders new compositions that comment on and amplify preexisting chants, often transforming not only the substance but also the meaning of the host text. Such works feature composite structures comparable to the compilations of Gregory of Catino in that they incorporate older materials into a new structure and comment upon them. The text of *Radix Iesse* is a case in point. It consists of four strophes, of which the first and fourth are taken from a much older text: the office hymn *Agnoscat omne seculum,* sometimes attributed to the sixth-century poet Venantius Fortunatus (see the italicized text in ex. 1.1).[115]

Agnoscat omne seculum, which was sung on Christmas, focuses on the In-

113. The transcription into modern notation with plain noteheads reflects the fact that the original neumes do not indicate note values or meter. Smaller notes indicate liquescences. A zigzag symbol over a note signals the presence of an ornamental neume called an oriscus.

114. For an overview of trope types in a representative and extensive repertory from one monastery, see Björkvall and Haug, "Tropentypen."

115. For a critical edition with an introduction on the hymn's authorship, see Walpole, *Early Latin Hymns,* 193–98.

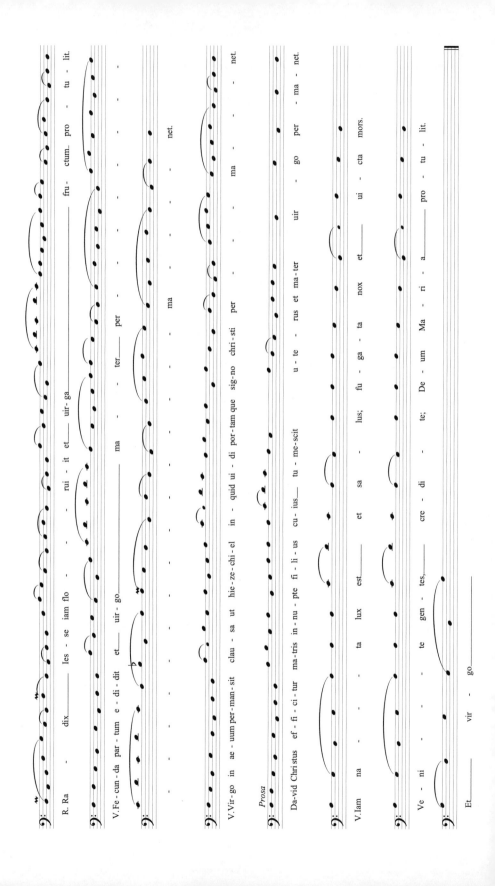

EXAMPLE 1.1. *Radix Iesse,* BAV Chigi C.VI.177, fol. 161r–v.

1	*Radix Iesse iam floruit*	The root of Jesse has now blossomed,
2	*et uirga fructum protulit*	and a virgin has brought forth fruit;
3	*v. Fecunda partum edidit*	the fecund one has produced a son
4	*Et uirgo mater permanet.*	and the mother remains a virgin.
5	v. Virgo in aeuum permansit	She remained ever a virgin,
6	clausa ut Hiezechiel	closed, as Ezekiel said:
7	inquit: Vidi portam que	"I saw a door," which
8	signo Christi permanet.	remains in the sign of Christ.
9	Prosa. Dauid Christus efficitur,	David is made into Christ,
10	matris innupte filius	the son of a pure mother
11	cuius tumescit uterus	whose womb swells
12	et mater uirgo permanet.	and the mother remains a virgin.
13	*v. Iam nata lux est et salus,*	Now is born light and salvation,
14	*fugata nox et uicta mors.*	night has fled and death is vanquished.
15	*Venite, gentes, credite:*	Come, nations, believe:
16	*Deum Maria protulit*	Mary gave birth to God
17	et uirgo [mater permanet].	and the mother remains a virgin.

2 uirga] *ms* uirgo

carnation and Nativity of Christ. The fourth strophe of the hymn, which is the first strophe of *Radix Iesse,* introduces the image of the root of Jesse in Isaiah 11:1: "And a rod shall come forth from the root of Jesse, and a flower shall ascend from its root, and the spirit of the Lord shall rest upon him" [Et egredietur uirga de radice Iesse et flos de radice eius ascendet et requiescit super eum spiritus domini]. Patristic and later commentators frequently fused the flowering rod of Isaiah's prophecy to the blossoming rod of Aaron in Numbers 17; allegorical readings cast the rod as the Virgin Mary, and the flower it produced as Christ.[116] As Margot Fassler has shown, the Marian interpretation of the flowering rod became an important image in the liturgy of the Christmas period and of feasts of the Virgin Mary, particularly her Nativity. Among the many medieval chant texts that echo Isaiah 11.1 is that of *Stirps Jesse,* a responsory for the Nativity of the Virgin Mary attributed to Fulbert of Chartres (ca. 960–1028): "The stock of Jesse produced a rod, and the rod produced a flower,

116. See Fassler, "Mary's Nativity," 414–15.

and upon this flower rests the kind spirit. The Virgin mother of God is the rod, and the flower is her son."[117] During Advent, the four-week season preceding Christmas, the image of the root of Jesse pervaded the liturgy of the office. Isaiah 11.1 was read during a weekday mass and set to music in a responsory performed at Matins during the third and fourth weeks.[118] Two other responsories performed at Matins on the third or fourth Sunday of Advent begin with the image of the ascending root of Jesse.[119] All these responsories could also be performed on the feast of the Annunciation, which also commemorated the Incarnation. On the fourth Monday of Advent, the antiphon for the Benedictus at Lauds begins with the first phrase of Isaiah 11.1.[120] One of the antiphons beginning with the word "O" sung with the Magnificat during the week before Christmas also draws upon this image: *O radix Iesse.*[121] The hymn *Agnoscat omne seculum* (containing the first strophe of *Radix Iesse)* was sung on Christmas Day, and *Radix Iesse* itself was performed at Matins on Christmas. After Christmas, the image of the root of Jesse appears in an antiphon for Lauds on the octave of Christmas, *Germinauit radix Iesse.*[122] Thus the opening strophe of *Radix Iesse* draws upon a motif that recurs throughout the liturgy of the Christmas season as well as on the feast of the Annunciation.

The other preexisting part of *Radix Iesse,* its fourth strophe (from the eighth strophe of *Agnoscat omne seculum*) places the Nativity of Christ in the context of salvation history rather than Old Testament prophecy; the phrase "death is vanquished" alludes to Christ's victory over death in the Resurrection. The preceding strophe in the original hymn text prepares for the idea of the Resurrection by contrasting the "old Adam" with Christ, the "new Adam," who cleansed what Adam had polluted through sin and redeemed with humility

117. *PL* 149:345B: "Stirps Iesse virgam produxit virgaque florem et super hunc florem requiescit Spiritus almus: Virgo dei genitrix virga est, flos filius eius." The music of the responsory *Stirps Jesse,* which was widely transmitted by the late eleventh century, is related to that of *Radix Iesse.*

118. For the text of *Egredietur virga de radice Iesse* see Hesbert, *CAO* 4, no. 6641. For a summary of readings from Isaiah during Advent see Flynn, *Medieval Music,* 111.

119. *CAO* 4, nos. 6606 (*Ecce radix Iesse ascendet*) and 7508 (*Radix Iesse qui exsurget*).

120. *CAO* 4, no. 2613: "A rod shall come forth from the root of Jesse, and the whole earth shall be filled with the glory of the Lord, and the whole [earth] shall see the salvific flesh of God" ("Egredietur virga de radice Iesse, et replebitur omnis terra gloria Domini; et videbit omnis caro salutare Dei").

121. *CAO* 3, no. 4075.

122. *CAO* 4, no. 2941. A rare chant for First Vespers of the Epiphany, *Flos illa de radice Jesse,* also evokes the root of Jesse (Rome, BV C.5, fol. 55v).

what Adam had lost through pride. Although it was not incorporated into *Radix Iesse,* this strophe would have been known to the creator of the new chant. The fact that the new composition lends greater emphasis to the Virgin Mary than does the source text may be connected to the composition of *Radix Iesse* in a monastery dedicated to her.

The newly composed strophes of *Radix Iesse* complement and expand on the themes in the preexisting hymn text, emphasizing Mary's postpartum virginity while incorporating allusions to prophecy and to the royal lineage of Christ. Lines 6–7 refer to Ezekiel 44:1–3, in which the prophet is shown the eternally closed door of the sanctuary through which God himself has passed:

> Then he brought me back to the way of the outer gate of the sanctuary, which was facing east; and it was closed, and the Lord said to me: "This gate shall remain closed; it shall not be opened, and [no] man shall pass through it, for the Lord, the God of Israel, has entered through it, and it shall be closed for the prince. And the prince himself shall sit in it [the gate] so that he may eat bread before the Lord. He shall enter by way of the vestibule of the gate, and he shall go out by the same way."[123]

Radix Iesse alludes to the common patristic identification of this closed door with Mary, as in Jerome's commentary on Ezekiel: "Some correctly perceive the closed door—through which only the Lord God of Israel enters . . . —as the Virgin Mary who both before and after childbirth remained eternally a virgin."[124] Even though *Radix Iesse* refers explicitly to Ezekiel, the phrase *uidi portam* itself is not derived directly from the Biblical text of the prophecy, but rather from an antiphon for the feast of the Annunciation, *Vidi portam:* "I saw a door in the house of the Lord, and the angel said to me: only the Lord will come, entering and leaving, and it will always be closed."[125] *De partu uirginis,* a treatise on the Virgin Birth by the Carolingian monk and commentator Paschasius Radbertus, provides a precedent for placing the words *uidi portam*

123. Ezek. 44:1–3: "et convertit me ad viam portae sanctuarii exterioris quae respiciebat ad orientem et erat clausa et dixit Dominus ad me porta haec clausa erit non aperietur et vir non transiet per eam quoniam Dominus Deus Israhel ingressus est per eam erit que clausa principi princeps ipse sedebit in ea ut comedat panem coram Domino per viam vestibuli portae ingredietur et per viam eius egredietur."

124. Jerome, *Commentarii in Ezechielem* 13.44, ed. Glorie, 646–47: "pulchre quidam portam clausam per quam solus dominus deus israel ingreditur . . . mariam uirginem intellegunt, quae et ante partum et post partum uirgo permansit."

125. *CAO* 3:537, no. 5405: "Vidi portam in domo Domini clausam, et dixit ad me angelus: Solus Dominus veniet, ingrediens et egrediens, et erit semper clausa."

in Ezekiel's mouth, even though they do not actually appear in his prophetic book: "the door that was shown to Ezekiel, about which he says: I saw a door in the house of the Lord, and it was closed."[126] Given the influence of *De partu uirginis* on the Marian theology of the Middle Ages, it is possible that the composer of *Radix Iesse* was referring to the text of Paschasius Radbertus as well as to the antiphon itself. The second newly composed strophe (lines 9–12) alludes to the Davidic lineage of Christ. At the same time, this strophe again emphasizes the virginity of Mary: the phrase *et mater uirgo permanet* in line 12 clearly echoes *et uirgo mater permanet,* the fourth line of the first strophe, taken from the hymn *Agnoscat omne seculum.* Moreover, lines 11–12 ("cuius tumescit uterus / et mater uirgo permanet") echo two verses of Ambrose's hymn *Intende, qui regis Israel:* "Aluus tumescit uirginis / claustrum pudoris permanet," in which the words *tumescit* and *permanet* occupy the same positions as in *Radix Iesse.*[127]

Like much medieval liturgical poetry, the newly composed strophes of *Radix Iesse* reflect adaptation of the meters of classical prosody to the principles of rhythmic poetry. Although the strophes borrowed from *Agnoscat omne seculum* are written in iambic dimeter, the newly composed strophes do not contain the requisite combinations of long and short syllables to make up quantitative verses. However, these strophes do contain the same number of syllables in each line as the preexisting strophes. Ancient Latin poetic meters are based on the lengths of the syllables combined in a verse, but in rhythmic poetry the structure of each verse is based on an accentual pattern and a fixed number of syllables per line.[128] The juxtaposition of strophes in quantitative and rhythmic iambic dimeter results from the troping of the hymn to create a new, hybrid poem.

Although the text of *Radix Iesse* maintains the strophic form of the office hymn on which it is based, the music is newly composed and the resulting musical structure is much more complex than that of a hymn, in which each strophe is sung to the same melody. The musical form of *Radix Iesse* is that of a responsory for the divine office, designated by the scribe with the standard abbreviation *R* for the first part (the respond) and *V* for the second part (the verse).

126. Paschasius Radbertus, *De partu uirginis* 1, ed. Matter, 68: "porta quae ostensa est Ezechieli, de qua dicit: Vidi portam in domo Domini, et haec erat clausa."

127. *Ambroise de Milan: Hymnes,* 273, vv. 13–14.

128. See Klopsch, *Einführung,* 8–16; Norberg, *Introduction,* 69–72 (translated in Norberg, *An Introduction,* 100–105); and Norberg, *Les vers latins iambiques et trochaïques,* 17–124.

In performance, the second half of the respond was repeated after the verse. The section marked *prosa* is a *prosula,* in which newly written poetry is sung to a passage of music that was originally textless, thereby transforming a melismatic melody (with several notes sung to each syllable) into a syllabic one (with a single note per syllable). When the respond of an office responsory was repeated, its final melisma could be replaced by a *prosula.* On a major feast, the *prosulae* corresponding to each melisma might be performed between the phrases of the original chant.[129] That the musical setting of *Radix Iesse* differs so radically in genre, form, and function from its textual source (a hymn) makes it an interesting example of transformation through musical composition. Textually, it is a troped hymn; musically, it is a troped responsory. Many medieval tropes for office and Mass employ the strophic form of office hymns, but the resulting musical structures usually do not reflect the combination of styles seen in *Radix Iesse.*[130] The florid melody of the first two lines is varied in the setting of the third and fourth; the addition of a melisma on *permanet* aptly expresses the meaning of the word "remains." This melisma furnishes musical material for subsequent sections of the piece. At the conclusion of the second strophe, the word *permanet* is set to the end of the melisma (see ex. 1.2a), while the middle of the melisma becomes a *prosula* in lines 10–11 and 13–16 (see ex. 1.2b) and to some extent in lines 5–8 (from *clausa* to *que*). The third strophe, the *prosa,* resets much of the music of the previous section to a new text. In the final *uersus,* the melody of the middle of the *prosa* (from *innupte* to *mater uir[-]*) is reworked and reset to text lines 13–14, then repeated to lines 15–16 (see exx. 1.1 and 1.2). This parallelism balances the differences in the musical settings of the previous strophes, in which lines 5 and 9 are set to variations of the same melody, while lines 6–8 and 10–12 are closely related in contour without being exactly the same. Within the final two strophes, designating each phrase by a letter of the alphabet, one can describe the musical form of lines 9–12 as A–B–C–A and that of lines 13–16 as A–B–A–B, both forms characteristic of hymn strophes. At the conclusion of the piece, the cue *et uirgo* signals a repetition of part of the respond, probably of line 4.

Radix Iesse is characteristic of chants composed in the eleventh and twelfth

129. On responsory prosulas, see Kelly, "New Music from Old" and "Melisma and *Prosula*"; Hiley, *Western Plainchant,* 204–7; and Hoffman-Brandt, "Die Tropen zu den Responsorien des Officiums." For the most recent discussion of troped responsories in Italian manuscripts, see Baroffio, "La tradizione dei tropi." Baroffio's study, however, does not mention *Radix Iesse.*

130. See Björkvall and Haug, "Tropentypen."

EXAMPLE 1.2. Musical Correspondences in *Radix Iesse.*

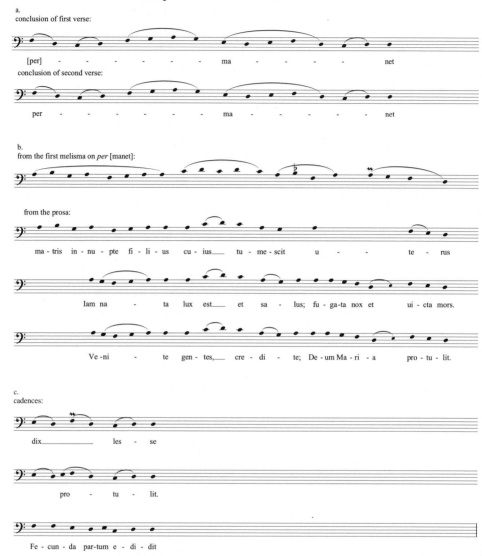

a.
conclusion of first verse:

[per] - - - - - ma - - - - net

conclusion of second verse:

per - - - - - ma - - - - net

b.
from the first melisma on *per* [manet]:

from the prosa:

ma - tris in - nu - pte fi - li - us cu - ius___ tu - me - scit u - - te - rus

Iam na - ta lux est___ et sa - lus; fu - ga-ta nox et ui - cta mors.

Ve -ni - te gen - tes,___ cre - di - te; De - um Ma - ri - a pro - tu - lit.

c.
cadences:

dix___ les - se

pro - tu - lit.

Fe - cun - da par-tum e - di - dit

centuries in that its mode (Dorian) is emphasized both by C–D–D cadences at the end of most lines and by a focus on the mode's tonal center, which spans the fifth from D to A.[131] The cadence is sometimes further enhanced by a decorative phrase turning around D, which recurs at the end of the respond and

131. On the tonal organization of new chants for the office, see most recently Hiley, "Style and Structure."

at the beginning of the first line (ex. 1.2c). This melodic contour recalls that of the initial phrases of the responsory *Stirps Iesse* discussed earlier.[132] The recurring verb *permanet* (remains) acts as a refrain that articulates the composition's broader textual and musical structures. The phrases sung to this word always end with the C–D–D cadence, heightening the rhetorical effect of the textual repetition and emphasizing the permanence of Mary's virginity. The use of a refrain, subtly varied repetition, and several types of troping link *Radix Iesse* to other eleventh- and twelfth-century musical compositions associated with Christmas, particularly those known as *uersus*, which are not based on preexisting chants.[133] Thus, although *Radix Iesse* is clearly identifiable as a versified office responsory, its form distinguishes it both from older examples of this genre and from the newer ones in manuscripts of the eleventh and twelfth centuries. The inexact melodic correspondence between the source melismas and *prosulae* attests to a degree of compositional freedom. *Radix Iesse* seems to have originated in the form found in the Chigi manuscript, for no known version of the piece lacks the *prosula* sections.

The distinctive features of *Radix Iesse* become salient through comparison with a related version of the piece in a twelfth-century manuscript that was copied in an unknown Roman monastery and is now preserved in the Biblioteca Vallicelliana (see ex. 1.3).[134] The most important difference between these two versions is the reversal, in the Vallicelliana version, of the sections corresponding to lines 9–12 and 13–17 in the Chigi version (see the italicized text in ex. 1.3). Thus in the Chigi manuscript the preexisting hymn strophes surround the newly written ones, while in the Vallicelliana version the hymn strophes alternate with the new poetry. The resulting structure separates two strophes that explicitly connect the Old Testament with the New, identifying the closed door seen by Ezekiel as the Virgin Mary and David as the type of Christ. In this version, the third strophe is the one that concludes the source

132. For a transcription of *Stirps Iesse*, see Fassler, "Mary's Nativity," 421. This chant appears in an early thirteenth-century manuscript from Beauvais with several proses, which, although much more extensive than those in *Radix Iesse*, reveal a similar compositional procedure. See Arlt, *Ein Festoffizium*, Editionsband, 149–52.

133. Examples include *Congaudeat ecclesia* (Paris, BNF lat. 1139, fol. 51r); and *Plebs Domini* (Paris, BNF lat. 3549, fol. 167v).

134. It is not known where Rome, BV C.5 was copied; it was used at the Roman convent of San Sisto in the early thirteenth century, then taken to the abbey of Sant'Eutizio in Norcia, and finally made its way back to Rome in the eighteenth century. It is closely related to BAV Archivio San Pietro B.79 from the Lateran Basilica. See Ledwon, "The Winter Office of Sant'Eutizio di Norcia," 90–93; and Supino Martini, *Roma*, 217.

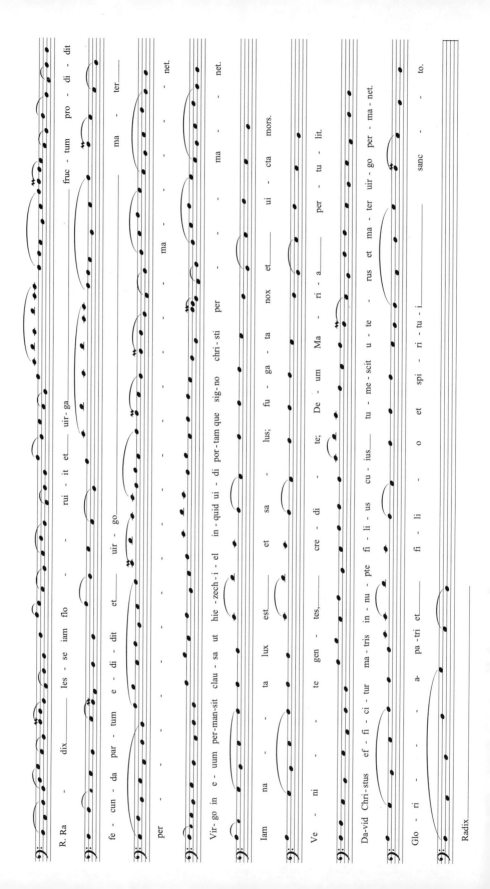

EXAMPLE 1.3. *Radix Iesse*, Rome, BV C.5, fol. 30r.

1	*Radix Iesse iam floruit*	The root of Jesse has now blossomed,
2	*et uirga fructum prodidit*	and a rod has brought forth fruit;
3	*fecunda partum edidit*	the fecund one has produced a son
4	*et uirgo mater permanet.*	and the mother remains a virgin.
5	Virgo in euum permansit	She remained ever a virgin,
6	clausa ut Hiezechiel	closed, as Ezekiel said:
7	inquid: Vidi portam que	"I saw a door," which
8	signo Christi permanet.	remains in the sign of Christ.
9	V. *Iam nata lux est et salus,*	Now is born light and salvation,
10	*fugata nox et uicta mors.*	night has fled and death is vanquished.
11	*Venite, gentes, credite:*	Come, nations, believe:
12	*Deum maria pertulit.*	Mary gave birth to God.
13	Dauid Christus efficitur	David is made into Christ,
14	matris innupte filium	the son of a pure mother
15	cuius tumescit uterus	whose womb swells
16	et mater uirgo permanet.	and the mother remains a virgin.
17	Gloria patri et filio	Glory be to the Father and to the Son
18	et spiritui sancto.	and to the Holy Spirit.
19	Radix . . .	The root . . .

text, the hymn *Agnoscat omne seculum.* This strophe refers to the Incarnation without drawing on Old Testament typology. It contains the exhortation "Come, nations, believe," a type of rhetorical gesture that usually appears at the beginning or end of liturgical poems, as in the hymn text and the Chigi version of *Radix Iesse.* For all these reasons it seems likely that the order of the strophes in the Vallicelliana manuscript is not the original one but instead reflects a later reworking of the piece.

The textual reversal in the Vallicelliana version also significantly alters the composition's musical structure by removing the symmetry in the Chigi version, where the melody shared by lines 5 and 9 sets up a parallelism that enhances resemblances between the settings of lines 5–8 and 9–12. In the Vallicelliana version the two lines beginning *Virgo in euum* and *Dauid Christus* are separated by the strophe beginning *Iam nata lux,* in which the musical settings of lines 9–10 and 11–12 are almost identical. As a result, the resemblance between the sections beginning *Virgo in euum* and *David Christus* is less prominent than in the Chigi version.

In addition to the structural contrast created by the reversal of sections, the version of *Radix Iesse* in Vallicelliana C.5 has none of the rubrics associated with troping that are found in the Chigi manuscript (*uersus* and *prosa*), even though such rubrics accompany other troped responsories in the same section of the manuscript. Another difference is that the Vallicelliana version contains the doxology *Gloria patri, filio et spiritui sancto* (Glory to the Father, the Son, and the Holy Spirit), followed by a cue to repeat the respond. The presence of the doxology may indicate performance as the fourth, eighth, or twelfth responsory of Matins.[135] Both the position of *Radix Iesse* among the supplemental responsories for Matins on Christmas in the Vallicelliana manuscript and the fact that its melody was notated by a different hand than the surrounding chants suggest that this responsory had recently been introduced as an alternate choice. In the Chigi manuscript, *Radix Iesse* was copied in the late eleventh century in a space that had been left blank at the end of a section; it is one of several recently composed works of liturgical poetry added to this part of the manuscript.[136]

The Farfa version of *Radix Iesse* as transmitted in the Chigi manuscript probably represents the original configuration of the work. It manifests a clearer structural logic than the Vallicelliana version and maintains the position of the final strophe as in the textual source, *Agnoscat omne seculum*. Moreover, the newly composed strophes of the text heighten the customary Marian emphasis of liturgical compositions associated with the Nativity, perhaps a sign of the particular veneration accorded Mary at Farfa.

The examples discussed in this chapter illustrate the various forms of written and performative memory in use at Farfa in the eleventh and twelfth centuries.

135. A note at the end of the version in the Vallicelliana manuscript suggests that *Radix Iesse* could be performed in place of the fourth, eighth, or twelfth responsory. The absence of the doxology from the Chigi version is not significant in itself. In manuscripts of the period responsories were not always accompanied by the doxology because it was not performed in every case, and its text could be sung to the melody of the verse. Hiley (*Western Plainchant*, 70) notes that the medieval performance practice of responsories varied widely but that in general, the doxology was sung only in the last responsory of each nocturn of Matins.

136. See Boynton, "Liturgy and History at the Abbey of Farfa." Other texts of recent composition that were added to this section of the Chigi manuscript are discussed in chaps. 4 and 5.

Juxtaposing the works of Gregory of Catino with liturgical compositions illuminates connections between the processes of their production. In both history and liturgy the elaboration of preexisting material through expansion and the interpolation of new ideas results in a new work with a complex, cumulative meaning. Similarly complex is the layering that results from the combination of contrasting yet linked temporalities—Old Testament and New Testament time, the recurring cycle of the church year and the linear immediacy of the present, Farfa's distant past and its present in liturgical celebration. Thus Gregory of Catino's foundation narrative in the *Chronicle* draws on liturgical references to create temporal connections; Paul the Deacon's poem for Benedict is remade through musical performance, and *Radix Iesse* builds a new trope upon the text of an earlier hymn.

Another dimension of the texts discussed here is the flexibility of genre. The Matins lessons for Thomas of Maurienne, which present a historical narrative in a liturgical context, furnish material for Gregory's *Chronicle*. The song for Saint Benedict was lifted out of the narrative framework of Paul the Deacon's *History of the Lombards*, inserted into that of Gregory the Great's *Dialogues*, supplemented with a new beginning, and adapted for musical performance. Preexisting poetry is also the basis of *Radix Iesse*, which in the Farfa version blurs boundaries between the genres of hymn, responsory, and trope. All these works represent possibilities for composition and innovation in the medieval monastic liturgy, which encompassed the manifold forms that are the subject of chapter 2.

the medieval liturgy wove texts from diverse sources into a tapestry rich with signification. The selection and combination of biblical texts in the chants and readings, and the juxtaposition of these texts with nonscriptural ones, created new layers of meaning. The resulting textual complex reflected the readings of scripture practiced by generations of commentators. Traditions of interpretation shaping the medieval Mass and office created inherently exegetical structures that were concretized through enactment in time and space through the performance of text, sound, and gesture. Treating the performative dimension of the liturgy as a type of active exegesis can be characterized as a hermeneutics of liturgical performance.[1] How does such a hermeneutics work? Particularly in the context of monastic life, the internalization of biblical texts through reading, hearing, memorization, and performance engendered interpretive traditions that influenced the liturgy's shape and content. The choice and composition of texts for worship services interacted with exegesis, and the synthesis of all these strata in the oral proclamation of sacred texts fed back into the commentary tradition. A liturgical hermeneutics centered on performance illuminates the circularity of these exegetical processes, seen in this chapter through the various aspects of the monastic liturgy at Farfa in the eleventh and twelfth centuries.[2]

In this chapter, I draw on liturgical manuscripts for the divine office to illustrate the varieties of interpretation that arose from and shaped the confluence of texts in the liturgy. In the first part of the chapter, several examples particular to Farfa illustrate the exegetical processes underlying the office of Matins. Expanding from the framework of Matins, I turn to various forms of commentary on the psalms that similarly reveal a dynamic interaction between performance and interpretation. The contents of several psalters from

---

1. For an analysis of a medieval liturgical drama in terms of a hermeneutics of performance, see Boynton, "Performative Exegesis." On the hermeneutic character of medieval musico-liturgical genres and repertories, see Flynn, *Medieval Music as Medieval Exegesis.*

2. On recent trends in biblical hermeneutics see LaCocque and Ricoeur, *Thinking Biblically.* A foundational essay on performance studies in ritual is Tambiah, "A Performative Approach to Ritual." For an overview of several approaches to performative hermeneutics in religious studies, see Sullivan, "Sound and Senses."

Farfa illustrate the intersection of ritual, exegesis, theology, pedagogy, and prayer in monastic life. In the second part of the chapter I consider the ritual functions and contexts of the prayer collections in the psalters. Although frequently characterized as "private," these texts are closely linked to liturgical performance and illustrate the elusive intersection of individual and communal prayer. In the context of the Adoration of the Cross on Good Friday, the prayers from Farfa reflect the gestures of individuals in a communal ritual.

Exegesis in the Monastic Office

Reading, performing, and interpreting the Bible were central activities in the lives of medieval monastic communities.[3] Monks sang and listened to the proclamation of biblical texts during the Mass and office (see table 2.1).[4] Approaches to scriptural interpretation that developed in the early centuries of Christianity influenced the selection and juxtaposition of scriptural texts in the chants and readings, making the liturgy itself a form of exegesis. The omnipresence of the psalms in the office and Mass reflected the Christian allegorical readings of the psalms.[5] The annual cycle of scriptural readings for the Mass, established by the early Middle Ages, influenced the formation of the liturgy around theological interpretations of the sacred events commemorated in the feasts and seasons of the church year.[6] Moreover, nonscriptural chants such as hymns, tropes, and sequences added a layer of commentary pertaining both to the liturgical occasions on which they were performed and to the biblical texts to which they alluded.

In addition to the modes of exegesis implicit in the structure of the liturgy itself, various forms of commentary on the Bible were ubiquitous in monks' daily life. Homilies on the Gospel readings of the Mass, which were gathered into collections in the early Middle Ages, furnished lessons for the office of Matins.[7] The writings of the church fathers and of early monastic authors were also read aloud to the community during meals in the refectory and at the collation preceding Compline. However, the lessons of Matins represent the

3. See Boynton, "The Bible and the Liturgy"; and Cochelin, "When Monks Were the Book."

4. For an overview of the readings at Mass and office, see Martimort, *Les lectures liturgiques*. Table 2.1 is not exhaustive; further details are supplied in this chapter.

5. Flynn, *Medieval Music as Medieval Exegesis*, 107–16; and Jeffery, "Monastic Reading and the Emerging Roman Chant Repertory."

6. An exemplary case study demonstrating this process is Fassler, "Sermons, Sacramentaries, and Early Sources for the Office."

7. On medieval homiliaries see Grégoire, *Homéliaires liturgiques médiévaux*.

TABLE 2.1. *Biblical texts in the daily monastic liturgical cycle.*

MATINS

Opening versicle: Psalm 69:1

Introductory psalms (Psalm 3 without an antiphon and Psalm 94 with an
  antiphon)

Psalmody at the beginning of the first and second nocturns

Pater noster

Three variable Old Testament canticles at the beginning of the third nocturn

First four lessons were often biblical

Gospel verse read before the ninth lesson

Gospel recited at conclusion of office

LAUDS

Opening versicle: Psalm 69:1

Psalms varying by day of the week

Psalms 66 and 50

Old Testament canticle

Psalms 148–50

Canticle (Luke 1:68–79)

Pater noster

PRIME

Opening versicle: Psalm 69:1

Psalms varying by day of the week

Sentence from the Bible

Pater noster

MORNING MASS

Epistle and Gospel readings

Psalm verses in Introit, Offertory, Gradual, and Communion

TERCE

Opening versicle: Psalm 69:1

Psalms varying by day of the week

Sentence from the Bible

Pater noster

continued

TABLE 2.1. *Continued*

HIGH MASS

Epistle and Gospel readings

Psalm verses in Introit, Offertory, Gradual, and Communion

SEXT

Opening versicle: Psalm 69:1

Psalms varying by day of the week

Sentence from the Bible

Pater noster

NONE

Opening versicle: Psalm 69:1

Psalms varying by day of the week

Sentence from the Bible

Pater noster

VESPERS

Opening versicle: Psalm 69:1

Psalms varying by day of the week

Sentence from the Bible

Canticle:

Magnificat (Luke 1:46–55)

Pater noster

COMPLINE

Opening versicle: Psalm 69:1

Psalms 4, 90, and 133

Sentence from the Bible

Pater noster

forms of biblical commentary and theological discourse that monks heard and read most frequently and at greatest length. While hagiographic lessons offered models of behavior for the monks to contemplate and emulate, exegetical lessons provided examples of interpretation and homiletic techniques. Our witnesses to the lessons of Matins at Farfa are two office lectionaries, one from the eleventh century and the other from the twelfth. These manuscripts contain the biblical readings, patristic exegesis, and hagiography, organized in the order of the church year, that were read as lessons.[8] In the quantity of their annotations, which include accentuation marks and musical notation, these manuscripts show the importance attached to the performative aspect of liturgical reading; in particular, they emphasize the correct pronunciation and oral punctuation of the text.

The lessons of Matins form part of the subdivision of the office known as a nocturn (see table 2.2). Each nocturn begins with the chanting of several psalms to a formulaic tone. Antiphons, which are brief chants set in a relatively unadorned style, often to scriptural texts, are sung before and after the psalms. In the form of Matins sung in cathedral, collegiate, and parish churches on Sundays and feast days, each nocturn has three psalms and antiphons and three lessons and responsories. The lengthier monastic form of Sunday Matins includes four lessons and responsories in each nocturn, as well as six psalms and antiphons in the first two nocturns; the third nocturn begins with three canticles from the Old Testament, preceded and followed by an antiphon. In both usages, the recitation of lessons, each followed by a responsory, begins after the recitation of a versicle and response, the Our Father, and an absolution. The third nocturn begins with a verse from the Gospel reading of the day; the lesson immediately following it is often taken from a homily on the Gospel.

The textual counterpoint embedded in the nocturns of Matins was enhanced in performance by contrasting musical styles and structures. Lessons, psalms, and canticles were chanted to syllabic reciting tones that consisted of a repeated pitch concluding with a cadence. While antiphons are relatively brief and sometimes rather simple chants, responsories are lengthier and usually more elaborate, with a florid respond and a sometimes formulaic verse. The manner of performance varied according to the genre of the chant. The leader(s) of the choir sang the first word of the respond, while the choir sang the remainder; the verse was performed by the leader(s) and the respond repeated by the choir.[9] For psalms, the leader of the choir intoned the first word or phrase, and the two halves of the choir chanted the psalm verses in alternation.

8. Rome, BN Farfa 32; and Farfa, Abbazia AF.278. Lessons for some feasts, along with chants, are also found in BAV Chigi C.VI.177 and Rome, BV F.29.

9. This summary description does not account for the variable aspects in the performance of Matins responsories during the Middle Ages, on which see Hiley, *Western Plainchant*, 69–74.

TABLE 2.2. *The nocturns of the monastic office of Matins on Sundays and major feasts.*

FIRST NOCTURN

6 psalms sung with 6 antiphons

Versicle and response, Pater noster, Absolution

Lessons and responsories, each preceded by a blessing

Lesson 1, Responsory 1

Lesson 2, Responsory 2

Lesson 3, Responsory 3

Lesson 4, Responsory 4

SECOND NOCTURN

6 psalms sung with 6 antiphons

Versicle and response, Pater noster, Absolution

Lessons and responsories, each preceded by a blessing

Lesson 5, Responsory 5

Lesson 6, Responsory 6

Lesson 7, Responsory 7

Lesson 8, Responsory 8

THIRD NOCTURN

3 canticles sung with 1 antiphon

Versicle and response, Pater noster, Absolution

Lessons and responsories, each preceded by a blessing

Lesson 9, Responsory 9

Lesson 10, Responsory 10

Lesson 11, Responsory 11

Lesson 12, Responsory 12

The juxtaposition of texts, integrated into the performative structure of alternating lessons and responsories, evoked various sets of associations and, in combination, created a multilayered interpretation of the liturgical occasion. The particular admixture of texts chosen for the liturgy could both reinforce certain themes and, by juxtaposition and contrast, create new meanings and associations. The formal and textual organization of the office of Matins for the feast of the Trinity from Farfa offers an especially interesting example of the liturgical exegesis in a medieval office.[10]

Liturgical commemoration of the Trinity, which in the central Middle Ages generally took place on the Sunday after Pentecost, lent itself well to the creative and hermeneutic possibilities inherent in the medieval office; the doctrine of the Trinity was inherently difficult to explain and consequently tended to inspire theological debate. The choice of texts for the lessons of Matins in this office varied from place to place, reflecting the traditions of individual institutions. In the Farfa office of the Trinity, the first nine responsories come from the set of chants composed for this office by Bishop Stephen of Liège in the tenth century.[11] These responsories form a series ordered sequentially according to the eight church modes.[12] The ninth responsory, which concludes the set, is in the fourth mode. Eleven of the twelve lessons in the Farfa Trinity office come from an anonymous patristic treatise, frequently misattributed in the Middle Ages to the fourth-century bishop Ambrose of Milan.[13] In the monastic office of the central Middle Ages, performance of these lessons in alternation with responsories taken from a variety of textual sources recontextualized the treatise, which was originally written during the doctrinal disputes of late antiquity. The third nocturn begins with a reading of John 15:26, the theme of the ninth lesson; this lesson is an excerpt from the beginning of a homily by the English monk Bede the Venerable (672 or 673–735).[14] This text effectively links the third nocturn to the second by continuing the thematic emphases of the preceding lesson.

Besides illustrating the combination of texts and responsories from various sources, the Farfa Trinity office represents the adaptation of preexisting material to monastic use. The nine responsories composed by Stephen of Liège were originally created for the cathedral office, and the entire set of responsories and antiphons comprising Stephen's office was rapidly adopted throughout western Europe. Because the cathedral office of Matins comprised only nine

10. The office is transmitted by three manuscripts: BAV Chigi C.VI.177, fols. 230r–239v; Farfa Abbazia AF.278, fols. 54v–57v; and Rome, BV F.29, fols. 87v–93r. The Chigi and Vallicelliana manuscripts contain the chants as well as the lessons of the office; the chants are notated only in the Chigi manuscript.

11. On this office see Auda, *L'École musicale liégoise*, 67–121 (including an edition); and Björkvall and Haug, "Text und Musik."

12. On office chants composed in modal order see, most recently, Hiley, "Style and Structure," which contains references to previous bibliography.

13. *PL* 17:509–16.

14. *Bedae Venerabilis Homeliarum Euangelii Libri II*, 290.

lessons and responsories, Stephen's office had to be adapted to monastic use through the addition of four more responsories. In the Farfa office, the particular selection and ordering of the variable chants as well as the texts for the lessons suggests an intention to give the office of Matins, and particularly its final nocturn, a coherent theological shape by creating connections among the chants and lessons. The juxtaposition of texts creates levels of meaning and places emphasis on certain aspects of the doctrine of the Trinity.

The first seven lessons of Matins, which correspond to the beginning of the treatise on the Trinity by Pseudo-Ambrose, set forth basic tenets of Trinitarian doctrine, emphasizing the incomprehensible, invisible nature of the Trinity; the indivisibility of its three persons; and its eternal existence outside time. The author then discusses and refutes the differing understandings of the Trinity according to the Arian and Sabellian heresies. The eighth lesson, which represents a significantly longer portion of the treatise than any of the previous seven, describes the persons of the Trinity by means of a logical demonstration that hinges on three categories of being, defined as the begotten, the created, and the born. The Father is neither born nor created; the Son is born but not created because he is begotten of the Father; and the Holy Spirit is neither born nor created because it proceeds from the Father.[15] The hierarchy of the universe is then articulated according to the same categories: heaven and earth are created but not born; humanity is created, born, and reborn; and the animals are created, born, but not reborn. The rest of the lesson is devoted to interpreting references to the persons of the Trinity in scriptural passage. It concludes by characterizing the Holy Spirit and its actions as "having neither beginning nor any end, just as he is coeternal with the Father and Son, he inspires with his own will where he wishes, and those whom he wishes, and as many as he wishes, and as much as he wishes, and as often as he wishes."[16] The conclusion of this passage seems to develop the first sentence of John 3:8, "The spirit breathes where it wishes" (*Spiritus ubi vult spirat*). The concluding theme of the eighth lesson is symmetrically mirrored in the opening of the tenth lesson. This parallel construction flanking the ninth lesson by Bede shows the care with which the third nocturn has been structured. The eighth responsory, which follows the eighth lesson, constitutes a communal affirmation of the

15. These statements are related to the description of Christ as "begotten, not made" (*genitum non factum*) in the Nicene Creed.

16. BAV Chigi C.VI.177, fol. 234v: "Neque initium, neque ullum finem habens, utpote qui patri ac filio et coeternus est, qui ubi uult et quos uult et quantos uult et quantum uult inspirat sua propria uoluntate."

Trinitarian doctrine set forth in the reading: "Let us praise the Father and Son with the Holy Spirit; let us praise and exalt him forever. Blessed art thou, Lord, in the firmament of the sky, and praiseworthy and glorious."[17] The respond is nonscriptural; the verse quotes Daniel 3:56.

The third nocturn begins with the Old Testament canticles and antiphons. The feast of the Trinity does not have its own proper canticles, so the texts are the standard ones for Sundays throughout the year: Isaiah 33:2–10 and 13–18, and Ecclesiasticus (Sirach) 36:14–19.[18] Although these texts have no evident connection to the doctrine of the Trinity, a special emphasis is added in the Farfa Trinity office by assignment of three antiphons to the canticles rather than the use of a single antiphon, as was customary. The texts of the antiphons present three aspects of the Trinity: its unity, the complementarity of God and Christ, and the fusion of the persons of the Trinity in God:

> Faith teaches that there are three persons in one, certainly to be vener-ated, but the believer venerates things that are undoubted; he worships and adores one.[19]
>
> God the Father from whom all things are is one, and the Lord Jesus Christ, through whom all things are, is one.[20]
>
> God the Father is one with his only son and the Holy Spirit; God is the one Lord, not in the singularity of one person, but in the Trinity of one sub-stance.[21]

Because all three of these antiphons are extremely rare, the second and third apparently unique, it is probable that they were composed at Farfa for the of-fice of the Trinity, or at least compiled for this purpose with an intention of thematic symmetry.

17. "R. Benedicamus patri et filio cum sancto spiritu laudemus et superexaltemus eum in saecula. V. Benedictus es domine in firmamento cęli et laudabilis et gloriosus."

18. This selection of canticles for Sundays was common to most monasteries; the texts appear in BAV Chigi C.VI.177, fols. 158v–159r.

19. BAV Chigi C.VI.177, fol. 234v: "Tres docet una fides personas nempe colendas sed credens confessa colit ueneratur adorat unum." This unusual antiphon is known from only three other manuscripts: Toledo, Biblioteca Capitular, 44.2, fol. 117v (Toledo, end of the eleventh century); Paris, BNF lat. 1090, fol. 113v (Marseilles, thirteenth century); and Rome, BV C.5, fol. 213v (Rome, twelfth century).

20. Chigi C.VI.177, fol. 234v: "Unus est deus pater ex quod omnia et unus dominus hiesus christus per quem omnia."

21. Chigi C.VI.177, fol. 234v: "Deus pater cum unico filio suo et spiritu sancto unus est deus unus dominus non in unius singularitate personę sed in unius trinitati substantię."

The scriptural passage read before the ninth lesson, John 15:26–27, is the basis for the first part of Bede's homily: "But when the Paraclete shall arrive, whom I shall send you from the Father, the Spirit of truth who proceeds from the Father, he will bear witness about me, and you too shall bear witness." The reference to the Paraclete fits with the emphasis on the action of the Holy Spirit at the end of the eighth lesson. This correspondence seems all the more significant because John 15:26 was the Gospel reading for the octave of the Ascension, not for the Sunday after Pentecost; the latter was the usual date for commemorating the Trinity. At Farfa, the Gospel on the Sunday after Pentecost was John 3:1–15.[22] However, the section of Bede's homily on John 15:26 seems thematically appropriate for use on the octave of Pentecost, for it begins with the statement that the advent of the Holy Spirit endowed the disciples with greater insight into divine mysteries. In commenting on the verses, the remainder of the brief ninth lesson reinforces the differentiation between the Father and the Son with regard to the operation of the Holy Spirit already seen in the eighth lesson.

The ninth responsory, which is the final one in the Trinity office by Stephen of Liège, emphasizes the same theological concepts as the lesson. The nonscriptural respond text reflects the distinction between the three persons as well as their indivisibility: "We confess, praise, and bless you, God, you only-begotten son, you the Holy Spirit Paraclete, the holy and indivisible Trinity, with our whole heart and mouth." The verse quotes the praise of God's power in Psalm 85:10: "Since you are great and you accomplish wonderful things, you alone are God."[23] The tenth lesson, considerably longer than the ninth, continues the description of the Holy Spirit from the eighth lesson, listing the traditional seven gifts (taken from Isaiah 11:2–3) and concluding with the exhortation to worship the Trinity as one: "Therefore we must worship the whole Trinity, since it is entirely royal, since it is of a single power, and it is of a single glory, above the world, above time, uncreated, invisible, incomprehensible, untraceable: it alone knows how it is ordered within itself; however, we must worship it equally."[24] The description of the Trinity as "royal" (regalis) in this

22. Madrid, BN Vitrina 20-6, fol. 52v.

23. BAV Chigi C.VI.177, fol. 235r: "Te deum patrem ingenitum te filium unigenitum te spiritum sanctum paraclytum sanctam et indiuiduam Trinitatem toto corde et ore confitemur, laudamus atque benedicimus: tibi gloria in saecula. V. Quoniam magnus es tu et faciem mirabilia, tu es deus solus." See also *CAO* 4:430, no. 7755.

24. BAV Chigi C.VI.177, fol. 235r; and *PL* 17:514: "Tota ergo a nobis sancta Trinitas adoranda est; quia tota regalis est, quia unius potestatis est, et unius gloriae est supra

passage evokes an image of earthly power, because the word *regalis* is almost never used in reference to the Trinity.[25] For monks at the imperial abbey of Farfa, the characterization of the Trinity in terms usually associated with earthly kings must have had a particularly significant resonance.

The responsory following the tenth lesson, *Tres docet* (ex. 2.1), echoes the lesson's exhortation to worship the Trinity as one: "R. Faith teaches that there are three persons in one certainly to be worshiped, but believing the things confessed, it rightly honors, venerates, and worships the one God who reveals heavenly things. V. Unanimously, with one mouth, let us honor the Lord and the father of our Lord Jesus Christ." This responsory is extremely rare; besides the versions from Farfa, it is attested in only one manuscript that was not produced at the abbey. It may have been composed at Farfa specifically for the office of the Trinity. Its text, which is based on the first of the three antiphons for the canticles performed at the beginning of the third nocturn, directly addresses the most important themes of the tenth lesson, namely, how one can recognize the persons of the Trinity and how one should worship them. The melody of the responsory emphasizes important points in the text. The first word of the respond, *Tres,* is sung to a long melisma, a rare feature shared by only a few compositions of the eleventh century, such as the responsory *Stirps Iesse* attributed to Fulbert of Chartres.[26] Lengthy melismas adorning the words *adorat unum* (worships one), beginning with a reminiscence of the opening melisma of the respond, realize musically the lesson's emphasis on the worship of oneness, which also uses forms of the verb *adorare* (to worship).

Although the responds in most office responsories can be divided into groups reflecting common structures and modes, *Tres docet* lacks modal consistency.[27] The opening phrases exhibit characteristics of responsories in mode 7, such as emphasis on the fifth from G to D and on the chain of thirds F–A–C, as well as frequent returns to G. The melodic range and the outlining

_____

mundum, supra tempora, increata, inuisibilis, incomprehensibilis, inuestigabilis: quae quo ordine apud semetipsam sit, ipsa sola cognoscit; a nobis autem aequaliter adoratur."

25. The only other example I have found is in an anonymous fifth-century North African theological treatise, *Liber de trinitate,* 8, in *Florilegia biblica,* ed. Fraipont, 252: "Nec dii, nec domini, nec reges dicti sunt, quia in trinitate nomina et personae discernuntur; nam una deitas, unum dominium, unum regale imperium."

26. Transcriptions of *Stirps Jesse* appear in Arlt, *Festoffizium,* Editionsband, 149–52 (with interpolated tropes); and Fassler, "Mary's Nativity," 421. I am grateful to Michel Huglo for pointing out this parallel.

27. The two sections bracketed in the example present difficulties of transcription because of inconsistencies in the notation.

EXAMPLE 2.1. *Tres docet una fides,* BAV Chigi C.VI.177, fol. 237r.

R. Tres docet una fides personas
nempe colendas, sed credens
confessa, colit, ueneratur,
adorat unum iure deo populi
qui celica pandit.

R. Faith teaches that there are three
persons in one certainly to be wor-
shiped, but believing the things confessed, it rightly honors, venerates, and
worships the one God who reveals
heavenly things.

V. Unanimes ex uno ore
honorificemus dominum
et patrem domini nostri Ihesa
Christi.

V. Unanimously, with one mouth,
let us honor the Lord and the
father of our Lord Jesus Christ.

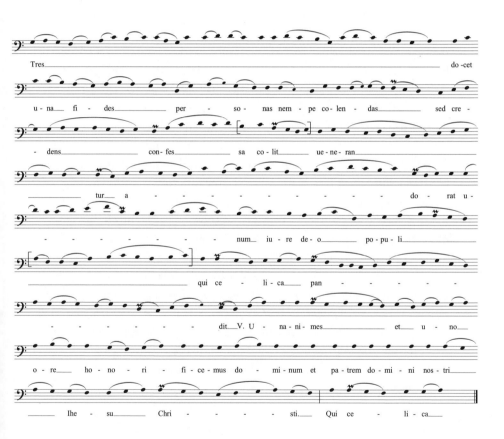

of F–A–C also suggest mode 5. By the word *pandit,* however, the melody has evidently shifted to mode 1, and the final cadence is on D. The change of mode is not startling to the ear because it is effected through a gradual lowering of pitch. The verse (*Unanimes. . .*) is sung to the usual melodic formula for mode 1 responsories, with a reciting tone on A and the customary cadence.

.The only other known version of *Tres docet* (ex. 2.2) is found in Rome, Biblioteca Vallicelliana C.5, an antiphoner produced at Rome in the twelfth century.[28] This manuscript contains several rare chants also found at Farfa, including the responsory trope *Radix Iesse* that was discussed in chapter 1. In the Vallicelliana manuscript, *Tres docet* begins on D (see ex. 2.2). The Vallicelliana and Chigi versions are almost identical beginning at "qui celica"; up to that point, their melodies are similar in contour. Although it would seem that the difference between the two versions reflects a scribal error, neither melody consistently manifests the conventions associated with responsories in a particular mode.[29] While the verse suggests mode 1, the first part of the Vallicelliana version lacks the tonal focus and characteristic melodic gestures of responsories in mode 1, seen, for instance, in *Radix* Iesse (ex. 1.1) and in the widely diffused *Domine ne in ira tua* (ex. 2.3 is the version found in manuscripts from Farfa). Unlike the respond in the Vallicelliana version of *Tres docet,* the melody of *Domine ne in ira tua* dwells on the pitches C, D, E, and F, frequently filling in the intervals with stepwise motion, turning around the interval of a third from D to F, and outlining the fifth from D to A. The respond of the Farfa version of *Tres docet* exhibits more similarities to responsories in mode 7, such as *O quam bonus,* the final responsory of Matins in the Trinity office from Farfa; like *Tres docet,* this responsory is preserved only in two manuscripts from Farfa and in Rome, BV C.5 (see ex. 2.4).[30] The melodies of *Tres docet* and *O quam bonus* share both a focus on the fifth from G to D and gestures outlining the chain of thirds F–A–C, but the scalar motion and recitation on D seen in *O quam bonus* does not appear in *Tres docet.* The unusual tonality of *Tres docet,* the rarity of its text, and its early appearance in two manuscripts from Farfa suggest that it may have been created there.

The two final lessons and responsories in the Farfa Matins of the Trinity continue the pattern of interlocking references already established. The eleventh

28. As seen in chap. 1, it is not known for which institution Rome BV C.5 was copied.

29. The two versions are closest to certain responsory types within these modes illustrated by Frere in the introduction to *Antiphonale Sarisburiense,* 19–20, 43–44.

30. Rome, BV C.5, fol. 195r. It is closely related to the responsory *Quinque prudentes* (BAV Chigi C.VI.177, fol. 277v).

EXAMPLE 2.2. *Tres docet una fides*, Rome, BV C.5, fol. 213v.

R. Tres docet una fides personas nempe colendas, sed credens confessa, colit, ueneratur (*ms*: uenerantur), adorat unum iure deum populus qui celica pandit.

R. Faith teaches that there are three persons in one certainly to be wor-shiped, but believing the things confessed, the people rightly honor, venerate, and worship the one God who reveals heavenly things.

V. Unanimes ex uno ore honorificemus dominum et patrem domini nostri Ihesu Christi.

V. Unanimously, with one mouth, let us honor the Lord and the father of our Lord Jesus Christ.

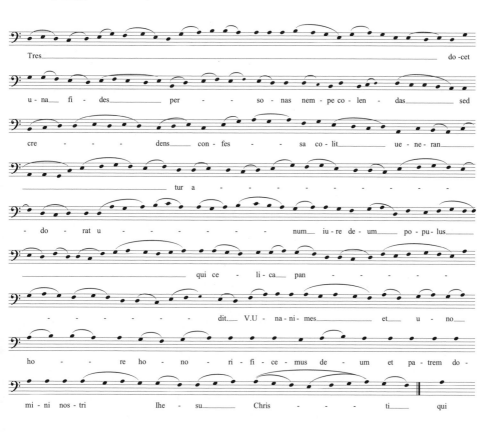

EXAMPLE 2.3. *Domine ne in ira tua,* BAV Chigi C.VI.177, fol. 283r.

R. Domine ne in ira tua arguas me
  neque in furore tuo corripias me;
  miserere mihi Domine,
  quoniam infirmus sum.
V. Timor et tremor uenerunt super
  me et contexerunt me tenebre
  et dixi . . .

R. Lord, do not rebuke me in your
  ire, nor reproach me in your
  fury; have mercy upon me,
  Lord, since I am infirm.
V. Fear and trembling came
  upon me and the shadows
  enveloped me and I said . . .

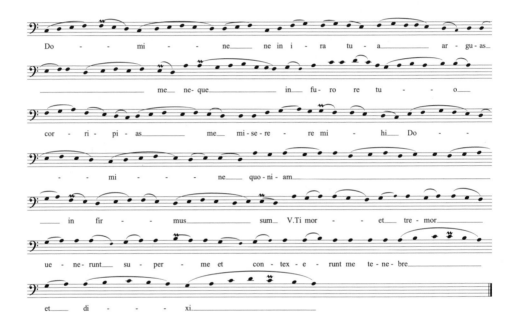

lesson describes the ways in which God and the Trinity surpass human understanding, which is limited by physical experience; the Holy Spirit is introduced as God's agent in salvation history.[31] The twelfth lesson expounds on the agency of the Holy Spirit, concluding with a statement of its crucial importance for personal redemption. Accordingly, the twelfth responsory of the Farfa Trinity office, *O quam bonus,* extols the presence of the Holy Spirit in the believer (ex. 2.4).[32] This particular combination of chants and lessons in the final nocturn is unique to the Trinity office from Farfa.

31. *PL* 17:515.
32. *PL* 17:516.

EXAMPLE 2.4. *O quam bonus*, BAV Chigi C.VI.177, fol. 239v.

R. O quam bonus et suauis est
   Domine spiritus tuus in nobis;
   ideoque hos qui oberrant partibus
   corripis et aequibus peccant; am
   mones et alloqueris ut relicta
   malitia credant in te Domine.

R. O how good and sweet, Lord, is
   your spirit in us; and therefore
   you reproach equally those who
   wander and those who sin; you
   admonish and exhort them so
   that, having abandoned evil, they
   may believe in you, Lord.

V. Parcis autem omnibus quoniam
   tui sunt Domine qui corripis
   noxios.

V. Spare all of them since they are
   yours, Lord, you who chide the
   guilty.

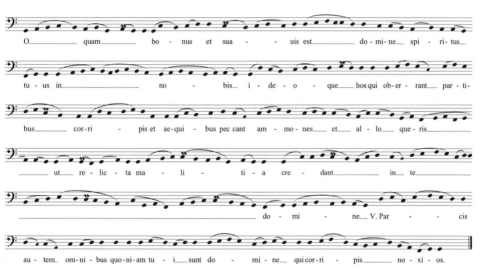

The interweaving of the scriptural and nonscriptural chants with the treatise on the Trinity and the passage from Bede's homily creates a network of interrelated meanings. The structure of this office suggests the composition of new chants and the selection of lessons to proclaim a particular understanding of the Trinity. The chants reaffirm and rephrase the doctrinal points in the lessons, while the lessons expand on the ideas evoked in the chant texts. By virtue of this exegetical structure, the office presents a synthesis of Trinitarian theology through which singers internalize doctrinal tenets while physically pronouncing them.

Another example of the didactic and hermeneutic design of the office can be perceived in the structure of Matins as celebrated at Farfa on Sundays in winter. All twelve lessons are taken from the first few chapters of Augustine's treatise on virginity.[33] The recitation of this text every week had two didactic functions: extolling the virtues of virginity, and explicating the simultaneous virginity and motherhood of the model virgin, Mary. Every week, then, the lessons of Sunday Matins invoked both the monastic ideal of virginity and the example of this state embodied in Mary, the monastery's patron saint.

Further enriching this network of associations are the responsories, all based on texts from the Old Testament. Each nocturn forms a thematically coherent group: the responsories of the first nocturn, set to verses from Psalms 6, 9, and 15, express supplication; those of the second nocturn, sung to verses from Psalms 17, 23, 25, and 142, praise God; and those of the third nocturn—sung to verses from Psalm 50, Jeremiah 17:14, Psalm 37, and Psalm 118—pertain to sin and penitence. Monasteries shared a common fund of responsories for Matins on ordinary Sundays in winter, with a selection and ordering that varied somewhat from place to place; however, this series from Farfa is unusual in maintaining a clear thematic structure in each nocturn.

As we have seen, although lessons and responsories can treat autonomous subjects in parallel, their performance in interlocking order (lesson-responsory-lesson-responsory) creates a new, layered text constituting a form of commentary on the separate elements. As a whole, the office juxtaposes and intersperses its recurring theological bases (praising God and beseeching his aid) with expressions of penitence and praise of virginity and of the Virgin. All these subjects pertain to the ideals of monastic life. As in the Trinity office, the patterning of Sunday Matins at Farfa constitutes a form of exegesis that encourages, through the regular performance of the office, a continuous reflection on the meaning created by the combination of texts.

The Psalms as Prophetic Song and Prayer

In addition to the practice of juxtaposing different texts and creating new meanings and associations from their confluence, individual psalms themselves were the locus of a hermeneutic practice. The psalms were the basis of medieval literacy for laypeople and clergy alike, and they were particularly familiar to monks, who had to memorize all the psalms as the first stage of their education. In the medieval liturgy, the psalms were omnipresent, whether chanted in their entirety or sung in the form of excerpts embedded in the chants of the Mass and office. Although the singing of psalms was a common

---

33. Rome, BV F.29, fols. 73r–76r; and Augustine, *De sancta uirginitate,* 235–40.

feature of all medieval liturgical traditions, the pervasiveness of the Psalter in performance was particularly characteristic of monasticism. The many hours monks spent singing the psalms gave rise to traditions of interpretation and teaching that were manifested in texts such as the *tituli psalmorum* found in psalters, sets of glosses on the psalms, and lengthier psalm commentaries.

In addition to standard texts such as the psalms, canticles, and hymns, the psalters from Farfa contain diverse materials for study, prayer, and ritual. Two of these psalters, BAV Chigi C.VI.177, copied around 1050–60, and Farfa, Abbazia A.209, from around 1100, are closely related to each other.[34] The Chigi manuscript also includes a useful collection of texts for the monastic life, beginning with a calendar and an excerpt from the seventh chapter of the Rule of Benedict, on humility (both the obits in the calendar and the excerpt from the Rule would be read in chapter). This manuscript unites several different groups of texts for the celebration of the office: a diurnal, a psalter followed by the litany, a hymnary with glosses, a capitulary (containing the short chapters from the Bible that were read during the office), rituals for visiting the sick and burying the dead, an orationale (containing the prayers known as collects that were recited during the office), and an incomplete section of offices.

Like the Chigi manuscript, Farfa, Abbazia A.209 comprises several sections of material for the office: a psalter and hymnary, a capitulary, a fragmentary orationale, and an extensive collection of prayers. Many of the texts in Farfa, Abbazia A.209 are glossed: the psalter, the canticle *Nunc dimittis,* the Athanasian Creed and *Confiteor,* and the hymnary. That the glosses on the hymns and many of the prayers also appear in the Chigi manuscript suggests a close relationship between the two books. Like psalm glosses, hymn glosses convey linguistic and other forms of commentary on chant texts, reflecting the didactic use of the liturgy.[35]

Two additional manuscripts from Farfa—a hymnary (Rome, BN Farfa 4)[36] and a psalter (Perugia, Biblioteca Comunale Augusta I 17)—both copied around 1100, also share many texts in common with the two psalters just discussed. The manuscript now in Perugia has the most diverse contents of the

34. For detailed descriptions of these two manuscripts see Boynton, "Eleventh-Century Continental Hymnaries," 202–13. Brief descriptions can be found in app. 1.

35. On the pedagogical implications of hymn glosses see Boynton, "The Didactic Function" and "Glosses on the Office Hymns."

36. On Farfa 4 see Supino Martini, *Roma,* 263; and Brugnoli, "Catalogus Codicum Farfensium," 291–97. The prayer collection is discussed later in this chapter, as is the ritual for the Adoration of the Cross.

group. The psalter is preceded by a ritual for penitence, *computus* tables, an excerpt from Bede's *De temporum ratione,* and instructions for singing the psalms. The Perugia manuscript was apparently designed as a companion manuscript to Rome, Biblioteca Vallicelliana F.29, a book for the celebration of the office. Pairs of books such as the Perugia and Vallicelliana manuscripts functioned both as collections of texts for the celebration of the monastic office and as manuals for priests to use when hearing confession and administering penitence.[37] The two manuscripts are almost identical in format, decoration, and script, and the texts they contain are complementary. The Vallicelliana manuscript contains an orationale, a capitulary, a ritual for confession, a breviary, and a ritual for the death and burial of monks.[38] In the Perugia manuscript, the complex *ordo penitentis,* which concludes with the confirmation of the penitent's intention to confess, seems to be completed by the confession ritual in the Vallicelliana manuscript.[39] The complementarity of the two rituals suggests that these two books were used by priests in the community at Farfa for pastoral care. That these manuscripts were produced around 1100 may reflect the increased proportion of ordained monks in the community since the mid-eleventh century.[40]

With contents both liturgical and didactic, the psalters produced at Farfa in the eleventh and twelfth centuries constitute a rich source of information on medieval hermeneutics and particularly on the reception of commentary traditions on the psalms. Three of the psalters from Farfa contain sets of descriptive headings for the psalms known as *tituli psalmorum,* which present allegorical interpretations derived from patristic psalm commentaries. These *tituli* reflect the Christian understanding of the Psalms as prophesies of the coming of Christ and his crucifixion and resurrection.[41] These *tituli* range in

37. On the administration of penance by monks see Hamilton, *The Practice of Penance,* 97–98.

38. On these manuscripts, see Supino Martini, *Roma,* 264–65. Descriptions are in app. 1.

39. Perugia, Biblioteca Comunale Augusta, I 17, fols. 1v–4r, unpublished; and Rome, BV F.29, fols. 70r–72v, ed. Schmitz, *Die Bussbücher* 2:760–62.

40. Constable, *The Reformation of the Twelfth Century,* 93; and Tappi-Cesarini, "Note sul reclutamento del 'conventus Pharphensis.'"

41. On patristic psalm commentaries and the origins of the *tituli,* see Salmon, Les "tituli psalmorum," 12–33; and Dyer, "The Psalms in Monastic Prayer." Perugia, Biblioteca Comunale Augusta, I 17, fols. 26r–113r contains a modified version of series 1, ed. Pierre Salmon, "Les *tituli psalmorum,* nouvelles séries," in *Analecta liturgica,* 12–14. BAV Chigi C.VI. 177, fols. 31r–105r contains an incomplete version of series 1, ed. Salmon, "*Tituli*

length from a brief phrase to several sentences. Many of the *tituli* identify who is speaking in the psalm and to what end, placing the psalms in the voice (*uox*) of Christ, God the Father, the church, or some other figure. For instance, Psalm 20 ("Lord, in your strength") is frequently identified as the voice of David speaking to God about Christ, while Psalm 21 ("God, my God, look upon me") is read as the voice of Christ speaking about the Passion.[42] Although most of the *tituli* reflect allegorical and messianic interpretations of the psalms, a few also project tropological or moral readings that treat the psalms as a guide for personal behavior. An example is the interpretation of Psalm 28 ("Bring to the Lord") as the psalmist's advice to believers to praise God by enumerating the seven gifts of the Holy Spirit.[43] Another example, the *titulus* of Psalm 150 in Farfa A.209, begins with a moral interpretation based on division of the Psalter into three groups of fifty: "The fiftieth psalm is about penitence, the hundredth about mercy and judgment, the hundred-fiftieth about the praise of God in his saints. For thus we strive for eternal life first by condemning our sins, then by living well so that, after condemning the evil life and behaving well, we may deserve eternal life."[44] In addition to the *tituli,* one of the psalters contains glosses on the psalms (Farfa, Abbazia A.209). Thus the monks who used these books at Farfa in the eleventh and twelfth centuries encountered the psalms in association with the synthesis of commentary traditions represented by the *tituli* and glosses.

A related form of psalm commentary also available to the monks of Farfa was a running commentary on the entire Psalter in the tradition of Augustine's *Enarrationes in Psalmos,* in which individual verses of each psalm are followed by exegesis of them.[45] A medieval example of this genre, attributed to the Italian monk Odo of Asti, was copied at Farfa in the early twelfth century.[46] The

---

psalmorum," 47–74. The longer *tituli* in Farfa A.209, fols. 2r–110r comprise Bede's excerpts from Cassiodorus's sixth-century commentary on the psalms (series 6); see Salmon, "*Tituli psalmorum,*" 158–86, but the *titulus* of Psalm 150 differs; see note 44 below.

42. Salmon, "*Tituli psalmorum,*" 57, 157–58.

43. Farfa A.209, fol. 6r; and Salmon, "*Tituli psalmorum,*" 159.

44. Farfa A.209, fol. 110r: "Quinquagesimus psalmus est de penitentia. Centesimus de misericordia et iudicio. Centesimus quinquegesimus dei laude in sanctis eius. Sic enim ad aeternam tendimus uitam primitus nostra peccata damnando, deinde bene uiuendo ut post condempnatam malam uitam et gestam bonam mereamur eterna."

45. An early twelfth-century fragment of Augustine's *Enarrationes,* now in the abbey archives, may have been produced there, but this cannot be demonstrated conclusively; see Boynton, "Frammenti," 335–36, 348–49.

46. Little is known about Odo of Asti, but he was probably a monk of Montecassino.

drawings added in the margins of the Farfa manuscript, like the *tituli psalmo-rum,* illustrate the Christian interpretation of the psalms. For instance, the first part of Psalm 2 ("Why do the nations rage?") is accompanied by a drawing in the margin depicting the Flagellation of Christ, apparently in response to Odo's interpretation of the uprising of the kings and princes of the earth against God and his anointed as prefigurations of the Crucifixion: "The kings of the earth rise up, and the princes take counsel together against the Lord and against his Anointed" (see fig. 2.1). In the lower margin the artist has depicted the Resurrection, expressing the Christological interpretation of the second half of the psalm, which begins with the verse "The Lord said to me: You are my son and today I bore you." This image also serves to illustrate the exposi-tion of Psalm 3, which begins on the subsequent page (facing this one) and is introduced by the abbreviated rubric at the bottom of the page.[47] The com-mentary on Psalm 3 develops the Christological reading of verse 6 ("I slept and lay at rest, and awoke") as Christ's words about his own passion and Resur-rection, an interpretation found in all the psalters containing the *tituli.* As noted by Hélène Toubert, the identification of Christ as the protagonist of Psalm 3:6 is unusual in the iconography of Latin psalters, which most often represent the psalmist, David, in illustrations of this verse.[48] Instead of fol-lowing the literal sense of the psalm as the words of David, the illumination embodies the interpretations found in Odo's commentary and in the *tituli* for Psalm 3.

Although Odo of Asti's psalm commentary seems to be intended primar-ily for study and meditation, it is nevertheless closely bound to the experience of liturgical singing and develops the implications of the psalm *tituli* in a man-ner that also illuminates the use of these texts in the liturgy. For instance, the verse "Lord, in your fury do not rebuke me" (*Domine ne in furore tuo arguas me*) in Psalm 6 is interpreted as the "voice of the church" (*uox ecclesiae*), while the same phrase in Psalm 37 is interpreted as the voice of a penitent (*uox cuius-libet penitentis*). The commentary on Psalm 37 explains further: "He says, re-buke me, but not in anger, or in fury, but rather in mercy and kindness."[49] Because the version of this phrase in the Roman Psalter was the text of the first

---

On the manuscript, see Toubert, "Contribution à l'iconographie des psautiers"; and Avril and Załuska, *Manuscrits enluminés d'origine italienne,* 32–33.

47. The abbreviated rubric, *tertii psalmi expositio,* is partly obscured by the drawing (see the lower margin of fig. 2.1).

48. Paris, BNF lat. 2508, fol. 1v; and Toubert, "Contribution," 599–600.

49. Paris, BNF lat. 2508, fol. 24r.

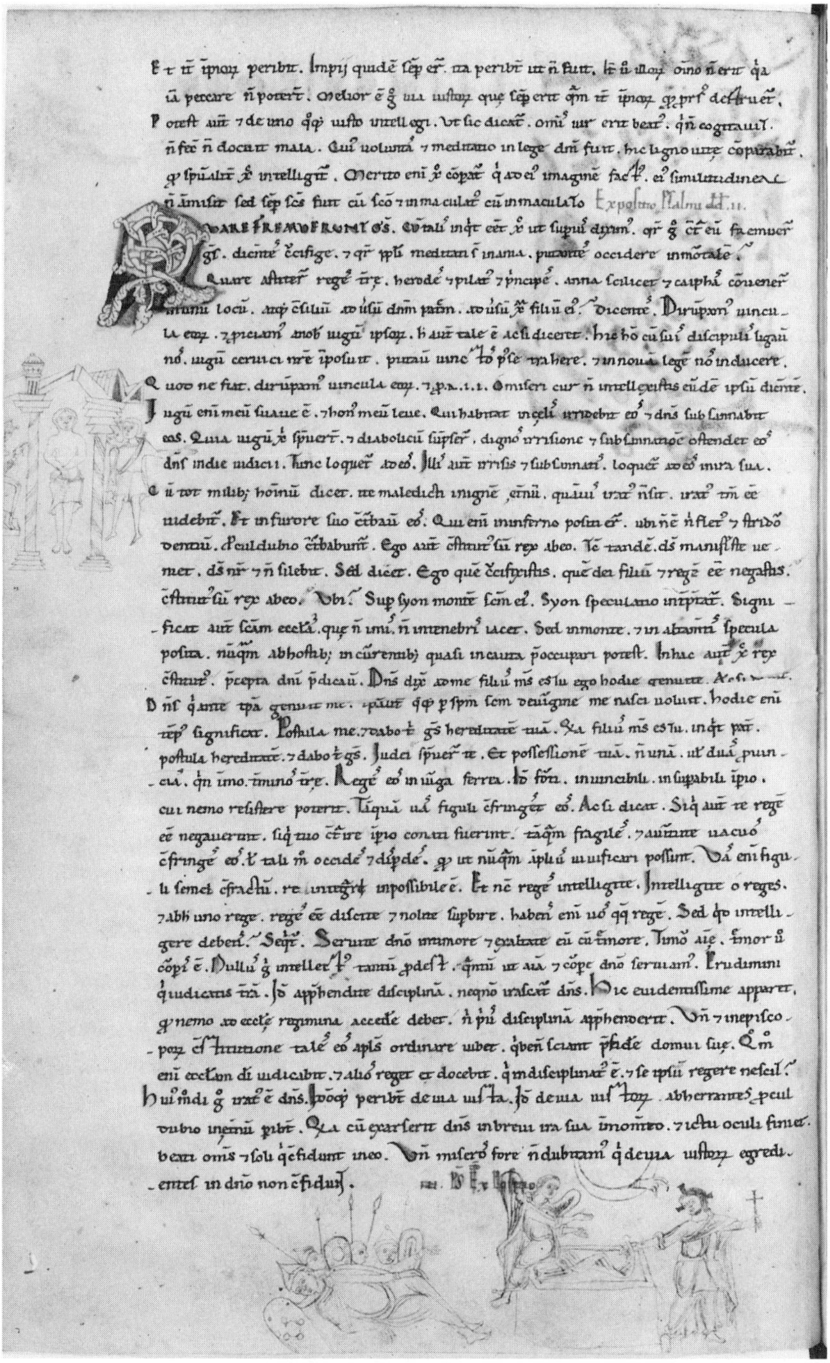

FIGURE 2.1. *Commentary on Psalm 2, with marginal drawings of the Flagellation and Resurrection, Paris, BNF lat. 2508, fol. 1v. By permission of the Bibliothèque Nationale de France.*

responsory of Matins on Sundays in winter (*Domine ne in ira tua arguas me*), monks assumed the penitential "voice" of this psalm verse every week in performing the office, thereby fulfilling the statement in chapter 49 of the Rule of Benedict that "the life of a monk ought to be a continuous Lent."[50] As a performance tradition, the psalms accumulated allegorical readings associated with the texts in the liturgy and incorporated into the commentary tradition. This cyclic process exemplifies the functioning of a hermeneutics of liturgical performance.

Thus the musical performance of psalms was closely linked to their interpretation through the singer's intimate spiritual identification with the voice speaking through the psalm. In addition to demonstrating modes of interpretation, the *tituli* of the psalms facilitate the appropriation of the psalmist's voice by those who are praying or singing them. As Joseph Dyer has remarked, "a singer tapped into the profound spiritual power of the psalms at the point when the words of the psalmist became in some manner his own."[51] The idea that the psalms offered a voice through which to express one's personal prayer appears in medieval texts such as the ninth-century preface to the treatise *On the Use of the Psalms* (*De psalmorum usu*), which combines the allegorical interpretations of the type seen in the *tituli psalmorum* with instructions for performance of the psalms. This text characterizes the psalms as prophecies of salvation history, and also identifies them as a form of prayer: "If you look with an attentive mind, in the psalms you will find a prayer so intimate that you cannot imagine it by yourself. In the psalms you will find the intimate confession of your sins and the whole supplication of divine mercy."[52] There follow specific recommendations for singing groups of psalms for particular purposes, such as the penitential psalms for penitence, the psalms beginning "Alleluia" for praising God, and Psalms 21 and 63 ("God, my God, look upon me"; "God, hear my prayer") for times of tribulation. Through this use of the psalms the singer appropriates the voice of the psalmist and makes it his own.

The idea of using psalms as prayers with specific intentions also informed

50. *RB 1980*, 253–54.

51. Dyer, "The Psalms," 64.

52. The preface and treatise exist in various forms, and the preface, attributed to Alcuin of York, is often transmitted separately from the rest of the treatise. I cite here one widely diffused and influential redaction of the preface edited in Black, "Psalm Uses," 50: "In psalmis invenies tam intimam orationem, si intenta mente perscruteris, sicut non potes ullatenus per te ipsum excogitare. In psalmis invenies intimam confessionem peccatorum tuorum et integram deprecationem divinae misericordiae."

the various practices of chanting groups of psalms in a certain order on behalf of specific beneficiaries. These forms of intercessory psalmody originated in the Carolingian period, and by the tenth and eleventh centuries, several such rituals were fixed components of the monastic schedule. The "threefold prayer" (*trina oratio*) involved reciting all or some of the penitential psalms in three groups, each for a specific intention and followed by the Our Father and a predetermined prayer of the type known as a collect.[53] The English *Regularis concordia* outlines the practice in detail: first the three penitential psalms (6, 31, 37) are sung on behalf of oneself, then Psalms 50 and 101 on behalf of the queen and her associates, and finally, Psalms 129 and 142 on behalf of the deceased faithful.[54] The *trina oratio* was recited three times a day: before Matins, before Terce (in winter) or Prime (in summer), and after Compline. Following the *trina oratio* that took place before Matins came the gradual psalms (*psalmi graduales*), which consisted of Psalms 119–33 in summer and Psalms 119–50 in winter. The seven penitential psalms were also sung after Prime. Two other forms of commemoration were the *psalmi familiares* (to be discussed in chapter 3), sung after each office with prayers on behalf of the monastery's patrons and benefactors, and the *psalmi speciales,* sung after Matins by decree of the Council of Aachen in 817.[55] The "special psalms" comprised sixteen psalms sung in groups before Prime in the summer or after the interval between Matins and Lauds in the winter. The first set of five psalms was for the king and all believers, friends or associates, and almsgivers (Psalms 50, 53, 56, 66, 69); the second was a single psalm (19) said for the king alone; the third group (5, 6, 114, 115, and 129) was for all deceased Catholics; and the fourth group, for all deceased monks and all faithful Christians, comprised psalms 22, 24, 25, 142, and 145.[56]

One of the Farfa psalters contains a set of instructions for another form of psalmody on behalf of beneficiaries: the chanting of psalms in groups of ten (*decadae*).[57] These instructions give this practice a ritual structure, beginning with the standard text to be recited before the psalms during the divine office:

---

53. The penitential psalms are those numbered 6, 31, 37, 50, 101, 129, and 142 in the Vulgate.

54. *Regularis concordia,* 81–82. See also Symons, "A Note on *Trina Oratio.*"

55. "Synodi secundae aquisgranensis decreta authentica (817)," XII and "Regula sancti Benedicti abbatis Anianensis sive collectio capitularis," XLIII, in *Initia consuetudines benedictinae: Consuetudines saeculi octavi et noni,* 475, 528: "Ut praetermissis partitionibus psalterii psalmi speciales pro elemosinariis et defunctis cantentur."

56. Tolhurst, *Introduction,* 72; see also *Regularis concordia,* 83.

57. Perugia, Biblioteca Comunale Augusta, I 17, fols. 7v–8v.

the versicle *Deus in adiutorium meum intende,* a chapter from scripture, and a prayer asking for God's indulgence on the monk who was about to sing the entire Psalter in his praise:

> Lord God omnipotent, you who are the beginning of all things, whose majesty is neither concluded by an end nor darkened by any change, look favorably upon me, I beg, about to sing psalms in praise of you, and enable me to sing without any mistakes all the psalms from the first to the last, so that they bring me, and those on whose behalf they are sung, salvation rather than judgment.[58]

The second part of the text lists the intentions for each of the fifteen groups of ten psalms: the Trinity, the Virgin Mary, the Cross, Saint Michael and all the angels, the apostles, martyrs, confessors, monks, virgins, and all the saints. After these comes a list of persons: the singer himself, his family, his friends and those of the monastery, and all the faithful deceased. After finishing the entire Psalter, the singer can also recite a litany, then sing canticles and hymns, and recite the Creed on behalf of the same beneficiaries; instructions follow for all the parts of this additional service. The final section of the text describes a similar service for singing the entire Psalter in groups of five psalms. Like the *trina oratio* and related practices, this set of directions from Farfa illustrates the conjunction of psalmody with intercessory prayer. The text suggests performance by an individual (perhaps in the company of others) who prays the psalms on behalf of himself and others, in a personal form of ritual also implied by some of the texts in Farfa's psalters that have been called "private" prayers.

Monastic Prayer and the Libelli Precum

The so-called private prayers in psalters from Farfa are found in text collections which modern scholars call *libelli precum* (booklets of prayers). Not separate books but sections within manuscripts (usually psalters), the *libelli precum* represent a genre that originated in the Carolingian period, although most of the extant examples were copied in the eleventh and twelfth centuries.[59] The Farfa psalters form part of a predominantly Italian tradition of

58. Ibid.: "Domine deus omnipotens qui es omnium rerum principium cuius maiestas nullo fine concluditur nullaque uarietate fuscatur, incipiente me queso in tua laude psallere, propitius respice et presta mihi sine aliqua offensione omnes psalmos canere a primo usque ad nouissimum quatinus mihi uel his pro quibus cantantur magis ad remedium quam ad iudicium proficiant."

59. On this type of collection, see Salmon, "*Libelli precum* du VIIIe au XIIe siècle"; and

monastic manuscripts that Pierre Salmon described in his analysis of the *libelli precum* in the Vatican Library. One of these books, from the northern Italian abbey of Nonantola (BAV Vat. lat. 84), contains, in addition to the psalter itself, a rich corpus of psalter prefaces and prologues, *tituli psalmorum*, and an abbreviated psalter. The second part of the collection consists of an office that can be performed during the Adoration of the Cross or for supplications to the saints, prayers on the seven penitential psalms, litanies, and prayers to saints and the Trinity.[60] A comparable collection from the abbey of Subiaco includes prayers to the Virgin Mary and the saints, a "psalmodic prayer" for daily performance, and rituals for confession and the Adoration of the Cross.[61] Some of these Italian prayer collections lack psalters but still contain unambiguously liturgical texts such as the order of Mass and offices.[62] The prayers are grouped in sections by intention. Fairly typical in their general outline, the *libelli precum* from Farfa include groups of prayers to the persons of the Trinity, the Virgin Mary, saints, and angels; as in all manuscripts of this kind, the precise selection and ordering of prayers in each book is unique. The texts in *libelli precum* are often considered "private" prayers. Although distinctions between public and private worship or between collective and individual prayer have sometimes been useful to modern scholars, a strict separation between the two creates a false dichotomy that finds little support in historical sources. As Jean Leclercq pointed out long ago, the varieties of monastic liturgical performance were profoundly interrelated, precluding a rigid distinction between personal and communal prayer.[63] Sarah Hamilton has also noted the lack of clear boundaries between private and communal prayer in the Middle Ages, both because prayer books for individual use can include texts of communal rituals, and because one could always pray personally during a public liturgical service.[64] Many texts associated with early monasticism (such as the *Sayings of the Desert Fathers*) make no distinction between private and liturgical prayer at all.[65] As cenobitic monasticism spread to the Latin West, there arose more prescriptive rules that took into account potential differences of behavior among the members of a community. Chapter 52 of the Rule of Benedict,

---

Wilmart, *Precum libelli.* For a recent list of editions of *libelli precum,* see Cottier, *Anima mea,* 276–79.

60. Salmon, "*Libelli precum,*" 129–39.

61. BAV Chigi D.VI.79; and Salmon, "*Libelli precum,*" 173–79.

62. See the description of BAV Chigi D.V.77 in Salmon, "*Libelli precum,*" 165–66.

63. Leclercq, "Culte liturgique et prière intime dans le monachisme au moyen âge."

64. Hamilton, "'Most Illustrious King of Kings,'" 270.

65. Taft, *The Liturgy of the Hours in East and West,* 68–71.

for instance, instructs monks to pray privately (*secretius*) in the oratory after the divine office or at other times.[66] The rule also distinguishes between personal and communal prayer in chapter 20: "Prayer should therefore be short and pure, unless perhaps it is prolonged under the inspiration of divine grace. In community, however, prayer should always be brief."[67] This sentence seems to refer to spontaneous prayer, whether within or outside the context of liturgical worship.

In the tenth and eleventh centuries, as the monastic liturgy acquired a more complex structure and a web of spiritual connotations, the prayer of a monastic community was understood to benefit those living and dead, both inside and outside the monastery.[68] Texts of the period offer abundant information on the intentions of liturgical prayer but relatively little evidence for a distinction between individual and community prayer. When such a difference is implied, it tends to be articulated in terms of the space in which prayer occurs. In monastic customaries, explicit provisions for personal prayer refer primarily to the interval between Matins and Lauds in winter, when individuals could move outside the communal space of the choir to pray. The earliest customs associated with Cluny, from around the year 1000, however, instruct monks to leave the choir briefly when they make a "particular" (*peculiaris*) prayer.[69] Similarly, the Cluniac customary copied at Farfa states that "should anyone wish to pray privately (*secretius*), he may pray outside the choir; let him be seated immediately upon returning to the choir."[70] An eleventh-century customary written for English monasteries by Archbishop Lanfranc of Canterbury refers to monks praying alone at side altars and other areas of a church.[71] The *Reg-*

66. *RB 1980*, 254–55.

67. *RB 1980*, 216–17: "Et ideo brevis debet esse et pura oratio, nisi forte ex affectu inspirationis divinae gratiae protendatur. In conventu tamen omnino brevietur oratio, et facto signo a priore omnes pariter surgant."

68. On monastic prayer for the dead, see chap. 4 of the present volume and McLaughlin, *Consorting with Saints*.

69. *Consuetudines Cluniacensium antiquiores*, ed. Hallinger, 17–18: "Si quis uero fratres uoluerit orationem facere peculiare, exeant et sub breuitate orationem faciant; postea iterum ueniant in chorum" (redactions B, B¹, B², G); "Si quis autem uoluerit orationem peculiarem facere, exeat et sub breuitate faciat et postea iterum in chorum redeat" (redaction C).

70. *LT*, 188: "Si cui secretius orare liberuerit, foris chorum orationem faciat et statim reueniens in choro sedeat." The later Cluniac customaries of Bernard and Ulrich (see chap. 3) do not make explicit reference to this kind of prayer.

71. *The Monastic Constitutions of Lanfranc*, ed. Knowles, 10–11.

ularis concordia, a customary established in England in the tenth century, implies that most of the monks remained in the choir to pray during the interval after Matins but does not describe this activity further.[72] The only customary to use the Latin term *priuata,* an early twelfth-century Cluniac customary from Vallombrosa, states that a "private" prayer is to be said by the whole community together, under the direction of the abbot or prior; this may refer to silent prayer.[73] Thus an activity termed "private" is clearly performed in common. Customaries also prescribe the performance of unspecified prayers by the community before other hours of the divine office, including Terce, Sext, None, and Vespers.[74] The early Cluniac customs state that monks say their own prayers in the choir (*faciant orationes suas in choro*) in front of the altar individually before Terce, as well as all together before None.[75] We do not know whether these prayers were extemporized or recited, but the main point to note in these texts is that they differentiate only slightly between the liturgical prayer of the community during the office and prayer by individuals between the hours of the office.

In the absence of a strong distinction between the prayer of the hours and personal prayer outside the office, one can presume a similar flexibility in the definition of the prayers included in the *libelli precum.* Indeed, many of the prayers in the Farfa *libelli precum* are closely bound to liturgical performance, either to various types of psalmody or to specific ceremonies of the church year. Several prayers commonly found in these collections propound a type of liturgical theology explicitly presenting psalmody as the sinner's offering to God.[76] Six of these texts, found in a great many monastic psalters of the eleventh and twelfth centuries, are intended for recitation after singing the psalms.[77] One of them refers to the melody of the psalms as the means of sal-

72. *Regularis concordia Anglicae nationis,* ed. Symons, in *Consuetudinum saeculi X/XI/ XII monumenta non-Cluniacensia,* 84: "in aecclesia orationibus dediti resideant."

73. *Consuetudines Cluniacensium antiquiores,* ed. Hallinger, 320: "Post haec agatur ab omnibus priuata oratio. Quantitas illius orationis fiat secundum uoluntatem abbatis uel prioris."

74. According to Tolhurst (*Introduction,* 195, 198, 202), the hours of Lauds, Prime, Terce, Sext, and None were all preceded by private prayers. *LT* (13, 42, 75, 82) refers to unspecified prayers before Terce, None, and Vespers.

75. *Consuetudinum Cluniacensium antiquiores,* ed. Hallinger, 11–13.

76. For a more extended discussion of prayers in *libelli precum,* see Boynton, "Prayer and Liturgical Performance."

77. Perugia, Biblioteca Comunale Augusta I 17, fols. 123v–124v: *Liberator animarum mundi redemptor* (Salmon, "*Libelli precum,*" no. 386); *Tuam Domine clementiam deprecor*

vation: "I, a sinner, supplicate you through your immense kindness and your great mercy, so that through the melody of the psalms which I, unworthy and a sinner, have sung, you may liberate my soul from sin and remove my heart from all petty and treacherous thoughts."[78] These prayers present psalmody as sung in the sight or view (*in conspectu*) of God,[79] recalling the final exhortation of the Benedictine Rule's chapter on the discipline of psalmody: "Therefore let us consider how to behave in the sight (*in conspectu*) of God and his angels, and let us stand to sing the psalms in such a way that our minds are in harmony with our voices."[80] References to psalmody just performed make such prayers appropriate for recitation after the structured groups of psalms described earlier, such as the psalms by decades, the *trina oratio, psalmi familiares,* and *psalmi graduales.* The connection with the intercessory character of these practices is particularly clear in a prayer that asks for salvation not only on behalf of the orant, but also for all his benefactors, those for whom he prays, and for all Christians living and dead.[81] Prayers associated with psalmody imply the singing of psalms by the individual reciting the prayer.

One of the *libelli precum* from Farfa, contained in the early twelfth-century psalter Rome, BN Farfa 4, begins with an unusual prayer to the Virgin Mary (ex. 2.5; boldface indicates repetitions within the text). Henri Barré, who edited the prayer from this manuscript, assumed that it was unique to Farfa and had originated there, in part because it shows special veneration of the abbey's patron and stands at the beginning of the prayer collection.[82] However, although the text is indeed rare, it also appears in an eleventh-century psalter from Subiaco that includes the beginning of the prayer, which is missing from Farfa 4.[83]

---

mihi (Salmon no. 485); *Domine Deus omnipotens creator celi* (Salmon no. 390); *Omnipotens et misericors Deus creator generis humani* (Salmon no. 402); *Suscipere digneris Domine Deus omnipotens istos psalmos consecratos* (Salmon no. 211). Nos. 386, 485, and 390 in Salmon also appear in BAV Chigi C.VI.177, fols. 113v–114r.

78. Perugia, Biblioteca Comunale Augusta, I 17, fol. 123v: "Supplico ego peccator per immensam clementiam tuam et per magnam misericordiam tuam ut per modulationem psalmorum quam ego indignus et peccator decantaui, liberes animam meam de peccato et abstollas cor meum de omnibus prauis et perfidis cogitationibus" (Salmon, "*Libelli precum,*" no. 386).

79. Perugia, Biblioteca Comunale Augusta, I 17, fols. 123v–124v: "in conspectu diuine maiestatis tue" and "in conspectu tuo."

80. *Benedicti Regula* 19, in *RB 1980,* 216–17.

81. Perugia, Biblioteca Comunale Augusta, I 17, fol. 124v (Salmon, "*Libelli precum,*" no. 211).

82. Barré, *Prières anciennes,* 246–47.

83. BAV Chigi D.VI.79, fols. 207v–208r; and Salmon, "*Libelli precum,*" 176, no. 511.

EXAMPLE 2.5. *Gloriosa et immaculata*, Rome, BN Farfa 4, fols. 50r–51v; BAV Chigi D.VI.79, fols. 207v–208r

Glorious and immaculate ever virgin Mary, mother of God, I humbly ask your holy majesty that you concede to me, your wretched servant, to praise and bless you always, since it is not sweeter to me to live than to praise you, o glorious one. **Blessed are you among women, and blessed is the fruit of your womb.** But when I contemplate your magnificence, soon all my innards shake, whence I beseech your holy intercession that you accord me, your servant, to say what I desire. Since while I faithfully believe you to be the mother of God and of the Lord, I see that you are the mistress of the angels and of men. **Whereupon there is nothing left for me to say except that I shall praise you always: Blessed are you among women, and blessed is the fruit of your womb. You holy and ever virgin immaculate lady. You are exalted** and glorious above all things. You imperial bedchamber from which proceeded the only son of God the father. You palace of the highest king, in which there are celestial secrets. You holy and ever virgin immaculate childbearer. From you, o blessed one, truth has been born; the holy spirit descended into you. From you, the sun of justice proceeded. O blessed and ever virgin Mary. O splendid morning star. The whiteness of the paternal light perfuses you entirely, virgin. The splendor of the father's glory reposed in your body. Your holy womb has been made the sky in

Gloriosa et immaculata semper uirgo Maria domini mater, suppliciter deprecor tuam sanctam maiestatem ut concedas mihi, misero seruo tuo, te semper laudare et benedicere. Quia non est mihi dulcius uiuere quam te gloriosa laudare. **Benedicta tu inter mulieres, et benedictus fructus uentris tui.** Sed dum considero tuam magnificentiam, mox contremescunt omnia uiscera mea. Unde precor tuam sanctam intercessionem ut concedas mihi seruo tuo loquor quae desidero. Quia dum te fideliter credo dei esse matrem et Domini, dominam te uideo angelorum et hominum. **Unde non restat mihi quid dicam, quam ut te semper benedicam. Benedicta tu inter mulieres, et benedictus fructus uentris tui. Tu sancta et semper uirgo immaculata domina. Tu excelsa** et gloriosa super omnia. Tu thalamus imperialis de quo processit unicus Dei filius patris. Tu aula summi regis, in qua sunt secreta cęlestia. Tu sancta et semper uirgo immaculata puerpera. Ex te o benedicta, orta est ueritas; in te spiritus sanctus descendit. Ex te sol iustitię processit. O beata et semper uirgo Maria. O stella splendida matutina. Candor paternę lucis te totam uirgo perfudit. Splendor paternę glorię quieuit in tuo sancto corpore. Uterus sanctus tuus factus est cęlum, in quo quieuit creator omnium rerum. Tua sancta brachia facta sunt cęlestia palatia et quem capere non potuit terra et cęlum, tuo sancta uirgo residet sinu. Arca

continued

EXAMPLE 2.5. *Continued*

which rested the creator of all things. Your holy arms have been made celestial palaces and that which the earth and sky could not contain, resided in your holy breast, virgin. The ark of your holy breast has become the throne of God, from whose breasts the creator of all things and of the angels sucked milk. Now what shall I say about your holy and melodious mouth which you gave to the Savior, puckered with a sweet kiss? And he whom the precious eyes were seeing, their son, and whom you were kissing, that very one was your God and creator. O inexpressible good, o admirable gift, o unspeakable joy that the archangel Gabriel announced to you saying, Hail Mary full of grace, the Lord be with you, with you in your womb, with you in aid. Rejoice and be happy, blessed and ever virgin Mary, behold your God and creator in your womb. **Now nothing remains to me to say except that I shall always praise you. Blessed are you among women, and blessed is the fruit of your womb. You holy and ever immaculate virgin, you are exalted** in the heavens, beatified on earth, your throne is elevated above the choruses of angels. The angels praise you, the archangels exult about you. The entire chorus of saints surrounds your throne. All the holy virgins return praise to you. Now the prophets rejoice, who were desiring to see you. The apostles who served you now rejoice with you. O glorious and exalted above all things, who alone were worthy of every honor and glory. Woe is me, unhappy and wretched, that I do not know how to convey

sancti pectoris tui facta est Dei thronus, de cuius uberibus lac suxit creator omnium et angelorum. Modo quid dicam de tuo sancto et mellifluo ore quem strictum dulci osculo dedisti saluatoris? Et quem pretiosi oculi uidebant filium suum, et quem osculabaris, ipse erat Deus et creator tuus. O ineffabile bonum. O ammirabile donum. O inenarrabile gaudium quem tibi nuntiauit Gabrihel archangelus dicens, Aue maria gratia plena Dominus tecum. Tecum in utero, tecum in auxilio. Gaude et lętare beata et semper uirgo Maria, ecce Deus et creator tuus in utero tuo. **Modo non restat mihi quid dicam, nisi ut te semper benedicam. Benedicta tu inter mulieres, et benedictus fructus uentris tui. Tu sancta et semper uirgo immaculata, in celis es exaltata.** In terris beatificata, Eleuatus est tuus thronus super choros angelorum. Te laudant angeli, de te exultant archangeli. Omnis chorus sanctorum tuum circumdant thronum. Omnes uirgines sanctę tibi referunt laudes. Modo gaudent prophetę qui te desiderabant uidere. Apostoli qui tibi seruierunt modo exultant tecum. O gloriosa et excelsa super omnia quę sola digna fuisti omni honore et gloria. Heu mihi infelici et misero quas laudes tibi referam nescio. Facilius possum a mea mente excedere quam tuam sanctam claritatem comprehendere. Ut uideo non est lingua qui te possit laudare dignę. Sed ipsa sola est laus quam tibi angeli canunt. Ego infelix et miser qui te laudare desidero, non te possum plus laudare, quam ut dico Dei esse matrem. Non possum dicere tibi plus laudem optimam, quam angelorum et hominum dominam. In cęlis sine te nulla laus, in terris sine te nulla salus. Qui te non credit semper esse uirginem et matrem Dei non introibit per portas cęli. Ego miser licet indignus te semper confiteor esse uirginem et Dei matrem cum omni honore quę genuisti Deum et Dominum saluatorem per quem sumus saluati et adiuuati, et a morte perpetua liberati. Modo et semper te deprecor Domini matrem, ut parcas mihi misero qui te presumpsi laudare, et si aliquid dixi indignum, tu mihi parce sancta et semper uirgo, quia ego miser et infelix, quid sum quam terra et cinis? In me nichil uideo bonum, nec rationem nec opus, nisi solam fidem karitatem et spem quam habeo in Deo et in te.

such praise to you. I may more easily be overwhelmed by my mind than understand your holy brightness. I see that there is no tongue that can praise you worthily, but that alone is praise which the angels sing to you. I, unhappy and wretched, who wish to praise you, I cannot praise you more than to say you are the mother of God. I cannot pronounce a more excellent praise than that you are the mistress of angels and of men. In heaven there is no praise without you, on earth there is no salvation without you. He who does not believe you to be ever virgin and the mother of God will not enter the gates of heaven. I, wretched, am permitted always to proclaim that you are virgin and the mother of God with all honor and that you gave birth to God and the Lord savior through whom we are saved and aided, and released from eternal death. And I beseech you always, mother of the Lord, that you spare me who has presumed to praise you, and if I said anything unworthy, spare me holy and ever virgin, for I, wretched and unhappy, what am I except for earth and ashes? I see nothing good in myself, neither judgment nor action, except for the faith, charity, and hope that I have in God and in you.

It is not unlikely that this prayer was composed at Farfa and subsequently taken to Subiaco, reflecting a long association between the two abbeys that manifested itself in both textual transmission and institutional connections during the eleventh century. Indeed, the relation between the two abbeys is reflected even in architectural similarities; for instance, the bell towers of Farfa and Subiaco, both constructed between 1050 and 1060, are so similar that they may have been built by the same masons. Ties between the monasteries were reinforced even further in 1068, when a monk from Farfa became Abbot Johannes V of Subiaco.[84] But two salient facts support the theory that the prayer to the Virgin Mary was written at Farfa and not at Subiaco: first, it occupies an unusual place at the beginning of the Farfa collection; and second, it associates the Virgin with the kingship of Christ in explicitly imperial terms: "You imperial marriage-bed (*thalamus imperialis*), whence proceeded the only son of God the Father. You palace of the highest king, in which there are celestial secrets. . . . Your holy arms have been made into celestial palaces. . . . The ark of your holy bosom is made the throne of God."[85]

The most distinctive epithet in this passage is *thalamus imperialis* (imperial marriage-bed), which is an extremely rare expression, although the individual words occur separately in many texts.[86] The word *thalamus* often signifies the womb of the Virgin Mary in allegorical readings of Psalm 18:6; early Christian writers such as Augustine interpreted the phrase *sponsus procedens de thalamo suo* (a bridegroom coming forth from his nuptial chamber) as a reference to the birth of Christ.[87] In his hymn for the Nativity, Ambrose interpreted Psalm 18:6 in light of the kingship of Christ, calling the *thalamus* a "royal palace of chastity" (*pudoris aula regia*).[88] Daniel Russo has pointed out the significance of Ambrose's architectural metaphor of the *aula* in fourth-century Milan, where the imperial palace was inaccessible and rendered sacred through the

84. See McClendon, *Imperial Abbey,* 77–78; and Schwarzmaier, "Der Liber Vitae von Subiaco."

85. Rome, BN Farfa 4, fol. 50r: "Tu thalamus imperialis, de quo processit unicus Dei filius patris. Tu aula summi regis, in qua sunt secreta caelestia. . . . Tua sancta brachia facta sunt caelestia palatia. . . . Arca sancti pectoris tui facta est Dei thronus" (ed. Barré, *Prières anciennes,* 246–47).

86. I have not found this precise phrase in any other published texts.

87. Influential examples of this interpretation are in Augustine's *In Iohannis euangelium tractatus* 124, 8.4.19, ed. Willems, 84; and Augustine's *Enarrationes in Psalmos,* Psalm 90, 2.5.18, ed. Dekkers and Fraipont, 1270.

88. Ambrose, *Intende qui regis Israel,* in *Hymnes,* ed. Fontaine, 275.

presence of the emperor.[89] In his tractate *De fide,* Ambrose developed this theme of inaccessibility further, applying the phrase *aula imperialis* to the kingdom of heaven: "Howsoever we may ascend to heaven. . . . The doors are closed, and they are not opened to anyone; no one who wishes enters, except he who believes faithfully. The imperial palace is guarded."[90] Similarly, a sermon of Petrus Chrysologus compares the imperial palace (*imperialis aula*) to a nuptial chamber (*thalamus*), both metaphors for the kingdom of heaven.[91] These early writings, in combination with the doctrine of Mary's virginity, provide a basis for characterizing her body as an inaccessible royal space. In the visual arts the association of Mary with an imperial or royal palace (*aula*) became an important theme in the Ottonian empire, as seen in tenth- and eleventh-century manuscript illuminations of the Adoration of the Magi.[92] In such images, the presence of the Virgin transforms the meaning of a space associated with secular power. Similarly, the phrase *thalamus imperialis* in the prayer from Farfa combines the multiple resonances of the two words in an allusion to both the imperial patronage of the abbey and its patron saint, Mary.

Although the language of royalty and empire is most concentrated near the beginning of the prayer, the text as a whole conveys an image of the Virgin's majesty so glorious that it defies expression in human language: "I see that there is no tongue that can praise you worthily, but that alone is praise which the angels sing to you." Despite the increasing emphasis in the eleventh century on Mary's intercessory role, supplication of her aid plays a remarkably small role in this prayer.[93] Only at the conclusion of the text does the speaker finally ask for her mercy: "And I beseech you always, mother of the Lord, that you spare me who has presumed to praise you, and if I said anything unworthy, spare me, holy and ever virgin, for I, wretched and unhappy, what am I except for earth and ashes? I see nothing good in myself, neither

89. Russo, "Les représentations mariales dans l'art de l'Occident," 184.

90. Ambrose, *De fide* IV.2, ed. Faller, 162: "Quomodo ascendemus ad caelum. . . . Clausae sunt portae, non cuicumque aperiuntur, non quicumque vult, nisi qui fideliter credat, ingreditur. Custoditur aula imperialis."

91. Petrus Chrysologus, *Sancti Petri Chrysologi collectio sermonum,* ed. Olivar, sermo 141, p. 858. Like Ambrose, Chrysologus wrote in an imperial city (Ravenna).

92. Russo, "Les représentations mariales dans l'art de l'Occident," 227–29.

93. On the theology of eleventh-century prayers to Mary, see Barré, *Prières anciennes;* and Fulton, *From Judgment to Passion,* 218–43. For two representative examples, see Cottier, *Anima mea,* 113–19, 230–39.

judgment nor action, except for the faith, charity, and hope that I have in God and in you."[94]

This passage evokes (albeit rather obliquely) Mary's ability to transmit the supplicant's petition to Christ. The middle of the prayer refers to the infant Savior whom she nursed and kissed, but makes no direct mention of his judgment or of her intercession. Instead, the speaker repeatedly invokes the exalted position of Mary, contrasting it with his own wretchedness, while lamenting his inability to offer her fitting praise. The text resembles a rhetorical exercise in the varieties of prayer. In colorful language, it conveys both praise of the Virgin and despair of attaining the supreme eloquence of the virgins, apostles, and angels who praise her. The words of Elizabeth to Mary in the Gospel of Luke ("Blessed are you among women") form a refrain as the only adequate words of praise. Unlike many other lengthy Marian prayers of the eleventh and twelfth centuries, this text does not dwell on the fear of judgment, instead expressing awe at the Virgin's majesty and the wish to praise her eternally.

Prayers to the Cross

Besides prayers to saints and prayers associated with psalmody, psalters from Farfa also include extensive collections of prayers to the Cross. The exceptionally rich series in Rome, BN Farfa 4 starts off with a rubric to the effect that the prayers are "for venerating the Cross on Good Friday and also to be said at other times."[95] Although these same texts are usually cited as examples of "private" devotion, prayer during the Adoration of the Cross on Good Friday, when monks prostrated themselves on the floor of the church in front of the crucifix and then went one by one to kiss it, was a profoundly personal action performed in community.

The ritual structure of the Adoration as performed in monasteries prescribed community prayer, but the selection of specific prayers was apparently variable. The development of the liturgy for the Adoration created a space for a variety of prayers in the service. By the ninth century, in the papal ceremony

94. Rome, BN Farfa 4, fol. 51v: "Modo et semper te deprecor domini matrem, ut parcas mihi misero qui te presumpsi laudare, et si aliquid dixi indignum, tu mihi parce sancta et semper uirgo, quia ego miser et infelix, quid sum quam terra et cinis? In me nichil uideo bonum, nec rationem nec opus, nisi solam fidem karitatem et spem quam habeo in deo et in te."

95. Rome, BN Farfa 4, fol. 79r: "Orationes ad crucem salutandam in parasceue, aliisque temporibus dicende." The entire series of prayers is edited in Wilmart, "Prières médiévales."

of the Adoration at Rome, after three genuflections before the cross, a moment of silent prayer preceded the osculation of the cross by the pope. In the Frankish kingdom this prayer became a three-part prayer sequence, for which there are three texts in *Ordo Romanus* 50; this custom then reached Rome through the Romano-Germanic pontifical.[96] Peter Damian wrote prayers for the ceremony which were widely transmitted along with preexisting texts.[97] These and other prayers for the Adoration are found in many psalters of the eleventh and twelfth centuries, including those from Farfa.

As stated earlier, the prayers to the Cross in Farfa 4 could be recited both during the Adoration of the Cross or on other, unspecified occasions. The sheer quantity of texts, twenty-four in all, raises the questions of how they were used in practice and whether the collection constitutes a set formulary to follow or an anthology offering a range of choices. A comparison of the collection's structure with the basic outlines of the Adoration ceremony suggests that the prayers also compose a ritual that monks can perform during the communal ceremony. On Good Friday, the monks prostrated themselves on the floor of the church in front of the crucifix for some time. Each monk then approached the crucifix in turn, knelt before it, and kissed it, while the choir sang chants about the Cross, including the antiphon "Let us venerate your Cross, o Lord" (*Crucem tuam adoremus, Domine*) and the long hymn "Banner of the king" (*Vexilla regis*).[98]

The prayer collection in Farfa 4 can be mapped onto the actions of an individual performing the Adoration ritual. The twenty-four prayers are divided into subsections that correspond to a series of gestures: genuflecting three times, kissing the ground in front of the crucifix, kissing each part of the cross, and finally rising from the kneeling position. Within each subsection the initial text, with instructions for its recitation, is followed by several others bearing the heading "another prayer" (*alia oratio*), suggesting that they may have been alternatives or that the number of prayers recited for each action was flexible. Presumably the Adoration would continue until every participant had kissed the cross, which meant that the length of the service was variable. Establishing a correspondence between the Good Friday liturgy and the Adoration ritual in Farfa 4 shows that this group of texts represents exactly what its initial rubric states: prayers to be said on Good Friday *and* at other times.

96. Römer, "Die Liturgie des Karfreitags," 77–78.

97. Wilmart, "Le recueil des poèmes."

98. On the Adoration of the Cross, see Schmidt, *Hebdomada sancta* 2:791–96. I refer specifically to the version of the ritual in *LT,* 81, because it was known at Farfa.

A closer look at individual elements of the Adoration ritual in Farfa 4 illustrates the difficulty of distinguishing between "private" and "public" prayer. Four of the prayers are indisputably liturgical in origin, for they are transmitted in sacramentaries (books containing Mass prayers for the use of the celebrant).[99] Other texts in the ritual come from the Carolingian *libellus precum* tradition; the ceremony begins with a widely diffused ninth-century prayer that describes the speaker as prostrate before the Cross.[100]

The subsection of the text pertaining to the osculation of the cross consists of instructional rubrics and verses to pronounce while kissing the different parts of the crucifix: "While kissing one foot, say: Cross, sure salvation for me; the Cross of the Lord [be] with me. At the other foot: Cross, my refuge. Kissing one hand: May the Cross be a true defense for me (kissing the other hand) that I adore always."[101] The verses are similar to short poems in several Carolingian manuscripts that share this text's terse evocation of the Cross as sure salvation, defense, and refuge,[102] and may ultimately derive from a text attributed to the fifth-century writer Calbulus.[103] Verses even more closely re-

99. "Crucem tuam adoro Domine per quam saluasti mundum" and "Sanctifica me Domine signaculo sancte crucis" (fol. 82r) are also found in Rome, BV B.23, fol. 116r–v; see Bragança, "A adoração da cruz," 280. "Deus cui cuncte obediunt creature" (fol. 82v) and "Deus qui unigeniti filii tui Deum nostri Ihesu Christi pretioso sanguine" are found in *GS* 3:272, nos. 4411 and 4414.

100. "Domine Ihesu Christi conditor mundi" (fol. 79r), ed. Wilmart, *Precum libelli,* 13–14; for a translation of this prayer and discussion of its theology in context, see Fulton, *From Judgment to Passion,* 150–51.

101. Rome, BN Farfa 4, fol. 85r: "In osculatione unius pedis dicatur: Crux mihi certa salus, crux domini mecum. Ad alterum pedem: Crux mihi refugium. Unam manum osculans. Crux mihi uera sit defensio. Alteram manum osculans: quam semper adoro."

102. Dhuoda, *Liber manualis,* ed. Riché, 128: "Crux tua sancta mecum. Crux est quam ut cognoui, semper amaui, semperque adoro. Crux mihi salus, crux mihi defensio, crux mihi protectio, semperque refugium"; Wilmart, *Precum libelli,* 55: "Crux mihi salus, crux mihi refugium, crux mihi protectio, crux mihi defensio, crux mihi uita"; Orléans, Bibliothèque Municipale, 184, p. 344, ed. *PL* 101:1412C: "Crux mihi refugium, crux mihi certa salus, crux domini mecum, crux est quam semper adoro"; and Cologne, Dombibliothek, 90, fol. 1v, ed. Ernest Dümmler in *MGH Poetae Latini aeui Carolini* 2:257 and ed. Friedrich Leo in *MGH Auctores antiquissimi,* 4:381: "Crux mihi certa salus, crux est quam semper adoro, crux domini mecum, crux mihi refugium."

103. See Bischoff, "Ursprung und Geschichte eines Kreuzsegens." The verses of Calbulus read: "Crux Domini mecum, crux est quam semper adoro, crux mihi refugium, crux mihi certa salus." They are found in the Latin anthology of the Codex Salmasianus (Paris, BNF lat. 10318), which dates to the late eighth or early ninth century.

lated to the ones in Farfa 4 appear in a complex diagram in the form of a cross, transmitted in several manuscripts from the eleventh and twelfth centuries, which forms part of the tradition of the *carmina figurata* (pictorial poems) represented by the *De laudibus sanctae Crucis* of Rabanus Maurus.[104]

One instance of this diagram can be linked, albeit indirectly, to one of Farfa's imperial patrons. As found in an eleventh-century pontifical from Eichstätt, the verses in the cross diagram can be translated loosely as follows: "Cross, sure salvation for me; it is the Cross that I adore always; Cross of the Lord, [be] with me; Cross, my refuge" ("Crux mihi certa salus, Crux est quam semper adoro; Crux domini mecum, crux mihi refugium").[105] At the center of the diagram is the word *crux*, forming the point of departure for reading each of the four verses in a different direction: up, then down, then to the right, and finally to the left.[106] Both the diagram and the osculation ritual order space through directed movement; in the diagram, successive verses are mapped onto different parts of the cross, and in the ritual the verses are pronounced while kissing the parts of the cross representing the extremities of the crucified Christ. The verses in the pontifical may reproduce an inscription on the silver pectoral cross belonging to Gundekar II (1019–72), who became bishop of Eichstätt after serving as chaplain to Empress Agnes from 1045 to 1057.[107] The pontifical states that the bishop placed on the altar in the Chapel of Saint John a cross "that he was accustomed to have hanging around his neck at Mass."[108] Gundekar's ownership and donation of the pectoral cross fits into a broader context of Ottonian and Salian prelates who manifested their piety

104. For an overview of the tradition see Ernst, *Carmen Figuratum.* On Rabanus Maurus see *De laudibus sanctae Crucis;* Ernst, *Carmen Figuratum,* 222–332; and Ferrari, "*Hrabanica*" and *Il "Liber sanctae crucis" di Rabano Mauro.*

105. Eichstätt, Diözesanarchiv B 4, fol. 14r; reproduced in *Das "Pontifikale Gundekarianum."* The verses are edited in *PL* 146:986, and the diagram in the pontifical is reproduced in "Gundechari Liber pontificalis Eichstetensis usque ad a. 1072," ed. Bethmann, *MGH Scriptores* 7:242. These verses are the conclusion of a longer poem beginning "Per crucis hoc signum fugiat procul omne malignum." Although I have translated the verses as addressed directly to the Cross, other interpretations are possible.

106. Ernst, *Carmen Figuratum,* 421.

107. Eberlein, "Die bildliche Austattung des 'Pontifikale Gundekarianum,'" 54–55; and Ernst, *Carmen Figuratum,* 424.

108. Eichstätt, Diözesanarchiv B 4, fols. 14r, 58v: "quam solitus erat in collo suo pendentem habere ad missam." See also "De beato Gundecharo episcopo," *Acta Sanctorum Augusti* 1:180.

through patronage of the arts.[109] Besides the Farfa manuscript, the other sources of the osculation ritual are Carolingian or Ottonian, raising the possibility that Farfa received the text through its imperial patrons. The extensive personal contact between Agnes and her chaplain Gundekar (whose candidacy for the episcopate she supported) makes it possible that she knew of the text on his pectoral cross.[110] The text of the inscription on the pectoral cross could have reached Farfa through this connection, perhaps in association with a gift from Agnes.[111]

From the Constantinian period onward, imperial devotion to the Cross formed part of a political theology in which the crucifix was simultaneously a sign of Christ's eternal victory and a symbol of his salvific act of humility, both images offering a model of behavior for earthly rulers. This complex of ideas found expression in the visual arts, particularly in precious metalwork of the Ottonian and Salian periods. Objects such as the Lothar cross (from around the year 1000) and the Herimann and Borghorst crosses (from the mid-eleventh century) reaffirmed, through their imagery and reuse of *spolia,* the theocratic ideology of the Germanic kings as Christian successors to the Roman emperors.[112] The monks of Farfa may well have known of the precious crosses and crucifixes produced for the Ottonian and Salian rulers and their associates; the images of these objects were perhaps echoed in the jewel-encrusted cross that was once visible in an eleventh-century fresco at the abbey.[113] Farfa itself had possessed at least one such decorated object: a document in the Farfa *Register* refers to a crucifix "encircled on all sides by marvelous gems" that was taken from the treasury in the early tenth century.[114] The same document refers to "two golden crosses with the wood of the Lord" (*cruces ii de auro cum ligno domini*), apparently signifying cross-shaped reli-

109. On this patronage see, most recently, North and Cutler, "Ivories, Inscriptions, and Episcopal Self-Consciousness in the Ottonian Empire."

110. Black-Veldtrup (*Kaiserin Agnes,* 359) notes the confidence Agnes had in Gundekar.

111. This suggestion is speculative because imperial gifts to the abbey are no longer extant.

112. See Forsyth, "Art with History." For descriptions and reproductions of some of these crosses, see Grodecki et al., *Il secolo dell'anno mille,* 264–65, 270–72; plates 260, 262–64, 271, 276.

113. The fresco, which apparently depicted a monk kneeling in front of the cross accompanied by saints, is no longer visible. It was indicated in a diagram by Markthaler ("Sulle recenti scoperte," 81).

114. *RF* 3:84, doc. 379: "Crucem unam purissimi auri longam plus unius brachi ex utraque parte circumdatam gemmis mirabilibus."

quaries containing fragments of wood from the True Cross that were in Farfa's possession before the abbey was abandoned in 898.[115] The abbey apparently also had some relics of the True Cross in the early twelfth century, when Abbot Guido (1119–25) sold them, according to the Farfa *Register*.[116] The presence of these relics in the eleventh century is suggested by two documents in the Farfa *Register* that refer to legal agreements made in front of a church door "of the Holy Cross," which was either the door of a separate small basilica or a door of the principal abbey church.[117] In the aggregate, this evidence for the cult of the Cross at Farfa in the central Middle Ages provides a context for the collections of prayers to the Cross copied there.

The prayers to the Cross in manuscripts from Farfa form part of a textual complex linked not only with the empire, but also with the abbey of Cluny. Material shared by prayers from Farfa and Cluny suggests a connection resulting from the relationship between the two abbeys in the eleventh century. A prayer from Farfa, to be said after kissing the cross, concludes with an expansion of the verses in the osculation ritual discussed earlier:

> Holy Cross of Christ, through you I have been redeemed, through you let me deserve to receive absolution and remission for my sins. Holy Cross, save me, because upon you perished God, the savior of the world. Save me, savior Christ, through the power of the Cross. You who saved Peter at sea, have mercy upon me. Cross of the Lord, be with me. The Cross of the Lord is with me that I adore always. Cross, my salvation. Cross, my refuge. Cross, my defense. Cross, my life. Cross, my protection and aid in present life and in future judgment.[118]

115. I am grateful to Holger Klein for pointing out that these objects were cross reliquaries.

116. *RF* 5:323.

117. Schuster, "Reliquie d'arte," 298; and *RF* 4:247, 263.

118. Rome, BN, Farfa 4, fol. 86v: "Sancta crux christi per te redemptus sum per te merear ueniam et indulgentiam recipere de meis peccatis. Sancta crux salua me quia in te passus est saluator mundi deus. Salua me christe saluator per uirtutem crucis qui saluasti petrum in mare misera mihi. Crux domini mihi sit mecum. Crux domini mecum est quam ego semper adoro. Crux mihi salus. Crux mihi refugium. Cruxi mihi defensio. Crux mihi uita. Crux mihi protectio et adiutorium in presenti uita et in futuro iudicio." This redaction of the prayer is apparently unique to Farfa. Wilmart ("Prières médiévales," 40, 53) pointed out its resemblance to a shorter prayer in an eleventh-century psalter from Nonantola that lacks the reference to the saving of Peter (BAV Vat. lat. 84, fol. 305r–v). Several of the same phrases appear in the prayer "Crux mihi salus est," which is found in

Given Farfa's association with Cluny, it is no surprise that some of the phrases in this prayer also appear in one by Abbot Odilo of Cluny for the Adoration of the Cross: "... since the Cross of the Lord is with me that I adore always. Cross, my refuge; Cross, my way and strength ... the Cross is my life."[119] Odilo reformed Farfa at the end of the tenth century with the help of William of Volpiano, and the two abbeys were in contact for at least half a century thereafter. This ongoing relationship makes it likely that the monks of Farfa were acquainted with Odilo's prayer. Another text of Odilo's for the Cross, certainly known at Farfa, was an inscription engraved on a processional cross at Cluny.[120] The text of the inscription quotes from the conclusion of Odilo's sermon for the feast of the Invention of the Cross, which employs the rhetorical device of anaphora in the manner of a litany, much like the conclusion of the prayer.[121] Each formulaic phrase begins with the word *crux* and continues with a definition of the quality or function of the Cross, usually in relation to a specific group within society:

The Cross is the guardian of the poor. The Cross is the leader of men. The Cross is the end of the elderly. The Cross is the light of those sitting in shadow. The Cross is the magnificence of kings. The Cross is a perpetual shield. The Cross is the wisdom of the foolish. The Cross is liberty for slaves. The Cross is the philosophy of emperors. The Cross is law for the impious. The Cross is the preaching of the prophets. The Cross is the union of the apostles. The Cross is the jubilation of the martyrs. The Cross is the abstinence of monks. The Cross is the chastity of virgins. The Cross is the joy of priests. The Cross is the foundation of the church. The Cross is the caution of the world. The Cross is the destruction of temples. The Cross is the refutation of idols. The Cross is the scandal of the Jews. The Cross is the perdition of the impious. The Cross is the strength of the lame. The Cross is the doctor of the sick. The Cross is the healing of lepers. The Cross is the repose of paralytics.[122]

two manuscripts from Farfa within series of prayers for the Adoration of the Cross: BAV Chigi C.VI.177, fol. 115v; and Farfa, Abbazia, A.209, fol. 130v.

119. Odilo of Cluny, *Ad crucem adorandam oratio*, Paris, BNF n.a.l. 1496, fol. 27r, ed. *PL* 142:1038: "... quia mecum est crux domini quem semper adoro. Crux mihi refugium, crux mihi uia et uirtus. ... Crux mihi uita est."

120. This text appears in the Cluniac customary copied for Farfa, the *Liber tramitis* (to be discussed in chap. 3).

121. The passage is from homily 13 of Pseudo-Chrysostom, and Odilo prefaces the series of epithets by attributing it to John Chrysostom; see Iogna-Prat, "La croix," 462–63.

122. *LT*, 260: "Crux paruulorum custos. Crux uirorum caput. Crux senum finis. Crux

As Dominique Iogna-Prat has shown, Odilo's sermon emphasizes the theme of the Cross as an imperial symbol, effectively presenting a political theology of the Cross that was an integral part of Cluny's spirituality.[123] The striking expression *crux imperatorum philosophia* is one of the first to appear in the text from the sermon inscribed on the processional cross at Cluny. The expression evokes ideas of importance to both Farfa and Cluny, particularly regarding the role of the emperor as a Christian ruler and the Cross as a triumphant symbol of empire. Both abbeys reserved special veneration for the Cross and enjoyed good relations with the emperors. Cluny was especially favored by Otto I, Otto II, Empress Adelaide, and particularly Henry II, who gave the abbey the imperial insignia and was commemorated in the liturgy there.[124] At Farfa, the patronage of the emperor must have given particular resonance to the phrase *crux imperatorum philosophia,* enriching an already complex network of associations. Some of the connections between devotion to the Cross at Farfa and at Cluny may have arisen from the affiliation between the two monasteries in the eleventh century, which is the subject of chapter 3.

---

lumen in tenebris sedentium. Crux regum magnificentia. Crux scutum perpetuum. Crux insensatorum sapientia. Crux libertas seruulorum. Crux imperatorum philosophia. Crux lex impiorum. Crux prophetarum praeconatio. Crux adnuntiatio apostolorum. Crux martyrum gloriatio. Crux monachorum abstinentia. Crux virginum castitas. Crux gaudium sacerdotum. Crux Ecclesiae fundamentum. Crux orbis terrae cautela. Crux templorum destructio. Crux idolorum repulsio. Crux scandalum Judaeorum. Crux perditio impiorum. Crux claudorum virtus. Crux aegrotantium medicus. Crux emundatio leprosorum. Crux paralyticorum requies." This passage from the sermon is edited in *PL* 142:1034. In the sermon, the presence of the verb *est* (elided thereafter) at the beginning of the passage from which the inscription is excerpted suggests a translation of each phrase beginning "The Cross is," rather than as an invocation construing the word *crux* as being in the vocative case.

123. Iogna-Prat, "La croix," 458–61. A similarly anaphoric praise of the Cross, which also evokes the submission to it of all earthly empires and rulers, is found in the middle and at the conclusion (a separate section entitled "Laus crucis") of Peter Damian's sermon 48 for the Exaltation of the Cross, which begins with the words "Standard of the eternal empire" (*Vexillum imperatoris aeterni*); see *Petri Damiani Sermones,* ed. Lucchesi, 298–99, 303–5.

124. On Cluny's relations with the emperors and commemoration of them, see Heath, *Crux imperatorum philosophia;* and Seibert, "Herrscher und Mönchtum," 222–23, 232, 241–42.

t he relationship between Farfa and Cluny illustrates several aspects of Cluny's influence on other monasteries in the tenth and eleventh centuries. As discussed in the introduction, Abbot Hugh of Farfa reformed his community at the end of the tenth century with the help of William of Volpiano (962–1031) and Odilo of Cluny (abbot 994–1049). Although never a dependency of Cluny, Farfa obtained information on Cluny's distinctive way of life during the first half of the eleventh century, and its abbots, beginning with Hugh, vowed to uphold the standards of a constitution they called Cluniac. Close reading of the sources suggests that the ramifications of Hugh's reform were both subtle and diverse. Taking a fresh look at the evidence, this chapter addresses Cluny's impact on Farfa's liturgy in the context of the reception of Cluniac customs represented by the *Liber tramitis*. To understand the function and meaning of the *Liber tramitis* for the monastic community at Farfa, one must analyze the use of Cluniac rituals there, which is the focus of the second part of this chapter. The nature of the extant manuscripts makes it difficult to determine whether practices originated at Farfa or Cluny, because the Cluniac customs themselves are reflected primarily in their dissemination to other institutions. The story of that transmission reflects the special status and unusual history of Cluny in the central Middle Ages.

Dedicated to Saints Peter and Paul, Cluny was founded in 910 by William III, duke of Aquitaine, whose foundation charter placed the monastery under the protection of the pope and guaranteed its freedom from aggression.[1] In 931 Pope John XI granted Cluny a privilege that gave Cluny's abbot the right to reform and take possession of other monasteries at the request of their abbots. Another a privilege granted by Pope Gregory V in 998 made Cluny into an autonomous sanctuary exempt from the jurisdiction of secular authorities and of the local bishop; in 1024 this extraordinary exemption was extended by Pope John XIX to all abbeys affiliated with Cluny regardless of their location.[2] Throughout the central Middle Ages, donors increased Cluny's property through

1. On the foundation of Cluny and its interpretation by Cluniac writers see Cochelin, "Quête de liberté."

2. On Cluny's privileges of exemption and immunity see particularly Rosenwein, *Negotiating Space*, 156–83.

their gifts, and a series of reforms enabled Cluny to appropriate jurisdiction over other monasteries and their lands. This potent combination of autonomy and patronage enabled Cluny to develop into an unprecedented monastic empire with an authority that was both temporal and spiritual.[3] From the time of Abbots Odo (927–942) and Maiolus (948–94), the community became associated with an ideal of reformed monastic life, and its abbots acquired a reputation of sanctity.[4] Odo was called to reform monasteries in Aquitaine, the Auvergne, and as far away as Rome, but the association between the houses he reformed and the abbey of Cluny itself remained loosely defined and somewhat informal. During the abbacy of Odilo (994–1049), however, Cluny began to develop a more structured network of dependencies: the *ecclesia Cluniacensis*. Odilo took the title of abbot in the monasteries he reformed, linking dependent priories more closely to the mother church. In the second half of the eleventh century, under Abbot Hugh of Cluny (1049–1109), the expanding *ecclesia Cluniacensis* became a congregation concentrically organized around the authority of Cluny and its abbot.[5] Dependent abbeys and priories venerated the Cluniac abbots Odo, Maiolus, and Odilo as saints.[6] Beyond the *ecclesia Cluniacensis*, interest in Cluny's way of life led several monasteries to obtain written versions of its customs, known as customaries. Compiled at various times from the late tenth to the late eleventh century, these texts provide a detailed description of daily life at Cluny, including copious information on liturgical practices.[7]

By the eleventh century, the celebration of the liturgy was an important factor in Cluny's prestige and renown; commemorative prayers and masses performed at Cluny were widely perceived as powerful instruments for saving the souls of the dead from damnation. For the eleventh-century chronicler Radulfus Glaber, the liturgy endowed the community with unprecedented spiritual powers of redemption. A monk at the abbey of Saint-Germain in Auxerre (which had been reformed by Abbot Maiolus of Cluny from 987 to 989),

3. On the history of Cluny's property see Rosenwein, *Rhinoceros Bound* and *To Be the Neighbor of Saint Peter*.

4. See especially Iogna-Prat, *Agni immaculati*.

5. For a recent summary of these developments see Iogna-Prat, *Ordonner et exclure*, 62–74 (translated in *Order and Exclusion*, 53–68). On the construction of the Cluniac network see Poeck, "*Cluniacensis Ecclesia*."

6. Iogna-Prat, *Agni immaculati* and "Panorama de l'hagiographie abbatiale clunisienne."

7. For the most recent overview of the Cluniac customaries see Cochelin, "Evolution des coutumiers monastiques." The various versions will be discussed later in this chapter.

Glaber spent little time at Cluny itself, but was a great admirer of the abbey and dedicated his *Histories* to Abbot Odilo.[8] In the *Histories* he included a short anecdote meant to illustrate the formidable efficacy of Cluniac worship. In a remote area of Africa, a traveler from Marseilles sought out and encountered a hermit who was reputed to have lived in isolation there for twenty years yet was able to attest to the power of the numerous masses performed at Cluny to rescue souls daily from the power of demons. After reporting this dialogue between the traveler and the hermit as proof of the widespread fame of Cluny's liturgy, Glaber remarked that the large number of monks at Cluny did indeed afford the continuous celebration of the Mass in a manner so pure and reverent that it appeared "more angelic than human" (*magis angelica quam humana*).[9]

Later in the eleventh century, the Italian monk and church reformer Peter Damian (ca. 1007–72) also praised the liturgy at Cluny as more divine than human.[10] In one of several letters he wrote to Abbot Hugh of Cluny in the 1060s, Peter expressed his admiration for the consummate splendor of worship at Cluny in terms that evoked the ancient monastic ideal of unceasing prayer, and referred to a promise he had obtained from the community to remember him in their prayers after his death and to clothe paupers in his memory.[11] Moreover, he contributed to the renown of the Cluniac monks' intercessory powers with a narrative he wrote at the request of Abbot Hugh of Cluny. This text was a new version of the *Vita Odilonis,* a biography of Abbot Odilo by one of his disciples and companions, the monk Jotsald of Saint-Claude (ca. 975–1052 or 1054). The *Vita Odilonis* includes a variant on Glaber's anecdote, transforming the traveler from Marseilles into a pilgrim returning from Jerusalem who encounters a hermit on a desert island. In this version, the hermit describes a chasm leading down to purgatory from which could be heard not only the cries of tortured souls but also the grumbling of demons complaining that their victims were being liberated by the prayers of holy men, above all by those of the monks of Cluny. The hermit advised the pilgrim to inform the monastic community of this phenomenon so that they would redouble their prayers.

8. *Abbaye Saint-Germain,* 287–89. On Glaber's life see Glaber, *Historiarum libri quinque,* xix–xxxiv. On Glaber as a Cluniac historian see France, "Rodulfus Glaber and the Cluniacs," 497–507; Ortigues and Iogna-Prat, "Raoul Glaber et l'historiographie clunisienne"; and Cantarella, "Appunti su Rodolfo il Glabro."

9. Glaber, *Historiarum libri quinque,* 234–37.

10. Peter Damian, letter 100, ed. Reindel, *Die Briefe des Petrus Damiani,* 105; and Resnick, "Peter Damian on Cluny, Liturgy, and Penance."

11. See Peter Damian, letters 100 and 103, ed. Reindel, *Die Briefe des Petrus Damiani,* 112–13, 138–41.

When the pilgrim reported his experience to the monks, they increased their prayers and Abbot Odilo established the annual feast of All Souls for the collective commemoration of the dead.[12] Peter Damian's reworking of Jotsald's *Vita Odilonis* became even more widely diffused than the original and helped to spread the fame of Cluny's liturgical efficacy.[13]

Through their writings, Radulfus Glaber and Peter Damian helped to shape an image of worship at Cluny that, however idealized, finds support in the Cluniac customaries of the eleventh century. These texts show that there was good reason for the wonderment manifested in accounts of the Cluniac liturgy: the complexity and attention to detail evident in these texts is striking even at a distance of almost a thousand years.[14] It is clear from other sources, too, that Cluny's commemoration of the dead, which extended to kings and emperors as well as to monks of the congregation, was perceived as efficacious in rescuing souls from perdition.[15]

In the tenth and early eleventh centuries, the influence of Cluny in the Italian peninsula was relatively limited.[16] Alberic, the prince of Rome in the early tenth century, invited Abbot Odo of Cluny to reform the monasteries in and around the city in 936, but with little success.[17] William of Volpiano, a monk from northern Italy, entered the abbey of Cluny during the abbacy of Maiolus, and although he founded several monasteries in Piedmont (including Fruttuaria, on his family estate), much of his career was spent reforming monasteries in Burgundy and Normandy.[18] In northern Italy, the Cluniac network began to develop in the later eleventh century with the foundation

12. Staub, ed., *Iotsald von Saint-Claude, Vita des Abtes Odilo von Cluny,* 218–20. For a recent analysis of these two texts see Longo, "Riti e agiografia."

13. See Iogna-Prat, "Panorama," 93–96.

14. The most extensive of the Cluniac customaries, that written by the monk Bernard around 1080, contains hundreds of pages of detail on the celebration of the liturgy. The text was published in *Vetus disciplina monastica,* 136–64. The critical edition of the text is in preparation for the *CCM;* the diplomatic edition with French and English translations, *Bernardus: Ordo Cluniacensis,* is forthcoming.

15. On the commemoration of kings and emperors at Cluny see Bishko, "Liturgical Intercession at Cluny for the King-Emperors of Leon"; and Heath, *Crux Imperatorum Philosophia,* 112–25. On Cluny's commemoration of the dead see Iogna-Prat, "The Dead in the Celestial Bookkeeping of the Cluniac Monks."

16. See Picasso, "'Usus' e 'consuetudines' cluniacensi in Italia."

17. Ferrari, *Early Roman Monasteries,* 403–4.

18. On William see particularly Bulst, *Untersuchungen;* and the introduction to Bulst's translation of the life of William in *Rodulfi Glabri Historiarum.*

around 1079 of the priory of Pontida (near Bergamo) and the transfer to Cluny of San Benedetto di Polirone (near Mantua) by Gregory VII in 1077.[19] And in central Italy, the reform of Farfa by William of Volpiano and Abbot Odilo of Cluny at the end of the tenth century seems to have been an isolated instance of Cluniac intervention in that period.

The Cluniac Reform of Farfa

The relationship between Cluny and Farfa grew out of the reform initiated by Abbot Hugh of Farfa. Hugh acquired the abbacy from Pope Gregory V in 997, thereby inciting the resentment of Emperor Otto III, who annulled the election and installed his own candidate (also named Hugh). Yielding to the monks' pleas, however, Otto finally invested Hugh with the abbacy in 998.[20] According to the *Relatio constitutionis*, a first-person narrative attributed to Hugh incorporated by Gregory of Catino into the Farfa *Chronicle*, Hugh decided to reform the abbey as a form of penance: "Realizing that I had gravely sinned, sighing, I began to think about this and about the renewal of this monastery, if perhaps God would have mercy on me because of this, and whether through the intercession of his most Holy Mother I could make any progress towards the recuperation of this monastery."[21] Hugh described the monks of Farfa as having abandoned monastic discipline, eating meat in the refectory and dressing almost like laypeople.[22] In order to introduce a new way of life, Hugh set about finding a model monastic community, and the first places to which he turned were two of the abbeys founded by Saint Benedict in the sixth century: Subiaco and Montecassino. At Subiaco he did not find the monastic observance he had sought; nor was he satisfied with monastic disci-

19. On the expansion of Cluny in Lombardy see *Cluny in Lombardia*. On Polirone and Cluny see Houben, "Il cosiddetto 'Liber Vitae' di Polirone"; and Poeck, "*Cluniacensis Ecclesia*," 107–10.

20. For a fuller account of these events see the introduction to the present volume. Seibert ("Herrscher und Mönchtum") suggests that Otto's quick change of mind may have been influenced by Odilo of Cluny.

21. *CF* 2:75: "recognoscens me graviter deliquisse, cepi de hoc ingemiscens cogitare et de huius monasterii redintegratione, si forte michi propter hoc miseretur Deus et per suę sanctissime Genitricis intercessionem si aliquem fructum efficere possem ad huius cenobii recuperationem."

22. There may be explanations for this way of life other than a lapse in monastic discipline: Carpegna Falconieri (*Il clero di Roma*, 160 n. 196) has pointed out that there were also secular canons at Farfa in the tenth century, who may have been among those wearing "almost secular clothing" (*vestimenta . . . quasi laicalia; CF* 1:55, 2:75).

pline at Montecassino.[23] While at Montecassino, however, Hugh heard of the more rigorous monastic observance practiced in Ravenna, at the monastery of Sant'Apollinare in Classe where Romuald was abbot. Hugh traveled there and brought some monks back to Farfa with him to help renew the community. The experiment failed, however: resources were in short supply and the monks from Ravenna frequently berated Hugh for the paucity of food.[24]

Finally, a visit from Abbot Odilo of Cluny and William of Volpiano decided Hugh's course of action. While he did penance for his simoniac acquisition of the abbacy, Hugh placed the administration of the abbey in their hands.[25] At the conclusion of their stay, Hugh established a new constitution at Farfa, declaring his intention to follow the observances of Cluny:

> We establish and confirm that we shall most wisely and constantly maintain and observe in all ways the same above-mentioned observance of the Cluniac monastery in ecclesiastical offices, and in worthy customs, and in the appearance of the clothing of the brothers, as well as in the quantity of daily nourishment, and in holy solemnities in as much as the possibility of this place may require, with God's assistance.[26]

Pope Sylvester II confirmed this constitution in 999.[27]

Hugh's phrase "in sacred solemnities" (*in sanctis sollemnitatibus*) refers to worship in very general terms; it is not clear to what extent he intended to adopt Cluniac liturgical practices at Farfa. Although information on Cluny's liturgy could have reached Farfa through contacts between the two monasteries,[28] there is no clear evidence of such direct transmission until the mid-eleventh century, when the earliest known copy of the *Liber tramitis,* a

23. *CF* 2:75–76.

24. *CF* 2:76.

25. Ibid.

26. *CF* 1:57, 2:77: "Statuimus et confirmamus ut eandem predictam religionem Cluniensis monasterii in officiis ecclesiasticis et dignis moribus et confratrum cultu vestium sive copia victus cottidie et in sanctis sollemnitatibus in quantum huius loci possibilitas Deo administrante exigerit, in hoc monasterio deinceps sagacissime et constantissime teneamus et omnimodis observemus." On these events see Schuster, "L'Abbaye de Farfa et sa restauration au XIème siècle sous Hughes I," 27–33.

27. *LT,* xxii; and Kehr, *Italia pontificia,* 62.

28. Books could have been transmitted when Italian monks visited Cluny, as recounted in the *Liber tramitis,* or when monks from Cluny came to Farfa. Moreover, Hugh of Farfa and Odilo of Cluny could have met at synods they both attended in 1014. See Weinfurter, *Heinrich II,* 237–38, 240.

collection of the customs of Cluny, was produced at Farfa. The story of Cluniac liturgy at Farfa is one of transformation and adaptation; Farfa preserved the distinctive local features of its liturgy even as it incorporated material from Cluny. Before turning to this document, however, it is necessary to understand the broader context for studying Cluniac liturgical influence at Farfa.

The Liturgy of Cluny and Its Influence

If the transmission of Cluny's liturgy to its priories has been somewhat neglected, even less is known about the liturgical influence of Cluny on abbeys that, like Farfa, remained independent, even while claiming a loose affiliation with Cluny. Indeed, the very definition of "the Cluniac liturgy" remains vague, in part because relatively few liturgical manuscripts have survived from Cluny itself, and almost none of these predate the late eleventh century.[29] As Dominique Iogna-Prat has pointed out in the case of the "Cluniac" literary tradition, the term is notoriously difficult to define. He employs the term "Cluniac nebula" for those writers who, like Radulfus Glaber, were only loosely associated with Cluny but were nonetheless representative of the phenomenon of Cluny's influence and of the ideas associated with Cluny.[30]

Iogna-Prat's distinction between the "Cluniac nebula" and the *ecclesia Cluniacensis* is a useful one for describing liturgical practices as well. While some scholars use the term *Cluniac* in reference to liturgical books from Cluniac priories or from Cluny itself, others expand the designation considerably to encompass books from monasteries outside the *ecclesia Cluniacensis* that exhibit features associated with Cluniac use. Such features include, for example, the selection and ordering of the responsories for Matins on the four Sundays of Advent, or the verses of the Alleluia for Mass on the Sundays after Pentecost.[31]

On the basis of these discrete liturgical elements, some manuscripts have

---

29. For an overview of extant chant books from Cluny, from the dependencies, and from the "broader Cluniac tradition," see Ferreira, "Music at Cluny," 47–71; for the office lectionaries see Etaix, "Le lectionnaire de l'office à Cluny." Wilmart, "Cluny (Manuscrits liturgiques de)" is an overview of all types of books; it is outdated but still useful. The only complete liturgical book that survives from before the late eleventh century is the office lectionary Paris, BNF n.a.l. 2390, described in Etaix, "Le lectionnaire," 136.

30. Iogna-Prat, *Ordonner et exclure,* 61–62 (translated in *Order and Exclusion,* 53–54).

31. The designations French Cluniac, Cluniac nuns, Lewes (Cluniac), and Payerne (Cluniac) for manuscripts containing the series of Matins responsories for Advent appear in Ottosen, *L'antiphonaire latin au Moyen-Age,* 59, 60, 109, 123, 153, 213, 214, 258, 260. On the presence of the Cluniac series of Alleluia verses for the Sundays after Pentecost in manuscripts from monasteries associated with Cluny see Hiley, *Western Plainchant,* 577–78.

been designated "Cluniac" in the scholarly literature even though they cannot be connected to the abbey of Cluny in any way; placing such books within a broader "Cluniac" liturgical tradition obfuscates the very notion of the Cluniac liturgy. Two central Italian manuscripts from the early eleventh century serve to illustrate the problem. The first is a missal-breviary from the abbey of San Salvatore on Monte Amiata (Rome, Biblioteca Casanatense 1907) which lacks any connection to the Cluniac network. Although its chant melodies for the Mass closely resemble those in the late eleventh-century gradual from Cluny (Paris, BNF lat. 1087), it does not contain the Cluniac series of Alleluia verses after Pentecost. The manuscript has nonetheless been cited as a witness to the Cluniac liturgy.[32] The second manuscript, a breviary of unknown origin, is also considered part of the larger Cluniac tradition despite the fact that it does not exhibit traits associated with the liturgy at Cluny itself.[33] Without adducing historical links between these manuscripts and the Cluniac reform, designating them as "Cluniac" liturgical books is problematic.

It is important to distinguish liturgical books produced at Cluny that reflect practices specific to the abbey from books that are associated with Cluniac dependencies, because the influence of Cluny varied considerably. An abbey reformed by Cluny did not automatically take over the Cluniac liturgy as a whole, but might introduce elements of it and adapt them in various ways. In some cases, Cluny played a direct role by providing liturgical manuscripts for the use of its priories. For example, around 1300, the abbey produced one of the most extensive extant records of its office chants for the priory of Saint-Victor-sur-Rhins.[34] In other cases, manuscripts used by dependencies were based on an exemplar from Cluny, such as a late eleventh-century breviary from northern France that is often cited as a manuscript from Cluny, even though it was probably not copied there.[35] At the abbey of Payerne, a depen-

32. See Ferreira, "Music at Cluny," 55–56.

33. Berlin, Staatsbibliothek Preussischer Kulturbesitz, Theol. Lat. Quarto 377. See Davril, "A propos d'un bréviaire," 122; and Ferreira, "Music at Cluny," 47. Although Achten (*Die theologischen lateinischen Handschriften in Quarto*, 2:233–34) localizes the manuscript to southeastern France, an Italian origin seems more likely.

34. The manuscript is now preserved in the Mairie of Saint-Victor-sur-Rhins; see Davril, "A propos d'un bréviaire manuscrit de Cluny."

35. Paris, BNF lat. 12601, probably copied at a Cluniac priory in Picardy such as Lihons-en-Sangterre and then used at Saint-Taurin l'Échelle (on these priories see Poeck, "*Cluniacensis Ecclesia*," 373, 498). The distinctive musical notation and non-Cluniac saints of this breviary distinguish it from contemporary products of the Cluny scriptorium. See Hourlier, "Le bréviaire de Saint-Taurin"; and Ferreira, "Music at Cluny," 47–50.

dency of Cluny since the late tenth century, both the architecture of the church and its liturgy reflected Cluniac influence. The two-storied structure at the west end of the eleventh-century church at Payerne emulated the Burgundian monastic form of the entry porch, called a narthex, found in many churches associated with Cluny. According to Kristina Krüger, in the eleventh century the upper story of the narthex at Cluny was used for the celebration of masses in memory of the deceased monks of the community.[36] By analogy, Payerne's narthex, built during the abbacy of Odilo of Cluny after Payerne had become a priory of Cluny, could have fulfilled the same liturgical function.[37] In the twelfth century, Cluny's scriptorium produced a breviary for use at Payerne that contains specifically Cluniac usages.[38]

One may more readily compare Cluny's liturgy with those of its priories after the mid-eleventh century, not only because more manuscripts survive from that period but also because the systematic influence of Cluny's liturgy on its dependencies is more typical of the abbacies of Hugh (1049–1109) and Peter the Venerable (1122–56) than of Odilo (994–1049).[39]

Beginning with the abbacy of Hugh, priories that were founded or transferred to Cluny were directly subject to the mother house, and were more likely to emulate its liturgical practices. For example, an office lectionary from San Benedetto di Polirone contains lessons for the office of Matins that are almost identical to those found in manuscripts from Cluny.[40] A thirteenth-century missal-breviary from Lewes, a Cluniac priory in England founded around 1080, also adheres rather closely to Cluniac usages, showing the lasting influence of the mother house centuries after the foundation.[41] Liturgical books from the abbey of Saint Bavo's in Ghent reflect the Cluniac reform there in 1117.[42]

36. Krüger, "Architecture and Liturgical Practice" and "Tournus et la fonction des galilées en Bourgogne."

37. See Krüger, "La fonction liturgique des *galilées* clunisiennes."

38. Fribourg, Bibliothèque cantonale et universitaire, L46; see Morin, "Un bréviaire clunisien"; and Leisibach, *Die liturgischen Handschriften,* 56–59. On Payerne as a Cluniac priory see Poeck, "*Cluniacensis Ecclesia,*" 419–20.

39. The Cluniac liturgies of Polirone and Lewes (see below) are a case in point.

40. Negri, "Il lezionario cluniacense."

41. Cambridge, Fitzwilliam Museum, MS 369; described in Hiley, "Cluny, Sequences and Tropes"; Leroquais, *Le bréviaire-missel du prieuré clunisien de Lewes;* and Holder, "The Noted Cluniac Breviary-Missal of Lewes." On the founding of Lewes see Poeck, "*Cluniacensis Ecclesia,*" 184–86.

42. Haggh, "Musique et rituel," 62–63.

Liturgical books from Cluny's dependencies did not always adhere closely to the usages of the mother abbey, however. As David Hiley has pointed out, some priories that adopted the Cluniac selection of chants continued to sing the same versions of the melodies they had used before the Cluniac reform of their community.[43] The liturgy of the Mass at Cluny apparently excluded most of the musico-poetic interpolations known as tropes; as a result, some monasteries apparently suppressed their trope repertories after reform by Cluny.[44] In other cases, liturgical changes were minor, as at the abbey of Moissac in southwestern France, where the Cluniac reform began in 1048 and continued through the 1060s.[45] In a manuscript produced at Moissac at the end of the eleventh century, Cluniac saints have been added to the calendar and the litany,[46] but other manuscripts of the period do not manifest the changes one might expect after the reform, such as the elimination of tropes.[47] In abbeys that remained only briefly in the Cluniac orbit, the degree of liturgical influence varied. Eleventh- and twelfth-century liturgical books from the abbey of Saint-Maur-des-Fossés, near Paris, reflect many aspects of Cluniac usage, although the monastery remained independent even after Abbot Maiolus of Cluny installed his disciples as abbots in the late tenth century.[48] Thus Cluny's liturgical impact on the abbeys it influenced ranged from profound to negligible. In the case of Farfa, it was somewhere in the middle.

Cluniac Liturgical Influence at Farfa

Determining the extent of Cluny's influence on the liturgy of Farfa is difficult because of the relative paucity of extant liturgical sources from this period in the history of both abbeys. No liturgical books of the early eleventh century survive from Farfa, precluding a comparison between Farfa's usages

43. Hiley (*Western Plainchant,* 578) cites Saint-Martial de Limoges, Marchiennes, Anchin, and Saint-Amand.

44. Hiley, "Cluny, Sequences and Tropes," 130–36. The idea of Cluny as an "anti-trope zone" was originally proposed by Gy, "Les tropes dans l'histoire," 9–10.

45. See Hourlier, "L'entrée de Moissac dans l'ordre de Cluny," 25–35; Kohnle, *Abt Hugo von Cluny,* 214–23; and Müssigbrod, *Die Abtei Moissac,* 65–100.

46. Oxford, Bodleian Library, D'Orville 45; for the most recent description of this manuscript see Boynton, "Eleventh-Century Continental Hymnaries," 228–29.

47. As Fassler observed in *Gothic Song* (114), "the apparent continuation of trope repertories at St. Pierre in Moissac, even after the church was reformed by Cluny," remains unexplained.

48. Iogna-Prat, *Ordonner et exclure,* 64 (translated in *Order and Exclusion,* 56); and Lauwers, "Mémoire des origines et idéologies monastiques," 161–66.

before and after Hugh's establishment of the Cluniac constitution. Some Cluniac influence can be discerned in office manuscripts copied at Farfa beginning in the middle of the eleventh century, particularly in those for the divine office.[49] The office was the aspect of the liturgy most characteristic of an individual monastery. Although some parts of the Farfa and Cluny offices show significant discrepancies, a few shared elements seem to indicate a connection between the two traditions; in particular, the Chigi manuscript (BAV Chigi C.VI.177) exhibits several features associated with Cluny. Abbot Maiolus of Cluny appears in the litanies of the saints,[50] and the manuscript contains an early appearance of the *psalmi familiares,* with four psalms rather than the traditional two. As seen in chapter 2, these *psalmi familiares* (familiar psalms) were recited after the hours of the monastic office on behalf of the monastery's royal patrons and other benefactors. It was at Cluny in the middle of the eleventh century that the traditional two psalms employed in this practice were doubled to four; the Chigi manuscript, copied around this time, is one of the earliest known books containing the fourfold familiar psalms.[51] The first psalm of each series was one of the seven penitential psalms, the second varied according to the hour of the office, and the third and fourth were fixed.[52] Farfa also employed the Cluniac order of daily commemorations, beginning with the Cross and the Virgin Mary, followed by the Archangel Michael, John the Baptist, apostles, martyrs, Saint Martin, Saint Benedict, confessors, the Trinity, and personal saints.[53] This series diverges from the Cluniac one only in the absence of Saints Odo, Maiolus, and Odilo, all abbots of Cluny who were venerated in the liturgy both at the abbey itself and in the churches of its dependencies.

Chants and readings for the office of Matins are an especially important body of material for tracing liturgical influence. Comparisons with manu-

49. Longo ("Dialettiche agiografiche," 126) states that Cluniac influence is not easily discernible at Farfa from a hagiographical standpoint, but he acknowledges that a detailed examination of the liturgical sources may yield more information.

50. BAV Chigi C.VI.177, fol. 23v. Maiolus also appears in the litany in the early twelfth-century manuscript Rome, BV F.29, fol. 74v.

51. BAV Chigi C.VI.177, fol. 21r; see Hallinger, "Das Phänomen der liturgischen Steigerungen Klunys (10/11. Jh.)," 217 n. 158. On the recitation of four familiar psalms at Cluny, see *CCM* 7.4 (1986): 17. According to Tolhurst (*Introduction,* 82), the use of four familiar psalms originated at Cluny.

52. The penitential psalms are those numbered 6, 31, 37, 50, 101, 129, and 142 in the Vulgate.

53. BAV Chigi C.VI.177, fols. 12r–13v.

scripts from other Italian monasteries suggest that the configuration of Matins as celebrated at Farfa is more closely related to Italian liturgical traditions than to the usages of Cluny or its northern dependencies.[54] In some liturgical practices, Farfa's traditions differed significantly from Cluny's, such as the performance of the Matins lessons from the Lamentations of Jeremiah at Matins during Holy Week. Whereas the *Liber tramitis* states that these lessons are read "without song" (*sine cantum* [*sic*]), meaning that they are recited but not chanted, in the eleventh-century lectionary from Farfa the texts are abundantly notated.[55] Another dimension of the liturgy that typically manifests a monastery's identity is the veneration of saints. But despite Farfa's connection with Cluny, commemorations of the major Cluniac saints (besides Maiolus) do not appear in Farfa's liturgical books.[56] The sanctoral at Farfa had a distinctly central Italian orientation, emphasizing the saints of particular importance to the abbey and its region.[57] The Farfa scriptorium does not seem to have produced copies of the lives or liturgical offices of Cluniac saints.[58]

It is not surprising that Farfa's liturgical books show few clear signs of Cluniac influence,[59] because Farfa was never a dependency of Cluny. Nevertheless, in the eleventh and early twelfth centuries there persisted at Farfa the idea that the community followed the Cluniac customs introduced by Abbot Hugh.[60] Near the end of the *Chronicle,* Gregory's account of the oath sworn

54. I compared all the chants of the office in BAV Chigi C.VI.177 and Rome, BV F.29 to those in office books from Cluniac dependencies. I also compared the lessons in these manuscripts and in the office lectionaries Rome, BN Farfa 32 (late eleventh century) and Farfa, AF278 (second half of the twelfth century) to the Cluniac ones analyzed in Etaix, "Le lectionnaire de l'office à Cluny." The limited number of concordances between the office lectionaries of Farfa and Cluny may result in part from the incomplete preservation of the offices from Farfa.

55. *LT,* 72; and Rome, BN Farfa 32, fols. 132r–v, 134v–135v, 137r–138r.

56. Longo, "Dialettiche agiografiche," 125.

57. Longo, "Agiografia e identità monastica."

58. Such texts did exist in priories of Cluny, such as the eleventh-century liturgical compilation from the collection of Saint-Martial de Limoges studied by Magne in "Saint Maïeul au miroir de la liturgie." I am grateful to the author for bringing this manuscript and the study to my attention.

59. Gregory of Catino's *Collectio canonum* offers evidence of another form of influence from Cluny. According to Theo Kölzer, the model for the collection appears to be West Frankish, perhaps indicating that a canon law manuscript was brought from Cluny to Farfa after the reform; see *Collectio canonum,* 43–44.

60. *RF* 5:160, 297–98.

by Abbot Guido III at his 1119 consecration invoked the abbey's Cluniac observance in the very words used by Hugh more than a century earlier (in my italics): "I promise to observe and maintain the constitution of Lord Hugh for this monastery, and agreed to by the entire community, that is the authentic observance of the Cluniac monastery, *in ecclesiastical offices and good customs, and in the appearance of the clothing of the brothers, as well as in the daily quantity of food and in holy solemnities.*"[61] The idea of Cluniac observance in Hugh's constitution related to the community's way of life as a whole, including the governance of the monastery and the monks' food and clothing. The celebration of the liturgy, evoked in the terse phrase "holy solemnities," is thus only one element in the ensemble of the customs. As we have seen, liturgical books offer only limited evidence for Cluniac practices at Farfa. For a fuller picture of Cluny's influence one must turn to the *Liber tramitis,* the book of Cluniac customs produced at Farfa in the eleventh century.

Cluniac Customs at Farfa

The *Liber tramitis* constitutes the first extensive account of daily life and liturgy at Cluny; it is the earliest customary of this length to survive from any Western monastery. For the liturgical dimensions of the relationship between Farfa and Cluny this text is particularly significant, because it contains a large corpus of Cluniac material that was compiled for use at Farfa and that was copied and preserved there for centuries. This document reveals not only eleventh-century liturgical practices at Cluny but also the adaptation and transformation of Cluniac practices at Farfa.

The contents of the *Liber tramitis* were compiled in the first half of the eleventh century, and the earliest extant manuscript copy was produced at Farfa around 1050–60.[62] An earlier, much more succinct group of texts known collectively as the *Consuetudines antiquiores* is thought to reflect Cluniac customs as they were known to other monasteries in the late tenth and early eleventh centuries. Although the *Consuetudines antiquiores* contain rather terse directions for performing the liturgy, the *Liber tramitis* offers numerous

61. *RF* 5:313, *CF* 2:296: "Promitto obseruare ac retinere constitutionem domni Hugonis abbatis huic monasterio et omni conuentui concessam, scilicet autenticam religionem Cluniacensis monasterii, in officiis ecclesiasticis et bonis moribus, et confratrum cultu uestium, sive copia uictus cottidie et in sanctis solemnitatibus."

62. See *LT,* xliii–lvi. Wollasch ("Zur Datierung des Liber tramitis") refined some of Dinter's conclusions regarding chronology. Supino Martini (*Roma,* 248) dates the earliest manuscript (BAV Vat. lat. 6808) to around 1050–87 but believes that it probably comes from the earlier part of that period.

details on such matters as the decoration of the church for important feasts, the performance of the chants on those occasions, and the daily activities of the community.[63] The *Liber tramitis* is divided into two parts: the first contains an account of the liturgy throughout the year, and the second is devoted to the regulations of the community and the duties of the monastic officers. The second book also includes prescriptions for the celebration of Mass, processions, prayers, funerals, and the office of the dead.

Until the early twentieth century, the *Liber tramitis* was known as the "customs of Farfa" because of the origin of the earliest known manuscript. However, Ildefonso Schuster pointed out in 1907 that the text refers predominantly to objects, people, and practices at the abbey of Cluny,[64] a conclusion confirmed once again by Peter Dinter in the introduction to his edition of the text.[65] In recent decades, most scholars have treated the *Liber tramitis* as a document that relates almost exclusively to Cluny. To be sure, many sections— such as the description of the church, its relics, and the rest of the monastic complex—portray Cluny rather than Farfa.[66] Furthermore, the liturgical calendar used in the *Liber tramitis* fits the cycle of celebrations at Cluny but does not mention the saints that were particularly venerated at Farfa.[67] Indeed, the customary contains few elements that seem indisputably to pertain to Farfa; these include the prologue and preface recounting the history of the compilation of the *Liber tramitis,* and the chapter on the election of the abbot. But even these latter passages present difficulties of interpretation; the abbatial election is a case in point and merits a brief digression here.

63. For a recent synthesis of the liturgical and musical significance of the *Liber tramitis* see Boynton, "Les coutumes clunisiennes au temps d'Odilon," in *Odilon de Mercoeur,* 193–202.

64. Schuster, "L'Abbaye de Farfa et sa restauration," 378–82.

65. *LT* xxxviii–xli. Although he cited Schuster's 1907 article in the bibliography at the end of the introduction to his edition, Dinter did not explicitly acknowledge that Schuster's article had already demonstrated the Cluniac origin of the text and had covered most of the same ground as Dinter.

66. The description of the monastery in *LT,* 203–6 provided the basis for the plans of Cluny II in Conant, *Cluny,* 44–45, 53–67. Excavations do not support all the details of the plans based on *LT,* however, and some of the buildings described in the customary had apparently not yet been built. See Stratford, "Les bâtiments de l'abbaye de Cluny," 386–9, 407–8; and Sapin, "L'abbatiale de Cluny II," 435–60.

67. The Cluniac character of the *Liber tramitis* was pointed out by Schuster in "L'abbaye de Farfa et sa restauration," 379–83; Dinter discusses the aspects of the text that refer specifically to Cluny in *LT,* xxxviii–xlii.

Scholars have long acknowledged that the procedure for electing the abbot described in the *Liber tramitis* cannot reflect the custom at Cluny, because it refers to the election of the abbot in the presence of the bishop and the person "to whom the abbey belongs."[68] Because Cluny was independent of the local bishop and of the aristocracy, it did not "belong" to anyone in the sense implied by the passage in the *Liber tramitis;* neither the bishop nor any other outsider could play a part in abbatial elections there. It is therefore assumed that this section of the *Liber tramitis* reflects the situation at Farfa, where the person "to whom the abbey belongs" was clearly the emperor. However, the abbatial election at Farfa did not require the presence of either the bishop or the emperor. The diploma by which Otto III reinstated Abbot Hugh stated that abbots should first be elected by the community, then presented to the emperor, and finally consecrated by the pope.[69] This electoral procedure was still in force in 1118, when it was reaffirmed in the privilege of Henry V.[70] Documents in the Farfa *Register* show that the emperor was never physically present at abbatial elections; the community sought his approval for candidates who had already been elected. They might make this petition by letter or by sending a delegation to the imperial court. The request for confirmation of the election of Abbot Berard I in 1047 similarly indicates that the emperor was not present at the election.[71] Moreover, although the *Liber tramitis* states that the local bishop should intone the antiphon by which the chorus celebrates the confirmation and then accompany the new abbot in announcing the result of the election to the monks, clergy, and populace, no other texts from Farfa mention or corroborate this procedure.[72] We do not know whether the chapter in the *Liber tramitis* on the abbatial election was formulated by the monks of Farfa or by those of Cluny; to make a purely hypothetical choice between these

68. Hallinger, "Cluniacensis SS. Religionis Ordinem Elegimus," 260–61. I am grateful to Gisela Drossbach for obtaining this article for me. *LT,* 208: "Primum eligitur ab omni congregatione in praesentia episcopi eiusdem diocesis et senioris ad quem abbatia pertinet."

69. *RF* 4:102.

70. *RF* 5:307: "Sed et hoc diuina optestatione sancimus, et hac nostra praeceptali pagina omnino firmamus, sicut quondam Otto imperator perpetuo roborauit."

71. *RF* 4:210: "Elegimus uno uoto parique consensu domnum Berardum nostrum monachum. . . . Quapropter domne imperator uestram flagitamus excellentiam, quatinus corroborare ac confirmare dignemini."

72. *LT,* 209: "incipit episcopus antiphonam *Confirma hoc deus quod.* . . . Tunc reuestiant se episcopus et electus, ueniant uterque ante altare et legitur iterum electio in ambone, ut audiatur et roboretur a monachis et a clero et ab uniuersis utriusque sexus."

two possibilities, it is more likely that this chapter represents guidelines offered by the Cluniac monks, who perhaps were not aware of Farfa's historical independence from the bishops of the Sabina. Thus the chapter on abbatial election in the *Liber tramitis,* which Cluniac historians frequently cite as emanating from Farfa, highlights the difficulty of differentiating the Cluniac parts of the text from those pertaining to Farfa.

In another case, however, the *Liber tramitis* was evidently understood as a set of prescriptive guidelines for the community at Farfa. Gregory of Catino's *Chronicle* reports a decree by Abbot Berard II prohibiting the monks of Farfa from making confession to monks from other monasteries. As Dinter has pointed out, the *Chronicle* quotes almost verbatim from the relevant section of the *Liber tramitis.* The prohibition is introduced by the phrase "and just as our Cluniac *ordo* requires" (*sicut ordo noster Cluniensis precipit*) and concludes by threatening excommunication for those who disobey without doing full penance.[73] On occasion, then, the monks of Farfa invoked the Cluniac customs as a source of rules for their own community, even though they were not subject to Cluny as a dependency.

The current scholarly consensus holds that the contents of the customary are so closely bound to Cluny as to preclude practical application of the text at Farfa.[74] This literalist approach to the *Liber tramitis* has its limitations. That the customary seems more prescriptive than descriptive with regard to Farfa does not diminish the fact that the monks there compiled the material, produced the manuscript, annotated it over time, and preserved it for hundreds of years. The question is not whether the monks of Farfa used or consulted the *Liber tramitis,* but how they applied its precepts to their own community. To answer this question in regard to the liturgy, one must first confront the ambiguous function of the document itself. Because abbeys adapted and altered the contents of the Cluniac customaries to fit their own usages, obtaining a copy of the customs of Cluny did not entail the wholesale adoption of Cluny's liturgy. Thus, although the *Liber tramitis* is the most concrete evidence for the transmission of liturgical practices from Cluny to Farfa, we do not know exactly how the community viewed the customary in relation to their own liturgical traditions, and it must be taken into account that the monks included material from Farfa in order to adjust parts of the text to their needs. Such adaptation is typical of the transmission of Cluniac customs.

In the tenth and eleventh centuries, Cluny's customs were recorded for the

73. *LT,* 279; and *CF* 2:200.

74. This was Dinter's conclusion (*LT,* xliii); however, practical use is implied by the annotation of Zurich, Zentralbibliothek 82 with liturgical texts from the *Liber tramitis.*

use of other monasteries but remained an oral tradition at Cluny itself.[75] Not until the years around 1080 were the customs recorded at Cluny itself, by the monk Bernard, in a form intended for internal use by the novices.[76] Another Cluniac monk, Ulrich of Zell, wrote a briefer version of the customs around the same time at the request of Abbot William of Hirsau.[77] The copies of these customaries made outside Cluny show that their recipients altered them at will.[78] In keeping with this tendency to adapt the Cluniac customs to local use, the Farfa manuscript of the *Liber tramitis* shows many subsequent liturgical annotations attesting to the continued practical use and adaptation of the manuscript.[79] To be sure, certain parts of the customary could not apply directly to Farfa's own liturgy, such as the commemorations of saints who were important to Cluny but who are not mentioned in any other manuscripts from Farfa. Nevertheless, several sections of the text were equally applicable to liturgical practices at both abbeys, such as the multiple commemorations of Henry II, who favored Farfa with two privileges (1014, 1019)[80] and also donated several precious liturgical objects to Cluny.

75. The *Consuetudines antiquiores*, like the *Liber tramitis*, survives only in manuscripts copied outside Cluny, and there is no evidence that either of these texts was known at Cluny. See Cochelin, "Evolution des coutumiers monastiques."

76. Nothing is known of Bernard besides the fact that he was a monk at Cluny. On the function of his redaction of the customs see Cochelin, "Evolution des coutumiers monastiques."

77. Ulrich, *Antiquiores consuetudines*, PL 149:643–779. William wished to refer to the Cluniac customs in preparing a customary for his own abbey. Ulrich arrived at Cluny for his monastic profession in 1061; see Tutsch, *Studien zur Rezeptionsgeschichte*, 18.

78. On this process of reception and modification see Cochelin, "Evolution des coutumiers monastiques"; and Tutsch, "Die Rezeptionsgeschichte," "Texttradition und Praxis," and "Zur Rezeptionsgeschichte."

79. All the annotations are mentioned in the critical apparatus of Dinter's edition. Because the manuscript from Farfa (BAV Vat. lat. 6808) is the earliest known copy of the text, it is not possible to determine whether it contains modifications of an earlier version. However, several of the annotations to the Vatican manuscript are assimilated into the text in a central Italian manuscript produced around 1100 (Abbazia di San Paolo fuori le Mura 92) which derives from the Vatican manuscript. The San Paolo manuscript lacks the description of the abbey of Cluny found in the Vatican manuscript. These interpolations and omissions in the San Paolo manuscript reflect the process of adaptation seen in other copies of Cluniac customaries, making it all the more likely that such changes were made when the *Liber tramitis* was written at Farfa. My study of the San Paolo manuscript is in preparation.

80. See *LT*, 199, 285.

The *Liber tramitis* could have been useful to Farfa for pragmatic considerations as well as spiritual ones. Charles McClendon has noted that the reconstruction of the Farfa abbey church, which reflects northern European
influences, was planned and undertaken at the same time the customary was
compiled. He has pointed out that the description of Cluny's architecture in
the *Liber tramitis* represents a valuable source of information about northern
monastic churches for the monks to use in their building campaign.[81] Recently, Kristina Krüger has observed that the *Liber tramitis* contains the earliest known reference to a two-story narthex as a *galilea* (galilee). As seen earlier,
Krüger associates the Cluniac form and function of this architectural element
with comparable structures in eleventh- and twelfth-century churches that
had ties with Cluny.[82] Because Farfa possessed a copy of the *Liber tramitis,*
Krüger argues that, by analogy with the other churches featuring Cluniac
galileae, the Romanesque church at Farfa must also have incorporated such a
structure.[83] In sum, it seems that the monks of Farfa put the Cluniac customs
to diverse uses.

Transmission and Adaptation in the Liber Tramitis

The story of the compilation of the *Liber tramitis,* as recounted in its prologue and preface, provides a fascinating example of the interaction of oral and
written transmission in the eleventh century. As in the narrative by Hugh of
Farfa quoted earlier, the prologue to the *Liber tramitis* recounts how he sought
to imitate at Farfa the monastic observance he had seen at Romuald's abbey
in Ravenna, and how he subsequently imposed on his monks the *usus* of
Cluny, "excelling in the path of the rule beyond all other monasteries in the
entire world at that time."[84] Hugh and Romuald agreed to study and introduce the Cluniac customs, and the prologue presents Hugh as following the
advice of Romuald, who had gained experience through building many monasteries:

81. McClendon, *Imperial Abbey,* 100–101.

82. See Krüger, "Architecture and Liturgical Practice," "La fonction liturgique," and
"Tournus et la fonction."

83. I am grateful to Kristina Krüger for sharing with me "Die Reichsabtei Farfa," which
expands on Krüger, *Die romanischen Westbauten,* 245–46. The preserved elevation of the
site, which has undergone many transformations over the centuries, does not confirm the
existence of the Cluniac-style *galilea.*

84. *LT,* 4: "per totum orbem cuncta ultra monasteria regulari tramite pollentis ipso
tempore."

And in fact, the fame of the aforementioned monastery [Farfa], and also of the aforementioned fathers, that is Romuald and most beneficent lord abbot Hugh, resounded far and wide; in short, these two fathers burning with great zeal and in agreement with each other, Lord Romuald shone forth splendidly in contemplation and in the construction of many monasteries, and father Hugh became his follower in the royal monastery, to such a degree that, for the study of the venerable Cluniac monasteries in Gaul (where venerable father Odilo still shines like a radiating lamp), for the salvation of their souls he imposed upon those who had been entrusted to them, and who had been gathered in the sheepfold of Christ, many things from their [Cluniac] customs for the benefit of the brothers.[85]

The prologue states that John, a monk from a community near Montopoli Sabina (in the neighborhood of Farfa) and a former disciple of Romuald, went with a companion to Cluny to observe the customs and write them down for others to read. The description of his mission clearly distinguishes between the actions of seeing and writing: "He hastened to see and write at that same Cluniac monastery. And thus he wrote down on small pages what he saw with his eyes, and he impressed [them] in books and delivered them to be read by future generations."[86] The rest of the prologue is devoted to assurances that those who follow the customs will succeed in the monastic life. Following the prologue is a preface that adds further information on the process by which the customary was compiled: whatever John learned from experience at Cluny he "wove into pure form through a double definition" (*quaecumque ibi probatae experientiae didicit, duplici hoc pro diffinitione ad purum contexuit*).[87] The meaning of this passage is not clear, but it might refer to the fact that the *Liber tramitis* contains two versions of several sections. Dinter has argued that John, visiting Cluny in the 1020s, found two written versions of the customs

85. *LT*, 4: "Insonante etenim longe lateque fama praelibati caenobii necnon et praedictorum patrum, Romualdo scilicet et domni Hugonis abbatis benignissimi, hi denique patres nimio zelo feruentes et inter se concordantes, domnus Romualdus in theoretica praeclarus effulsit uita necnon et in aedificatione multorum monasteriorum, pater uero Hugo sequipeda eius effectus in regali coenobio in tantum, ut ad Galliarum studia uenerabilium caenobiorum Cluniacensium ubi uenerabilis pater Ocdilo uelut lucerna radians adhuc fulget multa de illorum consuetudine ad utilitatem fratrum illi commissis et in ouile Christi aggregatis imposuerit ad salutem animarum."

86. *LT*, 4: "ad uidendum et scribendum properauit apud eundem Cluniacensem caenobium. Et ita exarauit in paginulis ut oculis uidit et in codicibus affixit posterisque legenda contradidit."

87. *LT*, 5.

and, from these, compiled a redaction that included both.[88] Dinter's assumption of predominantly written models conflicts with the language of the prologue and the preface, which seems to imply that John was recording an oral tradition learned "from demonstrated experience" (*probatae experientiae didicit*).[89] Although the preface's implication that a "double definition" (*duplex diffinitio*) was woven into a "pure form" (*ad purum contexuit*) could suggest that John ironed out inconsistencies, yet this "double definition" is clearly manifested in the structure of the text, which includes two contrasting versions of several sections, one immediately following the other, without offering any explanation for the contradictions between them. The double sections include prescriptions for manual labor, processions with relics, liturgical maledictions, the feast of All Souls introduced by Odilo, and extreme unction.[90] Except for the two chapters on manual labor, which are almost identical, the dual versions present contradictions.[91] Dinter argues that the dual versions arose from changes in the customs during the decades between John's initial visit to Cluny and the final redaction of the customary in 1050–60, during

88. *LT*, liv.

89. *LT*, 5. The section concerning processions on Wednesdays and Fridays (*LT*, 239–40), which Dinter thought manifested two different redactions (apparently because the second one begins with the word *item* [also]) opens with a general rule that monks should remain with the choir for the entire duration of the litany during processions. The next section is a more detailed prescription for chants and prayers performed during processions to the church of Saint Maiolus outside the monastery. Such a two-part structure does not necessarily arise from two different preexisting redactions. Similarly, the two sections on the commemoration of a monk from the Cluniac congregation who dies elsewhere complement each other without duplication (*LT*, 278–89), but Dinter listed them among the chapters with double versions.

90. Dinter (*LT*, liii) states that there were three versions of the statute for All Souls, but the text he describes as the third version (*LT*, 199–200) deals with the commemoration of Henry II and of deceased monks of Cluny (*pro nostrorum fratrum animabus*). What Dinter thought were multiple versions of the offices for the octaves of the feasts of Benedict and the Assumption are actually intended for two different liturgical occasions. One set of instructions is for the celebration of the liturgy during the eight days following the feast (*per octavas*), while the other set of instructions is for the octave of the feast day (*octava*). Dinter's reference to multiple versions of the liturgical instructions for the feast of the Nativity of the Virgin Mary (*LT*, 162–64) is also incorrect.

91. *LT*, 200–201, 213–14. The only noticeable differences between these two versions are the slightly greater length of the second version and its references to the performances of readings by a child oblate (*puer*).

which time a monk from Cluny was in residence at Farfa.[92] It is not clear why changes over time would entail the recording of two different versions of some texts by a single hand rather than revision or replacement of a single text. Another possibility is that the pairs represent two alternatives for the same action or text. The inclusion of alternative texts occurs fairly often in liturgical books, sometimes preserving texts that have been replaced or suppressed during a liturgical reform.[93]

Some of the pairs in the *Liber tramitis* may represent Cluniac practice juxtaposed with either an earlier version of the same ritual or a version adapted for use at Farfa.[94] For instance, the two sections of instructions for processions with relics share the same basic outline, but the second version lacks all the references that make the first version specific to Cluny. The first version uses Saint Marcellus, whose relics Cluny possessed, as an example of the saint being venerated and cites specific responsories from the liturgy of that saint. The second version refers only generically to "the saint whose relics are being carried" and the performance of responsories.[95] Otherwise, the liturgical actions and chants performed are similar. The second version could perhaps represent a simplified text intended for use outside Cluny. In this regard it may be significant that the two texts differ slightly with regard to the use of liturgical vestments; the first version specifies that the monks should wear copes and the oblates albs throughout the procession, while the second text prescribes albs for carrying the relic (*corpus sanctum*) outside and copes for bringing the relics back to the church. An adaptation of the original text for use in another monastery might explain this difference.

Rituals for Friends and Enemies

Although the *Liber tramitis* is often considered a purely Cluniac document, many of the ceremonies in it could have been adapted for use at Farfa. Revisiting these texts in consideration of their potential use at Farfa can offer new insight into their function and meaning. Two of these rituals, the reception of

---

92. *LT,* lii–lvi.

93. Some manuscripts copied in the duchy of Benevento after the suppression of the Beneventan chant contain "doublets," with the native Beneventan chants copied immediately after the Gregorian chants that had replaced them in common use; see Kelly, *Beneventan Chant,* 42–43.

94. I am grateful to Barbara Rosenwein for suggesting an interpretation of the phrase *hoc pro diffinitione* as referring to the juxtaposition of practices from Cluny and Farfa.

95. *LT,* 240–42.

a king at a monastery (the adventus) and a liturgical malediction (the *clamor*), would have served the same purposes at Farfa as they did at Cluny: the welcoming of visitors and the cursing of enemies.

Louis II spent Pentecost at Farfa in 872,[96] and in the following centuries the Ottonians and Salians stopped there on their way to or from Rome.[97] The visits of imperial patrons to Farfa would have occasioned the performance of a ritual, welcoming the ruler upon his arrival. The ordo in the *Liber tramitis,* which is the earliest known set of instructions for the reception of a ruler in a monastery, represents one version of the ceremonial that could be performed for the arrival of an imperial patron at Farfa.[98] Such ceremonies of welcome in the Middle Ages were based on the ancient tradition of a Roman emperor's triumphal entry into a city—his "advent" or arrival (*aduentus* in Latin, whence the origin of the term *adventus* for the ritual).[99] The ruler's arrival was symbolically linked to Christ's entry into Jerusalem on Palm Sunday.[100] The adventus had political as well as allegorical dimensions; as David Warner has observed, "a ceremonial entry indicated a king's relationship with a church or monastery as forcefully as a royal diploma."[101]

Central to the performance of an adventus were nonverbal forms of communication (such as music, gestures, special clothing, and ornaments) that heightened the meaning of the words pronounced in speeches and chants.[102] Accordingly, the *Liber tramitis* lists the objects to be carried in the procession greeting the king: a crucifix, holy water, a censer, candelabra, and a Gospel book.[103] Upon meeting the king, the abbot gives him holy water and censes the king, who kisses the Gospel book. Then, while all the bells are rung, the monks sing the responsory *Ecce mitto angelum meum,* a chant usually per-

96. *RF* 3:11–12 (May 18, 872).

97. Otto III visited Farfa on September 22, 999 (*CF* 2:5; *RF* 3:143–44); Henry II in 1022 ("Vita sancti Guidonis abbatis Casaurensis," *AASS Ordinis Sancti Benedicti,* saec. VI, 1:487); and Henry IV in 1082 (*RF* 5:94; *CF* 2:172).

98. Willmes, *Der Herrscher-'Adventus,'* 146.

99. On the adventus generally see Hack, *Das Empfangszeremoniell,* 4–7; and the bibliography in Warner, "Ritual and Memory." On the adventus's development in antiquity see Dufraigne, *Aduentus Augusti, Aduentus Christi.*

100. See Kantorowicz, "The 'King's Advent,'" 210.

101. Warner, "Thietmar of Merseburg on Rituals of Kingship," 56.

102. Hack, *Das Empfangszeremoniell,* 259.

103. *LT,* 242. For a translation of adventus ceremonies in the *Liber tramitis* and in the customary of Bernard, see app. 3.

formed on the fourth Sunday of Lent. With a text drawn from Exodus 23:20–24, this responsory is appropriate to the circumstance of welcoming a guest and symbolically taking him under the protection of the monastery: "Behold, I send my angel so that he may precede you and always watch over you. Observe and hear my voice, and I will be an enemy to your enemies, and I will cast down those who cast you down, and my angel will precede you."[104] After another chant, to be chosen by the abbot (and thus not specified in the text), the procession enters the church and two prayers are recited. The first, "Omnipotens sempiterne Deus qui caelestia," is found in an early ninth-century sacramentary among the "daily prayers"; it is assigned to the second Sunday after Epiphany in the supplement to the Gregorian sacramentary compiled in the early ninth century by Benedict of Aniane.[105] The second, "Omnipotens sempiterne Deus miserere famulo tuo," appears among the votive masses in the Aninian supplement.[106] If the visitor to the monastery is a queen, the ceremony is the same except for the special chant to be sung as the procession enters the church, *Cum sederit filius hominis.* This long and elaborate processional antiphon is sung to a text that paraphrases the conclusion of Matthew 25:

> When the son of God shall sit on the throne of his majesty and will have begun to judge the world by fire, then may all the choirs of angels stand before him, and all nations will be gathered before him; then shall he say to whose who will be on his right side: "Come, blessed ones of my Father, you possess the kingdom prepared for you from the creation of the world." And the impious ones will go into eternal suffering, but the just into eternal life, and they will reign with God forever.[107]

Singing *Cum sederit* at the moment a queen enters the church suggests an eschatological interpretation likening her arrival to the Second Coming of the

104. *CAO* 4:153 (no. 6598): "Ecce mitto angelum meum, qui praecedat te et custodiat semper. Observa et audi vocem meam, et inimicus ero inimicis tuis et affligentes te affligam, et praecedet te angelus meus." The *Liber tramitis* does not specify which verse follows this respond, but the most common one is "Israel, si me audieris."

105. *CO,* 3909, 6:93; *GS,* 922 and Supplement 1099, *Sacramentaire grégorien* 1:325, 382.

106. *CO,* 3859, 6:73; Supplement 1293, 238, *Sacramentaire grégorien* 1:432.

107. *CAO* 3:126, no. 2032: "Cum sederit Filius hominis in sede majestatis suae et coeperit judicare saeculum per ignem, tunc assistent ante eum omnes chori angelorum, et congregabuntur ante eum omnes gentes; tunc dicet his qui a dextris ejus erunt: Venite benedicti Patris mei, possidete praeparatum vobis regnum a constitutione mundi. Et ibunt impii in supplicium sempiternum, justi autem in vitam aeternam, et regnabunt cum Deo in saecula" (Matt. 25:31–34, 46).

Lord. In Matthew 25, this passage is preceded by the parables of the wise and foolish virgins and of the talents, so perhaps the antiphon was also meant to refer to the queen as one of the wise virgins. The fact that the same antiphon is sung during the Palm Sunday procession described in the *Liber tramitis* implies that the performance of *Cum sederit* during the adventus ceremony alludes to Christ's entry into Jerusalem.[108] Although *Cum sederit* was usually sung in other Lenten processions, its use in the *Liber tramitis* for Palm Sunday and the adventus of the queen aptly evokes the triumphal eschatology already implicit in the symbolism of both occasions.[109]

A rather different and more detailed version of the adventus appears in the later customary written at Cluny around 1080 by the monk Bernard. Translations of both texts appear in appendix 3.[110] According to Bernard, the procession to greet the king includes holy water, a censer, candelabra, and a Gospel book, but his text lacks the crucifix mentioned in the *Liber tramitis*. Bernard does not mention changes in the ritual when the visitor is a queen. Moreover, the chants and prayers performed in the ceremony described by Bernard are not the same as those mentioned in the *Liber tramitis*. Instead of the prayers specified by the *Liber tramitis*, Bernard prescribes two briefer and more common prayers: "Saluum fac seruum tuum" and "Miserere mei Deus."[111]

Despite the contrast between the versions of the ritual in the *Liber tramitis* and in the customary of Bernard, historians have never doubted that both represent the ceremony as performed at Cluny. The two rituals do share some elements: the monks in the procession for a royal visitor wear copes, the great bells are rung as the procession exits the choir, the procession takes place in si-

---

108. *LT*, 68.

109. *Cum sederit* is found among the processional antiphons for use throughout Lent in a manuscript roughly contemporary with the *Liber tramitis*: Paris, BNF lat. 903, fol. 35v. For a facsimile see *Le Codex 903 de la Bibliothèque Nationale*, 70. *Cum sederit* also appears in the thirteenth-century antiphoner Worcester, Cathedral Chapter Library, F.160, reproduced in *Antiphonaire Monastique, XIIIe siècle*, 206. On the type of processional chant collection in which *Cum sederit* is usually found, see Huglo, *Les manuscrits du processionnal*, 46*.

110. Bernard, *Ordo Cluniacensis*, ed. Herrgott, *Vetus disciplina monastica*, 217–29; and Paris, BNF lat. 13875, fols. 71r–72v. Bernard combines in a single chapter the provisions for different guests (kings, popes, bishops, archbishops, and abbots), while the *Liber tramitis* has three separate chapters for kings, bishops, and abbots.

111. Willmes (*Der Herrscher-'Adventus,'* 178–79) noted some of the differences between the ceremonies as described in *LT* and by Bernard but judged them ultimately inconsequential.

lence, and the visitor kisses the Gospel book after being censed and blessed with holy water. Both customaries call for carpets to be spread in front of two major altars in the church (the high altar and the altar of the Holy Cross). But the divergences between the texts suggest that they are two fundamentally different versions of the ceremony. Not only were the two customaries copied in different places and at different times, but no independent evidence from Cluny corroborates the performance of the ritual as described in the *Liber tramitis*. Although the differences between them could be attributed to change over time, it is also possible that the text in the *Liber tramitis* represents a version used at Farfa.

A ritual of welcome would have been performed at Farfa for the arrival of each royal or imperial patron, and the ceremony for the reception of a queen could have been used when Empress Agnes visited Farfa sometime between 1065 and 1072.[112] Unfortunately, neither the *Chronicle* nor the *Register* offers descriptions of these occasions. Even the account of Henry IV's 1082 visit, which is relatively informative (noting that the emperor was received into the brotherhood with the kiss of peace, and that his name was entered into the abbey's commemorative book), does not relate the details of his reception. It states only that "he was received most nobly and honorifically and affectionately by all the brothers" (*a cunctis fratribus nobilissime ualdeque honorifice et amantissime susceptus est*).[113] However loose the connection between the contents of the customary and Henry's visit to Farfa, it highlights the fact that medieval rituals and their meanings could be adapted to various circumstances.

The ceremony in the *Liber tramitis* shares several elements with the coronation ceremony found in the Romano-Germanic pontifical, a liturgical collection that was first compiled in the tenth century and then widely diffused in the Ottonian Empire and throughout Italy. Like the adventus, this ritual calls for a procession with a Gospel book and the spreading of two carpets in front of the altars in the church, as well as the performance of both the responsory *Ecce mitto* and the two prayers found in the *Liber tramitis*.[114] On the basis of these similarities, Dominique Iogna-Prat has suggested that the coronation ritual was the source of the adventus ceremony in the *Liber tramitis*. The adventus would thereby constitute a symbolic gesture of power toward the emperor that was particularly appropriate to Cluny's relationship with the

112. Black-Veldtrup, *Kaiserin Agnes*, 49.

113. Schuster, *Imperiale abbazia*, 207; *RF* 5:94; and *CF* 2:172.

114. Two versions appear in *Le Pontifical romano-germanique*, 246–60 (no. 77); see also Willmes, *Der Herrscher-'Adventus*,' 165–66.

papacy.[115] However, the textual components of the adventus ceremony (the responsory *Ecce mitto* and the prayers) had a long history of liturgical use before the compilation of the Romano-Germanic pontifical. The preceding analysis of the ritual in the *Liber tramitis* has shown that it indeed might not represent Cluniac practice in the eleventh century; it is suggestive that this version of the ceremony, contained in a manuscript written at Farfa for the use of that abbey, contrasts with the version in the customary of Bernard, which was compiled at Cluny for its own use. At the very least, the adventus ritual described in the *Liber tramitis* is appropriate for performance at Farfa and implies that the customary could have had practical applications there.

The *Liber tramitis* also contains instructions for two different rituals that medieval monastic communities could perform in order to curse their collective enemies. Such ceremonies made for a dramatic display of spiritual power in the face of a perceived material threat. By deprecating the enemy through prayer, by proclaiming biblical maledictions, and even by placing relics on the ground, monks verbally and visually evoked their role as the custodians of the saints and the purveyors of salvific prayer.[116] The two texts in the *Liber tramitis* represent a broader tradition of liturgical cursing that has been studied by Lester Little.[117] Although Little treated the two versions of the curse as variations on the same ritual, a closer comparison reveals significant differences, suggesting that one of the versions is intended for Farfa while the other reflects the Cluniac tradition.

The first text describes the placement during Mass of the crucifix, Gospel book, and relics of the saints on a hair cloth (*cilicium*) on the church pavement. The monks prostrate themselves and remain on the ground, silently reciting a psalm while two bells are struck. The priest stands alone before the altar and the saints' relics on the floor; he recites a long prayer, after which the relics are returned to their places. The ceremony concludes with a short prayer said silently by the priest.[118] The second version of the ritual in the *Liber tramitis* does not mention the deposition of relics at Mass; instead, after the chanting of the Creed, "the armarius ascends the pulpit and announces to the people the malice of the persecutors. Then another brother comes forth and reads the anathemas or maledictions of both the Old and New Testaments according to their usefulness and the order received from the Apostolic See and the provi-

115. Iogna-Prat, "La croix," 468–70.

116. See also Geary, "Humiliation of Saints," 95–103.

117. Little, *Benedictine Maledictions*, 27–29; and Little, "Anger in Monastic Curses."

118. *LT,* 245–47.

sion given by nearby bishops."[119] After the reading, the lights are extinguished and all the bells are rung. Then all the monks prostrate themselves singing psalms, after which all rise, sing the Offertory chant, and conclude the Mass. The greater part of this second *clamor* ritual is intended for performance at Mass on Sundays; the chapter closes with an alternative, simpler ritual for Mass on weekdays.

The two versions of the *clamor* in the *Liber tramitis* are explicitly contrasted by the rubric for the second version: *Item de eadem in alia diffinitione,* which can be loosely translated as "Another version of the same thing."[120] Perhaps the distinction between the two texts implied by *item in alia diffinitione* simply refers to the fact that the first version is for performance during the conventual morning Mass in which only the monks of the community were present, while the second version is intended for a Mass that laypeople would attend. The reference to the *alia diffinitio* in this rubric could mean that it was part of the *duplex diffinitio,* the double version of the customs mentioned in the preface of the *Liber tramitis.* Although the second version of the *clamor* in the *Liber tramitis* differs markedly from the first, it resembles the *clamor* in the Cluniac customary of Bernard.[121] Bernard's detailed account begins with instructions for the *clamor* at the community's morning Mass, which on this occasion had a penitential character: no bells are rung, no incense offered, no chasubles or copes worn, no candles lit in front of the altar, and the Creed is not sung. The remainder of the chapter, which describes how to perform the *clamor* when laypeople (*populares*) attend a Sunday Mass in front of the crucifix, is comparable to the second version of the *clamor* in the *Liber tramitis.* After the Creed (which, in the absence of the *populus,* would not be sung), a brother ascends the pulpit to announce (*manifestare*) the monastery's trouble to the people and encourage them to give alms. He is to add "something humble and persuasive, saying, 'You know that if our sustenance is taken away from us we cannot live; therefore, brothers, supplicate God and we will make a proc-

119. *LT,* 247: "Ad expletionem euangelii dicatur *Credo in unum deum.* Quo expleto ascendat armarius in pulpitum et nuntiet plebi malitiam persecutorum. Dein procedat alius frater et legat anathemata uel maledicta tam noui quam ueteris testamenti secundum utilitatem ac iussionem a sede apostolica acceptam et a uicinis episcopis praebitionem datam."

120. *LT,* 247.

121. Bernard, *Ordo Cluniacensis,* xlii; Paris, BNF lat. 13875, fol. 83r; and *Vetus disciplina monastica,* 230–31.

lamation to him.'"[122] The choir sings a response and all the bells are rung, after which the community chants psalms and recites prayers.[123]

The ritual described by Bernard expands on the second version of the *clamor* in the *Liber tramitis*, with the exception that the monks are not specifically instructed to prostrate themselves while they sing psalms. The humiliation of relics and the prostration of the community, which are the most striking ritual gestures in the first version of the *clamor* in the *Liber tramitis*, are absent both from the second version and from the customary of Bernard. Both the second version and Bernard's version refer explicitly to the presence of the laity, while the first version does not.[124] These aspects of the ritual structure, as well as the specific chants and prayers, differentiate the two versions of the *clamor* found in the *Liber tramitis*.[125]

The fact that only the second version agrees with Bernard's text suggests that it represents the Cluniac tradition of this ritual. The concluding reference to the Apostolic See and the local bishops fits the historical context of Cluny but contradicts both Farfa's imperial patronage and its long-standing independence from papal and episcopal control. The first version of the *clamor* in the *Liber tramitis* could reflect practices at Farfa. No other copy of this text survives from either Cluny or Farfa; indeed, almost nothing about the ritual suggests that it originated in either monastery. One element, however, may point to the place where it arose or at least was used. The prayer "In spiritu humilitatis," found in the first version of the *clamor* in the *Liber tramitis*, refers to Mary as the patron of the church: "Lord, this church of yours, which in ancient times you founded and raised up in the honor of the blessed and glorious ever-virgin Mary, now sits in sadness."[126] The text makes clear that the prayer is to be recited during the High Mass in the monastery's principal

122. Bernard, *Ordo Cluniacensis*, xliii; Paris, BNF lat. 13875, fol. 83r; and *Vetus disciplina monastica*, 230-31: "Adiungit quoque quaedam humilia persuasoria dicens, Scitis quia si aufertur nobis nostra substantia non possumus uiuere. Rogate ergo fratres Dominum et nos faciemus ad eum proclamationem."

123. There is only a limited correspondence between the specific texts mentioned in *LT* and Bernard at this point. The significance of this divergence is unclear.

124. The presence of the laity might be implied at the High Mass described in the first version of the *clamor*, but the text does not state that the priest addresses them directly.

125. Little (*Benedictine Maledictions*, 29) notes the difference between the two texts in the *Liber tramitis* without commenting on the implications of this contrast.

126. *LT,* 246: "Aecclesia tua haec domine quam priscis temporibus fundasti et sublimasti in honore beatae et gloriosae semper uirginis Mariae sedet in tristitia."

church, which at Cluny was dedicated to the apostles Peter and Paul, but which at Farfa was dedicated to Mary. This part of the prayer was customarily altered to name the patron of the monastery in which a manuscript originated.[127] Such an alteration might explain the reference to Mary. But it would conflict with the explicit mentions throughout the *Liber tramitis* of the monastic complex at Cluny, including the instructions for a procession to the basilica of Mary (the oratory of the Virgin in the monastic complex of Cluny II) following the second version of the *clamor*. Thus, while those performing the first version of the ritual are already implicitly located in a church dedicated to Mary (which would make sense at Farfa, but not at Cluny), the procession after the second version of the ritual implies movement from the principal church to a church dedicated to Mary (which would make sense at Cluny but not at Farfa). Clearly, the two versions of the *clamor* imply performance in two mutually contradictory locations, suggesting that they pertain to two different institutions: Farfa and Cluny. Although the second version corresponds to Cluniac liturgical tradition as recorded in the customary of Bernard, the first version seems designed for Farfa.

Farfa's frequent conflicts over property in the eleventh and twelfth centuries provided ample opportunities to perform liturgical maledictions on enemies. Individuals and institutions challenged the abbey's rights, sometimes invading its territories. The abbey was engaged in ongoing disputes with churches and monasteries in Rome, such as Sant'Eustachio, San Paolo fuori le Mura, and San Cosimato, over rights to landholdings both inside and outside the city. Competing claims by Farfa and San Cosimato to the priory of Santa Maria in Minione led to intermittent legal disputes for more than a century, from the first case presented to Emperor Otto I (962–73) until Henry IV's confirmation of Farfa's rights to the priory in 1084.[128] The noble families of the Sabina had frequent recourse to lawyers, and sometimes to armed warfare, in their attempts to annex Farfa's possessions or to reclaim those that earlier generations

---

127. To the sources for this prayer used by Dinter should be added the early twelfth-century chronicle of San Vincenzo al Volturno, which contains the same prayer with reference to the church "which you founded in honor of your blessed mother Mary and of your holy apostles Peter and Paul but then elevated to blessed Vincent priest and martyr" ("quam priscis temporibus fundasti et in honore beatissime genitricis tue Marie sanctorumque apostolorum tuorum Petri et Pauli sed et beatissimi Vincentii levite et martyris sublimasti"; *Chronicon Vulturnense*, 20, cited by Kölzer, "*Codex Libertatis*," 621, n. 58). On the relationship between Farfa and San Vincenzo see chap. 5.

128. For a recent discussion of these disputes with further bibliography, see Stroll, *The Medieval Abbey*, 30–47.

had given to the abbey. The Ottaviani, a branch of the influential Roman Crescenzio family, were involved in legal disputes with Farfa for more than a century.[129] In the 1050s, the Ottaviani invaded Farfa's lands repeatedly, leading Pope Nicholas II to summon the aggressors to a tribunal. After consecrating the altars in July 1060, Nicholas confirmed Farfa's privileges, liberties (*libertates*), and immunity (*emunitas*), and issued an anathema against all those who would violate them.[130]

The Farfa *Register* provides a detailed account of the ritual proclamation of this anathema. On September 14, 1060, the feast of the Exaltation of the Cross, three papal legates came to the abbey for the ceremony; one of them, Humbert of Silva Candida, pronounced the anathema at Mass after the singing of the Gospel. Then the legates placed the text of the anathema on the altar, and all those present subscribed it, including a monk who identified himself as "Martin of Cluny" (*Martinus Cluniensis*).[131] Thus, around the same time that the Farfa manuscript of the *Liber tramitis* was produced, a monk from Cluny witnessed a ritual of anathema performed at Farfa by a papal legate. We do not know what role Martin played in this ceremony except as a witness, but his presence among the monks suggests that he was involved in the transmission of Cluniac customs to the community, perhaps including more recent developments postdating the initial compilation of the *Liber tramitis*. In this regard, it may be significant that the document immediately following the anathema in the Farfa *Register* resembles the request to the laity for alms in the *clamor* ritual described by Bernard; this request reflects a later stage of Cluniac liturgy than the *Liber tramitis*.[132] Although it is not clear how the anathema pronounced at Farfa in 1060 relates to the *clamor* ritual in the *Liber tramitis* or to the later Cluniac ritual, the account in the *Register* provides an example of the performance of liturgical maledictions at Farfa.

The Death Ritual in the Liber Tramitis

Although the adventus and *clamor* rituals at Farfa may well have followed the prescriptions in the *Liber tramitis*, this cannot be proven beyond a doubt. However, the *Liber tramitis* does contain a text with much more direct and evident ties to Farfa's own rituals for the unction, death, and burial of monks. As

---

129. Bossi, "I Crescenzi di Sabina," 114–44; and Stroll, *The Medieval Abbey*, 30–47.

130. Schuster, *Imperiale abbazia*, 198–99; Stroll, *The Medieval Abbey*, 52–55; *RF* 5:294–95 (no. 1307, "Ob reverentiam"); Jaffé, *Regesta*, 563; and Kehr, *Italia pontificia*, 67.

131. On the presence of a Cluniac monk named Martin at Farfa, see *LT*, lv.

132. *RF* 5:295–96 (document 1308).

Frederick Paxton has shown, the *Liber tramitis* offers more information on the death ritual than any previous monastic text, and it preserves an early form of the Cluniac traditions seen in the later customaries of Bernard and Ulrich.[133] The death ritual in the *Liber tramitis* is the most suggestive example of Cluniac influence on Farfa, for it clearly shaped a text found in three liturgical manuscripts from the abbey, two of them copied there around the same time as the *Liber tramitis* and the third copied in the early twelfth century.[134] The Farfa ritual derives directly from the one in the *Liber tramitis,* with the addition of some elements characteristic of central Italy.

The similarities and verbal parallels between the Farfa text and the *Liber tramitis* suggest that the monks of Farfa adapted the Cluniac ritual to their own traditions. The Farfa ritual is summarized in example 3.1; in example 3.2, its text is compared to that in the *Liber tramitis,* with parallel passages in bold. The two texts exhibit the same ritual structure.[135] The unction and Communion in the Farfa death ritual are essentially abbreviated versions of those in the *Liber tramitis.* Even though the Farfa text appears to be based on the one in the *Liber tramitis,* it also includes some non-Cluniac elements that are found as well in a customary copied in the twelfth century at the central Italian abbey of Vallombrosa.[136] A significant contrast between the Farfa text and the death ritual in the *Liber tramitis* is the manner in which the ailing monk makes his confession. In the Farfa text, he confesses in the infirmary with the assembled community listening, before receiving extreme unction and Communion.[137] The *Liber tramitis* contains two different versions of the confession. According to the first version, the monk confesses privately to the abbot or prior, before the community visits him in the infirmary. The second version

---

133. I am grateful to Frederick Paxton for sharing with me his forthcoming study "Death by Customary at Eleventh-Century Cluny." He has generously offered me his advice since I first compared the *LT* to the Farfa death ritual in 1999.

134. Rome, BV F.29; BAV Chigi C.VI.177; and Zurich, Zentralbibliothek, Rheinau 82. My critical edition of this text is in preparation.

135. They differ in length because the manuscripts from Farfa, being practical books for the liturgy, include the entire text of nearly every prayer and litany, while the *Liber tramitis* contains only the incipits of these texts, as is to be expected in a customary.

136. This text is related to the Cluniac *Consuetudines antiquiores* of the tenth century, but the specific elements to be discussed here are not Cluniac. The text of the Vallombrosa customary was published as *Redactio Vallumbrosana,* ed. Vasaturo, in *CCM* 7.2 (1983):309–79. Hallinger analyzed in detail the relationship between the *Consuetudines antiquiores* of Cluny and the Vallombrosa customary in *CCM* 7.1 (1984):279–306.

137. This feature is also found in the *Redactio Vallumbrosana,* 368.

EXAMPLE 3.1. Summary of the death ritual at Farfa, Rome, BV F.29, fols. 113r–127v; BAV Chigi C.VI.177, fols. 182r–188v; Zürich, Zentralbibliothek, Rheinau 82, pp. 244–62.

CONFESSION, UNCTION, COMMUNION

The community goes in procession to visit the ailing brother, singing psalms, the Kyrie, and the Our Father, and then recites chapters and prayers. The ailing monk confesses in front of all the monks, who must then kiss him if the prior orders it. A priest administers unction and then brings the Eucharist while psalms are sung; the monks repeat the Kyrie, the Our Father, and the chapters and prayers recited earlier. The dying monk takes Communion while all stand, and then all return in silence to the cloister.

DEATH

When he is near death, litanies and prayers are recited, and when his final agony begins, a signal convenes all the monks, who arrive singing the Creed and then the responsory *Subuenite sancti Dei* until the soul has left the body. When the monk has expired, Matins and Vespers of the Dead are sung, while the body is prepared for burial and the commendation of the soul is recited along with other prayers.

VIGILS

The body is taken to the church accompanied by candles, a cross, incense, and holy water, while the responsory *Subuenite* is repeated. In the church, the monks sing the Psalter around the body. At nightfall, the prior selects those who will sing three vigils by the body, each comprising the entire Psalter.

FUNERAL MASS

The next day, Mass is sung with all the bells ringing; the body remains in the church until Sext. A priest vested in alb and stole stands next to the coffin and two singers stand at its head. The sacristan gives all the brothers candles. The singers sing the Kyrie while the priest says prayers. The responsories *Qui Lazarum* and *Subuenite* are sung while the priest censes the altar and body twice and recites prayers.

BURIAL

While the body is carried in procession to the burial place, the antiphon *In paradisum* is sung with the psalm "In exitu." All bells are to ring continuously until the tomb monument is closed. Other antiphons and psalms are sung as the body is placed in the tomb, which the priest censes and blesses with holy water while he recites prayers, and the community sings psalms. Afterwards, the priest recites the Our Father, followed by a final chapter and prayer.

EXAMPLE 3.2. Comparison of excerpts from the death ritual in Farfa manuscripts and in the *Liber tramitis*.

Rome, BV F.29, fols. 113r–127v

Quando congregatio ingreditur ad uisitandum infirmum hoc modo agatur. **Primitus uadant conuersi cum aquam sancta, candelabris, cruce, et incenso. Deinde omnes fratres, quibus ingressis et ordinatis inchoent vii.psalmos speciales,** hi sunt: *Domine ne in ira tua (i), Beati quorum, Domine ne in ira tua (ii), Miserere mei Deus, Domine exaudi (i), De profundis, Domine exaudi (ii).*

His ita expletis, **interrogetur a priore, si uult unctionem recipere, et cum dixerit se uelle, faciant facere eum confessionem** audientibus cunctis, dicendo ita: *Confiteor Deo omnipotenti.* Qua predicta absolutus, omnes respondentes: *Confiteor Deo.* Et infirmus respondet: *misereatur uestri,*[138]

Liber Tramitis, 269–72 (excerpts)

Tunc sint quattuor conuersi, quorum unus accipiat aquam sanctam, alius crucem, tertius turibulum, quartus oleum sacrum . . . sicque per ordinem incedant, in primis aquam sanctam et crucem et tunc subsequantur incensum atque uas cum oleo, deinde sacerdos post illos, ex hinc infantes et tunc domnus abbas. Alii ueniant bini ac bini sicut sunt priores. Cumque ibi fuerint, primum dicat sacerdos *Pax huic domui,* respondeant ceteri *Amen, Dominus uobiscum, Et cum spiritu tuo.* Tunc faciat incensum et aquam sanctam aspergat, oratio *Omnipotens sempiternae Deus qui per beatum apostolum tuum dixisti.* Post hanc orationem **omnis congregatio psalmos hos decantent, uidelicet septem speciales cum antiphonis sequentibus per unumquemque sicuti in collectario sunt inserte . . .**

Qualiter agendum est quando ingreditur congregatio in domum ad uisitandum infirmum. **Prior namque ante capitulum inspiciat ipsum infirmum et interroget, si uelit accipere corpus Domini aut ex oleo sancto ungeri.** Tunc infirmus **patefaciat suam uoluntatem et confessionem agat** cum abbate uel priore.

Quibus dictis, dicantur **Kyrie eleison, Pater noster, Et ne nos,** *Capitula Saluum fac seruum tuum, Deus meus; Mitte ei domine auxilio; Esto ei Deus turris; Nihil proficiat; Dominus custodiat; Domine exaudi.* **Oratio Deus qui famulo tuo Ezechie; Alia Respice Domine famulum tuum; Alia Deus qui facture tue;** *Alia Virtutum celestium.* **Qua finita osculetur ab omnibus** si iusserit prior. Quo pacto ungatur infirmus ipse hoc modo. Inchoet schola psalmos: *Beati immaculati, Deus in nomine tuo. Domine deus in adiutorium. Beati immaculati, Deus in nomine tuo. Domine deus in adiutorium.* Interim dum isti canuntur psalmi, usque ad *Dominum dum tibi.* Interim dum isti canuntur psalmi, **sacerdos ungat infirmum et dicat semper per unumquemque sensum ita: Per istam unctionem et suam piissimam misericordiam indulgeat tibi Dominus quicquid peccasti: Per uisum,** *Per auditum, Per odoratum, Per gustum, Per incessum, Per tactum, Per ardorem libidinis.*

Peruncto denique infirmo, lauet sacerdos manus suas et adducat corpus Domini cum canuntur psalmi. Et finitis dicit Kyrie, Pater noster. Oratio; capitula ut supra . . . Igitur hac dicta, **redeant omnes** in claustrum cum silentio.

Et **mox ut uiderint eum ad exitum approprinquare, communicetur etiam si comedit ipso die, quia communio erit ei ad adiutorium,** in resurrectione iustorum, et resuscitabit eum in nouissimo die.

Sacerdos incipiat ungere infirmum, in primis uisus siue ceteros sensus corporis et dicat repetendo per unumquemque **Per istam unctionem et suam piissimam misericordiam indulgeat tibi Dominus quicquit peccasti per uisum. Peruncto denique infirmo lauet presbiter manus suas** et tunc procurator infirmi accipiat ipsam ablutionem acquae et in ignem proiciat. . . . Dum haec patrantur, **sacerdos** cum quattuor conuersis pergat in ecclesiam et **tollat inde corpus Domini** et calicem. . . . Et tunc ueniant **hos psalmos decantando** *Miserere mei Deus secundum, Deus in nomine tuo, Deus misereatur, Deus in adiutorium meum. . . .* **Psalmos denique expletos dicant Kyrie eleyson, Christe, Kyrie, Pater noster, Et ne nos,** capitula *Ostende nobis,* **Mitte ei Domine, Nihil proficiat inimicus, Esto ei Domine turris fortitudinis et hanc orationem Deus qui famulo tuo Ezechiae et alias quae sequntur. Post hec osculetur** isdem infirmus crucem atque **omnes fratres, etiam infantes.** His expletis incipiat abbas psalmum *Miserere mei Deus* et sic **omnes cum silentio recedant.**

Mox ut anima ad exitum propinquasse uisa fuerit, **communicandus est** homo ipse corpore et sanguine Domini, **etiamsi ipsa die commederit, quia ipsa communio erit ei ad adiutorium** contra diabolum et insidias eius.

continued

EXAMPLE 3.2. *Continued*

Cum autem uenerit ad exitum **sonetur tabula et conueniant omnes fratres canendo:** *Credo in unum Deum.* Et incipiant *R. Subuenite sancti Dei* usque quo anima egrediatur canantur. Sacerdos autem dicat orationes subscriptas. Igitur egressa anima faciant **officium matutinum et uesperum mortuorum.**

Finito officium matutinum et uesperum mortuorum, leuetur corpus et sic **cum cereis siue crux atque incenso necnon cum aqua sancta deferatur in ecclesiam hunc decantant: R. Subuenite sancti dei V. Suscipiat.** Et sonent omnia signa et in ecclesia sit usque quo pro eo missa celebretur et offeratur ab omnibus.

Deposito igitur corpore in ecclesia **sedeant omnes circa corpus et cantent psalterium.** Igitur hoc modo fiat ordo psalmodiae. Si prima hora diei migrauerit, portato corpore in ecclesia et stantes uel sedentes fratres omnes circa corpus cantent psalterium. Quia si prima hora diei migrauerit, debet stare corpus in ecclesia usque ad horam sextam. Dicta hora sepeliatur si ad uesperam transierit siue ad nonam siue post completorium. Posito in ecclesia corpore, stent fratres et cantent psalterium usque dum nox fiat. **Facta autem nocte prior ordinet qui celebrent uigilias canendo psalterium. Scilicet totam noctem tribus uigiliis fratres partiendo. Et per unamquamque uigiliam totum psalterium cantatur.**

Cum uero iam anima e corpore uiam uniuerse carnis ingreditur et in extremis sicut consuetudo est **tabula sonuerit,** quocumque locorum **fratres** audierint, statim debent incipere **Credo in unum Deum.** . . . Tunc simul signa pulsentur et **officium mortuorum agatur. Post officium dicant Uesperum** et quinque psalmos.

Cunctisque fratribus **cum crucem et aquam benedictam, turibulum uel candelabris praecedentibus et hoc responsorium inponentibus** *Subuenite sancti Dei* **signisque sonantibus ad ecclesiam** prium sanctae Mariae posito feretro altare aromatizet.

Quandiu dies est, **iuxta corpus debent sedere omnes et psalmos dicere** praeter illos qui in talibus rebus occupati sunt quas omnino dimittere non possunt. **Armarius autem debet in tabula nominatim fratres mittere qui primam uigiliam faciant et secundam et ita sicut noctis est longitudo temperare aut ut in singulis uigiliis dicant psalterium** cum officio mortuorum et Matutina ipsorum et Uespera et quinque psalmis aut centum psalmos et officium.

Igitur facta die, hora prima dicta canatur ei sonantibus missa omnibus signis. Et tribus conuersis reuestitis in albis stent in suis gradibus.

Quando sepeliendi uenerit hora, hoc modo fiat. **Sacerdos reuestitus alba et stola**, stet iuxta feretrum et **duo cantores stent ad caput feretri** et **sacristanus det omnibus cereos**. Tunc cantores inchoent: *Kyrie eleison, Christe eleison, Kyrie eleison.* Deinde sacerdos dicit: Dominus uerbum. . . . *Oratio Ne intres in iudicium cum seruo tuo Domine* R. *Qui Lazarus.* Interim dum canitur R. sacerdos incenset altarem et corpus et cantores. **Dicunt iterum:** *Kyrie, Christe, Kyrie. Oratio Fac quesumus Domine hanc cum seruo tuo defuncto misericordiam* R. *Subuenite sancti dei.* Et sacerdos incenset sicut prius. Et cantores dicunt: *Kyrie, Christe, Kyrie.* Item oratio. *Inclina Domine quesumus aurem tuam ad preces nostras.* . . . Et iterum incensetur altare et corpus. Hoc facto eleuetur corpus defuncti. Vadant primitus infantes, deinde corpus, deinde sacerdos, deinde omnes fratres. Et inchoet schola antiphonam *In paradisum.* Ps. *In exitu.*

Postquam missum fuerit corpus in monumentum et finita antiphona in euangelium, Tunc sacerdos pronuntiet alta uoce ita *Pater noster* pro eius anima. Que omnis congregatio sub silentio dicit: *Et ne nos inducas* Cap: *Non intres in iudicium.* Quia. *Dominus uobiscum. Oratio: Tibi Domine commendamus animam famuli tui ut defunctus seculo tibi uiuat.*[139]

Missa uero matutinalis pro ipsa anima sollempniter celebretur in choro. Pulsentur signa. . . . Duo conuersi candelabra, tertius turibulum deferat.

Missa maiore completa prior signum tribus uisibus sonet, ut omnes conueniant **et candelas a secretario suscipiant**. Et obsequium mortuorum faciant et circa feretrum omnes stent. . . . **Duo fratres**, uidelicet armarius et unus ex aliis, **ueniant et stent iuxta defunctum et conclament** *Kyrie eleyson, Christe eleyson, Kyrie eleyson.* **Sacerdos qui ebdomadarius est sit uestitus alba cum stola** et dicat *Oremus.* Oratione *Ne intres in iudicium* peracta accipiat turibulum et incenset altare maius tantum et corpus. Illi duo ut supra incipiant responsorium *Heu michi domine,* dein *Kyrie eleyson,* sacerdos dicat orationem *Fac quaesumus Domine* et denuo aromatizet altare et defunctum. Duo ut supra fratres responsorium alium inchoent et *Kyrie eleyson,* sacerdos dicat orationem *Inclina Domine* et incenset aram et feretrum. Deinde leuetur corpus de aecclesia pulsentur signa. **Antiphona** *In paradisum* **cantantes procedant omnes sic per ordinem:** In primitus aquam sanctam, crux, incensum et duo candelabra, subsequantur infantes cum magistris, adiungantur eis conuersi qui nesciunt cantare, **dein alii duo et duo sicut sunt priores,** ad extremum sacerdos et illi qui deferunt feretrum. . . .

Cum uero post canticum *Benedictus* **antiphona fuerit dicta, sacerdos pronuntiet omnibus audientibus** *Pater noster.* Qua oratione finita dicat praeces solitas pro defunctis et orationem *Tibi domine commendamus.*

states that if the infirm monk can walk, he should confess publicly in chapter and be absolved by the abbot and all the brothers.[140] Public confession in chapter is also prescribed by the Cluniac customary of Bernard.[141] Perhaps the difference between the two texts in the *Liber tramitis* is simply one of degree; although a monk who cannot walk is compelled by necessity to confess in the infirmary, it was apparently preferable for the confession to take place in chapter if at all possible. Alternatively, the two sets of provisions for the monk's confession in the *Liber tramitis* might reflect contrasting customs—respectively, those of Farfa and those of Cluny—although with the small amount of information we have about monastic confession at Farfa in the eleventh and twelfth centuries this is difficult to determine. The ordo for routine confession preserved in a Farfa manuscript from the early twelfth century is to be performed by a priest, seemingly in private, but deathbed confession may have entailed a different kind of ritual.[142]

As soon as the monk's final agony begins, both the Farfa death ritual and the *Liber tramitis* quote the prescription of the early medieval Roman *Ordo* 49 that he must receive Communion even if he has eaten that day.[143] The monks run to the side of the dying brother singing the Credo. At this point, the Farfa text contains a distinctive feature: the performance of the responsory *Subuenite sancti Dei* immediately after the Credo. At Farfa this responsory is repeated two more times later on, while according to the *Liber tramitis* it is sung only after the Vespers of the Dead.

After nightfall the monks' vigils over the body begin. Here the Farfa death ritual agrees with the later customary of Bernard in dividing the night into three vigils, while the *Liber tramitis* mentions only two. According to Bernard,

138. In the manuscript, this section of text appears after the following one; I have reversed the order of these two passages for purposes of comparison.

139. Cf. Bernard, *Ordo cluniacensis*, BNF lat. 13875, f. 54r: . . . sub silentio premissa oratione dominica subinfert *Et ne nos inducas Domine in temptationem, Non intres in iudicium cum seruo tuo Domine, Dominus uobiscum, Oremus, Tibi Domine commendamus animam famuli tui.*

140. *LT*, 269–72.

141. Bernard, *Ordo Cluniacensis*, xxvi; Paris, BNF lat. 13875, fol. 47v; and *Vetus disciplina monastica*, 190.

142. Rome, BV F.29, fols. 70r–72v.

143. I am grateful to Fred Paxton for bringing to my attention the similarity between the opening rubric of the *Liber tramitis* death ritual and the one in *Ordo Romanus* 49 (Andrieu, *Les Ordines Romani* 4:525–30 [BAV Ottob. lat. 312, fol. 151v]). The rubric in the Farfa death ritual is closer to the *Ordo Romanus* than is the slightly modified rubric in *LT*, 272.

each of the first two vigils is sung by half the monastic choir and the third is assigned to the children and their teachers.[144] The vigils in the Farfa text consist of the recitation of the Psalter, while the *Liber tramitis* requires the performance of the Office of the Dead together with portions of the Psalter depending on the length of the night.

The funeral Mass and burial of the monk in the Farfa text resembles those in the *Liber tramitis* except for two unusual elements. While the priest censes the altar and the body, the responsory *Qui Lazarum resuscitasti* is sung.[145] This chant was usually part of the Office of the Dead but also appears in some early medieval burial services;[146] it is not performed in the ritual described in the *Liber tramitis*. This characteristic detail in the Farfa manuscripts does not alter the fact that the death ritual constitutes the most compelling piece of evidence for the influence of Cluny, through the *Liber tramitis,* on the liturgy at Farfa.

Rituals in the *Liber tramitis,* even if originally conceived at Cluny, could take on new meanings in performance at Farfa. The adventus, for instance, was equally pertinent to both abbeys, for each enjoyed a privileged relationship with the Ottonian and Salian monarchs, albeit in rather different ways. Some of the resemblances between these monasteries can be seen as parallels rather than as signs of influence. Farfa differed from Cluny particularly in the character of its relations with the popes. During his short pontificate, Nicholas II established a level of mutual cooperation between the papacy and the imperial abbey that was never attained again. During the investiture controversy, Farfa manifested its loyalty to the emperors in ways that suggested an adversarial relationship with the pope. Never officially a dependency of Cluny, in the late eleventh and early twelfth centuries Farfa moved ever further away from Cluniac ecclesiology, producing polemical treatises expounding the supreme place of the emperor in the church.[147] Support for this ideology at Farfa emanated from its identity as an imperial abbey, which presupposed a particular conception and reception of imperial patronage that will be explored in chapter 4.

144. Paris, BNF lat. 13875, fol. 52r.

145. *CAO* 4:367, no. 7477; Ottosen (*The Responsories and Versicles of the Latin Office of the Dead,* 400) notes that he has found 1,672 occurrences of this responsory.

146. Sicard (*Liturgie,* 73 n. 65) cites several examples.

147. Cantarella ("I Cluniacensi in Italia," 258) notes that Farfa had always maintained an identity quite different from that of Cluny, and that the *Orthodoxa defensio imperialis* simply confirmed it.

rom the time of Farfa's refoundation by Thomas of Maurienne at the end of the seventh century, patrons had a marked influence on the abbey's liturgical practices as well as on its possessions. Though the importance of donors was a common feature of monastic life in the medieval West, what set Farfa apart from many other monasteries was the sheer variety of patronage it enjoyed over its long history and the resulting wide range of influences from patrons seen in its liturgy, architecture, and manuscript production. This chapter addresses the effects of patronage on Farfa's liturgy and visual culture, placing the contributions of donors in the context of the abbey's political affiliations and networks of power during the eleventh and early twelfth centuries.

Relationships between Farfa and its patrons involved forms of exchange that addressed both material and spiritual concerns. Gifts presented to the abbey symbolized a bond and an ongoing relationship between donor and institution, a relationship that was acknowledged and expressed in various ways. Through ritual commemoration, for instance, absent patrons were made virtually present in the life of the monastery. Moreover, some gifts, such as textiles or books used in the liturgy, were invested with a symbolic dimension implying the metonymic presence of the donor during worship services. In this way, an integral part of the community's identity—its consciousness of its property and political affiliations—was incorporated into the performance of the liturgy.

The possible motivations of Farfa's benefactors resemble those described by Rosenwein for donations to Cluny.[1] Besides the hope of attaining salvation with the help of the monks' prayers, donors may have had other benefits in mind as exchange for their gifts.[2] For example, as Rosenwein suggests, their donations may have acted as a kind of long-term insurance for the upkeep of lands they transferred to the abbey; personal ties to members of the community could ensure that these possessions were maintained effectively. Con-

1. Rosenwein, *To Be the Neighbor of Saint Peter,* 35–48.

2. See also the analysis of donations in McLaughlin, *Consorting with Saints,* 133–77. White (*Custom, Kinship, and Gifts to Saints,* 26–31) describes the various benefits that accrued to donors.

ceived in this way, gifts would have represented far more than their discrete monetary value, taking on a range of meanings as "relational constructs."[3] Receiving donations of land and money, and of churches and the objects pertaining to them (such as books and liturgical vessels), was of crucial importance to Farfa's survival; the Farfa *Register* shows that managing this patrimony and maintaining the abbey's relationships with donors were among the community's central concerns. Land transactions formed an essential part of reciprocity that was closely tied to the liturgy.[4] As Eliana Magnani has written, it is by virtue of the gifts they presented to the abbey that lay donors were able "to enter the ritual community of the monastery"[5] through commemoration in the office and Mass.

Although information regarding Farfa's liturgical commemoration of its patrons is limited, one can extrapolate a fair amount from the Farfa *Register*. The donation charters copied in the *Register* comprise a series of standard elements: the date, the donor, the reason for the donation, designation of Farfa as recipient, a description of the gift, a promise that neither the donor nor the donor's descendants will retract the gift later on, and an anathema on all those who would take the donation from the monastery by force. Each copy of a document in the Farfa *Register* concludes with the name of the place in which the original charter was enacted, followed by the signatures of the donors, witnesses, and notary.

Donation charters often state the motivation for the gift as the salvation of the donor's soul (*pro anima*). Because the commemoration of benefactors was such an important aspect of monastic liturgical practice, it is likely that donors expected their gift to ensure intercessory prayer on their behalf; however, this expectation is not always expressly articulated in the formulaic language of the charters. In this context, it is rather exceptional to find a document that places the monks' prayers explicitly in a framework of exchange, as one from 1051 in which the donor, after describing the lands he has given to the abbot and his

3. Gadi Algazi, "Introduction: Doing Things with Gifts," in *Negotiating the Gift*, 22. Algazi's theorization of the gift complements the useful recent overview by Bijsterveld, "The Medieval Gift as Agent of Social Bonding and Political Power." I thank Isabelle Cochelin for this reference.

4. Costambeys ("Piety, Property," 172–90) indicates certain ideas shared by eighth-century charters (including those recording donations to Farfa) and contemporaneous liturgical texts, particularly prayers. White (*Custom*, 32–38) describes the association of ritual with gifts to monasteries.

5. Magnani S.-Christen, "Transforming Things and Persons," 279. I am grateful to the author for giving me this article.

monks, states that he has thereby obtained intercessory prayer on behalf of his father: "whence I received masses and prayers from that same abbot and from the monks and priests, that they might pray for my father to almighty God the Father and our lord Jesus Christ, so that he grant him mercy and redemption."[6] Presumably donors were aware of the types of commemorative practices described in chapter 2, in which the community sang psalms and recited prayers on behalf of the souls of benefactors. Several of the documents in the Farfa *Register* contain clauses referring to the salvific effects of prayers, psalmody, and masses performed by the monks. Some of these clauses specifically invoke the instrumentality of the monks' intercessory prayer: "so that through your holy prayers and psalmody and masses that are sung in the monastery indicated above, we may deserve to enter into the kingdom of heaven."[7] Many such formulas characterize the monks' prayer as ceaseless, stating that the gift has been made "in exchange for your holy prayers which you do not cease to address to God for the salvation and cure of the souls of all Christians,"[8] and some documents refer specifically to prayer both day and night.[9] Because the daily round of the divine office includes hours performed

6. *RF* 4:227 (dated 1051, no. 826): "Unde recepi missas et orationes ab ipso abbate et a monachis et praesbiteris, ut orent pro genitore meo ad deum patrem omnipotentem et dominum nostrum ihesum christum, ut misericordiam et redemptionem concedat ei."

7. *RF* 5:220, 246 (1058, no. 1270): "per sanctas orationes uestras et psalmodias et missas quae in suprascripto monasterio canuntur, mereamur introire in regnum coelorum." An earlier version of this formula is "in exchange for your holy prayers, psalmody, hymns, and canticles, and holy sacrifices" ("pro uestris sanctis orationibus psalmodiis ymnis et canticis atque sanctis sacrificiis"; *RF* 4:109 [1007, no. 707]).

8. *RF* 5:247 (1060, no. 1271): "pro uestris sacris orationibus quas pro salute et remedio animarum omnium christianorum ad deum facere non cessatis." Another formula that expresses the same idea in slightly different language appears in an earlier document, *RF* 4:67 (1013, no. 666): "And for your very holy and devoted prayers, which you perpetually endeavor to produce for the salvation of the souls of all Christians" ("uestrisque sacratissimis ac piis orationibus, quas pro salute omnium christianorum animarum iugiter exibere nitimini").

9. For instance, "In exchange for your sacred and holy prayers which you do not cease to perform forever, day and night, for the redemption of souls in perpetuity" *RF* 4:62 (1013, no. 662), 370 (1066, no. 990): "pro sanctis ac sacris orationibus uestris quas die noctuque non cessatis pro redemptione animarum facere in perpetuum." Another formula found in documents from the tenth and early eleventh centuries describes the ceaseless prayer of the monks as transpiring in a holy place; see *RF* 3:209 (no. 501), *RF* 3:233 (no. 524), *RF* 4:7 (1010, no. 608).

before dawn and after nightfall, it literally constitutes a prayer both day and night; however, in only one case is this ideal of ceaseless prayer linked explicitly to the office, which the monks sing "in melodious hymns and praise according to the rule of our holy father Benedict."[10] More emphatic versions of the formula specifically name the donor's own soul among those to be saved by invoking the "holy, sacred, and continuous prayers which you do not cease to perform, day and night, on behalf of the souls of all Christians, and [on behalf of] of ours"[11] and "your most holy and devoted prayers which for the salvation of all Christian souls, and of ours, you do not cease to perform and to offer the sacrifice." [12] The term "sacrifice" in the second of these phrases refers to the celebration of Mass as well as to intercessory prayer more generally.

A related form of commemoration mentioned in many documents in the Farfa *Register* is the inscription of donors' names in the "book of life" (*liber uitae*) or necrology. Necrologies contained the names of special patrons, deceased members of the monastic community, and the monks in other monasteries with which abbeys formed prayer confraternities.[13] A necrology formed part of a larger collection of texts for daily use, which also included the martyrology listing the saints commemorated on each calendar day.[14] In chapter, the daily meeting of the monastic community after the office of Prime, the names of patrons would be read aloud after the martyrology entry for the day.[15] No martyrology or necrology survives from Farfa, but the community

10. *RF* 4:321 (1062, no. 926): "sacrum obsequium persoluendam in ymnis canoris ac laudibus secundum pii patris nostri regulam sancti benedicti, quae die noctuque deo agere non cessatis."

11. *RF* 3:208 (no. 500), *RF* 4:65–66 (1013, no. 665), 177 (1043, no. 770): "pro uestris sanctis, sacris et assiduis orationibus quas die noctuque pro omnium christianorum et nostris animabus agere non cessatis."

12. *RF* 4:112 (1019, no. 710): "per uestras sacratissimas ac pias orationes quas pro salute animarum omnium christianorum, nostraeque, facere et sacrificium offerre non cessatis."

13. The *liber commemoratorius* in which the name of Henry IV was written was also the necrology. It might have resembled the *liber uitae* from Subiaco, which is still extant (see Schwarzmaier, "Der Liber Vitae von Subiaco"). On the terms *liber uitae* and *liber memorialis* see Houben, "Il cosiddetto *Liber Vitae* di Polirone."

14. On martyrologies and necrologies see Dubois, *Les martyrologes;* Huyghebaert, *Les documents nécrologiques;* and Lemaître, *Mourir à Saint-Martial*, 87–107. For a modern edition of a monastic martyrology-necrology from a monastery in eleventh-century southern Italy, see *The Necrology of San Nicola della Cicogna.*

15. On the books used in chapter see Lemaître, "'Liber capituli'" and *Mourir à Saint-Martial,* 61–85.

must have practiced this widespread observance.[16] In some eleventh-century documents, the inscription of donors' names in the *liber uitae* is accompanied by a request for offerings at Mass on their behalf after their death.[17] Offerings could be made during conventual masses or during masses celebrated specifically on behalf of the donors.[18] Such masses for the dead were probably performed frequently, and the pertinent prayers are found in an eleventh-century manuscript from Farfa that contains texts for daily use.[19]

Studying the influence of patronage networks on the liturgy at Farfa entails interpreting the evidence in liturgical books which, although standardized to some extent, can nonetheless reveal subtleties particular to Farfa when viewed in historical context. In the discussion that follows, I consider Farfa's relations with its patrons as networks of power that provide a context for the abbey's liturgical and visual culture. The patronage of the Germanic rulers had a discernible impact on some of Farfa's liturgical books and on other texts produced there. Turning to Farfa's patrons in southern Italy, I argue that their gifts to the abbey signal the kinds of cultural contacts that also influenced the southern Italian elements in Farfa's liturgy.

Imperial Patronage and Its Cultural Products

Certainly we should honor all the saints, but we need to venerate and prize especially, with all and beyond all, the saint of saints and more than virgin Mary, whom all saints strive to honor as their lady (*domina*), as the one

16. The monks of Farfa might have referred to the Cluniac formulas for recording names in the martyrology, as described in the *Liber tramitis* (*LT,* 286–87), but there is no necrological evidence besides the obits from the eleventh and early twelfth centuries added to the calendar of BAV Chigi C.VI.177, fols. 2r–6r, which provide only the names of the deceased. An eleventh-century martyrology from a dependency of Farfa near Rieti, the abbey of San Salvatore (Oxford, Bodleian Library Lat. liturg. D 6), does not illuminate this question.

17. *RF* 3:252 (1023, no. 543), 256 (1024, no. 546); 4:85 (1029 or 1030, no. 682), 218 (1048, no. 815), 312 (1062, no. 915), 328 (1063, no. 934); 5:3 (1070, no. 998), 43 (1078/9, no. 1040), 45 (1079, no. 1043), 68 (1072, no. 1083), 220 (1046, no. 1234): "Ita ut nomen nostrum in libro uitae conscribatur, uel pro nobis sanctum sacrificium post obitum nostrum pio domino offeratur." *RF* 3:240 (1019, no. 530) has only the clause "ut nomen nostrum in libro uitae conscribatur."

18. Some donations of the eleventh century allude to this practice: *RF* 4:74 (no. 672): "pro missabus et orationibus quas pro nobis facitis nocte ac die in omni decisione et deliberatione."

19. BAV Chigi C.VI.177, fols. 163v–164r.

through whom alone they are sanctified by the sole lord of all things. We, hoping to attain mercy through her, have prepared to honor the father of mercy, conceding from our property those things that we have been asked by our faithful to concede, to that monastery of Saint Mary which is in Farfa, where those who seek it faithfully particularly find her favor.[20]

This diploma of Henry IV from 1083 emphatically locates the exalted patron of his imperial abbey in the hierarchy of the saints. Henry was devoted to the Virgin Mary, whom he felt "could establish the crucial link between God and the king," and he particularly favored the cathedral of Speyer, which was dedicated to her.[21] As Patrick Corbet has pointed out, Marian devotion reached its apex with the Salian dynasty. The relationship of the Salian emperors to Speyer Cathedral is aptly represented by the dedication page of the Golden Gospels of Henry III (produced at Echternach in 1045–46), in which, in an architectural frame, the cathedral is personified as the Virgin receiving the manuscript from Henry III as she blesses his consort, Agnes of Poitou.[22] Likewise, the dedication page of the Farfa *Register* shows Gregory of Catino presenting his book to Mary, the abbey's patron saint. For Henry IV, then, the patronage of Mary may have been a link between Speyer, the ancestral burial site of the Salians, and Farfa, the imperial abbey near the Rome of the ancient emperors.[23] Just as the clergy of Speyer would commemorate Henry after his death, so too the community at Farfa would pray in perpetuity on his behalf, for his name had been written in the monks' *liber commemoratorius* in 1082 when they received him into their brotherhood of prayer with the kiss of peace.[24] The so-

20. Diploma of Henry IV, enacted at Rome, June 15, 1083; *Heinrici IV diplomata* 1:462 (no. 350); and *RF* 5:93 (no. 1098): "Omnes quidem sanctos honorare debemus, sed sanctam sanctorum plus quam uirginem Mariam cum omnibus et pre omnibus uenerari et diligere indigemus, quam ut dominam honorare student omnes sancti, ut puta per quam solam a solo omnium domino sunt sanctificati. Per quam et nos misericordiam sperantes consequi, patrem misericordiarum de nostra substantia honorare fuimus parati matri misericordiȩ concedentes illa, quȩ concedere a fidelibus nostris sumus rogati, ad illud monasterium sanctȩ Mariȩ quod est in Pharpha, ubi specialiter eius a quȩrentibus fideliter inueniuntur beneficia."

21. Weinfurter, *The Salian Century,* 158. See also Robinson, *Henry IV of Germany,* 352–53.

22. El Escorial, Biblioteca del Real Monasterio, Vitr. 17, fol. 3r; see Corbet, "Les impératrices ottoniennes," 129–30.

23. A diploma of 1080 donating land to Saint Mary of Speyer begins with an *arenga* that addresses the Virgin Mary in terms similar to the one in the diploma of 1083 cited above in n. 1; see *Heinrici IV diplomata* 1:325 (cited in Weinfurter, *Salian Century,* 158).

24. *RF* 5:94; *CF* 2:172; and Robinson, *Henry IV,* 353.

licitation of *memoria* was a defining feature of both the Ottonian and Salian rulers' relations with their imperial abbeys, almost all of which were situated within the Germanic lands of the empire.[25] In addition to being the most venerable Italian member in the network of imperial abbeys, Farfa had benefited significantly from Otto III's policy of Roman *renovatio*, as shown by his ten diplomas for Farfa.[26] This nexus of power, ritual, and devotion is the key to understanding the patterns of patronage and currents of influence at Farfa in the eleventh and twelfth centuries.

While the Ottonians' and Salians' diplomas for Farfa offer insight into how these rulers perceived their relationship to the abbey, some texts produced at Farfa in the eleventh and twelfth centuries show Farfa's response to imperial patronage. During the investiture controversy, Farfa sided with the emperors even at the most difficult of times, by tacitly and sometimes actively condoning their hostile actions toward the popes. In 1078 Gregory VII threatened Abbot Berard I with excommunication for his support of Henry IV.[27] But far from shaking Farfa's allegiance to the emperors, this period and later saw ever stronger affirmations of Farfa's imperial affinities. Abbot Berard III, upon his confirmation in 1099, swore to rule the abbey and all its dependents, down to the orphans and widows, in loyalty to the emperor.[28] Proimperial sentiment also characterizes the *Liber Beraldi*, a treatise written in 1105–6 in the context of ongoing conflicts between the abbey of Farfa and the local Ottaviani family; these quarrels resulted in several trials during 1103–5[29] concerning disputes over the ownership of castles and associated lands in the Sabina.[30]

25. On the administration of the imperial abbeys by the Ottonians and Salians, see Bernhardt, *Itinerant Kingship and Royal Monasteries;* and Vogtherr, *Die Reichsabteien der Benediktiner.* On the *memoria* of the Germanic kings see Metz, "Nekrologische Quellen zum Wirkungsbereich."

26. See Seibert, "Herrscher und Mönchtum," 233. On Otto's interventions on behalf of Abbot Hugh of Farfa in property disputes, see Warner, "Ideals and Action," 11–13.

27. Schuster, *Imperiale abbazia,* 206; and Kehr, *Italia pontificia,* 68.

28. *RF* 5:297, no. 1310.

29. The *Liber Beraldi* appears separately under the name of Abbot Berard III of Farfa in a manuscript copied in the fifteenth century by the Augustinian humanist Panvinius. The text is also transmitted within Gregory of Catino's *Chronicle.* Both Heinzelmann, *Die Farfenser Streitschriften,* 25–39, and Balzani, in the introduction to his edition of the *Chronicle* (*CF* 1:xxxii), suggested that Gregory was the author. Boesch Gajano, "Berardo," 771, supports the attribution to Berard III, while Longo, "Gregorio da Catino," 257, does not take a position.

30. For the most recent account of these trials see Stroll, *Medieval Abbey,* 75–132.

Another polemical text from Farfa, the *Orthodoxa defensio imperialis,* is associated with the scandalous events of 1111, when Henry V, outraged by Paschal II's terms for a resolution of the conflict over investiture, interrupted his coronation and imprisoned the pope and many of his cardinals in the fortress of Tribuco, which belonged to Farfa.[31] The *Orthodoxa defensio imperialis* defends Henry V, asserting the emperor as the head (*caput*) of the church. Although the authorship of the treatise is a matter of debate, the work was almost certainly penned by a monk of Farfa.[32] The precise date of the text is uncertain, but the explicit defense of the emperor in the title and in the text suggests that it was written after Henry V's coronation.[33] Exploiting the anatomical metaphor of the emperor as both literal and figurative head of the church, the author compares *regnum* and *sacerdotium* to the members of a single body that must work together in harmony for the proper functioning of Christian society.[34] Some of the arguments in the *Orthodoxa defensio imperialis* rely heavily on the rhetorical figures of metonymy and synecdoche. For instance, bishops must receive the investiture with staff and ring from the emperor before their consecration by the pope, because the head of the church (the emperor) must be present at the creation of the ministry of its members (limbs). The notion of sacral kingship supports the contention that if the bishop must be acclaimed by the people, then the emperor, leader of the people, must be involved in this process as well.[35] After referring to the protection of Farfa by the emperors, the author reserves the strongest statement for the conclusion:

> Therefore the congregation of the abbey of Farfa has retained faithfully from the beginning that these are teachings of Christ and the institutions of the saints concerning the imperial dignity, and will retain them forever,

31. Stroll, *Medieval Abbey,* 209; and Weinfurter, *Salian Century,* 170–71.

32. Balzani, *CF* 1:xxxiii–xxxv, suggested that the author was a follower of Gregory rather than Gregory himself, while Heinemann accepted Bethmann's attribution to Gregory. Heinzelmann (*Die Farfenser Streitschriften,* 25–39, 113–20) maintained that the *Orthodoxa defensio imperialis* exhibits too much stylistic contrast with Gregory's works for him to be its author. Boesch Gajano ("Berardo," 772) maintains that the attribution requires further study; Longo ("Gregorio da Catino," 257) does not offer an opinion on the attribution.

33. *Orthodoxa defensio imperialis.* See also Toubert, *Structures* 1:81, n. 3. Giorgio ("Il Regesto di Farfa," 459) dated the text to before the coronation of Henry V in April 1111, while Heinemann (*Orthodoxa defensio imperialis,* 535) placed it in the summer of 1111.

34. See Struve, "Die Stellung des Königtums," 237.

35. *Orthodoxa defensio imperialis,* 537–38.

preferring to suffer even the blasphemies and opprobrium of the adversaries of the empire than to deviate from the steps of the catholic fathers. . . . We have never wished to lose the patronage of the emperors, nor have we ever deserted their faith, since, as we know more venerable men to have said, whenever imperial dominion is lacking in this place, then its dignity is certainly diminished, and as long as the imperial dignity remains in vigor here, so the vigor of this holy monastery increases.[36]

The *Orthodoxa defensio imperialis* shows that at least one writer at Farfa understood imperial *regnum* as protection against its enemies. Although Kölzer has argued that the *Orthodoxa defensio imperialis* equates the emperor's patronage (*patrocinium*) with tradition rather than freedom,[37] the very status of the imperial abbey was understood as a form of liberty.[38]

In part because of the nature of the evidence, the political and economic effects of the Ottonian and Salian rulers on life at Farfa are far more evident than the liturgical ones. The Farfa *Chronicle* and *Register* make it clear that the abbey had many more liturgical books and objects, including gifts from the imperial family, than survive today. Another factor that must be taken into account is the elusive nature of such influence in the central Middle Ages, when oral transmission was still an important means of communication despite increasing use of the written word, and when it was customary in written records to evoke public rituals rather than to describe them in detail.

One of the most direct forms of imperial influence was occasional visits to Farfa by the Carolingian, Ottonian, and Salian emperors. The Carolingian abbey apparently had a royal *palatium*, equipped with a private chapel, for the use of the emperors when they visited.[39] Because the arrival of the emperor entailed a specific liturgy of welcome, it is no coincidence that the *Liber tramitis* preserves the earliest medieval adventus ritual for the reception of a ruler at a monastery (see chap. 3). Other vestiges of the imperial presence, now lost,

36. Ibid., 542: "Has igitur Christi doctrinas et institutiones sanctorum Pfarfensis cenobii unanimis coetus de imperiali fastigio fideliter ab initio retinuit et in evum retinebit, malens et blasphemias et obprobria adversariorum impii sufferre quam a patrum catholicorum semitibus deviare. . . . Patrocinium autem imperatorum numquam amittere voluimus, nec eius fidelitatem aliquando deserimus, quia, ut viros antiquiores prenuntiasse novimus, quotiens in hoc loco dominium imperiale deficit, eius pro certo dignitas totiens minuitur et in quantum hic fastigium imperiale vigescit, in tantum huius sacri cenobii vigor accrescit."

37. Kölzer, "*Codex libertatis*," 643.

38. Seibert, "Libertas und Reichsabtei."

39. *CF* 1:30, quoted by McClendon, *Imperial Abbey*, 8, 64.

were sumptuous gifts of textiles, books, and liturgical vessels mentioned in the Farfa *Register* and *Chronicle*.

Among these gifts, the northern manuscripts that reached Farfa through its imperial connections made a lasting contribution to the development of artistic styles in the abbey scriptorium. Manuscript production at Farfa in the eleventh and twelfth centuries reflects the influence of tenth- and eleventh-century manuscripts from imperial monasteries in the Germanic kingdom, such as Einsiedeln, Reichenau, and Saint Gall. As Edward Garrison first pointed out, the decorated initial letters in Farfa manuscripts constitute some of the finest examples of Ottonian-influenced or Ottonianizing styles in central Italy.[40] In Chigi C.VI.177, for instance, the ornate initial B of the first psalm, *Beatus uir,* is intertwined with golden strapwork interlace that has numerous parallels in Ottonian manuscripts (fig. 4.1). The subsequent development of this type of letter at Farfa can be seen in an antiphoner, now fragmentary, produced around 1100 (fig. 4.2).[41] The first responsory of Matins on the feast of Saint Benedict, *Fuit uir uenerabilis,* has an initial outlined in red, which is used also in the vegetal interlace, leaving much of the surrounding parchment bare. The shaft of the letter, divided into two fillets, is entwined with a leaf-sprouting vine. Parts of the letter are lightly washed with delicate shades of blue, green, and pale mauve. Continuing developments of Ottonianizing initials in the twelfth century appear in the psalm commentary of Odo of Asti and in a psalter now in the abbey archives.[42] Thus, over time, we see the forms of initial letters cultivated in the scriptoria of the empire gradually being assimilated at Farfa and transformed into a distinctive style of manuscript illumination.

Although decorated initials provide most of the evidence for Ottonian influence in manuscript production at Farfa, one book produced at the abbey contains full-page miniatures that are closely related to those in extant manuscripts from the empire. A liturgical book produced at Farfa in the third quarter of the eleventh century, now preserved in Madrid, exemplifies the adaptation of Ottonian iconography to a central Italian painting style.[43] This manuscript is an evangelistary containing the Gospel readings for Mass in the

40. Garrison, *Studies* 1:22–24.

41. Farfa, Archivio dell'Abbazia, AF 338, 4, fol. 3r. On this manuscript see Boynton, "Frammenti," 328–29.

42. Paris, BNF lat. 2508 (see fol. 29v in Avril and Załuska, *Manuscrits enluminés d'origine italienne,* plate XVII), discussed in chap. 2; Farfa, Archivio dell'Abbazia, A.209 (see fols. 133r and 182v in Garrison, "Random Notes," 199).

43. Madrid, BN Vitr. 20-6.

order of the church year. Of the four extant Gospel books created at Farfa in the eleventh and twelfth centuries,[44] the Madrid manuscript is the most luxurious and the only one that exhibits a clear relationship with Germanic manuscript illumination. Irmgard Siede has argued that the most likely iconographic model for this book is a manuscript produced at the imperial abbey of Reichenau in the middle of the eleventh century.[45] In this period Emperor Henry III was a frequent visitor to Reichenau, sojourning there in 1040, 1041, 1043, and four times in 1048.[46] Although we do not know when the Reichenau model reached Farfa, it is certain that Farfa possessed at least one precious book of Gospels donated to the abbey by Empress Agnes, for Gregory of Catino lists it among the items left to the monastery by Abbot Berard III, specifying that it had covers of ivory, gold and silver; such a book was probably richly illuminated.[47]

Of the extant manuscripts produced at Reichenau in this period, the one most similar to the Madrid manuscript is the Bernulphus Gospels, copied between 1040 and 1050.[48] Many scenes in the two manuscripts exhibit strikingly similar compositions. In the Pentecost scene, for instance, shared elements include the column that separates the apostles into two groups, the aureole in the middle of the composition symbolizing the Holy Ghost, and the use of architectural elements (see figs. 4.3 and 4.4).[49] The resemblance does not extend

44. The other three are BAV Chigi A.VI.164 (late eleventh century), Rome, BV E.16 (early twelfth century), and Farfa, Archivio dell'Abbazia, A.175 (first half of the twelfth century); on these manuscripts see Supino Martini, *Roma*, 234–35, 262–63, 266.

45. My discussion of the Madrid manuscript is much indebted to Siede, *Zur Rezeption ottonischer Buchmalerei*. Some aspects of Siede's analysis were anticipated by Garrison, *Studies* 4:250–64. Although Supino Martini, *Roma*, 328, has argued that the use of Caroline minuscule in this manuscript precludes attributing it to Farfa, I concur with Siede that several other aspects of the book support the idea that it originated there.

46. See the summary of imperial itineraries in Vogtherr, *Die Reichsabteien der Benediktiner*, 317.

47. *RF* 5:310 and *CF* 2:291: "textum euangelii, quem prefata regina huic monasterio dedit, cum tabulis eburneis et argenteis ac deauratis." Agnes could have donated the manuscript during a visit she made to the abbey sometime between 1065 and 1077. Black-Veldtrup (*Kaiserin Agnes*, 49) states that the visit took place between 1065 and 1077 but that no evidence supports any specific date in this period (although Schwarzmaier, "*Liber Vitae*," dated the visit to 1072).

48. Utrecht, Museum Catharijne Convent, ABM h3.

49. Madrid, BN Vitr. 20-6, fol. 53r; Utrecht, ABM h3, fol. 137v; Siede, *Untersuchungen*, 41; and Garrison, *Studies* 4:255–56.

to the colors, however; although both compositions share a gold ground and the vertical stratification of registers through contrast of colors and patterns, the Farfa miniature employs shades of red, blue, green, and pale mauve that recall the characteristic palette of other manuscripts produced at the abbey in the second half of the eleventh century.

Of all the scenes in the Madrid evangelistary, it is the combined Dormition and Assumption of the Virgin that most clearly indicates a model from Reichenau (see figs. 4.5 and 4.6).[50] The composition of the miniature closely resembles the corresponding one in the Bernulphus Gospels, with the exception of minor design elements such as the number of angels and columns. Standing behind Mary's bed, Christ holds her soul, which is depicted in a type of roundel termed "clipeus" because of its resemblance to the round shields or brooches on which portraits were painted in antiquity. Clipeus portraits (*imagines clipeatae*), common in Roman funerary imagery, were taken up in early Christian iconography as a common format for portraying saints.[51] The clipeus portrait in the Madrid manuscript, and the fusion of the Dormition and Assumption scenes, seems particularly influenced by book production at Reichenau, where the clipeus portrait was first added to the Byzantine iconography of the Dormition and Assumption, known as the *koimesis*.[52] The *koimesis* scene, which was diffused in the Ottonian empire through ivory carvings imported from Byzantium, appears almost identical in numerous Byzantine ivories of the tenth and eleventh centuries: the apostles gather on both sides of the Virgin, who lies on a bed placed horizontally across the middle of the scene; Christ stands behind the bed and lifts her soul to heaven while hovering angels witness the scene.[53] The image in the Farfa manuscript, inspired by

50. A similar composition is found in Utrecht, Museum Catharijne Convent ABMh3, fol. 173v; and Siede, *Untersuchungen*, 42–43; other examples are listed in Siede, *Untersuchungen*, 274. See also Garrison, *Studies* 4:258.

51. See Wirth, "La représentation de l'image," 10–11.

52. Kahsnitz, "Koimesis-dormitio-assumptio." The composition appears in two manuscripts from the early eleventh century: Bamberg, Staatsbibliothek, MS lit. 5, fol. 121v; and Munich, Bayerische Staatsbibliothek, clm 4452, fol. 161v; see Mayr-Harting, *Ottonian Book Illumination* 1:151–55, plate XXII, and 147, fig. 88.

53. A tenth-century example from Constantinople appears in *The Glory of Byzantium*, 154–55 (cat. 101). One of the many instances of the direct assimilation of the *koimesis* composition by the Ottonians in the art of the book is the tenth-century Byzantine ivory carving that adorns the jeweled cover of the Gospels of Otto III, produced in 998–1001 (Munich, Bayerische Staatsbibliothek, clm 4453); see Mayr-Harting, *Ottonian Book Illumination* 1:145, 158, figs. 85 and 92.

Ottonian rather than Byzantine sources, differs from the *koimesis* composition in employing a clipeus portrait rather than a small human figure to represent the Virgin's soul.[54]

An illuminator at Farfa probably encountered the model for this image in a book presented by one of the abbey's imperial patrons, possibly the sumptuous gift from Agnes mentioned in the Farfa *Register*. The liturgy at Farfa placed particular emphasis on the Assumption of the Virgin. Although the feast of the Assumption was one of the highest-ranking celebrations of the church year everywhere in Europe, the late eleventh-century office lectionary from Farfa accords it additional importance, with separate sets of lessons for Matins on the fourth, fifth, and sixth days after the Assumption and one set to be read on Sundays or other days within the octave.[55]

Seen against the historical background of Ottonian assimilation of Byzantine imagery, the Dormition-Assumption scene in the Madrid manuscript evokes an array of theological associations, including the perception of the Assumption as a multivalent symbol of power. As Henry Mayr-Harting has written, the Ottonians understood the Assumption as "analogous to the apotheosis of earthly emperors . . . thus, one function of belief in the Assumption, whether spiritual or bodily, in tenth-century society, was to enhance the political ideology of rule."[56] In the context of its reception at Farfa, the Ottonian iconography of the Assumption alluded implicitly to both the abbey's imperial patronage and the Virgin Mary's role as its patron saint.

Another imperial dimension of the imagery in the Madrid evangelistary is the visual echo of the adventus ceremony in the miniature of the Entry into Jerusalem on Palm Sunday. In addition to depicting the biblical event, the scene evokes the liturgical Palm Sunday procession with the word *osanna*,

54. A composition of the *koimesis* type can be seen on a carved ivory box given to the abbey by a patron in southern Italy (discussed later in this chap.). Another representation of this scene, no longer visible today, was at the east end of the eleventh-century church at Farfa in a wall painting uncovered in the 1920s; see Schuchert, "Eine unbekannte Elfenbeinkassette," 7, plate 5; and McClendon, *Imperial Abbey*, 44.

55. Rome, BN Farfa 32, fols. 69r–v, 71r–72v. The lessons for this feast day were among the folios of the manuscript that are now lost, but the lessons for the vigil were probably from the same text by Ambrose found in the twelfth-century office lectionary Farfa, Archivio dell'Abbazia 278, fols. 157r–158v: "Morale est omnibus ut qui fidem exigunt fidem astruant" (*Expositio euangelii secundum Lucam*, ed. Adriaen, 39–43). The only other occasions with an equivalent number of lessons in the Farfa lectionary are the feast of the Ascension and the feast of Saints Peter and Paul (fols. 63/148r–66/151r).

56. Mayr-Harting, *Ottonian Book Illumination* 1:140–41.

written next to the mouth of a boy spreading his cloak before Christ. This detail refers to one of the two antiphons performed during the blessing of the palms: "The Children of the Hebrews spread out their clothing in the road, and cried out, saying: Hosanna to the son of David; blessed is he who comes in the name of the Lord."[57] The depiction of a tonsured figure at the city (or monastery) gates welcoming Christ may echo an adventus, which would reinforce the association, common in Ottonian art, between the imperial adventus ritual into a monastery and the triumphal theology of Christ's entry into Jerusalem (fig. 4.7). The Madrid manuscript could even have figured in such a ceremony, which customarily entailed the use of a Gospel book. According to the Liber tramitis, the Gospel book is carried in the procession; when the ruler arrives, he is sprinkled with holy water, kisses the book, and is censed. Siede has suggested that the Madrid manuscript was used in such an adventus procession as well as in the mass that followed, perhaps during the visit of Henry IV in 1082.[58]

Some distinctive aspects of the Madrid miniatures seem to reflect specific elements of liturgy at Farfa, particularly the representation of the Ascension. In this scene, as Herbert Kessler has observed, Peter and Paul do not attempt to look up at Christ, who is a half-length figure in a clipeus carried by angels and obscured by a band of clouds:[59] "The two princes of the apostles have begun to see the Lord with the eyes of the mind" (see fig. 4.8). Thus the depiction of the Ascension in the Farfa evangelistary demonstrates what Kessler has called "the limits of corporal vision" by showing "that God's divinity is apprehensible only through the eyes of the mind."[60] Kessler's interpretation is reinforced by a text in a Farfa manuscript roughly contemporaneous with the Madrid evangelistary: the sermon of Pope Leo I (440–61) for the Ascension, which was originally preached at Mass on the feast, and which in the Middle Ages was read at the office of Matins during the week following the feast. The text is preserved in the late eleventh-century office lectionary copied at Farfa soon after the production of the Madrid manuscript.[61] In this sermon, Leo

57. CAO 3:418, no. 4416: "Pueri Hebraeorum vestimenta prosternebant in via, et clamabant dicentes: Hosanna Filio David; benedictus qui venit in nomine Domini."

58. Siede, Untersuchungen, 57–59. Henry was warmly received at Farfa on March 17; on this visit see Cowdrey, The Age of Abbot Desiderius, 157; and Robinson, Henry IV, 218.

59. Garrison (Studies 4:261) states that this particular manner of depicting Christ in an Ascension scene is unique.

60. Kessler, Spiritual Seeing, 131–32.

61. Rome, BN Farfa 32, fols. 56r–57r; Leo I, Tractatus 74, "Sacramentum, dilectissimi, salutis nostrae," in Sancti Leonis magni romani pontificis tractatus, ed. Chavasse, 455–61.

emphasizes the contrast between bodily and spiritual vision, describing the apostles at the Ascension as finally—having overcome the eyes of the body—understanding the mystery of salvation with the eyes of the mind. "For they raised the contemplation of the mind entirely to the divinity at the right hand of the Father seated with him, nor were they any longer impeded by the gaze of bodily vision that kept them from directing the keen glance of the mind upon the fact that neither was he absent when descending from the Father, nor had he disappeared from the disciples by ascending."[62] Later, the listeners are exhorted to follow the example of the apostles at the Ascension, drawing on the superior strength of spiritual vision to see the invisible: "Let us raise the free eyes of the heart to that altitude in which Christ exists."[63] Their souls, thus elevated, cannot be dragged down by earthly desires. The sermon concludes with a moral interpretation of the Ascension as inspiring the believer to resist sin by ascending to Christ in the spirit and reaching salvation through the eyes of the heart and mind. That this text was read aloud in the days following the Ascension must have had an effect on the monks' understanding of the feast. The effective rhetorical construction of the sermon, originally created for oral delivery to the Roman populace in the fifth century, could not fail to communicate its salient points. The presence of this text in a manuscript at Farfa and the distinctive composition of the Ascension scene in the Madrid manuscript suggest that the inspiration for the Ascension miniature was a liturgical text.

The connection between the Ascension miniature and the liturgy is heightened by the significance of Mary, the central figure in the scene. Although Kessler states that she symbolizes Ecclesia and that "[the] Church embodied in Mary thus is shown as the bridge between this world and the heavenly realm,"[64] she may also represent the patron saint of the monastery, to whom the high altar was dedicated at its consecration in 1060. The emphasis accorded Peter and Paul in this scene could reflect the fact that it was the octave of their feast that was chosen for the consecration of the altars in the Farfa abbey church. Siede has proposed that the Madrid manuscript was produced for the

62. Leo, "Sacramentum," 457; Rome, BN Farfa 32, fol. 56v: "Totam enim contemplationem animi in divinitatem ad patris dexteram consedentis erexerant, nec iam corporeae visionis tardabantur optutu, quominus in id aciem mentis intenderent, quod nec a patre descendendo afuerat, nec a discipulis ascendendo discesserat." Although the word *optutu*, equivalent to *obtutu*, appears in several manuscripts, the editor chose to print the variant *obiectu*.

63. Leo, "Sacramentum," 459; Rome, BN Farfa 32, fol. 57r: "liberos cordis oculos ad illam altitudinem in qua Christus est erigamus."

64. Kessler, *Spiritual Seeing*, 131.

recently consecrated altar of Mary, where it would display the imperial status of the abbey,[65] a theory supported by the important role of Mary in the Ascension miniature. The style of the miniature also supports the idea that the manuscript was produced in the same period as the dedication of the altars. According to Charles McClendon, the Ascension scene is closely related to the frescoes in the bell tower, which were executed in the years around 1060.[66] As he pointed out, both the illumination and the Ascension scene in the frescoes depict a scroll placed vertically in front of Peter's face.[67] As we have seen, this obstruction of Peter's vision is an important element linking the composition to the liturgy of the Ascension at Farfa.

The Ascension scene is one of several elements in the Madrid manuscript that, rather than suggesting northern influences, are characteristic of Farfa. The book's oblong format recalls the narrow shape of several other manuscripts produced at the abbey (such as Chigi C.VI.177) but has no parallel in contemporaneous Ottonian Gospel books. The distinctive musical notation and the melody for the Genealogy of Christ (*Liber generationis Christi*) sung on the Vigil of Christmas are both typical of Farfa (see fig. 4.9);[68] furthermore, it is quite unusual that the complete texts of the Gospel readings for the Vigil of Christmas, Christmas Day, the Octave of Epiphany, the Annunciation, and Easter are notated. It was the abbey's own hagiographic traditions, rather than Ottonian influence, that determined the choice of saints commemorated in the book, including Getulius, Lawrence of Syria and his sister Susanna, Valentine and Hilarius, Thomas of Maurienne, and Victoria, as well as other saints of particular importance in the Sabina (Sisinnius, Victorinus, Euticius, and Gregory of Spoleto).[69]

Reflecting northern models even as it remains closely bound to its local context, the Madrid evangelistary exemplifies the complex reception of imperial influence in a liturgical book at Farfa. Although the composition and

65. Siede, *Untersuchungen*, 56–57.

66. The frescoes are stylistically comparable to the ones in the lower church of San Crisogono in Rome, which were probably executed in the late 1050s; see McClendon, *Imperial Abbey*, 79–82; and McClendon, "Liturgical Furniture at Farfa Abbey," 197.

67. McClendon, *Imperial Abbey*, 81.

68. The intonation and conclusion of the Genealogy are found on the first leaf of a bifolium bound in a Gospel book from Farfa (Rome, BV E.16, fol. III).

69. Siede, *Untersuchungen*, 48; and Garrison, *Studies* 4:250–51. On the sanctoral of Farfa in the eleventh and twelfth centuries, see Garrison, "Saints Equizio, Onorato, and Libertino"; Gnocchi, "Un sondaggio"; and Longo, "Agiografia e identità monastica"; and "Dialettiche agiografiche."

iconography of the miniatures reflect predominantly Ottonian models, their style is patently central Italian.[70] In images such as the Pentecost and Assumption scenes, where the Farfa illuminator clearly sought to imitate a composition from Reichenau down to its every detail, the differences are clear. In the Farfa manuscript the faces of the figures are longer and less pigmented. The fluid rendering of their drapery, which employs contrasting light and dark shades to bring out the modeling of the folds, suggests more depth and volume than the flatter surfaces in Ottonian painting. McClendon has called this style "impressionistic and painterly" because of the layered application of paint and the bold surface patterning of the figures' garments.[71]

Like the miniatures, the decorated initial letters in the Farfa evangelistary also represent a fusion of Germanic and Italian sources. Ottonian models with vegetal interlace lie behind the initial *C* for the Gospel of Epiphany (see fig. 4.10),[72] whereas letters divided into rectangular compartments in contrasting colors (such as the letter *L* in fig. 4.9) instead resemble those in Italian manuscripts.[73] Minor initials with foliage and strapwork interlace outlined in red resemble those in Chigi C.VI.177. The mixture of Italian and northern-influenced styles in the initial letters of the Madrid manuscript can be compared to the eclectic blend of visual traditions seen in the section of the Chigi manuscript containing offices for the common of saints. There, Ottonianizing interlace letters are juxtaposed with clipeus portraits that evoke the early Christian art of Rome but also resemble the roundel portraits that Gregory of Catino drew in the Farfa *Register* to depict the seals on the documents he was copying.[74]

A synthesis of styles from Italy and northern Europe also characterized the architecture of the Romanesque abbey church at Farfa. As McClendon has shown, the square presbytery finds analogies in contemporary architecture of the empire. The form of the bell tower reflects both ultramontane and northern Italian influences, as does the blind arcading on the exterior of the presbytery and bell tower (see fig. 4.11). Although the blind arcading seen at Farfa

70. Siede, *Untersuchungen,* 49; and Toubert, *Un art dirigé,* 479–81.

71. McClendon, *Imperial Abbey,* 81.

72. The basic design of this letter resembles that of the corresponding letter in Brescia, Biblioteca Civica Queriniana F.II.1, fol. 24r, produced at Reichenau in the middle of the eleventh century.

73. Comparable letters appear in several eleventh-century manuscripts from the abbey of Montecassino, such as Montecassino, Archivio dell'Abbazia, Compactiones VI, a missal from the last third of the eleventh century; see *I fiori e' frutti santi,* 154, plate 37. Other examples can be found in *L'età dell'abate Desiderio,* vol. 1, *Manoscritti cassinesi del secolo XI.*

74. BAV Chigi C.VI.177, fols. 241v–281r.

FIGURE 4.11. *Bell tower, Farfa abbey church, ca. 1050–60.*
Photograph by Jens Ulff-Møller.

also appears in churches built in the first half of the eleventh century in the Rhine and Meuse valleys and also in Burgundy, the parallels with churches in northern Italy and Lotharingia are particularly strong.[75] This assimilation of both liturgical and visual elements from diverse sources was a natural result of Farfa's longstanding geopolitical position as an imperial abbey in central Italy.

The Emperor and the Cross

The distinctively central-Italian reception of imperial influences manifested in the visual arts at Farfa also affected the transmission of liturgical texts there. A particularly intriguing case of this transmission is the hymn *Salue crux sancta*. In the third quarter of the eleventh century, its text was added to the Chigi manuscript, where it is prefaced by the phrase *ymnus Heinrici regis* (hymn of King Henry), referring probably to Henry II (see ex. 4.1).[76] This use of the genitive case could be intended to associate the text with the emperor as patron or perhaps attribute the text to him as author. Although the same phrase also appears in two later, unrelated manuscripts, the hymn is usually credited to Bishop Heribert of Eichstätt (d. 1042) on the basis of the *Anonymus Haserensis,* a chronicle from a generation later.[77] The fact that the Chigi manuscript contains the earliest extant copy of the hymn suggests that the testimony of the anonymous chronicler should be reconsidered, however. The entire manuscript tradition of *Salue crux sancta* differs significantly from that of the other five hymns attributed to Heribert of Eichstätt. Although the other texts are found almost exclusively in manuscripts from Germanic regions, *Salue crux sancta* appears in four eleventh-century hymnaries from northern, central, and southern Italy, including the Chigi manuscript.[78] The hymn

75. McClendon, *Imperial Abbey,* 83–93 (details of the blind arcading on the bell tower are shown in plates 20–32).

76. BAV Chigi C.VI.177, fols. 154v–155r. On the date of the addition see Boynton, "Liturgy and History," 318 n. 3.

77. "Anonymus Haserensis de Episcopis Eichstetensibus," ed. Bethmann, 261; and *Die Geschichte der Eichstätter Bischöfe,* 55–56: "Here, inspired by the Holy Spirit, he composed six very beautiful hymns, one of them about the Holy Cross: *Salve crux sancta*" ("Hic Spiritu sancto afflatus sex ymnos pulcherrimos composuit; unum de sancta cruce: Salve crux sancta"). The attributions to "Henricus imperator" (in Chartres, Bibliothèque Municipale, MS 162, fol. 250) and "Henricus rex" (Rome, Biblioteca Alessandrina MS 93) are mentioned in *AH* 50, 292, but rejected there in favor of the testimony of the *Anonymus Haserensis.* On Heribert see Weinfurter, *Geschichte,* 147.

78. Besides the Chigi manuscript, they are Vatican City, BAV Vat. lat. 5776 (from Bobbio); Verona, Biblioteca Capitolare 109 (from San Zeno of Verona); and Naples, Biblioteca

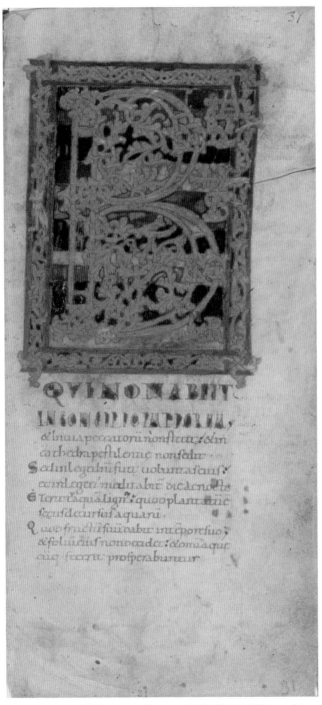

FIGURE 4.1. *Initial letter B of Psalm 1, BAV Chigi C.VI.177, fol. 31r.*
Copyright Biblioteca Apostolica Vaticana.

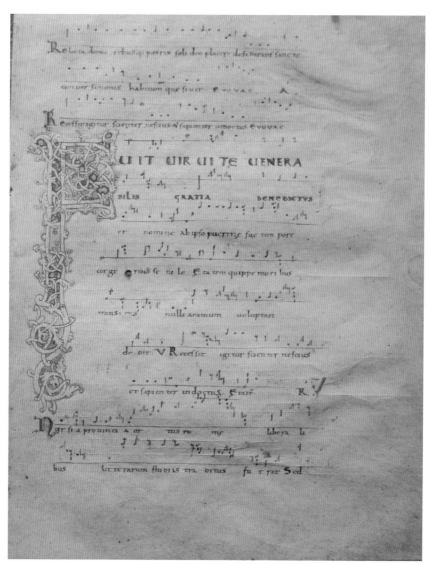

FIGURE 4.2. *Initial letter* F *in Farfa, Archivio dell'Abbazia, AF 338, IV, fol. 3r.*

FIGURE 4.4. *Pentecost, Utrecht, Museum Catharijne Convent, ABM h3, fol. 137v. By permission of the Museum Catharijne Convent.*

FIGURE 4.3. *Pentecost, Madrid, BN Vitrina 20-6, fol. 53r. By permission of the Biblioteca Nacional.*

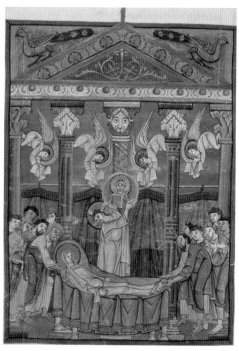

FIGURE 4.6. *Assumption, Utrecht, Museum Catharijne Convent, ABM h3, fol. 173v. By permission of the Museum Catharijne Convent.*

FIGURE 4.5. *Assumption, Madrid, BN Vitrina 20-6, fol. 76v. By permission of the Biblioteca Nacional.*

FIGURE 4.7. *Entry into Jerusalem, Madrid, BN Vitrina 20-6, fol. 25r.*
By permission of the Biblioteca Nacional.

FIGURE 4.8. *Ascension, Madrid, BN Vitrina 20-6, fol. 52r.*
By permission of the Biblioteca Nacional.

FIGURE 4.9. *Initial* L *of Genealogy of Christ (Matthew), Madrid, BN Vitrina 20-6, fol. 5r. By permission of the Biblioteca Nacional.*

FIGURE 4.10. *Initial letter C of Matthew 2, Madrid, BN Vitrina 20-6, fol. 12r. By permission of the Biblioteca Nacional.*

EXAMPLE 4.1. *Salue crux sancta,* BAV Chigi C.VI.177, fol. 154v–155r.

Ymnus Heinrici regis.

Salue crux sancta; salue mundi gloria.
Vera spes nostra, uera ferens gaudia.
Signum salutis, salus in periculis.
Vitale lignum, uitam portans omnium.

Te adoranda, te crucem uiuificam;
in te redempti, dulce decus seculi
semper laudamus, semper tibi canimus
per lignum serui, per lignum liberi.

Originale crimen necans in cruce
nos et a prauis Christe munda maculis
humanitatem miseratus fragilem
per crucem sanctam lapsis dona ueniam.

Pro lege salua benedic sanctifica
populum cunctum crucis per signaculum;
morbos auerte corporis et anime
hoc contra signum nullum stet periculum.

Sit Deo patri laus in cruce filii
sit coequalis laus sancto spiritui
ciuibus summis gaudium sit angelis
honor sit mundo crucis hec inuentio.

Hymn of King Henry.

Hail, holy cross, hail, glory of the world;
our true hope, bearing true joys.
Sign of salvation, safety in danger;
vital wood, bearing the life of all people.

You are to be venerated, you lifegiving cross;
redeemed in you, sweet ornament of the world,
we praise you always, we sing to you always,
made slaves by wood, liberated by wood.

Destroying original sin on the cross,
also purify us, Christ, of wicked stains;
having pitied fragile humanity,
through the Holy Cross give pardon to the fallen.

On account of the law, save, bless, and sanctify
the whole people with the sign of the cross;
avert illnesses of the body and soul;
against this sign may no danger stand.

Praise be to God, in the Cross of the son;
equal praise be to the Holy Spirit;
joy to the angels, celestial citizens; may
this invention of the Cross be an honor for the world.

seems to have circulated first in Italy but only later in northern Europe, where the manuscript transmission of the text dates to the late twelfth century, about a hundred years after the text was copied into the Chigi manuscript.[79] In this context, the phrase *ymnus Heinrici regis* can be reassessed in light of Farfa's imperial connections. If Henry II did indeed compose *Salue crux sancta* himself,

---

Nazionale, VI.E.43 (from Benevento), all copied in the second half of the eleventh century. See Boynton, "Orality, Literacy," 117–18. *Salue crux sancta* also appears, without attribution, in a late eleventh-century English manuscript (London, British Library, Cott. Vesp. D.XII).

79. Of course, *Salue crux sancta* might have existed in earlier manuscripts from northern Europe that have since been lost, but the early transmission throughout Italy suggests that the hymn existed there first.

it is not surprising that the text should have reached Farfa, where Henry apparently stopped with his troops in 1022 on his way back from southern Italy.[80] Whatever the authorship of the hymn, however, the reference to Henry constitutes a tribute to the emperor.[81] According to one hypothesis, Heribert may have been a member of the imperial chapel, where he would have composed the hymn for the feast of the Invention of the Cross; it would then have been diffused through the emperor's influence, which could explain the attribution to Henry.[82] It seems possible, however, that Henry wrote the text himself, perhaps in collaboration with an advisor such as Heribert. The rather simple construction of the hymn, particularly in its highly anaphoric first two strophes, would be within the reach of a relatively inexperienced poet, although it does not suggest an unskilled one.[83]

The text of the hymn resembles a catalog of the attributes and epithets of the Cross, invoking three aspects of the Cross commonly emphasized in the central Middle Ages: a symbolic instrument of salvation history, a powerfully redemptive object, and an apotropaic form of protection (in the sign of the cross). Typically for a poem of the early eleventh century, there is no consistent end rhyme, though a few lines rhyme and considerable use of assonance brings out the relationships between the words. Several lines in the first two strophes are divided in half by exact or nearly exact repetition, for example, the first, second, and fourth lines of the first strophe: "*Salue* crux sancta; *salue* mundi gloria / *uera* spes nostra, *uera* ferens gaudia . . . *uitale* lignum, *uitam* portans omnium" (italics mine). An exception to this pattern is the chiastic construction with the word *salus* in the third line of the first strophe: "Signum *salutis, salus* in periculis."

The very terseness of the phrases conveys symbolism, as in the use of *lignum*

---

80. "Vita sancti Guidonis abbatis Casaurensis," *AASS Ordinis Sancti Benedicti,* saec. VI, 1:487. This visit is not attested by any diploma, but it is logical that Henry would have stopped at Farfa on his way north from Rome, especially given his relationships with the imperial abbeys, described in Weinfurter, *Heinrich II,* 168–85.

81. Later examples of such honorific possessives can be cited, such as Josquin des Prez's chanson "Mille regretz," called "the song of the Emperor" because it was a favorite of Emperor Charles V; see Fallows, "Who Composed 'Mille regretz'?"

82. Schupp, "Der Dichter des 'Modus Liebinc,'" 36; and Delaporte, "L'hymne *Salve crux sancta,*" 84.

83. As noted by Delaporte ("L'hymne," 89), the prosody of the hymn derives from the quantitative iambic senarius, but because it is a work of rhythmic poetry, the only features of the quantitative model it retains are the number of syllables per line and the caesura after the fifth syllable.

(wood) in the fourth and eighth lines of the hymn: "*uitale* lignum, *uitam* portans omnium / *per lignum* serui, *per lignum* liberi." Whereas the *lignum* in the fourth line signifies the life-giving, salvific wood of the Cross, in the eighth line the repeated word refers to both the tree of the knowledge of good and evil that was instrumental in the fall of Adam and Eve, and to the wood of the Cross. The repetition of *lignum* here emphasizes its opposing and complementary significations in salvation history: "made slaves by wood, liberated by wood," an allusion that is elucidated by the ninth line ("destroying original sin on the Cross"). The symbolic analogy between the tree in the Garden of Eden and the wood of the Cross was proclaimed liturgically in the text of an antiphon that may have inspired the author of *Salue crux sancta,* for it was sung on the same feasts of the Cross on which the hymn was performed: "On account of the wood we were made slaves, and we were liberated by the Holy Cross; the fruit of the tree seduced us, the Son of God redeemed us, alleluia."[84] Similarly, in *Salue crux sancta,* connecting the wood of the Edenic tree to that of the Cross creates resonances across the first two strophes of the hymn.

The association of Henry II with *Salue crux sancta* makes sense, given his reputation for devotion to the Cross. He gave a relic of the True Cross to the church at Merseburg and, according to the eleventh-century historian Radulfus Glaber, evoked the symbolism of the Cross at his coronation in Rome in 1014.[85] According to Glaber's account, Pope Benedict VIII presented Henry with the newly fashioned imperial insignia, a golden apple surrounded by jewels and adorned with a golden cross; the emperor immediately sent the precious object to Cluny, stating that no one deserved such a gift more than "those who readily follow the Cross of the Savior, having scorned the pomps of the world."[86] The eleventh-century *Liber tramitis* lists the apple among the objects carried in procession on major feast days at Cluny.[87] This customary particularly singles out Henry II as a generous patron of Cluny who was received into the *societas* and *fraternitas* of the monks of Cluny. In the decretal of Abbot Odilo for the institution of the feast of All Souls on November 2, the instructions for the liturgy of the day refer specifically to the "memory of our dear

84. *CAO* no. 4398: "Propter lignum serui facti sumus, et per sanctam crucem liberati sumus, fructus arboris seduxit nos, Filius Dei redempti nos, alleluia."

85. On Henry's interest in liturgy and the donation of the relic, see Schupp, "Der Dichter," 36.

86. Glaber, *Historiarum libri quinque,* 40: "illis qui pompis mundi calcatis crucem expeditius sequuntur Saluatoris."

87. The apple (*pomum*) was carried in the processions described in *LT* 23, 42, 68, 108, 151.

emperor Henry" (*memoria cari nostri imperatoris Heinrici*), and the commemoration of his *memoria* is recorded in the section of the customary concerning necrology entries.[88] Since the second half of the eleventh century, when the earliest extant manuscript of the *Liber tramitis* was copied at Farfa, the monks there could read about Henry's importance for Cluny and about the ritual function of the golden apple. The *Liber tramitis* records the inscription of Henry's name on a processional cross at Cluny.[89] All this might well have led the monks of Farfa to associate Henry II with special veneration of the Cross, resulting in the ascription of *Salue crux sancta* to Henry in the Chigi manuscript. This suggests yet another way in which the *Liber tramitis* seems to have functioned as a reference text for Farfa.

Southern Italian Patrons and Their Gifts

Besides its northern affiliations, Farfa's patronage network extended to southern Italy as well. The Farfa *Register* and *Chronicle* record a donation to the abbey made in 1057 by Argyros, a Greek from Bari who was a *katapan* (governor) of southern Italy beginning in 1051.[90] According to the Farfa *Chronicle*, Argyros was so impressed by what he had heard about Abbot Berard and Farfa's monastic observance (*religio*), that he requested the prayers of the monks and asked to join the community. In a Latin epistle transcribed in both the *Register* and *Chronicle*, Argyros pledged future gifts in exchange for absolution of his sins and prayers on his behalf:

> I, Argyros, also called the son of Melis, by the grace of God master of the robe and *dux* of Italy, Calabria, Sicily, and Paflagonia, recommend and associate myself to the holy monastery of Mary, the most blessed mother of God, called Farfa . . . so that as long as I am alive in this mortal world, I should deserve to share in your very holy merits, according to the distinguished letter that your piety deigned to send to me, sinner and undeserving servant of my lady, the Virgin Mary the most holy mother of God. And so that, supported by your sacrosanct prayers and protected by your divine mercy, I may be made worthy to be acceptable, at first with fitting behavior and afterwards with earthly riches, so that after the chain of the flesh and after this habitation of clay, I might deserve to rejoice together in the joy of

88. *LT,* 199, 285. See also Heath, *Crux imperatorum philosophia,* 113–15.

89. *LT,* 259.

90. For a summary of Argyros' diplomatic career see von Falkenhausen, *Untersuchungen über die byzantinische Herrschaft,* 187–90; and Loud, *The Age of Robert Guiscard,* 95–97.

Elysium with you, my most beloved brothers and lords, for infinite ages. Amen. And may you all, present and future, acknowledge that, with concordant will and calm body and mind, I, a sinner and your brother, chose to carry these things out; I signed joyfully with my own hands for the absolution of my most numerous sins and for the salvation of my soul, and had it sealed with a silver seal, in the year 1057 of the Lord's redemption of our assumed flesh.[91]

The Latin epistle is followed by a much shorter text in Greek, presumably the words of Argyros in his own language, corresponding essentially to the first sentence of the Latin document.[92] It is doubtful that Argyros ever physically joined the community at Farfa, for his whereabouts after 1058 are unknown.[93] The *Chronicle* states that Argyros sent the abbey money both when he was received into the brotherhood of the congregation and again just before his death. With the second gift he also donated his robe of honor, a precious silk cape embroidered with gold.[94] This garment, like other rich textiles donated by patrons to medieval churches, was probably adapted for use as a liturgical vestment.[95] The conversion of secular clothing into vestments was common

---

91. *CF* 2:202–3; and *RF* 5:238–39 (no. 1261): "En ego Argiro Dei prouidentia magister uestis et dux Italię, Calabrię, Sicilię, Paflagonię, qui et Melis, commendo me et associor sancto monasterio beatissimę Dei genitricis Marię cognomento Farfę . . . ut, dum uiuus fuero in hoc mortali sęculo, merear fieri particeps uestris sanctissimis meritis secundum splendidum scriptum quod michi peccatori et immerito famulo meęque dominę et sanctissimę Dei genitricis Marię uirginis uestra dignata est dirigere pietas. Et ut uestris suffultus sacrosanctis orationibus et divina protectus clementia dignus fiam placere ibidem primitus utilibus moribus et postmodum terrenis opibus, quatinus post carnis uinculum postque domum luteam Elisii gaudiis una uobiscum, mei fratres dilectissimi et domini, congaudere merear per infinita sęculorum sęcula. Amen. Et ut cuncti pręsentes et futuri cognoscatis me congrua uoluntate placidoque corpore uel animo placuisse michi peccatori et confratri uestro talia peragere, pro absolutione meorum plurimorum scelerum et salvatione meę animę propriis meis subscripsi letanter manibus, et bullare fecimus uulla argentea. Anno millesimo .L. redemptionis nostrę assumptę carnis dominicę. VII."

92. On the use of Greek in this donation, see the last section of this chapter.

93. Von Falkenhausen, *Untersuchungen*, 190.

94. *CF* 2:203: "direxit ad hanc ecclesiam sive congregationem quędam cariora dona et non parvam pecuniam, videlicet bisantos sexmilia, et mantum pręciosum holosericum auroque textum quod erat pręclara vestis honoris sui, quę amplius valere ferebatur quam centum libras argenti purissimi. Nam quando huius societatem et fraternitatem suscepit congregationis, bisantos tria milia huic ecclesię mandavit."

95. Another example is the silk cope said to have belonged to Robert of Anjou, king of

in the Middle Ages, and the monks of Farfa also put to similar use the garments donated by the Empress Agnes.[96] Thus the commemoration of Argyros by the monks of Farfa took both ritual and textual forms. His *uestis honoris*, employed as a vestment, would recall his generosity; he would be remembered in the community's prayers as one of its members. Two records of his donations were inscribed in the collective memory, represented in textual form by the *Register* and *Chronicle*.

Argyros's decision to ally himself with the imperial abbey should be understood in the context of the network of relationships he had developed when he took part in negotations between Emperor Henry III, Pope Leo IX, and the imperial court at Constantinople in 1054, with the aim of renewing an alliance against the Normans. In response to an embassy sent by Argyros to the court of Henry III, Henry issued a privilege to protect the tomb of Argyros's father, Melos, in Bamberg. Almost immediately thereafter, Henry granted a privilege to the abbey of Santa Maria in the Tremiti Islands.[97] As McClendon has pointed out, Argyros was also a patron of Santa Maria in Tremiti. Both Farfa and Tremiti were dedicated to the Virgin Mary, both received the patronage of Henry III and Argyros, and both employed the same system of construction for their interior walls, which seems to be derived from a common north Italian source.[98] Thus Argyros's donation to Farfa fits into a strategy of patronage, perhaps combining Marian piety with cultivation of the emperor to secure his aid against the Normans.[99]

Within a few years of the donation from Argyros, another patron from southern Italy, the wealthy merchant Maurus of Amalfi, gave Farfa a richly carved ivory casket. Unlike many other objects the abbey possessed in the Middle Ages, this one is still extant and can be seen in the abbey museum (figs. 4.12–4.13).[100] Rectangular in shape, with a gabled lid, the solid ivory casket is

---

Naples; see May, *Silk Textiles of Spain*, 52 and fig. 37. The expression *auro textum* may refer to the practice of wrapping strips of gold around a core of silk thread (6–7). I am grateful to Constancio del Alamo and Elizabeth Valdez del Alamo for this reference.

96. *RF* 5:321: "Planetam purpurae nigrae et pluuialem purpurae clauatae quae fuerunt reginae agnetis. Dorsalem leonatum et tunicam reginae" are listed among the possessions dispersed by Abbot Guido in 1121.

97. Loud, *Age of Robert Guiscard*, 120.

98. McClendon, *Imperial Abbey*, 99, 172 n. 124.

99. I am grateful to Louis Hamilton for suggesting this interpretation.

100. For detailed descriptions of the casket see Bergman, *The Salerno Ivories*, 128–30; and Toesca, "Un cimelio amalfitano." Its dimensions are 33 cm long by 7 cm wide by 21 cm high.

FIGURE 4.12. *Dormition and Assumption of the Virgin, ivory casket, Museo di Farfa. Photograph by Jens Ulff-Møller, reproduced by permission of the Abbazia di Farfa.*

entirely covered with scenes carved in relief.[101] The long sides of the lid depict the Nativity cycle, with the Annunciation, the Visitation, and the Nativity on one side, followed by the Adoration of the Magi, the Presentation in the Temple, and the Flight into Egypt on the other. The Annunciation to the Shepherds and the Baptism of Christ appear on the ends of the lid. On the lower part of the box, the ends represent the Washing of the Feet and the Pentecost. One side shows the Crucifixion and the Descent into Limbo combined with the Ascension, while the other side is devoted entirely to the Dormition of the Virgin, perhaps in tribute to the patron of Farfa (fig. 4.12).[102]

As Robert Bergman has pointed out, the casket's iconographic program is a mixture of elements from East and West, but reflects the influence of earlier Italian art more than that of Byzantine sources.[103] Even though its models are

101. Bergman (*Salerno Ivories,* 129) noted that construction from solid ivory is found more often in Islamic or Carolingian caskets than in Byzantine ones.

102. Bergman, *Salerno Ivories,* 129–32, figs. 152–58.

103. Bergman, "A School of Romanesque Ivory Carving in Amalfi," 167–71.

FIGURE 4.13. *Crucifixion, Descent into Limbo, and Ascension, ivory casket, Museo di Farfa. Photograph by Jens Ulff-Møller, reproduced by permission of the Abbazia di Farfa.*

predominantly Western, the casket features a Dormition scene based on the Byzantine *koimesis* (fig. 4.12), and a Crucifixion scene derived from a composition that is common in Middle Byzantine ivories and is also found in some contemporaneous southern Italian works (fig. 4.13). The organization of scenes on the surface of the casket suggests careful planning of narrative sequence and visual design. The two carvers used architectural elements to set off the individual scenes in the Nativity cycle, three on each long side of the lid. The Baptism of Christ and the Annunciation to the Shepherds are placed at either end of the lid (not shown in figs. 4.12 and 4.13), where the smaller surfaces provide a natural frame for the scenes. Each of these two scenes is effectively articulated by elements that divide up the space, such as trees in the Baptism and a hut in the Annunciation to the Shepherds. The footwashing and Pentecost, depicted at each end of the body of the casket, both communicate a message of brotherhood, symmetrically contrasting an episode in which Christ humbles himself with one in which he is exalted. Another such contrast, this time one of directionality, appears in the choice of scenes for the long sides of the box, one representing Christ's Descent into Limbo, the other the ascent of Mary's soul in the *koimesis*. The figures are not as graceful as those in later ivories more directly influenced by Byzantine art; the modeling, however, is bold, vivid, and rather geometric. For instance, in the Descent into Limbo, Christ greets two stout figures (presumably Adam and Eve) whose parallel diagonal lines create a symmetrical counterpoint both with their overturned tombs and with Christ's outstretched arm and bent leg (see fig. 4.13).[104] Although the Descent into Limbo is organized horizontally, in the Ascension to its right the figures are vertically stratified to evoke the distance between the apostles standing on the ground and Christ rising above them.

The scenes are framed by a votive inscription in Leonine hexameters that begins next to the Nativity cycle and follows the events depicted in their narrative order, concluding with the Dormition. Traces of red and blue polychrome on some of the letters show that the inscription was once painted, making it an effective framing device for the figural carvings. The text of the inscription does not refer to the events depicted but rather to the donors:

> Take this modest vessel, appropriate for divine worship,
> and given to you with devout mind by your people.
> We ask that our names be known to you everywhere,
> but a salutary precaution led them to be engraved here.
> I am rightly called Maurus because I have associated with dark people;
> my children follow me, Johannes with Pantaleon,
> Sergius and Manso, Maurus, and their brother Pardo.
> Give absolution for sins, offer a celestial crown.[105]

The text names the donors as Maurus and his six sons. Maurus has been identified as an important merchant of Amalfi well known for his patronage of the abbey of Montecassino; in 1066, he donated a set of bronze doors made in

---

104. Bergman (ibid., 170) compares the rendering of the drapery and the figures on this panel to that in a casket made at Rome in the early ninth century; the hair and eyes are also similar.

105. Suscipe vas modicum divinis cultibus aptum
   Ac tibi directum devota mente tuorum.
   Nomina nostra tibi, quesumus, sint cognita passim.
   Haec tamen hic sgribi voluit cautela salubris.
   Iure vocor Maurus quoniam sum nigr[os] secutus;
   Me sequitur proles, cum Pantaleone Iohannes,
   Sergius et Manso, Maurus, frater quoque Pardo.
   Da scelerum veniam, caelestem prebe coronam.

I have followed the order of the verses as printed by Toesca ("Un cimelio," 538) and (Bergman, *Salerno Ivories*, 128), but I resolve the abbreviation *nig.* as *nigros* rather than *nigra.*

Constantinople for the new church, and in 1071 he became a member of the community. Because two of Maurus's sons died in the years immediately after the middle of 1072, Herbert Bloch originally concluded that the box was made in 1071–72 for presentation to Abbot Desiderius of Montecassino, reaching Farfa only some time later.[106] It used to be thought that the inscription referred to Maurus and all of his six sons taking the black Benedictine habit (*nigra*).[107] More recently, Bloch retracted his arguments concerning the casket, and demonstrated that the word *nigra* did not refer to the Benedictine habit but rather could be construed generally as "evil" or "sin."[108] I propose that by rendering the abbreviation *nigr.* as *nigr[os]* and translating the words *sum nigr[os] secutus* as "I have followed or associated with dark people" one can reveal a pun on the name Maurus, which can mean both "dark" and "a Moor."[109] The personal name Maurus could be an epithet conveying the association of Moors with darkness, as in the twelfth-century chronicle by William of Tyre, who refers to Manuel I, emperor of Constantinople, being nicknamed Maurus because of his dark skin and hair.[110] As a merchant from Amalfi, Maurus would have encountered Moorish populations through trade; Amalfitans maintained extensive commercial relationships with north Africa and Egypt in the eleventh century, even establishing trading posts in the Middle East. There were probably Amalfitan merchants at the Egyptian ports where ivory for carvings was exported to Europe.[111]

What little is known about the relationship between Maurus and Farfa is based on this inscription, but one can speculate that his donations to Farfa and Montecassino reflect a pattern of offering patronage to abbeys with imperial

106. See Bloch, "Monte Cassino, Byzantium, and the West," 208–12.

107. This interpretation was first presented by Schuchert, "Eine unbekannte Elfenbeinkassette"; and Hofmeister, "Maurus von Amalfi."

108. Bloch, *Monte Cassino in the Middle Ages* 1:155–60.

109. See *Oxford Latin Dictionary*, s.v. "Maurus" (Moroccan); and *Novum glossarium*, fasc. *Ma*, col. 276 (*Maurus* [a Moor]); more than a hundred instances can be found by searching various forms of the word in the *CLCLT*. *Maurus* (from the Greek μαῦρος) is a common synonym for *niger* in medieval Latin. For related words see *Novum glossarium*, fasc. *Ma*, col. 275 (*maura* [black clothes]; *mauriscus* [blackish]).

110. *Willelmi Tyrensis archiepiscopi chronicon*, 706: "He was of moderate height, and dark of skin and hair, whence he is even today also known by the name Maurus" ("Fuit autem statura mediocris, carne et capillo niger—unde et cognomento dicitur etiam hodie Maurus").

111. Bergman, *Salerno Ivories*, 113–15; and Citarella, "The Relations of Amalfi with the Arab World," "Patterns in Medieval Trade," and *Il commercio di Amalfi nell'alto medioevo*.

connections.[112] Maurus might have presented the casket to Farfa on a special occasion, such as the dedication of the altars in the abbey church in 1060. This theory, originally proposed by Robert Bergman, is supported by his dating of the carving through stylistic comparisons with contemporaneous and later ivories from southern Italy.[113] The particular prominence of the *koimesis*, which is the only scene that occupies an entire side of the casket, also implies a direct reference to the patron of Farfa. Because the final verse of the inscription encircles the scene, the viewer reads the request for absolution while viewing the Dormition of the Virgin. This juxtaposition suggests that the prayer in the inscription is meant to be addressed directly to the Virgin. The composition of the scene is characteristic of the Byzantine *koimesis*, with Christ standing behind the Virgin's bed and passing the diminutive figure representing her soul to an angel hovering on the right.

Beyond its manifestly votive purpose, the practical use of the casket at Farfa is unknown, although the inscription's reference to "divine worship" suggests a liturgical function. It might have served as a container for storing the host in preparation for the Eucharist.[114] In any case, the casket and the donation it represented had the ritual purpose of eliciting the monks' prayers for the soul of Maurus. The engraved supplication in the inscription exploits the written word in a lasting form; likewise, the letter accompanying the donation by Argyros was rendered more permanent when it was recorded in the *Register* and *Chronicle*. Maurus and Argyros, though men of different origins and occupations, were both powerful figures in southern Italy at a time of tension and

112. Louis Hamilton pointed out to me this implication of Maurus's patronage. On the relations between Montecassino and the emperors in this period, see Cowdrey, *Age of Abbot Desiderius*.

113. Bergman, "A School of Romanesque Ivory Carving," 166; and Bergman, *Salerno Ivories*, 87–89; I am grateful to Charles McClendon for discussing the ivory casket with me. Braca ("Lavori in avorio," 121) suggested that the casket's large size, more common in late antiquity than in the eleventh century, could indicate that it was composed from *spolia*. As far as I know, this suggestion has not been pursued through further physical analysis.

114. No records describe the casket's use as such; a lack of textual sources regarding a liturgical object is not unusual for this period. A ciborium for preserving the host was traditionally round, but few survive from before the twelfth century. The casket could have been an early form of tabernacle for keeping reserved hosts at the altar. From the thirteenth century on, tabernacles were produced in the shape of small shrines with pyramidal lids; see Parker McLachlan, "Liturgical Vessels and Implements," 399–401.

conflict with the Normans.[115] Farfa, which in the 1050s and 1060s was favored by pope and emperor alike, was implicitly (if not explicitly) anti-Norman. It is probably no coincidence that, within a few years of each other, Argyros and Maurus made valuable gifts to Farfa, thereby securing the beneficial prayers of its monks on their behalf, and at the same time associating themselves with a wealthy imperial abbey that had considerable power outside the contested lands of the south.

Liturgical Influences from Southern Italy

In addition to gifts from patrons in southern Italy, Farfa also possessed several liturgical chants of southern Italian origin. Although the precise paths of transmission are unknown, these compositions may have arrived at Farfa through patronage or through contact with abbeys to the south such as Montecassino. The most distinctive of the southern Italian elements in Farfa's liturgical repertory is the Beneventan melody for the *Exultet,* a long prayer sung during the benediction of the paschal candle during the Easter Vigil on Holy Saturday. After the abbot kindled new fire in a brazier, the deacon took the paschal candle to the pulpit and sang the *Exultet* while the candle was blessed; then the *Sursum corda* of the Mass and the Preface were sung. The *Exultet* was known in central Italy in two different versions: Beneventan and Franco-Roman. The Beneventan version originated in the early Middle Ages in the Lombard duchy of Benevento, which had a characteristic liturgy with a distinctive musical tradition that was officially suppressed in the second half of the eleventh century, although vestiges of the Beneventan usage survived.[116] The more widespread version of the *Exultet* is designated as Franco-Roman, because it forms part of the Gregorian chant that resulted from the fusion of Frankish and Roman traditions and became the standard repertory in much of Europe during the central Middle Ages.[117]

The melodies of both the Beneventan and Franco-Roman versions of the *Exultet* were apparently in use at Farfa by the early twelfth century. In an early

115. The role of Argyros in the struggle against the Normans was recounted by William of Apulia in the *Gesta Roberti Wiscardi;* see William of Apulia, *Guillaume de Pouille.* Recent discussions of Robert Guiscard are Loud, *The Age of Robert Guiscard;* and Hamilton, "Memory, Symbol, and Arson," 378–79. On the Norman expansion into Amalfi in the 1050s and 1060s see Schwarz, *Amalfi im frühen Mittelalter,* 53–56. Cowdrey (*Age of Abbot Desiderius,* 107–21) discusses relations between the papacy, the Normans, and Montecassino.

116. On the suppression of the Beneventan chant see Kelly, *The Beneventan Chant,* 39–40.

117. I use the term "Franco-Roman" following Kelly, *The Exultet in Southern Italy.*

twelfth-century office book from Farfa, Rome BV F.29, the first part of the *Exultet* combines the Franco-Roman text with the Beneventan melody, while the second part (the Preface) is set to the Franco-Roman melody (see fig. 4.14).[118] BV F.29 also contains a florid intonation of the words *Lumen Christi,* which preceded the performance of the *Exultet* itself; the deacon sang *Lumen Christi* three times to increasingly elaborate melodies. Thomas Kelly has suggested that some of the melodies set to the *Lumen Christi* may be those originally sung for the Beneventan *Exultet* and that they could predate the introduction of the Franco-Roman *Exultet.*[119] If this was the case at Farfa, the mixed *Exultet* there may reflect an early Beneventan influence that later gave way to the Franco-Roman version or perhaps the coexistence of multiple liturgical strata accumulated over time.[120]

Thus at Farfa, as in some other central Italian monasteries, the Beneventan and Franco-Roman melodies of the *Exultet* were combined in performance.[121] A fragment of another manuscript from Farfa copied around 1100 also contains the Preface with the Franco-Roman melody (see ex. 4.2).[122] Another melody at Farfa related to the Beneventan *Exultet* melody was the tone for the recitation of the Prayer of Jeremiah (*Oratio Jeremiae*), one of the lessons for Matins on Holy Saturday.[123]

Melodies for the *Exultet* are meant to convey the words of the text and ar-

---

118. Rome, BV F.29, fols. 36v, 7–8 (bound out of order); and Kelly, *Exultet,* 261. The melody, which is notated in neumes that are inconsistently heightened and lacks a clef, cannot be transcribed precisely, but it can be compared to the one in Kelly, *Exultet,* 80–81.

119. Kelly, *Exultet,* 153.

120. According to Kelly (ibid., 87–88), the presence of the partially Beneventan *Exultet* at Farfa would imply that the Beneventan practice predated the Roman one. On cities in which the *Exultet* changed over time, producing multiple versions, see Kelly, "Structure and Ornament in Chant," 259–62.

121. Kelly, *Exultet,* 77, 88.

122. Rome, BV E.16, fol. IV (later foliation added to the second leaf of a bifolium bound in at the beginning of a Gospel book); see Supino Martini, *Roma,* 263. This fragment was not included in Kelly, *Exultet.* The text is incomplete; it begins in the middle of the Preface.

123. Rome, BN Farfa 32, fols. 52v–53r; first pointed out by Boe, "Chant Notation in Eleventh-Century Roman Manuscripts," 48. The comparison between the melodies is necessarily approximative because the neumes are adiastematic (written between the lines of text without a staff line or clef). The Beneventan melody is transcribed from Rome, BV R 32, in Kelly, *Beneventan Chant,* 133; and Kelly, *Exultet,* 85. See also Boe, "Music Notation in Archivio San Pietro C 105," 27, 30.

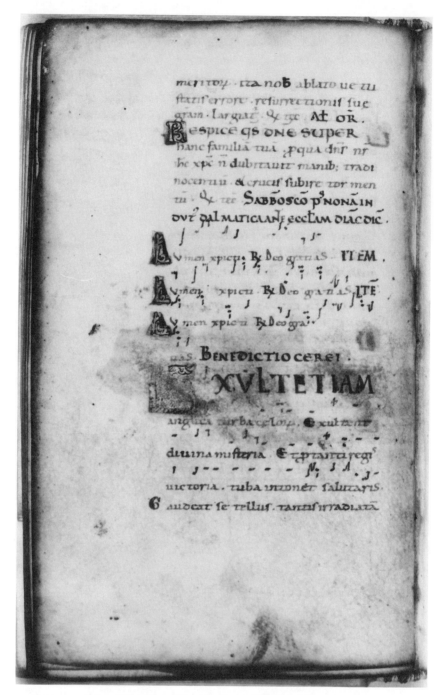

FIGURE 4.14. Lumen Christi *and* Exultet, *Rome, BV F.29, fol. 36v. By permission of the Ministero per i Beni e le Attività culturali, Biblioteca Vallicelliana, Roma.*

ticulate its structure, so the music consists predominantly of recitation on one of two pitches and concludes sentences with a cadence on a third pitch. In the fragmentary Franco-Roman Preface melody from Farfa, the interval between G (the final) and C (the reciting tone) is filled in by scalar motion; the melody then pauses on the secondary cadential note, B. Even such a simple melody can vary considerably from place to place, which is why it was often notated in liturgical books. In the Farfa melody, the only extended departure from recitation is the rhapsodic flourish moving up and down the scale on the crucial word *accendit,* drawing the listeners' attention to the central moment of the ceremony: the lighting of the paschal candle. The melody has a narrow range typical of reciting tones, staying within the fifth from G to D but rarely rising above C, except for the word *accendit.* An E is reached, appropriately, on the word *altissimus* (highest) in the last sentence. The concluding florid *amen* rises even higher to an F, then slowly descends to the final cadential note.

The blending of Beneventan and Franco-Roman traditions characterizes the melodies but not the texts. Both preserved versions of the *Exultet* from Farfa contain the Franco-Roman text, omitting most of the praise of the bees.[124] Both texts also lack the commemoration of the emperor, which appears near the end of some versions of the *Exultet* after the supplication on behalf of the pope. This omission seems anomalous in light of Farfa's imperial patronage, but the text used there may represent an early branch of the tradition that never incorporated the added clause. Nonetheless, the Farfa text of the *Exultet* is not entirely without imperial resonances, for it concludes with a sentence beginning "You who ever live, reign, and command" (*Qui semper uiuis, regnas, imperas*), echoing the *Christus uincit, Christus regnat, Christus imperat* that formed part of the medieval liturgical acclamations of kings (*laudes regiae*). Ernst Kantorowicz dubbed this conclusion to the *Exultet* the "Norman finale" because its earliest witnesses are manuscripts from Normandy and Norman Sicily.[125] Because the "Norman finale" first appears in manuscripts of the early twelfth century, the Farfa *Exultet* from around 1100 may be among the earliest witnesses to it outside the Norman orbit. The *Exultet* at Farfa, with its Beneventan, Norman, and Franco-Roman elements, represents the wide range of influences manifested in the abbey's liturgical culture.

---

124. Kelly labels this omission "Cut D" in his table (Kelly, *Exultet,* 66–67). This version is found in many manuscripts.

125. Kelly, *Exultet,* 74; and Kantorowicz, "The Norman Finale." On the *laudes regiae* see Kantorowicz, "*Laudes regiae.*"

Example 4.2. Rome, BV E.16, fol. IVr-v.

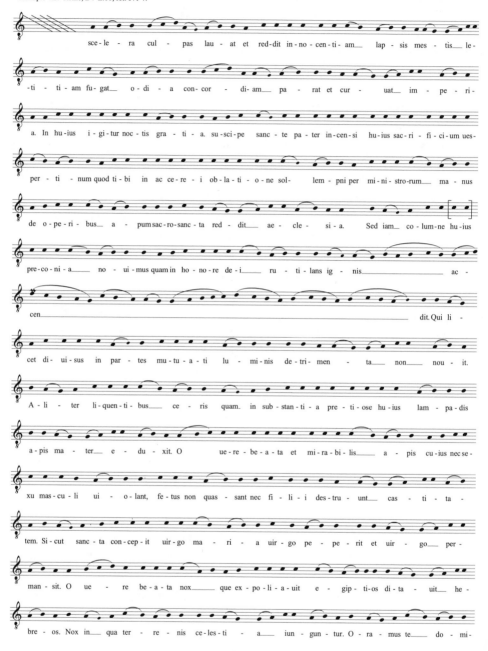

sce - le - ra cul - pas lau - at et red-dit in - no - cen - ti - am__ lap - sis mes - tis__ le-

-ti - ti - am fu - gat__ o - di - a con - cor - di - am__ pa - rat et cur - uat__ im - pe - ri-

a. In hu - ius i - gi - tur noc - tis gra - ti - a. su -sci - pe sanc - te pa - ter in - cen - si hu - ius sac - ri - fi - ci - um ues-

per - ti - num quod ti - bi in ac ce - re - i ob - la - ti - o - ne sol - lem - pni per mi - ni - stro-rum__ ma - nus

de o - pe - ri - bus__ a - pum sac-ro-sanc - ta red - dit__ ae - cle - si - a. Sed iam__ co - lum-ne hu - ius

pre - co - ni - a_____ no - ui - mus quam in ho - no - re de - i_____ ru - ti - lans ig - nis_____ ac -

cen_____ dit. Qui li -

cet di - ui - sus in par - tes mu - tu - a - ti lu - mi - nis de - tri - men - ta__ non__ nou - it.

A - li - ter li - quen - ti - bus__ ce - ris quam__ in sub - stan - ti - a pre - ti - ose hu - ius lam - pa - dis

a - pis ma - ter__ e - du - xit. O ue - re - be - a - ta et mi - ra - bi - lis__ a - pis cu - ius nec se-

xu mas-cu - li ui - o - lant, fe - tus non quas - sant nec fi - li - i des - tru - unt__ cas - ti - ta -

tem. Si - cut sanc - ta con - cep - it uir - go ma - ri - a uir - go pe - pe - rit et uir - go__ per -

man - sit. O ue - re - be - a - ta nox__ que ex - po - li - a - uit e - gip - ti - os di - ta - uit__ he -

bre - os. Nox in__ qua ter - re - nis ce - les - ti - a__ iun - gun - tur. O - ra - mus te do - mi-

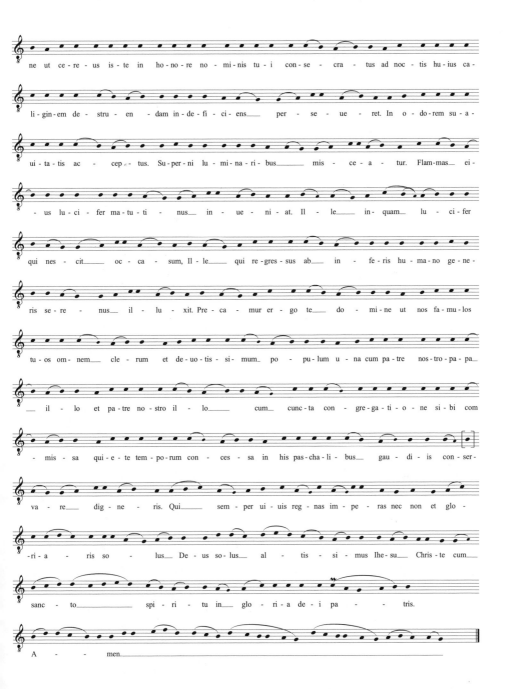

ne ut ce - re - us is - te in ho - no - re no - mi - nis tu - i con - se - cra - tus ad noc - tis hu - ius ca -

li - gin - em de - stru - en - dam in - de - fi - ci - ens___ per - se - ue - ret. In o - do - rem su - a -

ui - ta - tis ac - cep - tus. Su - per - ni lu - mi - na - ri - bus_____ mis - ce - a - tur. Flam - mas___ ei -

- us lu - ci - fer ma - tu - ti - nus___ in - ue - ni - at. Il - le___ in - quam lu - ci - fer

qui nes - cit___ oc - ca - sum, Il - le___ qui re - gres - sus ab___ in - fe - ris hu - ma - no ge - ne -

ris se - re - nus___ il - lu - xit. Pre - ca - mur er - go te___ do - mi - ne ut nos fa - mu - los

tu - os om - nem___ cle - rum et de - uo - tis - si - mum_ po - pu - lum u - na cum pa - tre nos - tro - pa - pa_

_ il - lo et pa - tre no - stro il - lo_____ cum_ cunc - ta con - gre - ga - ti - o - ne si - bi com

- mis - sa qui - e - te tem - po - rum con - ces - sa in his pas - cha - li - bus_ gau - di - is con - ser -

va - re___ dig - ne - ris. Qui_ sem - per ui - uis reg - nas im - pe - ras nec non et glo -

-ri - a - ris so - lus_ De - us so - lus_ al - tis - si - mus Ihe - su Chris - te cum_

sanc - to_____ spi - ri - tu in_ glo - ri - a de - i pa - tris.

A - men._

EXAMPLE 4.2. *Exultet* (incomplete), Rome, BV E.16, fol. IV. The text begins in the middle of the Preface. For a critical edition, see Kelly, *Exultet*, 280–86.

... scelera culpas lauat et reddit innocentiam lapsis, mestis letitiam fugat odia, concordiam parat et curuat imperia.

In huius igitur noctis gratia suscipe sancte pater incensi huius sacrificium uespertinum quod tibi in [h]ac cerei oblatione sollempni per ministrorum manus de operibus apum sacrosancta reddit aeeclesia.

Sed iam columne huius preconia nouimus quam in honore dei rutilans ignis accendit.
Qui licet sit diuisus in partes mutuati luminis detrimenta non nouit.

Alitur liquentibus ceris quam in substantia pretiose huius lampadis apis mater eduxit.
O uere beata et mirabilis apis cuius nec sexu masculi uiolant, fetus non quassant, nec filii destruunt castitatem.

Sicut sancta concepit uirgo Maria uirgo peperit et uirgo permansit.

O uere beata nox que expoliauit egiptios, ditauit hebreos, nox in qua terrenis celestia iunguntur.
Oramus te Domine ut cereus iste in honore nominis tui consecratus ad noctis huius caliginem destruendam indeficiens perseueret;
In odorem suauitatis acceptus superni luminaribus misceatur.

... evils, washes away sins, restores innocence to the fallen, bliss to the sorrowful, makes hatred flee, procures concord, and bows empires.

Therefore, in the grace of this night, receive, Holy Father, the evening sacrifice of this lighting, which, in this solemn offering of the candle [made] from the labors of bees, the holy church renders to you through the hands of [its] ministers.

But we already knew the praise of this column that the glowing fire ignites in honor of God, [the flame] which, although divided into parts, nevertheless knows no loss of its borrowed light.

It is fed by the molten waxes that the mother bee brought forth in the precious substance of this lamp.
O truly blessed and wondrous bee, whose chastity males do not violate by their sex; neither do offspring shatter it, nor do children destroy it,

just as the holy Virgin Mary conceived as a virgin, gave birth as a virgin, and remained a virgin.

O truly blessed night, which despoiled the Egyptians and enriched the Hebrews, night on which heavenly things are joined to earthly ones. We supplicate you, Lord, that this candle consecrated in honor of your name may persevere, unfailing, to destroy the darkness of this night, and that, received into the odor of sweetness, it may be mingled with the lights of heaven.

EXAMPLE 4.2. *Continued*

Flammas eius lucifer matutinus inueniat, ille inquam lucifer qui nescit occasum, ille qui regressus ab inferis humano generi serenus illuxit.	May the morning star find its flames, that morning star, I say, that knows no setting, that star who, having returned from the underworld, shone, serene, upon the human race.
Precamur ergo te Domine ut nos famulos tuos omnem clerum et deuotissimum populum una cum patre nostro papa illo et patre nostro illo cum cuncta congregatione sibi commissa quiete temporum concessa in his paschalibus gaudiis conseruare digneris.	Therefore, we ask you, Lord, to deign to preserve us in these paschal joys, your servants, all the clergy and the very devout people, together with our father the pope N and our father N with the entire congregation entrusted to him, granted the peace of ages.
Qui semper uiuis, regnas, imperas, nec non et gloriaris solus Deus solus altissimus Ihesu Christe cum sancto spiritu in gloria Dei patris.	You who ever live, reign, command, and are glorified, the one God, the only, the highest, Jesus Christ, with the Holy Spirit, in the glory of God the Father.
Amen.	Amen.

Another element that probably originated in southern Italy is a Latin transliteration of the Greek hymn *Doxa en ipsistis Theo* (Glory to God in the Highest), which was added to the Chigi manuscript in the last decades of the eleventh century (see ex. 4.3).[126] With a few omissions, the text corresponds to the Latin *Gloria in excelsis Deo* of the Mass.[127] This is the only known example of this text from central Italy. An earlier Greek Gloria text, widespread in the Carolingian empire, is very rare in Italian manuscripts.[128] Perhaps the

126. BAV Chigi C.VI.177, fol. 162r–v. The same anthology contains *Radix Iesse* (see chap. 1 in the present volume) and *Salue crux sancta.*

127. Various versions of the Gloria were sung in East and West from late antiquity; the earliest version of the common Latin text appears in the *Antiphonary of Bangor,* copied in Ireland around 690. For a summary of the history of the Gloria see Jungmann, *The Mass of the Roman Rite* 1:346–59.

128. See Atkinson, "Zur Entstehung und Überlieferung der *Missa Graeca*"; "The *Doxa,* the *Pisteuo,* and the *Ellinici Fratres*" and "Further Thoughts on the Origin of the *Missa Graeca.*" Of seventy manuscripts known to contain one or more Greek texts of a Mass Ordinary chant, just five are Italian, all from the north of the peninsula, and a *Doxa* text ap-

EXAMPLE 4.3. *Doxa en ipsistis Theo*, BAV Chigi C.VI.177, fol. 162r–v, compared to the Latin Gloria.

Doxa en ipsistis theo	Gloria in excelsis Deo	Glory to God in the highest,
kepigis yrini en · antropis · evdochian	et in terra pax hominibus bonae voluntatis.	and on earth, peace to men of good will.
eunumense eulogumense · Prosilugumense	Laudamus te, benedicimus te, adoramus te,	We praise you, we bless you, we adore you,
	glorificamus te.	we glorify you.
· eudar istomense ·	Gratias agimus tibi	We give thanks to you
Dyatyn meglasinsu doxan ·	propter magnam gloriam tuam.	on account of your great glory.
kyrie othee · Basileo · Epuranye	Domine Deus rex caelestis	Lord God, heavenly king,
theae patyr · pantocraton ·	Deus pater omnipotens	God, almighty Father,
kyrie yemonogeni ·	Domine fili unigenite	Lord, only-born Son
yosxpycte ·	Ihesu Christe	Jesus Christ,
kyrie otheo · oamostotheo · Oyos to patros	Dominus Deus, Agnus Dei, filius patris	Lord God, Lamb of God, Son of the Father,
· Oerontin · amartian to · cosmo ·	qui tollis peccata mundi	you who take away the sins of the world
eleyson ymas ·	miserere nobis	have mercy upon us,
Oerontin · amartian to · cosmo ·	qui tollis pecata mundi	you who take away the sins of the world,
Prodesche · Dinteisin ymon ·	suscipe deprecationem nostram	hear our prayer,
Ocathemenos · Endexian to patros ·	qui sedes ad dexteram patris	you who sit at the right hand of the Father,
eleyson ymas ·	miserere nobis	have mercy upon us,
ochisimonos · agyos symonos	quoniam tu solus sanctus	since you alone are holy . . .
[. . .] theos patros amin.	Dei patris. Amen.	of God the Father. Amen.

Doxa in the Chigi manuscript reached Farfa by means of a book or other gift presented to the abbey by a Greek-speaking patron from southern Italy, such as Argyros, whose letter of donation was copied both in Greek and in Latin transliteration.[129] The donation of Argyros and the ivory box given to the abbey by Maurus of Amalfi reflect influences that might also have brought the *Doxa* text to Farfa. It is unlikely that the *Doxa* came to Farfa through its connection with the duchy of Benevento; though some of the chants in the traditional Beneventan liturgy were performed in Greek, the *Gloria* was not one of them.[130] The presence of the *Doxa* in a collection of recently composed texts suggests that it was new to the abbey in the second half of the eleventh century.

In this chapter I have placed patronage in the framework of the broader influences on ritual and cultural production at Farfa in the eleventh century. Although many of the connections described here are indirect, influence from the empire appears in the Farfa manuscripts, and parallels can be drawn between the abbey's liturgical practices of southern Italian origin and gifts from southern benefactors. As in all medieval monasteries, the impact of patrons on ritual and the contexts for the transmission of liturgical influence varied. In addition to influences from the outside, concerns internal to the community shaped the liturgical compositions created there. The next chapter focuses on several works, unique to Farfa, that manifest political motivations and subtexts in the context of the divine office.

------

pears in only one (Berlin, Deutsche Staatsbibliothek, Hamilton 552, from ninth-century Milan). For a more extended discussion see Boynton, "Liturgy and History."

129. *CF* 2:202; Rome, BN Farfa 1, fol. 335v; *RF* 5:238; BAV Vat. lat. 8487, fol. 481v; and Supino Martini, *Roma*, 275 and Tav. LXXVI.

130. For instance, the brief processional antiphon *Doxa en ipsistis Theo/Gloria in excelsis Deo* was performed on Holy Saturday in the Beneventan liturgy, first in Greek and then in Latin. See Kelly, *Beneventan Chant*, 57, 90, 195, 214, 216, 269, 273.

CHAPTER 5 LITURGY, POLITICS, AND THE CONSTRUCTION OF HISTORY

Just as Farfa's liturgy reflected external influences ranging from Cluniac customs to southern Italian melodies, so too it was shaped by events and ideas originating in the internal politics of the monastery itself. In the eleventh and twelfth centuries, the cult of saints who had special importance to Farfa inspired the creation of new texts and chants that enriched the liturgical celebration of the feasts commemorating these saints. Memorization, writing, and annual communal performance of a saint's liturgy reaffirmed, in song and in the hagiographical lessons of Matins, the power and authority of the saints. For the monastic community, the ritual retelling of the stories of the saints through liturgical performance reinforced ideas about the abbey's traditional spiritual connection to certain saints. But the veneration of saints also served the more indirect purpose of establishing Farfa's ownership of saints' relics that were, in some cases, also claimed by other religious institutions. The material location of the body or relics of a saint venerated by the community played a crucial role in the abbey's perceived spiritual and material power. Consequently, the physical presence of a saint's relics in a church owned by Farfa not only fostered an increased liturgical emphasis on that saint in the abbey's textual and musical production, but could also implicitly support contentious claims over territories and churches elsewhere. These material claims were sometimes embedded in the creation and performance of the liturgy for saints venerated at Farfa. By interpreting liturgical compositions in the context of Farfa's history, we can reach beneath the surface of their words and imagine what connotations these texts might have had for the monks who performed them.

This chapter takes up the political dimensions and implications of poetic and prose works from eleventh- and twelfth-century Farfa. First, building on recent studies of the construction of Farfa's monastic identity through the production and reception of hagiography,[1] I situate the origins of some office hymns in the political context of controversies regarding the location and appropriation of saints' relics in churches near Farfa.

I revisit the Matins lessons for Thomas of Maurienne as a vivid instance of

---

1. Longo, "Agiografia e identità monastica"; and Susi, "Strategie agiografiche."

how the abbey mobilized the authority of the liturgy to support contentious claims. Finally, I turn to the political turmoil at Farfa in the early twelfth century, the context for the emergence of a new kind of song that exemplifies the general transformation of musical style occurring at the time. These examples illustrate the ways in which conflicting accounts of the past, whether played out between monasteries or within a single community, could lead to the production of new liturgical, hagiographic, and historical texts as a means of revising or reclaiming communal memory.[2]

New Hymns for Old Saints

Among the new liturgical compositions created at Farfa in the eleventh and twelfth centuries, the hymns of the divine office were the ones most likely to be performed by the entire monastic community. The hagiographic lessons were recited by a single reader, but hymns were sung from memory by the whole choir. Each strophe of text was sung to the same tune, facilitating the memorization of the poetry. The repetitiveness and relatively simple structure of office hymns made them a powerful conduit for the transmission of ideas and consequently an important didactic tool from the time of their introduction into the Latin liturgy by Ambrose of Milan (ca. 340–97).[3] The enduring fame of Ambrose's hymns caused some writers to refer to most hymns as *ambrosiani* (Ambrosian, meaning "by Ambrose"), an association that invested the genre with considerable authority.[4] Only the most erudite medieval scholars dared to point out that Ambrose could not possibly have written so many hymns of such varying quality.[5] The influence of the name manifested itself in stylistic continuity as well: for more than a millennium, poets favored the

2. For a recent case study of this process in monasteries see Lauwers, "Mémoire des origines."

3. According to Augustine's *Confessions* (*Confessionum libri XIII*, 191–92), Ambrose introduced hymns at Milan in 385. After he refused to offer the Arian imperial family a basilica for their own worship, his basilica was surrounded by imperial troops, while he sang hymns inside with the congregation.

4. The Rule of Benedict refers to *ambrosiani* in the hours of Matins, Lauds, and Vespers; see *RB 1980*, 202–3, 206–7, 208–9, 212–13. The commentary on the Benedictine Rule written by Hildemar of Corbie in the middle of the ninth century equates *ambrosianus* with *hymnus;* see his *Expositio Regulae*, 296. The Cistercians, in an attempt to render their hymn repertory authentically Ambrosian, assumed that all the hymns in the Milanese rite were composed by Ambrose; see Waddell, *The Twelfth-Century Cistercian Hymnal* 1:19–22.

5. Walahfrid Strabo, "Libellus de exordiis et incrementis quarundam in obseruationibus ecclesiasticis rerum," 506; see the translation and commentary by Harting-Correa, *Walahfrid Strabo's "Libellus,"* 161.

strophic form and characteristic metrical patterns of the hymns called "Ambrosian," which endowed the newly composed additions to the hymn repertory with a venerable and timeless character.

Hymns had become part of the monastic liturgy by the sixth century, when the rules of Caesarius of Arles and of Benedict mandated their performance in each of the hours of the office.[6] Between the ninth and the twelfth centuries, hymns were sung primarily in monasteries.[7] Why the hymn repertory became so closely associated with monasticism is not clear; it may have been a result of the widespread adoption of the Benedictine Rule, which prescribes the performance of a hymn at each hour of the office. Because most of the components of the office were fixed, hymns presented an opportunity to create new compositions, making them a natural choice for poet-composers at Farfa.[8] Hymns tended to be written in a few common meters (iambic, trochaic, or sapphic), so newly composed texts could easily be sung to existing hymn melodies. A hymn could be sung, at least in theory, to any tune that fit its metrical structure; the melodies were rarely written down before the twelfth century.[9] A new hymn for the feast of a saint would fit readily into the preexisting liturgy of the day by replacing a text taken from the common of saints. The common was a collection of liturgical texts and chants that would be performed on a saint's feast in the absence of liturgical compositions specifically composed for that saint; the material would be chosen according to the classification of saints as martyrs, virgins, confessors, or bishops.

In the central Middle Ages, proper hymns were sung only on the feasts of saints who were either universally celebrated (such as the Virgin Mary, John the Baptist, and Peter and Paul), of particular regional significance, or institutional patron saints. In a monastery, the composition of a proper hymn signaled a saint's importance to the community by rendering the liturgy of the day more specific to the individual being commemorated. Moreover, a proper hymn reaffirmed the saint's association with the monastery, whether it was an ancient link renewed by a rediscovery of the saints' relics or a more recent con-

6. Taft, *The Liturgy of the Hours*, 103–4.

7. Hymns were transmitted almost exclusively in monastic manuscripts until the twelfth century; see Jullien, "Les sources de la tradition ancienne."

8. Although the composition of a new hymn was the most common way to alter a preexisting office, entirely new offices for saints were also composed; for recent discussions of such offices see Goudesenne, *Les offices historiques;* Berschin and Hiley, *Die Offizien des Mittelalters;* and Fassler and Baltzer, *The Divine Office.*

9. For an overview of hymns and their transmission through the twelfth century, see Boynton, "Hymn, II. Monophonic Latin" and "Orality, Literacy."

nection arising from the translation of a relic to a new location. Understood in their historical context, some proper hymns can be seen as articulating an abbey's claims on the saint.

The fact that many saints did not have their own proper hymns clearly troubled some monks, such as Peter the Venerable, abbot of Cluny (1122–56), who stipulated that, on certain feasts, hymns from the common of saints should be replaced by more appropriate ones composed especially for the occasion. To this end, Peter himself wrote two new hymns for feasts of Saint Benedict.[10] In the eleventh century composers at Farfa expressed the same sense of liturgical propriety by creating new hymns for saints who were not elsewhere honored in this way. The new chants complemented the hagiographic narratives performed on the saints' feasts, enhancing or adding further detail to the commemoration of their lives and martyrdoms.[11] In addition to heightening the solemnity of the celebration, these hymns can be interpreted as subtly polemical statements stressing the abbey's possession of the saints' relics. For example, liturgical compositions for the Roman virgin martyr Victoria supported Farfa's claims on the relics of a relatively well-known saint, while the hymn for the eastern clerics Valentine and Hilarius illustrates the commemoration of saints who were venerated primarily at Farfa itself.[12] In both cases, Farfa claimed ownership of the churches in which the martyrs lay, and enterprising abbots translated the martyrs' remains to new resting places belonging to Farfa. Subsequently, disputes arose over the abbey's possession not only of the relics themselves but also of the churches from which they had been removed. Thus the hymns for Victoria and for Valentine and Hilarius, which are found only in manuscripts from Farfa, were created during periods when more than one institution asserted possession of the saints' bodies. In this context, it is all the more significant that these hymns are the only known examples of liturgical poetry for these saints from the central Middle Ages.

According to her *passio,* Victoria was a Roman virgin persuaded by her companion Anatolia to lead a life of chastity against the will of her betrothed,

10. "Statuta Petri venerabilis abbatis Cluniacensis IX (1146/7)," ed. Constable, in *Consuetudines Benedictinae variae,* 99 (no. 68). For the hymns and the letter introducing them see Peter the Venerable, *The Letters of Peter the Venerable,* 1:317–20 (letter 124).

11. These are not the only examples of hymn composition at Farfa in the eleventh and twelfth centuries. In fact, hymnaries from Farfa contain several apparently unique melodies set to widely diffused texts; see Boynton, "Glossed Hymns," 103–4. I focus here on the hymns for Victoria and Valentine and Hilarius because their texts are unique.

12. This is not the Saint Valentine commemorated on February 14 but a rather more obscure martyr bearing the same name.

Eugenius. She was sequestered at his property in Trebula Mutuesca, an ancient town in the Sabina not far to the east of Farfa, and when she refused to worship pagan gods, she was beheaded on his orders.[13] Although Victoria was widely venerated in the Middle Ages, proper chants for her feast are quite rare.[14] The composition of proper hymns at Farfa shows that her feast received particular emphasis there. At the abbey on her feast day (December 23), the *passio* was read at Matins; proper hymns were sung at Vespers, Matins, and Lauds; and proper prayers were recited during the office.[15] The hymns and prayers differentiated the liturgy for Victoria's feast from that of other virgin martyrs to a degree that was unusual at the time for this saint.

The three hymns for Victoria are transmitted in four Farfa manuscripts.[16] *Virginis Christi merita beatae,* a hymn for Vespers on the eve of the feast, is a composition in ten strophes of sapphic meter which tells the story of Victoria's conversion and exile, during which she killed a dragon that was menacing the population of Trebula (ex. 5.1). Its G-mode melody, apparently unique to Farfa, emphasizes motion around the final of G and a descent from C to G, twice turning around the intermediary pitch B. The hymn *Iam festa fulgent au-*

13. A *passio* is a narrative account of a saint's martyrdom. The *passio* of Victoria (*BHL* 8591) is edited in Mara, *I martiri della via Salaria,* 172–92; see also Paschini, *La "passio" delle martiri sabine Vittoria e Anatolia,* 33–44. Excavated ruins of the ancient Trebula Mutuesca can be seen near the church of Santa Vittoria, located in the town now known as Monteleone Sabino. On Trebula see, most recently, Fiocchi Nicolai and Ricciardi, *La catacomba,* 9–11.

14. On the early cult of Victoria see Fiocchi Nicolai and Ricciardi, *La catacomba,* 11–14; Mara, *I martiri,* 151–55; and Paschini, *La "passio,"* 3–5. The only other known proper hymn is *Virgo Christi Victoria,* which was added in the later Middle Ages to a fourteenth-century manuscript (edited in *AH* 43:304–5). Proper antiphons are found in an early twelfth-century manuscript from Rome (Rome, BV C.5, fols. 23v–24v).

15. Victoria's feast appears in the calendar of BAV Chigi C.VI.177, fol. 8r; the *passio* is found in the late eleventh-century office lectionary Rome, BN Farfa 32, fol. 8r–v. The feast of Victoria was indicated on other days in some early martyrologies; see Mara, *I martiri,* 153. The prayers appear in BAV Chigi C.VI.177, fol. 190r–v; Rome, BN Farfa 30, fol. 55v; Rome, BV C.93, fol. 29v; and Zurich, Zentralbibliothek, Rheinau 82, pp. 161–62.

16. The hymn is found in the eleventh-century manuscripts BAV Chigi C.VI.177; Zurich, Zentralbibliothek, Rheinau 82; and Rome, BN Farfa 4, from the early twelfth century. In the Chigi manuscript all three hymns are notated with staffless neumes. The hymn texts were also added in the thirteenth century to Farfa, Biblioteca dell'Abbazia, A.209, fols. 132v–133r, and staff lines were prepared for the first strophes of the first two hymns. The melody of *Virginis Christi* was notated, but the staves of *Assiste nunc* and the space intended for staves in the first strophe of *Iam festa* were left blank.

EXAMPLE 5.1. *Virginis Christi merita beatae*, BAV Chigi C.VI.177, fol. 122r–v.

Virginis Christi merita beatae
martyris nec non Victoriae sacrae,
socii, simul colite deuote
Deum laudantes.

Companions, honor piously together
the merits of the blessed and holy
virgin of Christ, Victoria,
praising God.

Quae fido corde suam castitatem
coniuge spreto monitis sacratae
collegae suae Anatoliae docta
obtulit Deo.

With a faithful heart she offered her chastity
to God, having spurned her spouse,
and having learned the advice of
her associate Anatolia.

Suis nam gazis egenis tributis
perosa sponso dehinc facta suo
seuera mente praediis squalidis
exsulem fecit.

For after bestowing his destitute treasures,
the despised bridegroom,
with terrible intent, made her
an exile among squalid farms.

Adfuit sibi ab illo solamen
qui nunquam in se deserit sperantes
incolis illis annotauit eam
quibus faueret.

She was sustained by consolation from the
one one who never deserts those who trust in
him; he pointed her out to those inhabitants
so that she would favor them.

Quorum rogatus furuo hinc de antro
expulit anguem a quo arcebantur
rapido cursu extra illis factus
uirtute Christi.

At their entreaty, she expelled from a dark
cave there a dragon by which they were
closed in; with swift progress it was forced
out by the power of Christ.

Post hinc per trinos annos in diuinis
laudibus uacans uirginibus gregatis
quas et instruxit studiis in quibus
beari queant.

Afterwards, for three years there she devoted
herself in divine praise to assembled virgins,
whom she also instructed in endeavors in
which they could be made blessed.

Toruus deinde spiculator adit
eam precatu adlocutus sponsi
ut ad culturam numinum fandorum
mentem mutaret.

Then the grim executioner arrived;
he spoke to her at the request of the
bridegroom, so that he might change her
mind to worship the prophecies of the gods.

Imperiali iussu ensem dextra
laeuaque gestans, monstrum exsecrandum,
quo sanctam spreto illico percussit
infelix illam.

By imperial order, bearing a sword in the left
and right hands, the evil monster, on behalf of
the one who had been spurned, the unhappy
man immediately struck that holy woman.

Sicque ad coeli moenia uolauit
martyrum choro pie socianda
uirginum sertis simul inserenda
martyr opima.

And thus she flew to the walls of heaven,
to be joined to the holy choir of martyrs,
at the same time to be inserted among the
garlands of virgins as a splendid martyr.

Gloria Deo, qui ubique potens,
Gloria nato simul atque sancto
Spiritui sit omnia per saecla
hic et in aeuum.

Glory be to God, who is powerful
everywhere, glory also to the Son and to the
Holy Spirit for all ages,
now and forever.

EXAMPLE 5.1. (cont.) Melody from Farfa, Abbazia A.209., f. 132v.

Vir - gi - nis— Chris - sti me - ri - tae be - a - te

mar - ti - ris— nec non vic-to - ri - e——— sa-cre

so - ci - i si - mul co - li-te de-vo - te

De - um lau - dan-tes.

rea, for Matins, comprises eight iambic strophes; only the text of this hymn survives (ex. 5.2).[17] These two hymns form a pair, contrasting in meter and thematic emphasis.[18] Both texts present Victoria as heroic and fearless, but whereas *Virginis Christi* focuses on her exploits and significance for the community, *Iam festa* dwells on the saint's virginity, referring to her exile and torture only in passing. Each of these hymns, in its own way, draws on the *passio* of Victoria. The narrative of *Virginis Christi* effectively condenses the plot of the *passio* and occasionally echoes its text.[19] The emphasis on virginity in *Iam festa* seems to have been inspired by the section of the *passio* in which Victoria's companion Anatolia and an angel extol virginity in eloquent monologues.[20] That the two hymns stress different aspects of Victoria's story may also reflect didactic considerations. Both the heroism and the chastity of the virgin martyr were models of behavior for the monks to imitate, but while

17. The texts have been published in *AH* 22:280–82; my exx. 5.1–3 are new transcriptions of the texts from the Chigi manuscript.

18. The pairing of a Vespers hymn in sapphic strophes and a Matins hymn in iambic strophes is a compositional strategy found in some eleventh-century saints' offices. The same combination appears in two hymns for the office of Saint Heribert of Cologne composed by Lantbert of Liège in the later eleventh century. In London, BL Add. 26788, the rubrics of these hymns explicitly identify their meters. See Lantbert of Deutz, *Lantbert von Deutz: Vita Heriberti,* 288–90.

19. Some of the textual echoes are *praediis squalidis,* in strophe 3 (Mara, *I martiri,* 184, 190); and *rapido cursu,* in strophe 5 (Mara, *I martiri,* 188: *cursu rapidissimo*).

20. Mara, *I martiri,* 174–82.

EXAMPLE 5.2. *Iam festa fulgent aurea*, BAV Chigi C.VI.177, fol. 122v.

Iam festa fulgent aurea
quae palma compsit inclita
saluo pudore candida
fuso cruore fulgida.

Now shine the golden feasts
which the glorious palm adorns;
radiant with intact chastity,
glistening with spilled blood.

Victorias Victoriae
Christi canamus milites
et uirginis certamina
pangamus almae fortia.

Let us, soldiers of Christ,
sing the victories of Victoria
and let us sound the courageous struggles
of the tender virgin.

Haec uirgo missa uirginem
moecho pudicam dedere
non esse crimen autumans
proci pati conubia.

This virgin was sent to give the chaste virgin
to a suitor, asserting
that it was not a crime
to suffer marriage with an adulterer,

Quod spreuit Anatholia
Christo pudorem dedicans
docetque sic Victoriam
sponsi cauere copula.

which Anatolia spurned,
dedicating her chastity to Christ;
and thus she taught Victoria
to fear the embraces of a bridegroom.

Imbuta sacro famine
tunc castitas Victoriae
calcauit mundi lubrica
et sanguinis dispendia.

Imbued with the holy discourse,
then the chastity of Victoria
trampled the dangerous things of the world
and the losses of blood.

Te, Christe, huius sedula
solum dilexit caritas
te concupiuit anxia
tormenta risit promptula.

You, Christ, her zealous
love alone adored;
troubled, she desired you;
resolute, she laughed at her torments.

Non urbis hanc seclusio
carcer, fames, metus, furor,
nec separarunt omnia
a te, Deus, supplicia.

Neither the closing off of the city,
prison, hunger, fear, fury,
nor did all tortures
separate her from you, God.

Huius precamur, meritis
culpae solutis uinculis
aeterna dones praemia
per saeculorum saecula.

Let us pray that, released from the
chains of sin by her merits,
you will give us eternal rewards
throughout the ages.

martyrdom represented a figurative state for the monks of Farfa, who were unlikely to undergo actual torture and death, the virtue of chastity was a much more pragmatic ideal.

Evidence of the monks' close study of the text of the hymns can be seen in the Latin glosses added in the eleventh century to the phrase *proci pati* in *Iam festa*.[21] A scribe at Farfa annotated the genitive *proci* between the lines with the gloss "that is, of the bridegroom" (*id est sponsi*) and the infinitive *pati* with "that is, to suffer" (*id est sustinere*). In the margin, the same writer added the two words *sponsus* and *procus*. Despite its two appearances in Isidore of Seville's seventh-century *Etymologies*, the term *procus* was quite rare in medieval Latin.[22] But one might conjecture that the author of *Iam festa* referred to Eugenius as *procus* to distinguish him from Christ, who in the *passio* is also called the *sponsus*.[23] This is clearly an allusion to the parable of the wise and foolish versions in Matthew 25, a passage that was read in the liturgy on feasts of virgins and therefore also on the feast day of Victoria. The philological approach to the text seen in this manuscript represents the intersection of didactic liturgical commentary with linguistic pedagogy that produced medieval hymnaries with Latin glosses.[24] As poems to be memorized and performed by all monks from an early age, and as the first examples of poetry to which students were exposed, hymns were an efficient tool for teaching Latin vocabulary, grammar, syntax, and prosody. Glosses on the hymns may reflect teachers' explanations of the texts to their students. The hymn glosses that appear in manuscripts from Farfa are predominantly synonyms, providing common equivalents for rare words.

Although *Virginis Christi* lacks unusual words, it features the enjambment

21. The two words are in close proximity so that they appear to form the word *procipati*, which might have confused a reader unfamiliar with the word *procus*.

22. Isidore of Seville, *Isidori Hispalensis Episcopi Etymologiarum* 9.7.7, 10.214. *Procus* is also found in the two works praising virginity written by the English monk Aldhelm of Malmesbury in the early eighth century; they refer to Eugenius as Victoria's *procus*: *Prosa de uirginitate*, chap. 52, and *Carmen de uirginitate*, line 2416; in Aldhelm of Malmesbury, *Aldhelmi Opera*, 309, 451.

23. Mara, *I martiri*, 178: "This virginity has deserved to have as a bridegroom the son of God" (*Haec virginitas sponsum dei filium habere promeruit*); "O virginity, you who do not have a mortal husband but an immortal bridegroom" (*O virginitas, quae mortalem virum non habes sed immortalem sponsum*).

24. See Boynton, "The Didactic Function." In this context it may be significant that the hymn for Saint Agatha, a virgin martyr, is the most heavily glossed of all those in a manuscript used by the nuns of Santa Giulia in Brescia in the eleventh century; see Boynton and Pantarotto, "Ricerche sul breviario di Santa Giulia."

and chiastic constructions typical of sapphic meter, compelling the reader to parse the phrases in order to follow the colorful plot. In the course of singing the hymns and memorizing them, monks would also internalize their basic metrical patterns. By singing *Virginis Christi* one learned the outline of a strophe in sapphic meter; the text of *Iam festa* embodied the rhythms of iambic dimeter.[25] Like many medieval hymns, those for Victoria reflect the adaptation of the meters of classical prosody to the principles of rhythmic poetry. Ancient Latin poetic meters are based on the lengths of syllables combined in a verse, but in rhythmic poetry the structure of each verse is based on an accentual pattern. Though medieval hymns imitate the accentual patterns of quantitative meters, as examples of rhythmic poetry they have a fixed number of syllables per line.[26] Nonetheless, rhythmic poetry occasionally includes vestiges of the classical quantitative meters; one of these features is elision, as illustrated by *Virginis Christi*. Each of the hymn's strophes reflects the accent pattern of a sapphic meter, despite an inconsistent observance of quantities. Most of the lines have a regular syllable count, reflecting the fact that the same melody was sung to each strophe, though there are exceptions in the form of hypermetric lines (containing extra syllables).[27] In the third line of strophe 2, the word *suae* must be elided to the immediately following word, *Anatoliae*, in order to maintain the correct number of syllables in the line. The second line of strophe 6 has twelve syllables instead of eleven, which a singer must accommodate by slightly altering the melodic distribution across the syllables of the text. This small irregularity of the rhythmic meter in *Virginis Christi* is not unusual for a composition of the eleventh century, when various forms of sapphic meter (both quantitative and rhythmic) were employed.[28]

In contrast to these two hymns, the third hymn in the group, *Assiste nunc precatibus,* is a modest composition consisting of four iambic strophes (see ex. 5.3).[29] This hymn may have been adapted from an earlier text from the common of virgins, for it does not allude to the events of Victoria's life and martyrdom, and only the inclusion of her name in the first strophe makes it specific to her feast. The fact that this hymn is not as extensive as the other two

25. In iambic dimeter, each verse has four iambs (short–long).

26. See Klopsch, *Einführung*, 8–16; Norberg, *Introduction*, 69–72 (translated in *An Introduction*, 100–105); and Norberg, *Les vers latins iambiques et trochaïques*, 17–124.

27. I am grateful to Gunilla Iversen for pointing out the implications of this hypermetricity.

28. On the variety of sapphic poetry in the Middle Ages see Stotz, *Sonderformen*.

29. *AH* 15:236–37; and BAV Chigi C.VI.177, 122v.

EXAMPLE 5.3. *Assiste nunc precatibus*, BAV Chigi C.VI.177, 122v.

Assiste nunc precatibus	Aid now the prayers
tuorum, uirgo, supplicum	of your supplicants,
Victoria, mirabilis	Virgin Victoria,
Deo atque placabilis.	wonderful and pleasing to God.
Quae mundi huius noxia	You who have rightly overcome
Tempsisti rite omnia,	the harmful things of this world,
Da nobis tecum perpetim	enable us to be joined to you
Iungi aeternis gaudiis	forever in eternal joys,
Ut Christo grates debitas	So that our fragility
Possit nostra fragilitas	may give the thanks owed to Christ
reddere in etheriis	[when we are] united with
associati angelis.	the angels in heaven.
Praestet hoc idem Dominus,	May God provide this very thing,
qui exstat indiuiduus	he who is indivisible,
cum patre et sancto spiritu	with the Father and the Holy Spirit,
mundi ante principium.	before the beginning of the world.

is not surprising in the larger scheme of the liturgical commemoration of Victoria; the office of Lauds in which it was sung is neither as long or as complex as Vespers and Matins, and rarely features proper hymns.[30] In any case, the very existence of three proper hymns for the saint clearly indicates the particular significance of her feast at Farfa.

The addition of musical notation to the hymns for Victoria may indicate that they were recent and unique compositions.[31] *Virginis Christi* and *Assiste nunc precatibus* are among the only hymns in the Chigi manuscript to which musical notation was added not long after the production of the manuscript in 1050–60.[32] As mentioned earlier, notating hymns was a rare practice at this time, because the melodies were learned through oral transmission. Because any hymn in sapphic meter could be sung to the same melody as any other sapphic text, a range of melodies could have been used for *Virginis Christi.*

30. I am grateful to Bill Flynn for pointing out this fact.

31. See Boynton, "Orality, Literacy."

32. The staffless neumes with which the melody has been notated in Chigi C.VI.177 cannot be transcribed, but those for *Virginis Christi* seem to correspond to the melody added in square neumes to Farfa, Abbazia A.209 during the thirteenth century.

But how can we understand the conspicuous importance of this local saint at Farfa? The emphasis on Victoria's feast at Farfa arose from the abbey's proximity to the church near Trebula Mutuesca, which had been built over the traditional site of the saint's tomb.[33] Farfa must have had control over this church by the ninth century, for the diplomas of Pope Stephen IV (814), Emperor Lothar (840), and Emperor Louis II (858) list it among the abbey's possessions.[34] In 934 Abbot Ratfred of Farfa took a drastic step to secure the abbey's claims on the relics of Victoria. Citing the destruction at Trebula Mutuesca wrought by Arab raids at the end of the ninth century, he transferred Victoria's body to safety in a priory of Farfa situated in the Piceno region of the Marches, where some of the monks had taken refuge in 899.[35]

After making their way through the Sabina, Umbria, and the Marches with Victoria's relics, Ratfred and his companions arrived on June 20, 934 at the priory, which then came to be known as Santa Vittoria in Matenano. As Patrick Geary has pointed out, among the many motivations for monasteries to acquire relics in the early Middle Ages the assertion of authority was of foremost significance.[36] In the instability of the early tenth century, the translation of Victoria's body to the Marches strengthened Farfa's influence there by enhancing the prestige of its priory and affirming the mother abbey's control over the cult of the saint. According to Hugh of Farfa's *Destructio*, Ratfred consolidated the abbey's properties in the area of Santa Vittoria and undertook a building campaign there; both actions reflected a broader agenda of enlarging Farfa's holdings.

> He gathered a great many other properties there as well, and in that same place, he himself had consecrated and newly constructed the same church and monastery that is clearly visible. Having restored these and many other ancient places and having recovered them for the said monastery, he began to be very powerful in the world and to enrich the monastery considerably, above all because he was the nephew of a powerful king, and very well versed in worldly knowledge.[37]

33. For the most recent analysis of the site see Fiocchi Nicolai and Ricciardi, *La catacomba*.

34. Paschini, "*Passio*," 10.

35. They had abandoned the monastery after seven years of Arab raids; see Hugh of Farfa, *Destructio*, in *CF* 1:36; and Schuster, *Imperiale abbazia*, 90–91.

36. Geary, *Furta Sacra*, 58, 85.

37. "Aliaque plura beneficia ibi contulit; et ipse in eodem loco de novo ecclesiam ipsam et monasterium consecrari et fabricari fecit, ut evidenter apparet. Hec et alia multa antiqua restaurata loca et dicto monasterio restituta, cepit valde potens secundum secu-

With the new church, its sacred space enhanced by the presence of the saint, Ratfred strengthened the presence of Farfa in the Piceno. The history of Farfa's landholdings in the Piceno confirms that the establishment of Santa Vittoria in Matenano was a significant factor in the expansion of the abbey's network of power.[38] Thereafter, both the priory and the saint remained important to Farfa. The abbey's possession of the priory was confirmed by the emperors Otto I (967), Otto II (981), and Otto III (996) and the empress Theophano.[39] The translation of Victoria to the Piceno was celebrated annually at Farfa on June 20, followed by a festive observance of the octave on June 27.[40] The hymns would have been performed on these occasions, as well as on Victoria's principal feast day of December 23.[41]

Farfa's ownership of the relics of Saint Victoria did not go unchallenged, however. A text written sometime before the mid-twelfth century reports that from her original resting place in the church at Trebula Mutuesca her body had been transferred for safety to another part of the catacombs beneath the church, implying that Abbot Ratfred had taken the wrong body to Santa Vittoria in Matenano.[42] Moreover, even as local tradition held that Victoria's body remained on its original premises in the church at Trebula Mutuesca, Farfa's pretensions to the ownership of that church seem to have been denied or forgotten. As early as 944 the bishop of the Sabina had claimed jurisdiction over the church. This was perhaps a gesture of defiance toward Farfa, which, though located in the Diocese of the Sabina, was independent of its bishop. By 1153, the church at Trebula Mutuesca had reverted to the Diocese of Rieti, whose bishop, Dodo, had it rebuilt. In 1156 Dodo consecrated an altar to the Virgin

---

lum esse, et monasterium satis locupletare; precipue quia potentis regis nepos et prudens valde in scienta seculari" (*CF* 1:36).

38. Schuster, *Imperiale abbazia,* 95–96. On Farfa's possessions in the Piceno see Pacini, "I monaci di Farfa nelle valli picene" and "Possessi e chiese farfensi nelle valli picene"; and Saracco Previdi, "Il patrimonio fondiario."

39. *CF* 1:36, 303; and Paschini, "*Passio,*" 11–13.

40. Paschini, "*Passio,*" 12; Schuster, "Martyrologium Pharphense, suite," 83; and Schuster, "De fastorum," 12. Strangely, the translation of Victoria does not appear in the calendar of Chigi C.VI.177.

41. Mara, *I martiri,* 156.

42. Leggio, "I rapporti agiografici tra Farfa e il Piceno," 89–99; Leggio, "Rieti e la sua diocesi," 141–51; and Paschini, "*Passio,*" 15. This text is preserved only in an early seventeenth-century manuscript: Rome, Biblioteca Alessandrina 96, fols. 491r–492v, 499r–500v; and Poncelet, *Catalogus codicum hagiographicum Latinorum bibliothecarum Romanarum,* 186. For a recent transcription see Fiocchi Nicolai and Ricciardi, *La catacomba,* 83–4.

Mary, and in 1171 he rededicated the renovated church to Saint Victoria. Dodo is thought to have removed the relics of Victoria from the catacomb and deposited them in the high altar dedicated to her. But although Dodo's two consecrations are documented by inscriptions that can still be seen in the church today, the inscription recording the deposition of Victoria's relics in the high altar is lost, and what is thought to have been its text is preserved only in a much later breviary from Rieti.[43]

That the location of Victoria's relics was disputed illustrates both the prestige inherent in the possession of saints' bodies and the expansion of networks of power that could be accomplished by translating relics and thus establishing new cult centers for their veneration. It may have been a proprietary sentiment that motivated the composition of the hymns in honor of Victoria found in eleventh-century manuscripts from Farfa. By giving Victoria special commemoration in the liturgy, these chants reaffirmed the importance of the saint's cult for the monastic community. The hymns, then, could have formed part of a broader hagiographic strategy by which the community at Farfa aimed both to appropriate Victoria's prestige and to expand its influence in central Italy.

Liturgical poetry for Saints Valentine and Hilarius relates to another instance of contested claims that similarly involves a translation of relics by an abbot of Farfa from one of the abbey's churches to another. Although the remains of Victoria were removed from their resting place to a priory of Farfa, the bodies of Valentine and Hilarius were translated to Farfa itself.

Valentine and Hilarius were saints from the east who were martyred on the via Cassia outside Viterbo under the emperor Maximian (286–305, 307–8). According to the Matins lessons for the feast of Thomas of Maurienne in the late eleventh-century office lectionary from Farfa, Abbot Sichardus (830–42) brought the bodies of the saints to Farfa from a church near Viterbo in the province of Tuscia Romana.[44] Adjacent to the abbey church he built an oratory with a crypt where the bodies of the saints were then buried along with the body of Saint Alexander, son of Felicity. Charles McClendon has identified this oratory with the apse, transept, and ring-shaped crypt that were added in the early ninth century to the west end of the eighth-century abbey church.[45]

---

43. Fiocchi Nicolai and Ricciardi, *La catacomba*, 13–14.

44. Rome, BN Farfa 32; see chap. 1 of the present volume.

45. Gilkes and Mitchell ("The Early Medieval Church at Farfa") argue for an earlier dating of the crypt, to the later eighth century during the abbacy of Probatus (770–81), based primarily on the style of the fragmentary frescoes. For McClendon's response see "The Carolingian Abbey Church at Farfa."

The remains of the crypt, which are visible below the south transept of the present abbey church, still preserve fragments of wall paintings that seem to have depicted scenes from the lives and martyrdoms of the saints interred there.[46] McClendon situates the construction of the crypt in the context of the emulation in Rome of the plan of Old Saint Peter's. A Roman design for the new complex at Farfa would have been suitable for housing the relics of Saint Alexander, who was brought from Rome with the permission of Pope Gregory IV in what was perhaps a political gesture on the part of the pope toward the imperial monastery.[47]

In the Matins lessons, Sichardus's building campaign is the material counterpart that parallels and supports the spiritual construction of the monastic community:

> For the increase of this place and of its inhabitants, he took pains to construct spiritual edifices; thus too he did not neglect to devote himself diligently to the temporal ones. For this oratory that we see in honor of the Lord Savior, joined to the church of Saint Mary, he himself constructed, with a crypt below, where he honorably interred the bodies of the martyrs Saints Valentine and Hilarius translated from the regions of Tuscia, along with the body of Saint Alexander, the son of Felicitas. And he applied himself [to rebuild] many other churches in the various places of that monastery, both to rebuild the ancient ones that were destroyed, and to construct very many new ones, as can be seen even today. And he acquired many other fine riches for this place, such as lands, various church ornaments, and innumerable other things.[48]

---

46. McClendon, *Imperial Abbey,* 30–31, 58–59. A comparable structure in a better state of preservation can be seen north of Farfa at Santa Maria di Vescovio, which served as the cathedral for the Diocese of the Sabina in the early Middle Ages. On annular or ring crypts in Rome and at Farfa during the Carolingian period, see Crook, *The Architectural Setting of the Cult of Saints,* 80–89; on the origins of the annular crypts at Rome see McClendon, *The Origins of Medieval Architecture,* chap. 2.

47. McClendon, *Imperial Abbey,* 158; and McClendon, "The Carolingian Abbey Church at Farfa." McClendon cites Smith, "Old Saints, New Cults," on the political ramifications of relic translations from Rome in the early ninth century, which provides a broader context for the transfer of Saint Alexander to Farfa.

48. "Ad augmentum quoque huius loci atque habitantium sicut spiritalia studebat edificia construere, ita et temporalia diligenter accomodare non neglegebat. Nam oratorium hoc quod cernimus in honorem Domini Salvatoris, adiunctum aecclesie sancte Marie, ipse construxit cum cripta deorsum, ubi corpora sanctorum Valentini et Hylarii martyrum de Tuscie partibus translata, cum corpore sancti Alexandri sancte Felicitatis filii co-

This account places Sichardus's translation of Valentine, Hilarius, and Alexander in the context of his other construction projects and, more generally, of his contributions to the prosperity of the abbey. Hugh of Farfa, in the *Destructio Farfensis,* portrayed Abbot Ratfred's building campaign at Santa Vittoria along similar lines a century later, in the context of the acquisition of wealth. Both texts emphasize that the physical evidence of these achievements, the newly built churches, were visible at the time of writing. Thus in the historical sources from Farfa, the translations of Victoria in the tenth century and of Valentine and Hilarius in the ninth are fundamentally linked to the creation of new sacred spaces that take their place among the abbey's spiritual and earthly possessions.

Long after the cult of Valentine and Hilarius was introduced at Farfa in the ninth century, Gregory of Catino refers to them in his *Chronicle,* where he reproduces the text of the Matins lessons and adds that Sichardus had brought the body of Saint Alexander from Rome to Farfa with the permission of Pope Gregory IV. The passages regarding Valentine and Hilarius in the Matins lessons and the *Chronicle* are based on the *passio* of the saints found in a manuscript, copied at Farfa between 842 and 898, which contains lives of the saints for reading during the liturgy.[49] Eleventh- and twelfth-century liturgical books from Farfa also refer to the abbey's ownership of the relics.[50] A proper prayer for the saints in the Chigi manuscript invokes the *patrocinia* of Valentine and Hilarius, "which we have taken care to gather in this present church," thereby affirming the bodily presence of the saints in the abbey.[51] A second prayer in the Chigi manuscript, also found in an early twelfth-century

---

niuncta, honorifice sepelivit. Multasque alias aecclesias per diversa loca istius monasterii et antiquas studuit reedificare destructas, et noviter plures construere ceu usque hodie apparet. Alia quoque multa bona huic loco acquisivit lucra, scilicet terras, ornamenta diversa aecclesiastica et alia innumerabilia" (*CF* 1:21–22).

49. Rome, BN Farfa 29. See Susi, "Strategie agiografiche," 280–81. The *passio* (*BHL* 8469–70) is edited in *AASS Novembris* 1:626–29. This text was also probably Gregory's source for the translation of Alexander from Rome with the agreement of Gregory IV. Although the cult of Valentine and Hilarius was rare in the eleventh and twelfth centuries, their *passio* also appears in a manuscript produced at Montecassino in the eleventh century (Rome, BV Tomus XVI, fol. 73r–v).

50. On the cult of the saints and their liturgy at Farfa see Schuster, "Martyrologium," 364–72.

51. BAV Chigi C.VI.177, fol. 218r: "Auxilium tuum domine nobis placatus impende, et intercedentibus sanctis tuis ualentino et hylario, quorum in hac presenti ecclesia pretiosa patrocinia colligere curauimus, fac nos ab omni aduersitate liberari et aeterna letitia gaudere cum illis." See Susi, "Strategie agiografiche," 281.

EXAMPLE 5.4. *Splendor decusque martyrum*, BAV Chigi C.VI.177, fol. 154r.

1	Splendor decusque martyrum	Splendor and glory of the martyrs,
2	robur deus fortissimum;	God, the mightiest strength;
3	uotis faueto supplicum	favor the prayers of the supplicants
4	melos tibi pangentium.	sounding songs to you.
5	Strophosus anguis prelia	The deceitful serpent
6	ausus subire maxima;	has dared to enter the greatest battles;
7	armat dolones tabidos	he arms his poisonous lances
8	tuos necare seruulos.	to kill your servants.
9	Nam bella mouit rabula	For the prosecutor began
10	in Ualentinum pluriam;	a great many attacks against Valentine,
11	Hilariumque parili	and he attacks Hilarius in
12	aggreditur certamine.	an equal combat.
13	Quos nulla quippe uerbera	Of course, no flogging,
14	equuleique gabula	nor the yoke of the rack
15	perterruerunt Herculi	frightened them so completely
16	beata colla flectere.	as to bend the blessed necks to Hercules.
17	Templi labuntur culmina,	The roofs of the temple give way,
18	prostrata quassant ydola,	and shatter the prostrate idols;
19	gemunt inormi pondere,	the foul divinities, having been brought low,
20	depressa foeda numina.	groan from the huge weight.
21	O mira, o prodigia:	O wonders, o marvels:
22	saxo ligati guttura	with their throats bound to a stone,
23	illesi, Christi gloriam	unharmed, they proclaim the glory of Christ
24	mersi fluentis predicant.	while submerged in the stream.
25	Post haec beatos perfidus	After these things, treacherous Demetrius
26	ferro truncat Demetrius;	finishes off the saints with a sword;
27	cęli capessunt premia	they seize the rewards of heaven
28	omnesque calcant dęmonas.	and trample on all demons.
29	Aeger dehinc Demetrius,	Then Demetrius, ill,
30	spelea sacra martyrum	goes to the sacred tomb of the martyrs;
31	adit; salutem nactus est,	he is healed,
32	demumque martyr factus est.	and finally is made a martyr.

EXAMPLE 5.4. *Continued*

33	Pręcemur ergo supplices	Therefore, let us pray, suppliants,
34	utrosque polo preclues	that both the glorious ones in heaven
35	piacla soluant noxia,	free us of harmful sins,
36	et alma dent suffragia.	and grant us sweet intercession.
37	Deo patri sit gloria . . .	Glory be to God . . .

14 equuleique] aequuleique *ms.*

Interlinear glosses:
2 robur: id est fortitudo
4 melos: id est dulces cantus | pangentium: id est canentium
5 strophosus: id est dolosus | anguis: id est serpens
6 subire: id est inire
7 dolones: id est dolosa gladio | tabidos: id est saucios
9 rabula: id est inuidus
14 gabula: id est patibula
15 Herculi: id est ydolo
17 labuntur: id est cadunt
18 quassant: id est confringunt
20 foeda: id est sordida | numina: id est dii
21 prodigia: id est signa
25 beatos: id est santos
27 capessunt: id est capiunt
30 spelea: id est sepulcra
31 adit: id est ibit | nactus est: id est consecutus
32 demumque: id est postremo
34 preclues: id est preclaros
35 piacla: id est crimina
36 suffragia: id est adiutoria

manuscript office book from Farfa, contains the less explicit phrase "whose patronage we venerate here" (*quorum hic patrocinia ueneramur*).[52] The unique liturgical commemoration of Valentine and Hilarius at Farfa is further illustrated by an office hymn, *Splendor decusque martyrum* (see ex. 5.4).The only known copy of this text appears in the Chigi manuscript, where it was added in the second half of the eleventh century to a group of recently composed

52. BAV Chigi C.VI.177, fol. 218r; and Rome, BV, F.29, fol. 25v.

chants.[53] Given the limited diffusion of Valentine and Hilarius's cult, and the fact that their bodies reposed in the abbey, it is very probable that the hymn was created at Farfa.[54] No other comparable composition is known from the central Middle Ages. That liturgical compositions specific to the feast of Valentine and Hilarius were apparently performed only at Farfa at this time suggests that the abbey enjoyed a veritable monopoly on the veneration of these saints.

In time, however, conflicting claims arose regarding the location of the saints' bodies. Local tradition in Viterbo maintained that Valentine and Hilarius had remained in their original resting place near the church of San Valentino until they were discovered and translated to the cathedral of Viterbo in 1303, whereupon they became the patron saints of that city.[55] Historians have proposed various explanations for the disagreement between the Farfa *Chronicle* and traditions in Viterbo: perhaps the bodies were translated from Farfa, or perhaps Abbot Sichardus had removed only parts of the saints' bodies to Farfa, leaving the remainder in place.[56] The monks of Farfa never relinquished their claims on Valentine and Hilarius, however, and they continued to honor the saints with proper liturgical texts. The two prayers in the eleventh-century Chigi manuscript, which refer to the saints' *patrocinia* (patronage) in "this present church," appear with slight but significant alterations in a breviary copied at Farfa in the early fifteenth century.[57] Changes in the later book suggest that the prayers were altered to heighten their emphasis on the material presence of the saints' bodies in the church. Where the eleventh-century manuscript refers to the saints "whose precious patronage we have taken care to gather in this present church" (*quorum in hac presenti ecclesia pretiosa patrocinia colligere curauimus*), the same text in the fifteenth-century breviary has "whose precious bodies rest in this present church" (*quorum in hac*

53. BAV Chigi C.VI.177, fol. 154r; see Boynton, "Liturgy and History."

54. Schuster ("Martyrologium Pharphense, suite," 366–68; and "Reliquie d'arte," 315–16) argues that, because of the lack of references to the crypt of Sichardus in the eleventh century, the saints' relics had been translated into the abbey church in the tenth.

55. See *AASS Novembris* 1:619–22. Two hymns for the 1303 translation (one of which states the date explicitly in the final strophe) are published in *AH* 22:131–32. Prayers for the translation are published in *AASS Novembris* 1:632–44.

56. Andreucci, *Notizie storiche dei gloriosi santi Valentino Prete e d'Ilario diacono martiri Viterbesi*, 89–114; LaFontaine, *Le traslazioni dei ss. martiri Valentino ed Ilario*, 11, 27; and Signorelli, *Viterbo nella storia della chiesa* 1:306–10.

57. Rome, BN Farfa 30, fols. 155v–156r. See also Schuster, "Spigolature farfensi, II," 51; and Schuster, "Martyrologium Pharphense, suite," 365–67.

presenti ecclesia pretiosa corpora requiescunt). The second prayer in the earlier manuscript concludes with the phrase "whose patronage we venerate here" (*quorum hic patrocinia ueneramur*), while the later version again substitutes *corpora* for *patrocinia*. Thus, in a manuscript copied at Farfa a century after the purported 1303 translation of the saints to the cathedral of Viterbo, the word *patronage* was replaced by the more concrete *bodies*. These changes to liturgical texts constitute the only indication that Farfa made any response to the claims on the saints by the clergy of Viterbo.

That the dispute over the location of the saints arose earlier than 1303 is suggested by a controversy over the ownership of the church of San Valentino in Silice, on the via Cassia near Viterbo. According to tradition, San Valentino had been built on the site of the saints' martyrdom, and it was apparently from this church that Sichardus removed their bodies between 830 and 842. Farfa's possession of the church was confirmed by a privilege of Otto I (967),[58] but in 1084, in the presence of Henry IV, Bishop Rainerius of Vercelli once again invested Abbot Berard I of Farfa with the church.[59] The emperor's participation suggests that he was called on to resolve a conflict; an imperial privilege of the same year had already reconfirmed Farfa's ownership of the church and its possessions.[60] Moreover, Gregory of Catino's account of the event in his *Chronicle* obliquely mentions a challenge to Farfa's claims on the church:

> When the emperor Henry was staying in the *burgus* of San Valentino and he heard that that same church belonged to our monastery *for certain*, on his order, the bishop Rainerius of Vercelli, with door and key, invested Abbot Berardus with that same church of San Valentino as the property of our monastery, as is contained in the privilege of the emperor Otto the Great.[61]

With this diploma Henry once again confirmed Farfa's ownership of the church on the via Cassia at the site of the saints' martyrdom. The idea that the

58. *RF* 3:111, no. 404; and *CF* 2:338–39: "Et cellam sanctę Marię infra castrum ueterbense. Et ęcclesiam sancti ualentini in burgo cum eorum omnibus pertinentiis."

59. *RF* 5:100, no. 1100.

60. *RF* 5:95, no. 1099; *Heinrici IV diplomata* 1:480–81 (no. 361): "Infra castrum biterbense aecclesiam sanctae Mariae. Et aecclesiam sancti ualentini in burgo, cum omnibus suis pertinentiis."

61. *CF* 2:179: "Cum autem Heinricus imperator in burgo Sancti Valentini maneret audiretque *pro certo* ipsam ęcclesiam huic monasterio pertinere, eo iubente, Rainerius Vercellensis ępiscopus per hostium et clavem investivit domnum B[erardum] abbatem de ipsa ęcclesia Sancti Valentini ad proprietatem huius monasterii, sicut continetur in precepto imperatoris maioris Ottonis" (italics mine).

emperor's intervention resolved a dispute is supported by an undated document of Henry V in the Farfa *Register* which refers to his father, Henry IV, as having "restored" to Farfa its property in the *burgus Sancti Valentini* near Viterbo.[62]

In 1139 Pope Innocent II gave the church of San Valentino to Azo, the archpriest of the church of San Lorenzo in Viterbo. Innocent had stayed in the village of San Valentino (around the church) during the papal schism of 1130–32; his sojourn there led to the destruction of the place by the troops of the antipope Anaclet II in 1137.[63] The papal bull of 1139 states that the church of San Valentino had been destroyed and neglected but then rebuilt by Azo; the document does not refer to the location of the saints' bodies, perhaps implying that they were still presumed to be at Farfa at that time.[64] In 1192 Viterbo became the episcopal seat of Tuscia Romana, which had previously been situated in the nearby city of Tuscania.[65] The process by which Viterbo became an episcopal seat may be linked to its reacquisition of the church of San Valentino and its subsequent claims on the relics of Valentine and Hilarius.

Given this background of apparent contestation, it is significant that the hymn and the prayers from Farfa are the only known liturgical compositions dating from the central Middle Ages that are specifically intended for the feast of Valentine and Hilarius.[66] This can be explained by the fact that the cult of the two saints was not widespread and by the supposition that the monks of Farfa had reason to create proper liturgical texts for them. The direct intervention of Henry IV suggests that the stakes were high and that the creation and performance of new hymns in this case, as in the case of Saint Victoria, was a gesture of appropriation through the liturgy.

The hymn for Valentine and Hilarius, *Splendor decusque,* presents a narrative based on the *passio* known at Farfa (see ex. 5.4). In contrast to the other, much briefer redaction of the saints' passion,[67] the longer *passio* contains a great many details that were probably added to the story at Farfa. Valentine (a

---

62. *RF* 5:304, no. 1319: "In burgo s. ualentini quam olim Beatae Mariae genitor noster Heinricus imperator, et omne monasterium restituit."

63. Signorelli, *Viterbo* 1:122.

64. *AASS Novembris* 1:613, 619.

65. Gams, *Series episcoporum,* 737. According to Andreucci (*Notizie,* 35–42), Viterbo was a bishopric before 1191, perhaps already in the eleventh century.

66. The cult of Valentine and Hilarius was not widespread, and few liturgical texts for their feast are known. The liturgical poetry for the saints in *AH* 22:129–32 is from the later Middle Ages and the early modern period.

67. The shorter *passio* is edited in *AASS Novembris* 1:625.

priest) and Hilarius (a deacon) are arrested by the proconsul Demetrius, who orders them to sacrifice to Hercules; they refuse and are tortured on the rack; as they pray, the temple of Hercules collapses in an earthquake. Demetrius then has the saints thrown into the Tiber with their necks bound to heavy millstones, but an angel rescues them. They return to Demetrius and are decapitated at his order. Later Demetrius becomes ill and goes to the saints' tombs to ask for their aid; he converts to Christianity and then becomes a martyr when he is executed on the instructions of the emperor.

Found only in the Chigi manuscript, the hymn *Splendor decusque* seems to have been composed at Farfa. The relative lack of errors in the text suggests that the redaction of the hymn was fairly close in time to the copying of the manuscript. Although the frequent use of end rhyme suggests a date of composition possibly as late as the middle of the eleventh century, the rarefied lexicon of the hymn creates an impression of greater antiquity. Words such as *dolones, tabidos, rabula, gabula, spelea,* and *capessunt* are unusual in Christian Latin. *Strophosus,* a Graecism favored by Insular Latin authors of the early Middle Ages, may be intended to evoke the saints' eastern origins.[68] All these unfamiliar terms are among the many that are glossed with more common equivalents between the lines of the text. The numerous glosses added to the hymn reflect its abstruse vocabulary as well as the particular importance of these saints for the abbey. The fact that the melody of *Splendor decusque* does not appear in the manuscript is not unusual; as we saw in the case of the hymns to Saint Victoria, the text could have been sung to any tune that fit its metrical structure. Sung in the divine office, the hymn would join the prayers to the saints in reaffirming their continued physical presence at Farfa despite challenges from the clergy of Viterbo.

The hymns for Victoria and for Valentine and Hilarius were created in the context of claims on saints' relics and on their churches. Abbots of Farfa removed relics to the monastery's own churches, at the same time affirming jurisdiction over the churches where the saints had previously lain. Another example of this phenomenon is the cult of the martyrs Getulius, Cerealis, Amantius, and Primitivus. In 724 the church containing the relics of San Getulio was conceded to Farfa by the Lombard duke Transmundus II at the request of Abbot Lucerius. Lucerius then established a colony of monks at

---

68. Forms of the word *strophosus* appear in four works of Sedulius Scotus: *Carmina,* II.1.26 and II.21.24, in *MGH Poetae latini medii aeui* 3:167, 188; *MGH Epistolae* VI:203; *Liber de rectoribus christianis,* 42; and "Aenigmata Bonifatii," *De uitiis* 3, vv. 21 and 56, in *Collectiones aenigmatum,* 319, 323.

the saints' tomb.[69] Prayers in the eleventh-century Chigi manuscript state that the bodies of the martyrs lay in the church at Farfa, where they had been translated, probably in the tenth century.[70] These proper prayers lent authority to the association of these saints with Farfa.

Thus the composition of hymns could encode a response to political and hagiographic challenges to the legitimacy of Farfa's claims on saints. Perhaps the choice of the hymn, a characteristically monastic genre, was a calculated gesture on the part of the unknown poets who created these works. Not only did the repetitive strophic form of their melodies help the monks commit these texts to memory and internalize their messages; the choral performance of hymns also ensured that the entire community sang them together, both hearing and actively proclaiming the stories of these saints whose relics were preserved in a church belonging to Farfa.

Constructing History through Liturgy

The commemoration of another saint important to Farfa, the second founder Thomas of Maurienne, reveals a more explicit way in which the monastery could claim ownership of a church through the liturgy. The Matins lessons from Farfa for Thomas's feast day constitute a narrative text that eloquently demonstrates the political potential of the divine office. As seen in chapter 1, this text recounts the abbey's history from its refoundation by Thomas to the early ninth century. Although preserved only in a liturgical book, an office lectionary (Rome, BN Farfa 32), the lessons present a strange hybrid of history and sacred biography which, through performance, commemorated the life of Thomas of Maurienne both as an individual and in the context of his illustrious role in the community's history. As such, it also constitutes a rhetorical gesture asserting Farfa's jurisdiction over the southern Italian monastery of San Vincenzo al Volturno.

The narrative links the two abbeys through the foundation of San Vincenzo by Thomas of Maurienne, who, while passing through the Roman province of Samnium on his way back from the East, found an oratory dedicated to Saint Vincent, revealed to him by the Virgin Mary in a vision. According to this text, the site, flanked by dense forest on both sides of the river Volturno, was uninhabited except for wild beasts and robbers' dens.[71] Some time later, Thomas

69. Cignitti, "Getulio, Cereale, Amanzio e Primitivo"; *RF* 2:36, 3:124; and Susi, "I culti farfensi," 64–68.

70. BAV Chigi C.VI.177, fol. 208v. Getulius and companions also appear in capital letters in the calendar of the Chigi manuscript (June 9).

71. *CF* 1:13–14: "Siquidem isdem vir Domini dum de Orientis partibus Italiam reme-

warmly received Paldo, Taso, and Tato, three young noblemen from the duchy of Benevento who had stopped at Farfa on their way to Gaul. Thomas advised them to found a community at the oratory he had discovered.[72] Paralleling Thomas' vision, Gisulf I, the Lombard duke of Benevento, had a dream in which he saw Thomas accompanied by the Virgin Mary. Mary instructed Gisulf to grant any requests made by Thomas, whom she described as a pilgrim and a holy man who would pray on the duke's behalf. The next day Gisulf instructed his ministers to seek out and bring into the palace a tonsured pilgrim clad in monastic clothing. The ministers found the pilgrim, Thomas, without difficulty, for he was standing outside as if awaiting them. Upon seeing Thomas, Gisulf threw himself to the ground and venerated him, promising to give him whatever he might request; Thomas asked Gisulf to concede to him the oratory of Saint Vincent so that he could establish a monastery there.[73] Having received the donation charter, Thomas then brought the three young men to the site, instructed them on the construction of the new monastery, and returned to Farfa,

> but over the course of many years the aforementioned men and their successors came at mutually agreed times to the abbey of Saint Mary the mother of God, and they carried out their weekly duties in the kitchen just as the other brothers in that monastery were doing; and for many years the monastery of Saint Vincent continued to be administered through the arrangements made by Abbot Thomas and his successors.[74]

The stipulation that the monks of San Vincenzo should perform kitchen service at Farfa (perhaps according to the Rule of Benedict) implied that they inherently belonged to the monastic community at Farfa.[75] This statement expresses a hierarchical relationship between the two abbeys, however, for which

---

asset, per Samnii provinciam habuit iter; in qua videlicet super Vulturni fluminis ripam, a mille fere passibus a quo initium sumit, repperit in honore beati Vincentii martiris oratorium dedicatum, quod densissima quoque ex utraque parte fluminis silva ambiebat, et nulla ibidem erat habitatio preter ferarum ac latronum fortasse latibula."

72. *CF* 1:9–14.

73. *CF* 1:15.

74. *CF* 1:16: "at vero memorati viri successoresque eorum multa per annorum curricula congruis temporibus ad monasterium sancte Dei genitricis Marie veniebant, et ebdomadas suas in coquinae officio sicut et alii fratres in ipso faciebant monasterio; atque per dispositionem domini Thome abbatis successorumque eius ipsum sancti Vincentii monasterium ordinabatur."

75. Regulations for weekly kitchen service are in chap. 35 of the rule (*RB 1980*, 232–35).

there is no historical basis in the eighth century or, indeed, at any time before the imperial diplomas of the late eleventh century.[76] The descriptive detail of kitchen service at Farfa performed by the monks of San Vincenzo was more likely intended to reinforce an image of subordination that would resound both figuratively and literally when the narrative was recited at Farfa every year during Matins on the feast of Thomas of Maurienne.

In the medieval office of Matins, each of the lessons was followed by a responsory, and the lessons themselves were chanted to a reciting tone somewhere between speech and song. The alternation of lessons and responsories, the linear narrative progression of the hagiographic lessons of Matins, and the chants that were sometimes drawn from other offices or from the common of saints, reflected and played off one another, creating a complex nexus of meaning. Even chants from the common of saints served a hagiological purpose, for they signaled the membership of the saint in a group, reaffirming through this typology the saint's possession of virtues characteristic of that group. Thus the choice of the responsories for Matins created intricate networks of associations that intersected with and added to both the historical and symbolic dimensions of the lessons.[77]

The complete office with the chants for Thomas of Maurienne does not appear in any extant manuscript from Farfa, but it may have resembled the one preserved in an early twelfth-century breviary from the abbey of Sant'Eutizio in Norcia, an important Benedictine monastery north of Farfa.[78] The chants in this office derive mostly from the common of confessors, with some antiphons and responsories proper to Thomas after the fourth and twelfth lessons.[79] However, the hagiographic connections between Farfa and Sant'-

76. Schuster, "Spigolature," 23–24.

77. A good example of this layering is the medieval monastic office of Saint Benedict. Although this office exhibits some variation from place to place, the readings are generally from the second book of Gregory the Great's *Dialogues*, a text that was the source of most but not all the chants. Although the readings follow the order of the narrative, the chants generally do not; for transcriptions of the chants in six manuscripts see *CAO* 2:210–15, 243–45; other manuscripts containing this feast are inventoried in the Cantus database, http://publish.uwo.ca./~cantus/, accessed June 25, 2003. See also Steiner, "The Music for a Cluny Office." The Benedict office from Farfa survives incomplete in the fragment Farfa, Archivio dell'Abbazia, AF 338 Musica IV.

78. Rome, BV C.13, fols. 55v–58v. On this manuscript see Ledwon, "The Winter Office" 1:38–67.

79. The proper chants are indicated in the breviary by their incipits; because they seem to be unique to this manuscript from Sant'Eutizio, they cannot be reconstructed on the

Eutizio in this period are not limited to this office.[80] Saint Euticius, the patron saint of Sant'Eutizio, had been venerated at Farfa since the early Middle Ages, as attested by a *passio* of the saint written there. This veneration, according to Eugenio Susi, exemplifies Farfa's strategy of appropriating local devotions and often rewriting the origins of the saints in question to suit Farfa's politico-religious needs.[81] One sign of the enhanced relations between the two abbeys and of the veneration of Saint Euticius at Farfa is an episode reported by Gregory of Catino in the *Chronicle*. In a dream, one of the monks of Farfa saw Saint Euticius tell an ancestor of Abbot Berard III that he would favor the abbot's endeavors if Berard celebrated the saint's feast day with great solemnity. The feast of Euticius was also the day on which Berard had assumed the abbacy.[82] Thus the dreamer, according to Gregory, establishes a connection between the two abbeys by symbolically joining the veneration of the patron saint of Sant'-Eutizio with the installation of the abbot of Farfa.

The community of Sant'Eutizio also commemorated some saints of particular importance at Farfa, including Valentine and Hilarius as well as Victoria.[83] It is not happenstance, then, that the office for Thomas of Maurienne is preserved in a manuscript from Sant'Eutizio. The lessons of Matins in this office, however, do not simply reproduce the ones in the late eleventh-century lectionary from Farfa (Rome, BN Farfa 32); the text is distributed differently and lacks several of the episodes concerning the three young men from Benevento.[84] Significantly, the twelfth lesson in the Sant'Eutizio manuscript omits the statement that San Vincenzo was subject to Thomas and his successors, a sentence found only in the Farfa office lectionary. As Umberto Longo has pointed out, the sections lacking in the Sant'Eutizio breviary are precisely those that make the most convincing case for Farfa's claims on San Vincenzo as described by Gregory of Catino.[85]

In the *Chronicle,* Gregory summarizes the foundation narrative of San

---

basis of other manuscripts. Ledwon ("The Winter Office" 2:74–79) presents a complete inventory of the chants for the office (First Vespers, Matins, Lauds, and Second Vespers) on the vigil and feast of Thomas.

80. On the relationship between Farfa and Sant'Eutizio in this period, see Longo, "Dialettiche agiografiche," 107–23; and Pirri, *L'abbazia di Sant'Eutizio,* 31.

81. Susi, "L'agiografia picena tra l'Oriente e Farfa," 57–84.

82. *CF* 2:228. On the context of this passage see Longo, "Dialettiche agiografiche," 114–16.

83. Longo, "Dialettiche agiografiche," 121–22; and Ledwon, "The Winter Office" 1:59.

84. Longo ("Agiografia e identità monastica," 339) discusses the relationship between the texts in BV C.13 and BN Farfa 32.

85. Ibid., 340.

Vincenzo as it appears in the Matins lessons, adding that the abbey had been subject to Farfa until it was, in Gregory's account, misguidedly granted its independence by Abbot Fulcoald of Farfa (740–59).[86] To demonstrate the jurisdiction of Farfa over San Vincenzo, Gregory cites a series of passages from scripture and canon law, including twelve texts from the *Collectio canonum* he had compiled for the Farfa *Register*.[87] Near the conclusion of his tirade, Gregory states that soon after the loss of San Vincenzo, Farfa's property had become so diminished that the abbey, far from being able to acquire distant possessions, was unable even to maintain those in its vicinity. Gregory goes on to admonish the reader to attend to the recovery of Farfa's lost property, citing a decretal of Pope Hilary (461–68) stating that the faults of an official must be emended by his successor and one by Pope Sylvester (314–35) that goods taken away from a monastery must be restored. Gregory further implies that the removal of San Vincenzo from Farfa's jurisdiction was invalid because it constituted alienation of church property without written justification.[88] This passage can be interpreted as a vain attempt to incite Berard III, the abbot of Farfa at the time Gregory was writing the *Chronicle*, to act on Gregory's contentions. It is more likely, however, that it reflects Gregory's wish to memorialize his fabricated claims on San Vincenzo in order to influence future abbots in their perception of Farfa's relations with San Vincenzo.[89]

The claims established by the foundation narratives of San Vincenzo in the Matins lessons and in Gregory's *Chronicle* are also found in the privileges of Henry IV and Henry V, both of which included San Vincenzo and all its holdings among Farfa's properties.[90] Because none of the imperial privileges before 1084 refer to San Vincenzo as a possession of Farfa and because the only previous textual source for this assertion is the Matins lessons, Pierre Toubert has concluded that it was Gregory himself who revived a claim that had been

86. *CF* 1:141. Because neither the Matins lessons nor the Farfa *Register* refer to Fulcoald's actions with regard to San Vincenzo, Gregory's source of information for this is unknown.

87. *CF* 1:142–44; see *Collectio canonum*, 111–12.

88. *CF* 1:146–47.

89. It should be noted that in the prologue to the Chronicle (*CF* 1:114) Gregory said he would strive not to attribute anything fraudulently to the monastery.

90. *CF* 2:175, 282; *RF* 5:97, no. 1099; *RF* 5:304, no. 1318: "in Samnii partibus, super Vulturnum flumen, monasterium Sancti Vincentii cum castellis et omnibus suis pertinentiis, quod sanctissimus Thomas Pharphensi monasterio a duce Gisulfo per preceptum acquisivit."

made in the original *Constructio*.[91] Indeed, Gregory had ample opportunity to interpolate San Vincenzo among Farfa's possessions when he copied the imperial diplomas in the *Register*.[92]

No evidence for Farfa's claims appears in documents from San Vincenzo.[93] The San Vincenzo chronicle, written by the monk John during the second and third decades of the twelfth century, incorporates two earlier texts that recount the foundation of the abbey by the three brothers from Benevento on the advice of Thomas of Maurienne. The first was written by Ambrosius Autpertus, abbot of San Vincenzo in the 770s, and the second by a priest named Peter in the late eleventh century.[94] John copied these two versions into his chronicle in the early twelfth century, adding his own redaction of the story after the two preexisting texts.[95] This triple foundation narrative lacks the colorful episodes, such as the dream of Gisulf, that support Gregory of Catino's contentions. Furthermore, no mention is made of San Vincenzo's juridical dependence on Farfa. Instead, John's chronicle relates that Thomas simply described the location of the oratory of Saint Vincent to the three Beneventans, who subsequently took up an ascetic existence there. Thomas's role is limited to the choice of the location, for according to Ambrosius Autpertus and John, and in contrast to the apprenticeship model described by Gregory of Catino, Thomas neither accompanies the three men to the site nor maintains a master-disciple relationship with them after they have established their new community. The priest Peter's account lies somewhere in between those of John and Gregory of Catino. He makes reference to a visit by Thomas to San Vincenzo to advise the brothers, but, as if to affirm the independence of San Vincenzo from any other monastery, this version of the foundation concludes

91. Toubert, *Structures* 1:80–81.

92. Federici ("L'origine") suggested in 1940 that the passages in the diplomas and in the Matins lessons affirming Farfa's claims on San Vincenzo were interpolations of the eleventh century, but he did not state explicitly that they were the work of Gregory of Catino.

93. Felten, "Farfa und S. Vincenzo al Volturno," 25–26. As noted by Longo, references to a relationship between Farfa and San Vincenzo appear in documents regarding Sancta Maria in Apinianicis, a female monastic community dependent on Farfa ("Agiografia e identità monastica," 339 n. 90: *RF* 2:199; 3:115–16, 123, 136; 5:97, 274, 302, 304).

94. For the foundation narratives by Ambrosius Autpertus and Peter, see *Chronicon Vulturnense* 1:104–11, 124–29.

95. The beginning of John's chronicle is *Chronicon Vulturnense*, 145. On the compilation see Sennis, "Tradizione monastica," 194–201; and Wickham, "The *Terra* of San Vincenzo al Volturno in the 8th to 12th centuries," 229.

with a description of Gisulf's patronage of the abbey, followed by purported transcriptions of diplomas (both false) from Gisulf and Charlemagne. These falsifications may constitute a response to Farfa's claims on San Vincenzo as indicated in the late eleventh-century imperial diplomas copied in Gregory's *Register.* Given that the original diploma from Gisulf was lost and that there were no diplomas from Charlemagne, Peter might have found it expedient to invent them.[96] Perhaps he was aware that it was the early privileges from the local Lombard duke and from Charlemagne that were the basis of Farfa's independence. Indeed, Farfa and San Vincenzo had many things in common: both attained importance in the eighth and ninth centuries through the patronage of local Lombard nobility; both were abandoned by the monks from the time of the Saracen raids at the end of the ninth century and were reinhabited by their respective communities more than thirty years later; and both sought to expand and rebuild in new locations at the end of the eleventh century. Farfa's building campaign on Monte Acuziano was abandoned, but the new building complex of San Vincenzo was completed in the early twelfth century.

The compilation of the San Vincenzo chronicle coincides with the period of the building of the new monastery. An unfinished version of John's text was presented to Pope Paschal II in 1117 when he consecrated the new abbey church. After its consecration, the pope conceded a privilege to the abbey guaranteeing its independence from secular authorities and the local bishop while subjecting it directly to the Apostolic See. According to Paolo Delogu, the community sought to define its new identity through both the physical reconstruction of the abbey and the historical reconstruction of its past. The compilation of its chronicle and the retelling of its origins therein were part of this process of self-determination and renewal.[97] Both the diplomas forged by Peter and John's version of the foundation narrative need to be seen in political context and can be interpreted as responses to Gregory's nearly contemporaneous account.[98] As Richard Hodges has pointed out, the subtext of the

96. Delogu, "I monaci," 50–51.

97. Ibid., 45–47.

98. According to Federici (*Chronicon Vulturnense* 1:xxi–xxii), John's chronicle was a response to Farfa's claim of jurisdiction over San Vincenzo from its foundation to the mid-eighth century, a claim recently supported by Sennis, "Tradizione monastica," 200. However, Toubert (*Structures* 1:79–83) concludes that Gregory and John worked simultaneously, though without knowledge of each other, during a period of hostile relations between the abbeys. Because neither chronicle can be dated with absolute precision, chronology alone cannot rule out the possibility that John had some knowledge of Greg-

differing foundation legends of San Vincenzo is the parallel between Farfa, an important abbey on the frontier of the Lombard duchy of Spoleto, and San Vincenzo, on the frontier of the Lombard duchy of Benevento.[99] In light of the Lombard patronage of both abbeys, it is particularly significant that Thomas's solicitation of funds from Gisulf I is absent from the account by Ambrosius Autpertus, which is the earliest text relating to the foundation of San Vincenzo and was apparently one of the sources for the Matins lessons.[100]

The story of Gisulf's dream clearly originated at Farfa, where it served to support the imperial abbey's claims over San Vincenzo.[101] The Matins lessons from Farfa present the foundation of San Vincenzo as primarily a result of negotiation between Thomas and Gisulf (and only secondarily a result of Thomas's advice to the three Beneventans). It was the supernatural character of Gisulf's first encounter with Thomas in the company of the Virgin Mary that invested Thomas, and by extension Farfa, with spiritual authority, making Thomas in some sense the true founder of San Vincenzo. In his *Chronicle*, Gregory of Catino repeatedly invokes Gisulf's dream, stating that the abbey of San Vincenzo was granted to Thomas by Gisulf on the order of the Virgin Mary and without the direct involvement of the three Beneventans. Gregory describes Fulcoald as acting "inadvisably" (*inconsulte*) in liberating San Vincenzo, for he violated the privilege granted by Duke Faroald to Thomas of Maurienne in 705, a privilege which protected Farfa from the alienation and usurpation of its property.[102] By casting both Gisulf and Faroald as patrons of Farfa with a direct connection to Thomas, Gregory strove to present a strong case for Farfa's jurisdiction over San Vincenzo. Gregory's contentions found support only in the two diplomas he had himself transcribed into the *Register* and in a sentence in the Farfa lectionary's version of the Matins lessons for Thomas of Maurienne which concluded: "and for many years the monastery of Saint Vincent continued to be administered through the arrangements made by Abbot Thomas and his successors."[103]

---

ory's *Chronicle*. Delogu ("I monaci," 50–51) argues that the priest Peter was aware of Farfa's claims on San Vincenzo and wrote his account of the foundation in response to them.

99. Hodges, *Light in the Dark Ages*, 25.

100. Toubert (*Structures* 1:82) noted that the author of the *Constructio* used Ambrosius Autpertus's text.

101. Ugo Balzani pointed this out in *CF* 1:16 n. 1.

102. *CF* 1:142–43.

103. *CF* 1:16.

The appropriation of authority over San Vincenzo in documents from Farfa is one instance of a broader phenomenon in the eleventh and twelfth centuries, when varying versions of a foundation legend could lend authenticity to conflicting claims made by different abbeys. Such disputes could easily arise when, as in the case of Farfa and San Vincenzo, one monastery claimed possession of another as a dependency in its archival documents and history writing, while the subjugated abbey represented itself as independent through its own version of the foundation legend.[104] Both such foundation narratives and legal documents such as diplomas and charters—texts not ordinarily considered liturgical—acquired a powerful ritual function when read aloud during services in a monastic church.[105] The lessons for Thomas of Maurienne are more historical than hagiographic in character; thus, performing them on his feast enhanced the role of the foundation narrative as an affirmation of Farfa's jurisdiction over San Vincenzo.[106]

Scrutinizing Farfa's glorious Carolingian past and comparing it to an uncertain future, Gregory represents the "loss" of San Vincenzo as emblematic of poor abbatial stewardship. Abbot Fulcoald's decision in the mid-eighth century was precisely the kind of misguided judgment that Gregory most feared from the abbots of Farfa in his lifetime. It was for this reason that he had begun compiling the Farfa *Register* in 1092, during the abbacy of Berard II, and the *Collectio canonum* soon after the death of Abbot Oddo in 1099. Thus the long tirade about San Vincenzo was intended as an admonition to the abbots of Farfa to manage its patrimony with care. Even Gregory must have been reassured by the auspicious abbacy of Berard III, who in the first two decades of the twelfth century not only expanded the abbey's domains to an unprecedented extent but also cultivated arts and letters at Farfa, leaving an important legacy of manuscript production. According to the *Register,* the divisions in the community that followed on the death of Berard III in 1119 compromised the abbey's traditions of governance. As is so often the case, the only perspective we have on the events of 1119–25 is Gregory's own. His account of these years highlights his lifelong vision of Farfa's identity as defined by its independence and by its imperial patronage. In this context, changes in liturgical performance reflect the disintegration of the community, and in the eyes of

104. On this phenomenon in southern France see Remensnyder, *Remembering Kings Past,* 259–61.

105. Ibid., 297–98.

106. For another example of rewriting a monastic foundation through hagiography, see Cochelin, "Quête de liberté et récriture des origines."

Gregory change in the monastery's musical practices come to symbolize a growing threat of spiritual decay.

Novelty and Decadence

For Gregory, the quality of liturgical celebration was emblematic of the state of the abbey and the character of the abbot, and imperial patronage was an essential component of both. It is no surprise, then, that the *Register* portrays the social unrest and loss of imperial status in the 1120s as the low point in Farfa's history . The complex events of those years are recounted in a narrative that portrays the eruption of social tensions around the abbatial election following the death of Abbot Berard III.[107] According to this account, some of the monks who were sympathetic toward the lay population subject to the abbey (*populus abbatiae*) opposed the election of an abbot from one of the noble families of the region. When a debate ensued, the monks agreed among themselves to elect the sacristan, Guido, because his lower social status would help prevent the conflicts that might be provoked by a more aristocratic candidate. In the midst of the traditional three-day fast before announcement of the election results, Guido's name was leaked to the *populus* "by a certain seducer of peasants" (*per quendam seductorem rusticanorum*). Some of the abbey's knights acclaimed Guido publicly, bearing him off to the church in triumph. Outraged at the disruption of the three-day fast mandated by their electoral procedure, the monks unceremoniously expelled the peasants (*rusticani*) from the church. Riotous disorder ensued, and the monks decided to elect Rainaldus, a monk of Farfa who was residing at one of the abbey's priories. However, the *populus* became so violent that Rainaldus was forced to flee. Under duress, the monks finally compromised with the *populus* and accepted Guido. The election of Guido, however, clearly violated both the Benedictine Rule and Farfa's own customs, forcing the monks to follow the will of the people.[108] According to the *Register,* this was a subversion of the social order and nothing less than a reversal of the natural order itself:

> Therefore it is evident to all that he was elected neither by clerics nor by monks, but rather by townspeople and peasants. And the will of the laity

107. These events are recounted at the end of the Farfa *Register* (BAV Vat. lat. 8487, II, fols. 514r–520v; *CF* 2:291–313; and *RF* 5:311–25), which was copied by Todino, Gregory's nephew; see Supino Martini, *Roma,* 275. Because the narrative resembles Gregory's other works in style and content, I believe that he composed it, perhaps dictating it to Todino. The crucial passage about music, discussed later in this section, has a parallel in the *Chronicle.*

108. *CF* 2:295; *RF* 5:312.

was not turned to that of the clergy, but rather the will of the clergy was bent to that of the laity. And it can be said that the tail is made into the head of the body, and out of the exalted head is created the base extremity.[109]

For reasons that go unexplained in the *Register*, Guido secretly sent a letter to Emperor Henry V declining his own election because of his modest station. Henry, accordingly, sent no confirmation of Guido's abbacy. However, when Henry subsequently dispatched imperial legates to Farfa with orders to install as abbot the emperor's candidate, Berard Ascarellus, Guido refused to step down. Supported by the monks who hoped that he would be useful to them in the future as an ally of the *populus*, Guido stood his ground as abbot of Farfa. But Guido soon disappointed the community's expectations by abusing his position and dispersing the abbey's property. Finally, the *Register* tells us, the monks ousted Guido and accepted Berard Ascarellus, creating thus an abbatial schism from which the old imperial affiliation of Farfa would never fully recover.[110]

At this point in the narrative, a conflict seemingly based on tensions between the monks and the lay population around the abbey takes on connotations of papal-imperial politics. Guido, in an effort to reinstall himself as abbot, enlisted the support of those villages among Farfa's properties that were still loyal to him. Moreover, he forged an alliance with Pope Calixtus II (1119–24), with the intention of wresting the abbey from imperial control altogether and sending into exile any monks who might resist. To escape this fate, most of the monks left the abbey voluntarily with Berard Ascarellus and wandered among Farfa's dependencies.[111] Hearing the rumor that some of the abbey's knights wanted to install as abbot Adenulf, the son of a local count, Calixtus accompanied Guido to Farfa with an army in June 1121, only to find the abbey virtually abandoned. Guido proceeded to sell off the liturgical vessels, vestments, and church ornaments, an act rendered all the more reprehensible by the fact that these were the very objects that had been in his charge when he was sacristan.[112] Beginning in 1122, as a result of the Concordat of Worms concluded in that year by Henry V and Calixtus II, abbots in monasteries that were located outside the

109. *CF* 2:296; *RF* 5:313: "Notum ergo omnibus videtur quia electio eius non fuit clericorum nec monachorum, sed potius villanorum et rusticorum. Et non laicorum ad clericorum, sed magis clericorum voluntas conversa est ad laicorum, et, ut dici potest, corporis cauda caput est facta, et de capite sublimi fit extremitas vilis."

110. *CF* 2:305; *RF* 5:318–19.

111. *CF* 2:306–7; *RF* 5:319–20.

112. *CF* 2:307–10; *RF* 5:320–22.

Germanic kingdom but considered to be part of the empire, such as Farfa, had to be consecrated by the pope before their investiture by the emperor. This condition placed the abbacy of Farfa more or less in the hands of Calixtus, who excommunicated Berard Ascarellus during the Lateran Council of 1123. Because associating with an excommunicate was forbidden under canon law, the monks were compelled to return to Farfa under Guido's abbacy.[113]

According to the Farfa *Register*, after the monks returned, Guido took his revenge on them by deforming the solemnity of the liturgy, making them wear tattered, dark garments in the choir instead of the sumptuous vestments Guido had sold off in their absence. To make matters worse, the younger brothers no longer sang the traditional chants with spiritual sincerity or solemnity:

> The adolescents and younger brothers refused the melodies of chants and customary *organa*. They were eager to sing in the manner of actors, and they busied themselves with introducing many ditties (*nenias*) and foreign songs; they did not care to cultivate the custom of this place but instead frivolities and flighty things from elsewhere, which they had heard or seen in the foreign places where they had stayed. When the older or more serious brothers heard or saw all these things, they were deeply saddened and afflicted, because they were unable to oppose them.[114]

This passage exemplifies a tradition of polemical criticism, represented in a number of medieval texts, in which detractors of certain kinds of musical performance describe it pejoratively as histrionic or theatrical.[115] Judging from the vitriolic critiques of actors by twelfth-century ecclesiastical writers, it is clear that comparing a monk to an actor was the strongest possible condem-

---

113. On these events see also Stroll, *Medieval Abbey*, 235–47.

114. *CF* 2:311; *RF* 5:322: "Adolescentes uel iuniores fratres cantuum neumas et organa solita respuebant, et non spirituali honestate aut grauitate, sed istrionum more canere studebant, et multas nenias extraneasque cantilenas introducere satagebant, nec huius loci consuetudinem sed diuersarum partium leuitates et extollentias, quas in exteris locis quibus degebant audierant uel uiderant, exercere curabant. Quae omnia cum maturiores uel grauiores fratres audirent uel cernerent, contristabantur diutissime et affligebantur, quia eis non poterant resistere." I have substituted the reading *iuniores* from the manuscript (BAV Vat. lat. 8487, II, fol. 519v); the word *minores* in the edition is apparently a mistake of transcription.

115. See the context for this passage, discussed in Van Dijk, "Saint Bernard and the *Instituta Patrum* of Saint Gall." For a useful overview of such polemics see Casagrande and Vecchio, "Clercs et jongleurs."

nation.[116] The word *nenia* (or *naenia,* ditties) evokes connotations of secular song.[117] When associated with *histrio,* meaning actor or entertainer, *nenia* implies singing as light entertainment.[118] In the *Gesta Tancredi,* an early twelfth-century crusaders' chronicle by Ralph of Caen, *naenia* signifies the playful, whimsical song of a child.[119] All these contemporaneous uses of the word *naenia* suggest that the passage in the Farfa *Register* deplores the new music introduced by the younger monks by associating it with the kinds of secular song performed by actors and entertainers.[120] Thus the "ditties and foreign songs" stand in opposition to the customary chant and polyphony (*organa*) of the liturgical repertory. The fact that the older monks were saddened by things they "heard or saw" shows that musical style was a crucial element of Farfa's tradition, violated by the new style of singing associated with the younger monks. As instigators of musical disorder in opposition to their seniors, the younger monks not only broke with liturgical tradition but also defied the hierarchies of seniority that governed life in a Benedictine monastery.

Analyzing the rhetoric of this account as a polemical statement about rit-

116. One of the most famous attacks on actors is found in the *Policraticus* of John of Salisbury, I.viii, 52–55.

117. In medieval Latin, *nenia* could denote the various musical genres of funeral dirge, secular song, or nursery rhyme, the latter two with connotations of humor and frivolousness. In Gregory's *Chronicle, nenia* is generally understood to signify secular song. See *Novum glossarium mediae Latinitatis, L–Nysus,* 1202–03; and *Latinitatis Italicae medii aevi lexicon,* 144. I disagree with the translation of this word as "laments" in Ziolkowski, "Women's Lament," 145.

118. The fourth-century African writer Arnobius of Sicca (*Disputationes aduersus nationes,* VI.12, 321) describes a depiction of Apollo as "maintaining the postures of a lute player, and even of an actor about to sing ditties" (*citharistae gestus servans, cantaturi et nenias histrionis*). In *Arnobius of Sicca: The Case Against the Nations* 2:463, McCracken translates *cantaturi et nenias histrionis* as "about to sing dirges," but the context of the passage suggests that entertainment rather than funeral music is implied.

119. Radulfus Cadomensis, "Gesta Tancredi in expeditione Hierosolymitana," lxi; *PL* 155:535A; and *Receuil des historiens des Croisades* 3:651: "inde est quot adhuc puerorum decantat naenia: *Franci ad bella, provinciales ad victualia.*" According to the introduction to *Recueil,* xxxix, Ralph wrote between 1112 and 1118.

120. A comparable passage appears in the prologue to the *Chronicle,* where Gregory, addressing God, enumerates the diverse gifts offered by mankind (*CF* 1:110): "For some give you beneficial actions, others empty words, others adulations, others pleasing songs, but others [give you] deceitful trifles (or jokes), like actors" ("Alii namque vobis referunt quędam acta proficua, alii verba inania, alii adulationes, alii placitas cantiones, alii vero ioca lubrica, ut mimones").

ual, one can easily see that the narrative uses musical innovation as a symbol for the social unrest and reversals caused by the unconventional election of Abbot Guido. The degeneration of liturgical music, manifested in a new and foreign repertoire, suggests the spiritual and political decay of Farfa. The "insiders" within the monastic community (monks of the upper classes struggling to manage the *populus*) have been transformed into impotent "outsiders" by their subjection to an abbot reigning without the assent of the emperor. However, the text can also be situated within another rhetorical tradition, that of the reactions in the twelfth and thirteenth centuries to music associated with youth and the expression of levity and modernity. The new music created during this period for the feast of Saint Nicholas and the other festivities of the Christmas season did not always meet with the approval of clerical authorities. The liturgical compendium by Guillaume Durand, bishop of Mende (1286–96) describes an abbot who refused to let his monks sing the new office of Saint Nicholas because of its novelty and what he perceived as its resemblance to the secular songs of minstrels.[121] This anecdote recalls the comparison of the monks to *histriones* in the Farfa text.

The most striking and unusual aspect of the account in the Farfa *Register* is its vivid characterization of musical style. Judging from the liturgical repertories of the period, one can extrapolate what music would have seemed foreign to a central Italian monk. A manuscript from Farfa offers an apt example of such a piece. *Splendor patris,* added to a manuscript at Farfa in the early twelfth century (quite possibly in the 1120s), is a troped *Benedicamus Domino,* a type of composition that was new to the region at the time (ex. 5.5 and fig. 5.1). The text is based on the liturgical versicle *Benedicamus Domino; Deo gratias* (Let us bless the Lord; let us give thanks to God), which was traditionally sung as a dismissal at or near the conclusion of the divine office. Various melodies for this text survive, including several florid, wide-ranging ones for performance on feast days.[122] Beginning in the late eleventh and early twelfth centuries, tropes of the *Benedicamus Domino* were recorded in manuscripts from southern and northern France. The more elaborate among these compositions combined additions to the original text with greatly expanded melodies. Characterized by rhyme and the recurrence of refrains, these tropes with their extended structures are often called "Benedicamus" songs.[123] *Splen-*

121. Boynton, "Work and Play in Sacred Music," 65–78.

122. For *Benedicamus Domino* melodies from this period see Huglo, "Les débuts de la polyphonie à Paris," 150–54.

123. See Arlt, *Festoffizium,* Darstellungsband, 160–206.

EXAMPLE 5.5. *Splendor patris*, Rome, BN Farfa 4, fol. 77r–v.

1	Splendor patris et sol iustitię	The splendor of the Father and the sun of justice
2	fit particeps nostre materię	is made to share in our substance;
3	intrat uentre sed sine semine	he enters the womb, but without seed;
4	egreditur ex matre uirgine.	he exits from the virgin mother.
5	Ergo *benedicamus Domino.*	Therefore *let us praise the Lord.*
6	Hic egressus et haec ingressio	This exit and this entry
7	Deitatis fiunt probatio;	are rendered the proof of his divinity;
8	probat namque matris integritas	for the integrity of the mother proves
9	quod filius eius est Deitas.	that her son is God.
10	Ergo *Deo* dicamus *gratias.*	Therefore let us say *thanks to God.*
11	*Benedicamus Domino.*	*Let us praise the Lord.*
12	Orthodoxorum cętus	Let the assembly
13	cherichorum iubilorum.	of orthodox rejoicing clerics
14	*Deo* dicamus *gratias.*	give *thanks to God.*

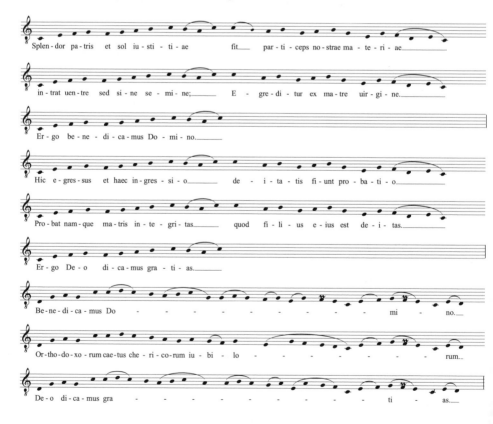

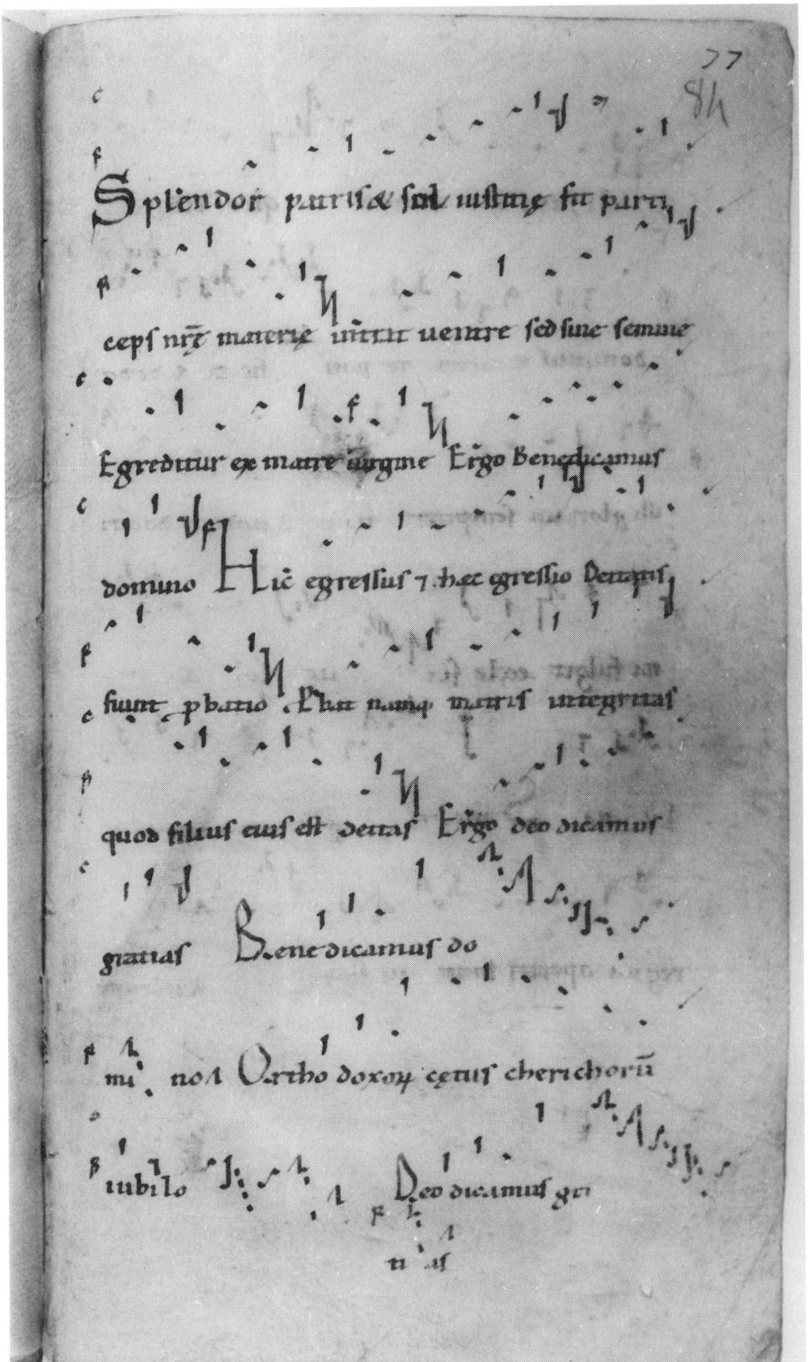

FIGURE 5.1. *Splendor patris*, Rome, BN Farfa 4, fol. 77r. By permission of the Ministero per i Beni e le Attività culturali, Biblioteca Nazionale.

dor patris is one of these songs; the text interweaves newly composed rhymed verse with the preexisting versicle (shown in italics in ex. 5.5). As a whole, *Splendor patris* most resembles the "Benedicamus" songs and *uersus* found in northern French manuscripts of the early twelfth century. In fact, a related text appears, though with a different melody, in a manuscript copied in Norman Sicily for the Cappella Palatina around 1140 (Madrid BN 289; see ex. 5.6).[124] This manuscript contains many works that originated in northern France, including several new compositions; like the other books copied for the use of the Norman rulers in Sicily, it reflects little contact with native Italian traditions.[125] Madrid 289 has more "Benedicamus" songs than any other Norman-Sicilian manuscript, including several that are not found elsewhere.[126] Thus, although the version of *Splendor patris* known at Farfa may be unique, it is related to a corpus of new Norman or Norman-Sicilian works in the first half of the twelfth century, and could be one of the "imported" compositions mentioned in the Farfa *Register*. Various scenarios could explain how *Splendor patris* reached Farfa, all of them reflecting the abbey's far-flung connections in western Europe. Perhaps a monk of Farfa learned the song while in Normandy or Palermo or southern France during the self-imposed exile of the community during the abbacy of Guido. Conversely, a traveler from one of these places could have brought new music to the monks of Farfa during a visit there.[127]

Whatever the means of transmission, *Splendor patris,* a *Benedicamus Domino* chant in the new style often called the "New Song," was without question a type of music that would have been practically unknown in Lazio in the early twelfth century.[128] The designation "New Song" describes both a distinctive corpus of music with specific stylistic features and a general principle of musico-poetic composition in which musical settings are closely fitted to the text—where individual compositions are not modeled on preexisting pieces but rather are built around newly conceived structures, with the result that each work represents a unique form.[129] As an example of "New Song," *Splen-*

124. Madrid, BN 289, fol. 134r. On this manuscript see Hiley, "Quanto c'è di normanno," 6–7; and Hiley, "The Liturgical Music of Norman Sicily," 199–204.

125. Arlt, *Festoffizium,* Darstellungsband, 176; and Hiley, "Quanto c'è di normanno," 20.

126. Hiley, "The Liturgical Music," 127, 699.

127. A similar hypothesis might explain the presence of the "Norman finale" in the *Exultet* at Farfa (see chap. 4).

128. Baroffio, "La tradizione dei tropi," notes that *Benedicamus Domino* tropes were quite rare in medieval Italy.

129. In the context of music, the designation *neues Lied* ("New Song") for this reper-

EXAMPLE 5.6. *Splendor patris*, Madrid, BN 289, fol. 134r.

Splendor patris et sol iusticię	The splendor of the Father and the sun of justice
fit particeps nostre materię	is made to share in our substance;
intrat uentrem sed sine semine	he enters the womb, but without seed;
egreditur de matre uirgine.	he exits from the virgin mother.
Hic ingressus et haec egressio	This entry and this exit
deitatis fiunt probacio.	are rendered the proof of his divinity.
Ergo *benedicamus domino.*	Therefore *let us praise the Lord.*
Caro deus et factor omnium;	God, the maker of all things, [has become] flesh;
dominator cunctorum hominum,	the ruler of all men,
regem regum et lumen luminum	the king of kings and the light of lights
enixa est regina uirginum.	is born from the queen of virgins.
Probat namque matris integritas	For the integrity of the mother proves
quod filius eius est deitas.	that her son is God.
Deo dicamus *gratias.*	Let us say *thanks to God.*

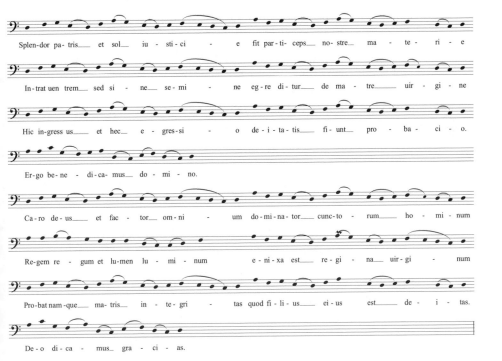

dor patris represents the opposite of the poetic and musical traditions seen in the hymns discussed at the beginning of this chapter, even though as a "Benedicamus" song it is clearly intended for performance in the divine office.[130] The text exhibits consistent end rhyme, tight construction, and a rather simple vocabulary that nevertheless plays deftly with language. In older genres of liturgical poetry such as the office hymn, musical form is determined by the patterns and structures of poetry, limiting the shapes of new compositions to the possibilities represented by preexisting examples of the genre. In the "New Song" corpus, musical and textual forms are infinitely variable. Building on the dialogic structure of the *Benedicamus Domino* versicle, songs such as *Splendor patris* created new forms of expression for a liminal moment near the end of the office,[131] giving voice to theological ideas of the twelfth century through expansions of the original liturgical text. As a modification of a traditional genre, they introduced new stylistic, formal, and doctrinal elements into the liturgy. *Splendor patris* seems to illustrate this process of musico-liturgical innovation in the microcosm of Farfa during the abbacy of Guido, as described by the passage in the Farfa *Register*.

The transparent structure of the Farfa version of *Splendor patris* is based on textual rhyme and extensive melodic repetition (see ex. 5.5). The first part (set to lines 1–10 of the text) is predominantly syllabic, while the second part (lines 11–14) is more melismatic. Ascending and descending passages, subdivided into antecedent and consequent phrases that begin and end on C, lend symmetry to the musical settings of lines 1–4 and 6–9. The same melody, rising through the octave from C to C, is sung to lines 1, 3, 5, 6, 8, and 10, and acts as a refrain in lines 5 and 10 after the strophic settings of lines 1–4 and 6–9. The strongly directed contour of this recurrent melody and its concluding decora-

tory was coined by Arlt, "Sequence and *Neues Lied*," "Das Eine und die vielen Lieder," and "*Nova cantica*." Among the more recent interpretations of the corpus are Grier, "A New Voice in the Monastery"; Haug and Björkvall, "Altes Lied—Neues Lied"; and Hiley, *Western Plainchant*, 238–50.

130. The manuscript context of *Splendor patris* shows that it was understood as belonging to the repertory of the office; on the reverse of the folio (fol. 77v) the same scribe copied a piece from the standard liturgical corpus, the eighth responsory for Matins on feasts of apostles (with the same melody as that in BAV Chigi C.VI.177).

131. Gunilla Björkvall, in a forthcoming paper on the "Benedicamus" songs, notes that many of these works consist only of the first part of the versicle (the words *Benedicamus Domino*), but that about half the known compositions include both halves of the versicle text. The two-part type of composition predominates in the Sicilian-Norman collection in Madrid, BN 289.

tive cadence (B–A–C) both serve to reinforce the role of C as a goal. The B–A–C cadence, sometimes called an "under-third" cadence, appears more frequently in music of the late Middle Ages; here, it gives B the role of a leading tone, strengthening the listener's expectation of the repeated C. Rapid scalar passages, multiple repetitions of phrases, and the use of refrains all distinguish *Splendor patris* from the traditional chant melodies that were sung at Farfa in the twelfth century and reveal its stylistic affiliations with music from northern and southern France.[132]

Splendor patris strikes the modern ear as being in the key of C, a bright sound found in several new compositions of the eleventh and twelfth centuries, including the secular songs of the troubadours.[133] These pieces resist conventional methods of classification under the system of the eight modes, each of which is associated with a typical range, final pitch, and melodic gestures. Moving rapidly up and down from C to C, the melody of Splendor patris frequently outlines the chain of thirds C–E–G or the third C–E and concludes on D. In combination, the final and range could suggest mode 1, but chants in mode 1 tend to emphasize the sequence of pitches D–F–A, with extensive recurrence of A, as seen in the responsories *Radix Iesse* (ex. 1.1) and *Domine ne in ira tua* (ex. 2.3). Chants that emphasize the chain of thirds C–E–G can be interpreted as a transposition of mode 5 or as a combination of mode 5 with mode 8.[134] However, such melodies have a C final, whereas *Splendor* patris ends with a rather inconclusive-sounding cadence on D. One could perhaps describe the mode of the melody as mode 7 transposed with a final on D, but this interpretation would not account for the emphasis on C throughout the composition.

The distinctive sound of *Splendor patris* is certainly unusual, but two comparable examples can be cited, both of them hymn melodies. One is a well-known tune associated with the Christmas hymn *Christe redemptor omnium*,

132. I am grateful to David Cohen for pointing out, several years ago, the importance of recurring gestures and the inchoate refrain structure in *Splendor patris*. For a recent discussion of the structural role of refrain in the "New Song," see Haug, "Ritual and Repetition."

133. Two widely diffused examples are the eleventh-century sequence *Letabundus exultet fidelis chorus* and the twelfth-century conductus *Orientis partibus* (particularly the version preserved in Madrid, BN 289, fols. 146v–147r). For a transcription of Letabundus see Arlt, *Festoffizium,* Editionsband, 11. Peire Vidal's *Pus tornatz sui* is a good example of this tonality in troubadour song; see the edition in *Teaching Medieval Lyric* after Milan, Biblioteca Ambrosiana, R71, fol. 42v.

134. McGrade, "Modal Contrast."

EXAMPLE 5.7. *Tibi Christe splendor patris*, BAV Chigi C.VI.177, fol. 140r.

Tibi Christe splendor Patris,	To you, Christ, the splendor of the Father,
uita uirtus cordium	the life and strength of hearts,
in conspectu angelorum	in the presence of angels
uotis uoce psallimus	we sing with a voice in prayer,
alternantes concrepando	resounding in turn,
melos damus uocibus.	we produce melodies with our voices.

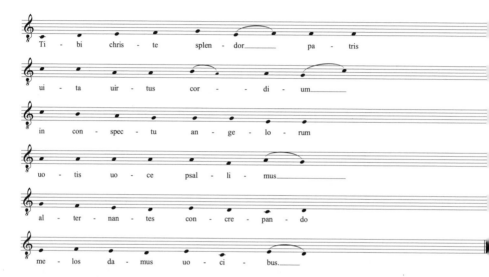

which outlines C–E–G and has an octave range from C to C.[135] The other is a much rarer melody, perhaps unique to the Chigi manuscript from Farfa, where it was notated in the margin below the widely diffused text *Tibi Christe splendor patris* (ex. 5.7).[136] Like *Splendor patris*, this tune ascends from C, soon reaching the octave above. The repetition of the A and final cadence on D suggest mode 1, but the emphasis on the pitches C–E–G distinguishes it from other Dorian chants. Because *Tibi Christe splendor patris* was a traditional hymn text, only the tonality of the melody is unusual, whereas both the text and music of *Splendor patris* represent the new forms of the twelfth century. To a twelfth-century singer accustomed to a more traditional chant idiom, *Splendor patris* would have sounded unfamiliar enough to strike the ear as "foreign."

135. Melody 142 in *Die Hymnen: Die mittelalterlichen Hymnenmelodien des Abendlandes*.
136. This melody was added in the early twelfth century to BAV Chigi C.VI.177, fol. 140r.

The style of *Splendor patris* and the period in which it was copied suggest that it may have represented one of the new compositions deplored in the Farfa *Register*. The *Benedicamus Domino* versicle was traditionally sung by boys,[137] and the texts of many "Benedicamus" songs refer explicitly to their youthful performers.[138] The association was so common that the twelfth-century liturgical commentator John Beleth assigned to the performance of the versicle by boys a symbolic meaning of purity and innocence.[139] The fact that *Splendor patris* is a "Benedicamus" song means that it was probably performed by the younger singers, strengthening the connection to the account in the *Register*, which identifies the singers of the new and "foreign" songs as a distinct group composed of the adolescents and junior monks (the *adolescentes* and *iuniores fratres*). The broader context linking this "new song" to the younger monks at Farfa makes the *Register*'s portrayal of the *adolescentes* and *iuniores fratres* as agents of change all the more convincing. Young singers played an important role in the transmission of medieval music, and they may also have been instrumental in the emergence of the "New Song" corpus, many of whose earliest examples are "Benedicamus" songs.[140] In combination, the description in the Farfa *Register* and the musical evidence of *Splendor patris* illustrate the introduction of new genres at Farfa in the 1120s during the abbacy of Guido.

The atmosphere of desolation and neglect conveyed by the account in the *Register* extended through the rest of Guido's abbacy. After he had reduced the community to utter poverty, a delegation of twenty monks went to Rome in 1124 to obtain the assistance of Pope Calixtus II, who remained impervious to their protests and unwavering in his support of Guido. Calixtus died on December 13, 1124, and was succeeded by Honorius II (1124–30). Honorius did not support Guido's abbacy, and in 1125, six years after the tumultuous events

137. See, for example, *Consuetudines Fructuarienses—Sanblasianae* 2:215–16; and Ulrich of Zell, *Antiquiores consuetudines*, PL 149, col. 654D. The *Liber tramitis* and the Cluniac customary from Vallombrosa, among other sources, are cited by Robertson, "Benedicamus Domino," 5–9.

138. I am grateful to Jan Ziolkowsi for bringing to my attention this aspect of his commentary on the texts in a forthcoming edition by Gunilla Björkvall.

139. John Beleth, *Iohannis Beleth summa de ecclesiasticis officiis*, 31e, 53c, pp. 61, 92. I am grateful to Gunilla Björkvall for bringing to my attention Beleth's commentary on the *Benedicamus Domino.*

140. "Benedicamus" songs constitute a large part of the repertory in the earliest manuscripts of "New Song" from southern France (see Björkvall, *Liturgisk versdiktning*) and the majority of pieces in what is possibly the earliest northern French manuscript of the "New Song," described in Arlt, "Neues zum neuen Lied."

surrounding Guido's appointment, the monks elected Adenulf to replace Guido. Lacking the support of both the monastic community and the abbey's *populus,* Guido obtained permission to renounce the abbacy, and Honorius sent two cardinals to the abbey to preside over Guido's abdication.[141] The proceedings reflected the subjection of Farfa to the pope; after Guido had abdicated, the monks asked the cardinals to authorize them, on behalf of the pope, to elect Adenulf. After the departure of the cardinals, the community held the election "for the original liberty and restoration of this church, in agreement with and according to ancient custom" (*autenticam huius ecclesiae libertatem et restaurationem, concorditer et iuxta antiquam consuetudinem elegimus*). Clearly, this statement was a paradox: even if the internal procedures for election had not changed, the abbey no longer enjoyed the freedom from outside intervention that had been guaranteed by its imperial patrons. What is more, the requirement of the pope's approval was a radical innovation. The irony of the situation did not escape Gregory of Catino, who commented that, after a long history of avoiding papal control, the community had realized that there was no other way to extricate itself from its difficulties.[142]

Thereafter, Farfa's changed relationship with the papacy was reflected in its textual and artistic production. In the *Liber floriger,* written during the papal schism of 1130–32 which opposed Honorius II's successor, Innocent II, to the antipope Anaclet II, Gregory of Catino recounted that Lawrence of Syria had been ordained deacon in Rome by Pope Urban I, adding a connection to the papacy that had not previously appeared in Gregory's accounts of the history of Farfa.[143] According to Charles McClendon, the twelfth-century throne that once stood in the abbey church at Farfa may have commemorated the consecration of Pope Eugenius III there in 1145, "a poignant symbol of papal authority in the middle of the twelfth century at what had formerly been the most important imperial abbey in the region."[144] Eugenius chose Farfa as the site of his consecration and intervened on its behalf in property disputes while reaffirming the papacy's jurisdiction over the imperial abbey. Although in the

141. Kehr, *Italia pontificia* 1:68. It is not clear why Guido fell out of favor with the *populus;* the *Register* simply states that they considered him despicable (*RF* 5:318).

142. *RF* 5:323–24.

143. See the discussion of the prologue to the *Liber floriger* in chap. 1 in the present volume.

144. McClendon, "Liturgical Furniture at Farfa Abbey," 205. The throne, along with the twelfth-century chancel, might also have been created between 1138 and 1144, during the abbacy of Adenulf, who was a close associate of both Innocent II and Eugenius III. I am grateful to Charles McClendon for sending me this study.

second half of the twelfth century Frederick Barbarossa asserted his right to control Farfa, this attempt to reinstate imperial patronage did not outlast his reign.[145]

The case studies in this chapter show that the monastic liturgy, and specifically the divine office, provided the opportunity both for new compositions and for the articulation of power through the expression, implicit or explicit, of the monastery's relationships with the saints. Both poetry and prose served rhetorical purposes: the hymns, "Benedicamus" song, and Matins lessons discussed here were all meant to be performed during the office, while the narrative account in the Farfa *Register* articulates a condemnation of changes in liturgical and musical practice.

Contested spaces are crucial to all these examples. Disputes over the relics of Victoria and of Valentine and Hilarius concern the ownership of church spaces and the implications for Farfa of the saints' presence in those spaces. In the case of the Matins lessons for Thomas of Maurienne versus the chronicle of San Vincenzo, the contested space was the abbey of San Vincenzo, which lay far from Farfa but remained subjected to it in the discursive space of some texts from Farfa. Finally, during the abbacy of Guido, Farfa itself became a contested space. According to the account of this abbacy in the *Register,* Guido's election brought on multiple ruptures of boundaries. When the *populus* burst into the abbey church acclaiming Guido, it disrupted the traditional electoral procedure. Guido's abuse of the monks, which led to their departure, enabled him to appropriate temporal control over the monastery and many of its lands despite the fact that his election had never been confirmed by the emperor. Therein lies the ultimate significance of the crisis represented by the abbacy of Guido: he subverted the abbey's imperial patronage, which had been central to the identity of Farfa since the early ninth century. In describing these years, Gregory reveals once again the links between property, identity, and history that had been at the heart of the abbey's culture for at least the previous hundred years.

145. Stroll, *Medieval Abbey,* 256–73.

CONCLUSION

this book places the development of liturgical and musical traditions at Farfa in the context of the reworking of historical memory and the formation of institutional identity. As the manuscripts produced at the abbey in the eleventh and twelfth centuries indicate, however, Farfa's was not a unitary identity but one that was continuously shaped by a multiplicity of influences and affiliations. At the end of the period studied here the community was riven by conflicting loyalties that seem linked to the process by which Farfa's independence inexorably came to an end. But already throughout the course of its long history, Farfa had repeatedly been transformed, as its patronage shifted from the Lombard aristocracy to the Carolingians, then to that of the Ottonians and Salians before its final transition into papal jurisdiction. These vicissitudes fostered the continual reinvention and negotiation of identity and status. As an imperial abbey of long standing, Farfa enjoyed special privileges and immunities that were repeatedly reaffirmed; nonetheless, the community was continually engaged in the regional politics that threatened to dominate the outcome of each abbatial election. As an abbey reformed by Cluny at the end of the tenth century, Farfa adopted some aspects of Cluniac ritual while maintaining its own traditions; although independent of Cluny, Farfa received the Cluniac customs and proclaimed the Cluniac character of its constitution. Patrons of all stripes, including the Germanic rulers, southern Italian potentates, and the local families and clergy of the Sabina, all made their mark on the abbey's culture in their own ways.

Studying liturgical evidence from Farfa opens a new window onto this profusion of influences and affiliations, enriching and broadening the particular account of the abbey's history in the works of Gregory of Catino. The contents of Farfa's liturgical manuscripts attest to its role as a cultural crossroads in the central Middle Ages. Its visual culture manifests equally diverse sources originating in southern Italy, Rome, Subiaco, and Reichenau. Although the contributions of these influences to painting and carving at Farfa were already known, the analogous connections with both northern and southern Europe seen in the liturgical books shed new light on the abbey's history, further illuminating its reception of diverse traditions. Imperial patronage exposed the monks of Farfa to religious texts from the north and to illuminated manuscripts and other precious gifts. For instance, the hymn to the Cross associated with Henry II in the Chigi manuscript is not just a text with an attribution; it represents the transmission of an entire complex of ideas regarding the Germanic emperor and his attitude toward the Cross. A prayer that addresses the Virgin Mary in terms evoking empire demonstrates Farfa's self-identification as an imperial abbey; some prayers to the Cross in manuscripts from Farfa reflect the transmission of Carolingian devotional traditions there. In the illuminated Gospel book discussed in chapter 4, northern elements were taken up and fused with central Italian ones, resulting in a product typical of Farfa but redolent of imperial influence. Connections with southern Italy were also manifested in material culture and liturgy, but in combination with central Italian traditions, as in the *Exultet* chant that unites Franco-Roman and Beneventan features. The mixed reception of elements from north and south characterizes the assimilation of influences in the liturgy and the visual arts at Farfa.

Another important influence from afar was that of Cluny. The Cluniac reform of Farfa established a loose affiliation that added yet another feather to Farfa's cap: throughout the eleventh and early twelfth centuries Farfa could claim "Cluniac" status while remaining juridically independent of Cluny. The *Liber tramitis* promoted a dual identity, incorporating both Cluniac customs and Farfa's own traditions. The dual versions of some sections in the text reflect a "double definition" (*duplex diffinitio*), juxtaposing what appear to be two different monastic identities. The reevaluation of the *Liber tramitis* in light of Farfa's own traditions has shown that the liturgical use of this customary was both more flexible and more extensive than was previously thought. The monks of Farfa drew on the text selectively, annotating its contents to adapt them for their own use, combining the liturgical texts with the abbey's own rituals, and assimilating Cluniac liturgical practice in its death rituals. In this way the community fashioned for itself a modified Cluniac identity.

A recurrent theme in the history of Farfa is the factionalization within the monastic community and the tensions with its neighbors that inspired the production of texts. Abbot Hugh recounted the troubles of the tenth century in his *Destructio Farfensis* and described the challenges of monastic reform in his *Relatio constitutionis*. Gregory began to compile the *Register* and the *Collectio canonum* during periods of internal conflict in the 1090s, then made a final attempt to perfect his catalogs of the abbey's holdings with the *Liber floriger* during the papal schism of 1130–32. The causes of disagreement often revolved around the abbots' interactions with the lay landowners of the region. Of course, these stories have reached us only through the eyes and hands of Gregory, in the documents he copied in the Farfa *Register* and his narrative accounts, so we are compelled to listen to his version of events. Gregory condemned Abbots Rainald, Berard II, Oddo, and Guido for favoring lay landowners, interpreting their actions as misguided neglect of the abbey's property, which led to outside encroachment and, inevitably, to disaster. Tensions with the local laity seem to have become particularly severe after the death of Berard III in 1119, when the polarization of factions around Guido's election was directly related to the role of the *populus abbatiae*. Guido's alliance with Calixtus II once again polarized the community, this time around papal and imperial factions. The only narrative source for these events is the *Register*, which reflects the strong imperial sentiment seen in Farfa's production, during the investiture controversy, of texts such as the *Orthodoxa defensio imperialis* and the *Liber Beraldi*. The *Register*'s description of the changed atmosphere under Abbot Guido after the Concordat of Worms suggests the emergence of yet another identity within the community, that of younger monks adopting new ways of singing the divine office. Such junior members of the community were the performers and possibly the creators of the "Benedicamus" song *Splendor patris*. With the introduction of this composition to Farfa, we have come full circle, from the poem for Saint Benedict from the *History of the Lombards* notated in the early eleventh century to another kind of new song. When the younger monks performed songs such as *Splendor patris*—new songs made from old ones—they were perhaps unaware that they were continuing a long tradition of innovation seen a century earlier in the song for Saint Benedict. That the *Register* makes musical performance and style emblematic of the abbey's situation at this crucial moment in its history attests to the central importance of liturgy in monastic life and identity. The liturgy does not follow a linear trajectory of change over time, but it does reflect the vicissitudes of an institution's history and forms an integral part of the narrative that has come down to us. Liturgy constructs history, and to understand the character of Farfa in the central Middle Ages, we must listen for its song.

Brief Descriptions of Liturgical Manuscripts from Farfa Discussed in the Text

The bibliography listed below is limited to the most recent studies of each manuscript; they contain references to earlier scholarship.

All manuscripts have drypoint ruling on the hair side of the parchment except where otherwise indicated.

Farfa, Archivio dell'Abbazia, AF 338, III–V

Leaf and two bifolia from an antiphoner, late eleventh century. Romanesca script, Latian neumes.

One column, 60 lines.

Page 285 × 185 mm; ruled space 193 × 120 mm.

CONTENTS

Chants for the office: Agatha, Scolastica, Chair of Saint Peter, Gregory, Benedict, Holy Week from Tuesday to Good Friday

BIBLIOGRAPHY

Boynton, "Frammenti," 328–29, 337.

Farfa, Archivio dell'Abbazia, A.209

Glossed psalter and glossed hymnary, end of the eleventh century. Romanesca script, Latian neumes. 183 leaves.

Two columns, 30 lines. Page 330 × 235 mm; ruled space 260 × 177 mm.

GATHERING STRUCTURE

a^4, I^{8-1}, $II–III^8$, IV^{8-1}, V^8, $VI–XII^8$, XIII^2, $XIV–XXV^8$, XXIV^{8-1}

At least two quires are missing at the beginning; the psalter begins in the middle of Psalm 21.

HANDS

1: Text, fols. 1–143v, and occasional glosses throughout the psalter

2: Text, 144r–183v

3: Glosses, 1r–9r (line 4 of marginal gloss), 9v (line 2–29 of marginal gloss), (lines 1–27), 24r–65r, 70v–78v, 101r–114r, 117v–123r

4: Glosses, 9r (line 11 of marginal gloss)–17r; 17v (lines 28)–22v

5: Glosses, 23r–v, 65v–70r

6: Glosses, 79r–95v

7: Glosses, 96r–100v

8: Glosses, 115r–117r

9: Main gloss hand, 133r–159v

10: Group of glosses, 137v–138r, 141v, 143r

11: Glosses, 153v–159v

CONTENTS

fols. 1–120v: Glossed psalter and glossed Old Testament canticles

121r: Creed

121r: Glossed *Nunc dimittis*

121v: Te Deum in two columns, notated *Te decet laus*

122r: *Quicumque vult,* glossed by two different hands

123v–125r: Litanies

125r–132v: Prayers and absolutions

133r–159v: Hymnary

160r–165r: Canticles

165r–182r: Capitula

182r–183v: Orationale (incomplete; ends with proper prayer for feast of Saint Nicholas)

BIBLIOGRAPHY

Boynton, "Eleventh-Century Continental Hymnaries," 210–13; Supino Martini, *Roma*, 257–59.

Farfa, Archivio dell'Abbazia, AF.278

Office lectionary for Matins in summer, second half of the twelfth century. Caroline minuscule. 206 leaves. Ruled on the flesh side.

Two columns, 31–33 lines. Page 420×310 mm; ruled space 315×225mm.

GATHERING STRUCTURE

I–IV^8, V^4, VI–VII^8, VIII$^{6-1}$, IX–XVI^8, XVII$^{6-1}$, XVIII–XIX^8, XX$^{6-1}$, XXI$^{10-1}$, XXII^8, XXIII$^{10-1}$, XXIV^4, XXV–XXVII^8, XXVIII^4

HANDS

1: fols. 1r–32v; 37v line 15–52v; 59r–126v (except for 65r column B, line 23 ("tympanum") to 65v line 13–); 175r–199r

2: 127r–173r column A, line 13; 199v–205v

Later additions:

1: 33r–34r column A, line 29 ("causam"); 35r column B–36r column B, line 5; 36v –37v, line 15 ("habent")

2: 34r column A, line 29 ("pacifus")–35r column A

3: 36r column B, lines 6– 33

4: 53r–57v, 174r– v

5. 173r column A, line 13– 173v

CONTENTS

Old Testament readings and sermons and some passions for saints, from the vigil of Pentecost through the Dedication of a Church

Madrid, Biblioteca Nacional, Vitr. 20-6

Evangelistary, third quarter of the eleventh century. Caroline minuscule (one hand throughout), Latian neumes. 94 leaves.

One column, 24 lines. Page 267×170 mm; ruled space 204×107 mm. Musical notation on 5r–6v, 8v–9v, 10v, 13r–15v, 19v–20r, 30v, 31v, 34v, 44v–45r

Passion letters: + C S E P

GATHERING STRUCTURE

I–VIII⁸, IX⁸⁻¹, X–XI⁸, XII⁸⁻¹

GATHERING STRUCTURE

I–VIII^8, IX$^{8-1}$, X–XI^8, XII$^{8-1}$

CONTENTS

Gospel pericopes for Mass from the first Sunday of Advent to the Dedication of a Church, concluding with the Gospels for the Friday Mass in honor of the Cross and the Saturday Mass in honor of the Virgin Mary

BIBLIOGRAPHY

Garrison, *Studies* 4:250–64; Siede, *Untersuchungen*, 18–61, 236–42, plates A1–A23; Supino Martini, *Roma*, 328.

Perugia, Biblioteca Comunale Augusta, I 17

Psalter, early twelfth century. Romanesca script and Caroline minuscule, Latian neumes on fol. 1r.

This manuscript is almost identical in format, decoration, and script to Vallicelliana F 29.

One column, 26 lines. Page 177×123 mm; ruled space 127×75 mm.

GATHERING STRUCTURE

I–IV^8, V^{4+1}, VI^4, VII–XVI^8; one bifolium (fols. 41–42) is bound out of place between fols. 47 and 48

HANDS

1r (first half of the twelfth century)

1v–7r, 17–121

7v–8v

CONTENTS

fol. 1r: Lesson for the Virgin Mary, and hymn *Terrena cuncta iubilent* (Peter Damian)

1v–4r: Ordo for penitence

4v–5r: *Computus* tables

5r–7r: *De loquela digitorum*

7v–8v: Instructions for singing the psalms in decades

17r–24v: *Computus*

25r: blank

25v–113r: Roman Psalter, concluding with Psalm 151

113r–120r: Old and New Testament canticles, *Te decet laus,* Te Deum and Gloria

120v–122v: Pater noster, Apostles' Creed, Nicean Creed, *Quicumque vult saluus esse*

122v–123r: Litany

123r–129v: Prayers

BIBLIOGRAPHY

Supino Martini, *Roma*, 264–65.

Rome, BN Farfa 2, fols. 1–2, 411–12

Two bifolia from a notated antiphoner, late eleventh century. Romanesca script, Latian neumes.

One column, irregular number of lines; would have 59 or 60 in a complete folio.
Page 260×160 mm (heavily cropped at top); ruled space ca. 158×121 mm.

CONTENTS

fols. 1–2: Matins and Lauds of Maundy Thursday, beginning with the second
responsory of Matins

411–412: Office chants for the fourth week of Lent, from the third nocturn of
Matins on Sunday to the beginning of Matins on Wednesday

BIBLIOGRAPHY

Boynton, "Frammenti," 328–29; Supino Martini, *Roma*, 276–80.

Rome, BN Farfa 4

Psalter with hymnary, ca. 1100. Romanesca script, Latian neumes. 144 folios, not
counting modern paper quires at beginning and end.

One column. Page 175×106 mm. fols. 1–77v: 23 lines, ruled space 118×69 mm; fol.
78: 22 lines, ruled space 113×69 mm; fols. 79–144: 17 lines, ruled space 118×71
mm. Latian neumes on fols. 77r–v and 133r–134r.

GATHERING STRUCTURE

I^6, $II–IV^8$, V^4, $VI–X^8$, XI^{4+1}, $XII–XIX^8$, XX^{2+1}

HANDS

1. 1r–65v
2. 66r–74v
3. 79r–88r
4. 89r–144r
Additions on 75r–v, 76r–v, 77r–v, 78r–v

CONTENTS

fols. 1–49v: Psalter (Psalms 1–77 only)
50r–88r: Prayers
88v–132r: Hymnary
132r–144r: Canticles

BIBLIOGRAPHY

Barré, *Prières anciennes*, 245–48; Brugnoli, "*Catalogus codicum Farfensium*,"
291–97; Jullien, "Sources," 115–16; Supino Martini, *Roma*, 263; Wilmart,
"Prières médiévales."

Rome, BN Farfa 32

Office lectionary, late eleventh century. Romanesca script, Latian neumes. 128
leaves.

GATHERING STRUCTURE

I^6, 7, 8, II^8, III^6, IV^8, V^6, $VI–IX^8$, X^6, $XI–XVI^8$, XVII^6
Outer bifolia missing from I, III, V, X, and XVII. Two *quaternia* are missing
between X and XI. Ten gatherings are missing from the beginning of the
manuscript.
Two columns, 39 lines (40 lines on some folios, 45 on fols. 1–8). Page 475×335

m; ruled space 291×276 mm (fols. 1–8); elsewhere varies in the range of 370–75 ×267–70 mm.

HANDS

1: 1–5v column B, line 32

2: 5v: column B, lines 33–38v; 24r

3: 9r–11r; 12r–23v; 24v–26r column B, line 33

4: 26r: column B, line 33—128

5: 11v

CONTENTS

Lessons from the feast of Thomas of Maurienne (Dec. 10) to the common of martyrs

BIBLIOGRAPHY

Supino Martini, *Roma*, 253–54, tavola LXVI; Brugnoli, "*Catalogus codicum Farfensium, Pars altera*," 113–17.

Rome, BV E.16, fols. III, IV

Leaves from two liturgical books, late eleventh century. Romanesca script, Latian neumes.

Currently serve as flyleaves in an evangeliary from the early twelfth century.

One column, 50 lines. Page 268×173 mm; ruled space 195×120 mm.

CONTENTS

fol. III: Notated Genealogy of Christ in the Gospel of Matthew with a red F line, F clef, and custos

fol. IV: Notated *Exultet* (incomplete at beginning) with a C clef and custos

BIBLIOGRAPHY

Supino Martini, *Roma*, 263.

Rome, BV F.29

Collection of texts and chants for the divine office, early twelfth century. Romanesca and Caroline scripts, Latian neumes. 127 leaves.

One column, 26 lines. Page 198×120 mm; ruled space 126×75 mm.

GATHERING STRUCTURE

a⁴, I ⁶, II–IV⁸, V¹⁰, VI–XV⁸, XVI⁷⁻¹. The outer bifolium from the first gathering is incorrectly inserted in the fifth gathering. Fol. 35 should be the first leaf of the manuscript. Fol. 36 should be between fols. 6 and 7.

HANDS

Romanesca hand: 1–30v, 35r–36v, 97r–110r line 6, 112v–127r

First Caroline hand: 31r–34v, 37r–64r, 6, 64v–73r, 8

Second Caroline hand: fols. 110v–112v

CONTENTS

fols. 1r–30r: Orationale (collects)

31r–70r (line 5): Capitula, lessons, responsories, verses, and versicles

70r (line 6)–72v: Confession ordo

73r–112v: Diurnal

113r–127v: *Ordo visitandi infirmos, et sepeliendi mortuos*

BIBLIOGRAPHY

Supino Martini, Roma, 264–65; Kelly, *Exultet*, 67, 77, 88, 261; Kelly, "Structure and Ornament," 251.

Vatican City, BAV Chigi C.VI.177

Collection of texts and chants for the divine office and other services, ca. 1050–60. Romanesca script, Latian neumes. 300 leaves.

One column, 28–34 lines. Page 300×142 mm; ruled space 205×96 mm.

GATHERING STRUCTURE

I–III⁸, IV⁶, V–XIX⁸, XX¹², XXI–XXXVII⁸

HANDS

First main hand: 9r–152v, 154v line 92–162r; 165r–177r line 31; 177v line 8–227v

Second main hand: 229r–300v

Other hands:

1r–8r

8v

153r lines 1–12, 153v–154r

153r, lines 14–35

154r, lines 16–154v

163r–v line 10, 163v line 11–164v

177r line 32–177v line 7

CONTENTS

fols. 1r–8r: Calendar

8v: Excerpt from the Rule of Benedict

9r: Erased liturgical texts, followed by notated invitatory (Psalm 94)

9r–v: Hymnary preface

9v–30v: Diurnal

31r–105r: Roman Psalter

105r–110v: Canticles

110v–112v: Te Deum, Pater noster, Credo, *Quicumque uult*

113r: Litany

113v–120v: Prayers

121r–152v: Hymnary with glosses

153r–164v: Supplement to hymnary

163v–164r: Mass for the Dead

164v: *Missa pro patre et matre,* Sunday collects

165r–182r: Capitula

182r–188v: Ritual for the unction, death, and burial of a monk

189r–227v: Orationale, mixed temporal and sanctoral

229r–300v: Offices for the Trinity, common of saints, Sunday, and Monday; responsories, antiphons, and lessons

BIBLIOGRAPHY

Boe, "Music Notation," 18–21; Boynton, "Eleventh-Century Continental Hymnaries," 202–9; Boynton, "Liturgy and History."

Zurich, Zentralbibliothek, Rheinau 82

Collection of texts and chants for the divine office and other services, late eleventh century. Romanesca script, Latian neumes (with Germanic neumes added on p. 1). 262 pages.

One column, 24 lines. Page 230 x 135 mm; ruled space 152 x 70 mm.

GATHERING STRUCTURE

I^8, II^{8+2}, III^6, IV^{8+1}, V–IX^8, X^6, XI^{6+1}, XII^8, XIII^{8-1}, XIV^8, XV^6, XVI^{8-1}, XVII^{8+2}

HANDS

p. 1: twelfth-century addition

2: 2–30, 32–77

3: 31, 78–96

4: 97–232

5: 233–262

CONTENTS

pp. 1–113 Hymnary

113–27 Canticles

127–53 Capitulary

154–220 Orationale and litanies

221–41 Sanctorale

241–44 Common of saints

244–62 Ordines for visiting the sick and death ritual; Office of the Dead

BIBLIOGRAPHY

Jullien, "Sources"; Supino Martini, *Roma,* 252–53.

Table A.1. Texts and Contexts Related to the Abbey of Farfa, ca. 998–1125

Decade	Abbots of Farfa	Emperors	Popes	Important dates	Texts from Farfa	Abbots of Cluny
990	Hugh 998–1009 Guido I	Otto III 983–1002	Gregory V: 996–999 Silvester II: 999–1003	998–1000 Cluniac reform of Farfa 998 Privilege of Otto III 999 Otto III visits Farfa		Odilo 994–1049
1000	Guido I 1009–13	Henry II 1002–24	John XVIII: 1003–9 Sergius IV: 1009–12		1002–9 Hugh of Farfa, *Destructio monasterii Farfensis*	
1010	Hugh 1014–27		Benedict VIII 1012–24	1014, 1019 Privileges of Henry II		
1020	Guido II 1027–35	Conrad II 1024–39	John XIX 1024–33	1022: Henry II visits Farfa 1027: Privilege of Conrad II 1027–32 Abbot Hugh of Farfa visits Cluny (?)	ca. 1020–40 *Liber tramitis* compiled	
1030	Hugh 1036–38 Almeric 1039–47 Suppo elected in 1039 ruled in 1047	Henry III 1039–56	Benedict IX: 1033–44			
1040	Berard I 1047–89		Gregory VI: 1044–46 Leo IX: 1048–54	1049, 1051 Privileges of Leo IX		Hugh I 1049–1109

Year	Emperors	Popes	Abbots	Events	Texts / Manuscripts	Cluny
1050	Henry IV 1056–1106	Victor II: 1055–57 / Stephen X: 1057–59 / Nicholas II: 1059–61		1050 Privilege of Henry III	ca. 1050–1060 *Liber tramitis* MS copied at Farfa BAV Chigi C.VI.177 Madrid BN Vitr. 20-6	
1060		Alexander II: 1061–73		1060 Consecration of altars by Nicholas II / 1060 Privilege of Nicholas II / 1065 Privilege of Henry IV	ca. 1060–90 additions to BAV Chigi C.VI.177	
1070						
1080		Gregory VII: 1073–85 / Victor III: 1085–88 / Urban II: 1088–99	Rainald 1089–90	1082 Henry IV visits Farfa / 1084 Second privilege of Henry IV	late 11th c. Rome BN Farfa 32 (lectionary with *Constructio Farfensis*)	
1090		Paschal II: 1099–1118	Berard II 1090–99 / Oddo 1099 / Berard III 1099–1119	1099 Construction of new church initiated, then interrupted	1092–99 *Regestum Farfense*	
1100	Henry V 1106–25				1103–7 *Liber largitorius* / 1107–19 *Chronicon Farfense* / 1105–6: *Liber Beraldi*	Ponce 1109–22
1110		Calixtus II: 1119–23	Guido III 1119–25	1111 Imperial coronation interrupted: Paschal II and cardinals imprisoned in one of Farfa's fortresses / 1118 Privilege of Henry V	ca. 1111: *Orthodoxa defensio imperialis* early 12th c.: *Splendor patris* added to Rome, BN Farfa 4 Perugia I 17, Rome, BV F.29	
1120				1122 Concordat of Worms		Peter the Venerable 1122–56

Adventus Ceremonies in the Liber tramitis *and in the Customary of Bernard*

Liber tramitis, 242–43

For the reception of a king. When the arrival of the king is announced in the monastery, then let all convene in the church, with the abbot or prior signaling to the brothers, if it is not the time for talking in the cloister. And they should wear copes, even the lay brothers, and the children should put on tunics. The sacristans shall prepare the procession, and the two principal bells shall be rung. Setting forth, they should process in the order indicated here: cross, water, cross; thurifer, cross, thurifer; candelabra, Gospel book, candelabrum; candelabrum, Gospel book, candelabrum; candelabrum, Gospel book, candelabrum. The lay brothers should go two by two, then the oblates with their teachers, then the abbot and then the other brothers two by two like the previous ones, but they should walk in silence. On reaching the king, let the abbot give him holy water, and he shall kiss the Gospel book and be censed. Then the responsory *Ecce mitto angelum meum* is begun, and the servants should strike all the bells. In the church, two carpets are arranged, one before the altar of the Holy Cross and the other in front of the main altar. Then the abbot should begin an appropriate antiphon or responsory of his choice. After this is finished, he should say the chapter and these prayers: "Omnipotens sempiterne Deus qui caelestia simul et terrena moderaris," and another: "Omnipotens sempiterne Deus miserere famulo tuo," and they should return to the cloister. For a queen, let them do the same thing, but while entering the church, let them sing this antiphon: *Cum sederit filius hominis.*

For the reception of a bishop. As soon as the arrival of the bishop will have been announced in the monastery, the prior or whoever is in charge should signal to the brothers, if there is no talking in the cloister, that all should gather in the church, and they should all be vested in copes and the children in albs. Then the lay brothers receive the holy water, cross, two candelabra, and the Gospel book, and they should go in silence. They should give [the bishop] the holy water and he should kiss the Gospel book and be censed. Then let him begin the responsory *Ecce uere Israelita* or *Audi Israel.* All the bells shall be rung, and they should go into the church. Let two carpets be arranged, one of which is before the principal altar, but the other is at the altar of the Holy Cross, and thus let them return to the cloister.

The same, for an abbot. For an abbot the bells are not rung, nor are all vested, but only those who make the procession. They should never sing, neither going nor returning. But nevertheless, if his rank merits it, all the brothers can be in copes, the boys in albs.

2. *Bernardus: Ordo Cluniacensis,* **Paris, BNF lat. 13875, cap. 35, fols. 71r–72v;** *Vetus disciplina monastica,* 217–19.

On processions for receiving persons. If any person is received in a procession according to his rank or to the extent to which he is known by those receiving him, let the same procession be made, that is, in albs or in copes. But, whereas an abbot or prior is received in albs, and those who lead the procession are in copes, the abbot has ordered that no person should be received in copes, unless at his order, except for the king and the pope. But after all are vested and the procession is prepared, with holy water, and a censer, and candles, and the Gospel book, before they set off the guest-master should find out whether the person to be welcomed is too far away. As the brothers leave the choir, the two big bells should begin to sound, and they shall not fall silent until, when that which was begun for the reception has been completed, *Saluum fac seruum tuum* or *Saluos fac seruos tuos* is said by the abbot or prior, and then the abbot proceeds with the procession, or the prior in the same procession, arranged with those preceding who bear the censer, and the water, and those following in the same order who carry the Gospel book and the candelabrum, with the Gospel book in the middle. After them follow the children with their teachers, and then their elders, the others following in the same way in which they are accustomed to go in procession to the cross. Then while all the others remain within the monastery, the abbot alone, or the prior, goes with the procession toward the person who is to be welcomed at the entrance to the porch. And if it is a king or pope who is received, both he and the community go outside the walls of the monastery. If, however, a bishop or archbishop is received, and the abbot greets him, he should prepare for him a casket with incense, and the bishop or the archbishop places the incense in the censer. But if an abbot is received or a person of another rank, the abbot places the incense in the censer. The prior should do the same if a person of higher status is received; he should prepare for him a casket with incense. If he is a layperson, he places the incense in the censer himself. And as soon as the water and incense are given by the abbot, and the Gospel book has been offered for osculation, the procession returns in the same manner in which it came, with the abbot or prior leading by the hand the person who has been received, near the procession that precedes them. Then, when the chant has been begun by the *armarius* (or, if the person who is welcomed is an abbot, *Miserere mei Deus*), they enter the monastery, passing through the group of children to the crucifix, and the guest prostrates himself, until released by the abbot, on a carpet of rushes that has been spread according to custom in front of the crucifix; the abbot, standing, waits for him to finish his prayer. Those who serve the procession stand in order in front of the altar of the crucifix, outside the enclosures, with their faces turned to the community, who hold the Gospel book in the middle, and holding the candelabra next to it on either side; those who hold the water and censer are at the end, one on one side, and another on the other, until when the chant is finished (or until, as stated, if it is an abbot who is welcomed, *Miserere mei Deus, Kyrie eleison, Pater noster,* and *Saluum fac seruum tuum*), he who was lying there prostrate arises. Then, with those preceding who lead the procession, and the children following, and after them the novices, all return to the choir in silence, each in his place, and the abbot or prior and the one who is received arrive last in the choir. If, however, that person is an abbot, or a bishop monk for whom the procession is made, he prays again, with those in the procession standing on the presbytery step, and the community standing in the choir; in the same way, they should stand with their faces turned toward the community, just as before, in front of the crucifix, until the prayer is finished. After the prayer is finished, the abbot or prior leads him into the place he pleases, that is the sacristy, and converses with him. At the same hour the procession recesses and all are unvested. If, however, the person who is welcomed is dressed in secular clothing, the abbot leads him to the high altar by another path than through the choir, whether he is a bishop or a layperson. And when a prayer has been recited there, if he is a layperson he is led immediately into the guesthouse. If, however, he is a bishop, the abbot leads him into the sacristy, or another place fitting for this purpose, which (as was recently decreed) has been decorated with seat covers and things of this kind, and there, when the blessing has been given to the reader by the bishop, the abbot has the reader recite in front of him for his edification two or even four biblical verses from a passage that should be relevant to him, such as *Ego sum pastor bonus* or other pertinent things of this kind. Then the abbot indicates to the reader that he should finish, and having said *Benedicite,* he should kiss him, and the other brothers who are with him, seeking forgiveness at his feet, as is customary, and afterward he speaks with him about his life, and about those things which he knows to be appropriate. When this has been done as much as seems honorable and fitting, he has him led into the guesthouse, and he sees to it that he and all his appurtenances are well treated in every way.

Glossary of Technical Terms

Advent: the four weeks preceding Christmas

adventus: ceremonial entry or arrival of a ruler

ambrosianus (Ambrosian): refers to hymns of the divine office attributed to Ambrose of Milan

antiphon: brief liturgical chant, usually sung before and after a psalm or series of psalms; the text is usually scriptural and often taken from the psalms

armarius: monastic librarian (in some contexts also entrusted with the direction of the liturgy)

breviary: liturgical book containing chants, readings, and prayers for the divine office

cadence: in medieval chant, conclusion of a melodic phrase

canticle: passage of Biblical text chanted during the divine office

cantor: choir director

capitulary: collection of brief texts (called *capitula;* see *chapter [reading]*) recited during the divine office, organized in an annual liturgical cycle

cartulary: volume containing copies of charters, usually in chronological order

chapter (meeting): daily gathering of a monastic community during which a chapter of the Benedictine Rule was read

chapter (reading): a short text, often from scripture, read during the divine office

collation: reading aloud of a text to the community before Compline

common of saints: collection of liturgical texts and chants for performance on the feasts of saints in the absence of material composed specifically for that saint

customary (monastic): compilation of prescriptions for the liturgy and daily life in a monastery

divine office: daily cycle of liturgical prayer centered on recitation of the psalms; consists of eight services performed at certain hours of the day (Matins, Lauds, Prime, Terce, Sext, None, Vespers, and Compline)

evangeliary: book containing the complete texts of the four Gospels

evangelistary: liturgical book containing the Gospel readings for Mass in the order of the church year

elegiac distich: line of dactylic hexameter followed by a line of elegiac pentameter.

epanalectic elegiac distichs: elegiac distichs in which the first part of the hexameter line is repeated in the second part of the pentameter line

hymn: Latin liturgical poem in strophic form sung during the divine office

lesson: from *lectio;* liturgical reading during the office of Matins

libellus: "booklet"; a small self-contained manuscript, often a section of a book

liber vitae: see necrology

litany: liturgical series of petitions to God and the saints with repeated refrains

liturgy: ritual actions with a predetermined structure, carried out in the church, primarily by members of a monastic or clerical community

martyrology: list of the martyrs commemorated on each calendar day, with the locations in which they were martyred

mass: religious ritual centered on the consecration of bread and wine, in which the celebrant commemorates and reenacts the words and actions of Christ at the Last Supper

Matins: liturgical office performed in the predawn hours

melisma: series of notes sung to a single syllable of text

melismatic: musical style of a vocal composition in which syllables of text are sung to phrases comprising numerous notes

mode (musical): term used to classify medieval chants by final note, melodic range, and other musical characteristics

necrology: written record of the names and death dates of deceased members of the monastic community, of its patrons, and of monks in associated monasteries; sometimes called the *liber vitae*

neumes: approximative graphic form of musical notation

nocturn: division of the office of Matins comprising psalmody, lessons, and responsories

octave: the eighth day following a feast day

office lectionary: liturgical book containing the biblical, hagiographic, and patristic readings for Matins

osculation: ritual kissing, as in the osculation of the cross during the Adoration on Good Friday

passio: narrative of a saint's martyrdom

pericope: selection from the Gospel read during Mass

pontifical: liturgical book used by a bishop for officiating at particular ceremonies

processional hymn: liturgical poem sung during a procession

proper (liturgical): texts designated for a particular liturgical occasion

prosula: type of trope in which a preexisting melody is set to a newly composed poetic text

psalmody: chanting of a group of psalms

responsory: liturgical chant for the divine office, composed of a respond and a verse

sacramentary: liturgical book containing prayers used by the celebrant during Mass

sanctoral: calendar of saints to be venerated in the liturgical year

sequence: liturgical poem sung during Mass, structured in paired versicles

strophic form: musical structure in which each strophe of a text is sung to the same melody

syllabic: musical style of a vocal composition in which each syllable of the text generally corresponds to a single note of the melody

trope: interpolation or addition to a prexisting liturgical chant

BIBLIOGRAPHY

MANUSCRIPT SOURCES

Bamberg, Staatsbibliothek, Lit. 5

Berlin, Staatsbibliothek Preussischer Kulturbesitz, theol. lat. quarto 377

Brescia, Biblioteca Civica Queriniana, F.II.1

Cambridge, Fitzwilliam Museum, MS 369

Eichstätt, Diözesanarchiv B 4

El Escorial, Biblioteca del Real Monasterio, Vitr. 17

Farfa, Archivio dell'Abbazia A 278

Farfa, Archivio dell'Abbazia AF 338

Farfa, Archivio dell'Abbazia A.175

Farfa, Archivio dell'Abbazia A.209

Farfa, Archivio dell'Abbazia A.281

Farfa, Archivio dell'Abbazia, A.278

Fribourg, Bibliothèque cantonale et universitaire, L46

London, British Library, Add. 26788

London, British Library, Cott. Vesp. D.XII

Madrid, Biblioteca Nacional, 289

Madrid, Biblioteca Nacional, Vitrina 20-6

Montecassino, Archivio dell'Abbazia, 506

Montecassino, Archivio dell'Abbazia, Compactiones VI

Munich, Bayerische Staatsbibliothek, clm 4452

Munich, Bayerische Staatsbibliothek, clm 4453

Naples, Biblioteca Nazionale, VI.E.43

Orléans, Bibliothèque Municipale, 184

Oxford, Bodleian Library, D'Orville 45

Paris, Bibliothèque Mazarine, 364

Paris, BNF lat. 903

Paris, BNF lat. 1087

Paris, BNF lat. 1092

Paris, BNF lat. 2508

Paris, BNF lat. 10318

Paris, BNF lat. 12601

Paris, BNF lat. 13875

Paris, BNF n.a.l. 2390

Perugia, Biblioteca Comunale Augusta, I 17

Piacenza, Biblioteca Capitolare 65

Rome, Abbazia di San Paolo fuori le Mura 92
Rome, Biblioteca Alessandrina 93
Rome, Biblioteca Alessandrina 96
Rome, Biblioteca Casanatense 1907
Rome, BN Farfa 1
Rome, BN Farfa 2
Rome, BN Farfa 4
Rome, BN Farfa 29
Rome, BN Farfa 30
Rome, BN Farfa 32
Rome, BV B.23
Rome, BV C.5
Rome, BV C.9
Rome, BV C.13
Rome, BV E.16
Rome, BV F.29
Rome, BV Tomus XVI
Saint-Victor-sur-Rhins, Mairie, s.c.
Utrecht, Museum Catharijne Convent, ABM h3
Vatican City, BAV Archivio S. Pietro D 164
Vatican City, BAV Chigi C.VI.177
Vatican City, BAV Chigi D.VI.79
Vatican City, BAV Ottob. lat. 145
Vatican City, BAV Pal. lat. 265
Vatican City, BAV Reg. lat. 801
Vatican City, BAV Urb. lat. 585
Vatican City, BAV Vat. lat. 84
Vatican City, BAV Vat. lat. 5776
Vatican City, BAV Vat. lat. 7172
Vatican City, BAV Vat. lat. 6808
Vatican City, BAV Vat. lat. 8487
Verona, Biblioteca Capitolare 109
Worcester, Cathedral Chapter Library, F.160
Zurich, Zentralbibliothek, Rheinau 82
Zurich, Zentralbibliothek, Rheinau 91

PRINTED PRIMARY SOURCES

Acta sanctorum quotquot toto orbe coluntur. Ed. Joannus Bollandus and others. 69
   vols. Antwerp: Victor Palme, 1643–1940.
Aldhelm of Malmesbury. *Aldhelmi opera.* Ed. Rudolf Ehwald. *MGH Auctores
   antiquissimi* 15. Berlin: Weidmann, 1919.

Ambrose of Milan. *Ambroise de Milan: Hymnes.* Ed. Jacques Fontaine and others. Paris: Cerf, 1992.

——. *Expositio euangelii secundum Lucam.* Ed. Marcus Adriaen. *CCSL* 14. Turnhout: Brepols, 1957.

——. *De fide.* Ed. Otto Faller. *CSEL* 78. Vienna: Hölder-Pichler-Tempsky, 1962.

Analecta hymnica medii aeui. Ed. Guido Maria Dreves and others. 55 vols. Leipzig: O. R. Reisland, 1886–1922.

Andrieu, Michel. *Les ordines romani du haut moyen âge.* 5 vols. Spicilegium Sacrum Lovaniense 11, 23, 24, 28, 29. Louvain: Spicilegium sacrum Lovaniense, 1931–61.

"Anonymus Haserensis de Episcopis Eichstetensibus." Ed. Ludwig Bethmann. In *MGH Scriptores 7*, ed. Georg Heinrich Pertz (Hannover: Hahn, 1846), 253–66.

Antiphonaire monastique, XIIIe siècle, codex F. 160 de la Bibliothèque de la Cathédrale de Worcester. Paléographie musicale 12. Tournai: Desclée, 1922. Reprint, Bern: Lang, 1971.

Antiphonale Sarisburiense. Ed. Walter Howard Frere. London: Plainsong and Mediaeval Music Society, 1901.

Arnobius of Sicca. *Arnobius of Sicca: The Case against the Nations.* Trans. George E. McCracken. Ancient Christian Writers 8. Westminster, MD: The Newman Press, 1949.

——. *Disputationes aduersus nationes.* Ed. Concetto Marchesi. Turin: Paravia, 1957.

Augustine of Hippo. *Enarrationes in psalmos.* Ed. Eligius Dekkers and Jean Fraipont. *CCSL* 39. Turnhout: Brepols, 1990.

——. *Confessionum libri XIII.* Ed. Martin Skutella. Stuttgart: Teubner, 1981.

——. *In Iohannis euangelium tractatus.* Ed. D. Radbod Willems. *CCSL* 36. Turnhout: Brepols, 1990.

——. *De sancta uirginitate.* Ed. Joseph Zycha. *CSEL* 41. Vienna: Tempsky, 1900.

Bannister, Henry. *Monumenti Vaticani di paleografia musicale Latina.* 2 vols. Leipzig: Harrassowitz, 1913.

Bede the Venerable. *Bedae venerabilis homeliarum euangelii libri II.* Ed. David Hurst. *CCSL* 122. Turnhout: Brepols, 1955.

Bernardus: Ordo Cluniacensis (Paris, Bibliothèque Nationale de France, ms latin 13875). Ed. and trans. Susan Boynton and Isabelle Cochelin. Turnhout: Brepols, forthcoming.

Bibliotheca hagiographica Latina. Ed. Society of Bollandists. 2 vols. and supplement. Brussels: Société des Bollandistes, 1898–1911.

Björkvall, Gunilla, ed. *Liturgisk versdiktning under 1100-talet i Frankrike och dess europeiska reception. Källor, transmission, edition.* Forthcoming.

Canones apostolorum et conciliorum saeculorum IV–VII. Ed. Hermann Theodor Bruns. Berlin: Reimer, 1839.

Cetedoc Library of Christian Latin Texts. Release 3 (*CLCLT*-3). 3 CDs. Turnhout: Brepols, 2003.

Chronicon Vulturnense del monaco Giovanni. Ed. Vincenzo Federici. 3 vols. Fonti per la storia d'Italia 58–60. Rome: Istituto Storico Italiano, 1925–37.

Chrysologus, Peter. *Sancti Petri Chrysologi collectio sermonum.* Ed. Alexandre Olivar. *CCSL* 24B. Turnhout: Brepols, 1975.

Le Codex 903 de la Bibliothèque nationale de Paris (XIe siècle): Graduel de Saint-Yrieix. Paléographie Musicale 13. Tournai: Desclée, 1925. Reprint, Bern: Lang, 1971.

Collectio canonum Regesto Farfensi inserta. Ed. Theo Kölzer. Monumenta Iuris Canonici, ser. B, Corpus Collectionum, vol. 5. Vatican City: Biblioteca Apostolica Vaticana, 1982.

Collectiones aenigmatum Merovingicae aetatis. Ed. François Glorie. *CCSL* 133. Turnhout: Brepols, 1968.

Concilios visigóticos e hispano-romanos. Ed Juan Vivez. España cristiana, Testo, 1. Barcelona: Consejo Superior de Investigaciones Científicas, Instituto Enrique Flórez, 1963.

Consuetudines Benedictinae variae (saec. XI–saec. XIV). *CCM* 6. Siegburg: Franz Schmitt, 1975.

Consuetudines Cluniacensium antiquiores cum redactionibus derivatis. Ed. Kassius Hallinger. *CCM* 7.2. Siegburg: Franz Schmitt, 1983.

Consuetudines Fructuarienses—Sanblasianae. Ed. Luchesius Spätling and Peter Dinter. 2 vols. *CCM* 12. Siegburg: Franz Schmitt, 1987.

Consuetudinum saeculi X/XI/XII monumenta non-Cluniacensia. Ed. Kassius Hallinger. *CCM* 7.3. Siegburg: Franz Schmitt, 1984.

Corpus antiphonalium officii. Ed. Réné-Jean Hesbert. 6 vols. Rome: Herder, 1968–79.

Corpus Christianorum, continuatio medaeualis. Turnhout: Brepols, 1971–.

Corpus Christianorum, series Latina. Turnhout: Brepols, 1954–.

Corpus consuetudinum monasticarum. Siegburg: Franz Schmitt, 1963–.

Corpus orationum. Ed. Eugene Moeller and Jean-Marie Clément, completed by Bertrand Coppieters 't Wallant. 13 vols. *CCSL* 160. Turnhout: Brepols, 1993–2003.

Damian, Peter. *Die Briefe des Petrus Damiani* 3. Ed. Kurt Reindel. *MGH Briefe der deutschen Kaiserzeit* 4. Munich: Monumenta Germaniae Historica, 1989.

——. *Petri Damiani sermones.* Ed. Giovanni Lucchesi. *CCCM* 57. Turnhout: Brepols, 1983.

Dhuoda. *Liber manualis.* Ed. Pierre Riché. Paris: Cerf, 1991.

Early Latin Hymns. Ed. A. P. Walpole. Cambridge: Cambridge University Press, 1922.

Festtagsevangelistar mit Kanontafeln: Brescia, Bibliotheca Civica Queriniana Codex F.II.1. Commentary by Satoko I. Parker. 3 vols. Studien zur Bibliotheksgeschichte 6. Graz: Akademische Druck- und Verlagsanstalt, 1991–92.

Florilegia biblica Africana saec. V. Ed. Jean Fraipont. *CCSL* 90. Turnhout: Brepols, 1961.

Die Geschichte der Eichstätter Bischöfe des Anonymus Haserensis. Ed. Stefan Weinfurter. Eichstätter Studien, Neue Folge 24. Regensburg: Pustet, 1987.

Glaber, Radulfus. *Rodulfi Glabri historiarum libri quinque/Rodulfus Glaber, The Five Books of the Histories.* Ed. and trans. John France. Oxford: Clarendon Press, 1989.

Gregory of Catino. *Il Chronicon Farfense di Gregorio di Catino.* Ed. Ugo Balzani. 2 vols. Fonti per la Storia d'Italia 33–34. Rome: Istituto Storico Italiano, 1903.

——. *Il "Liber floriger" di Gregorio da Catino.* Ed. Maria Teresa Maggi Bei. Miscellanea della Società Romana di Storia Patria 26. Rome: Società Romana di Storia Patria, 1984.

——. *Il Regesto di Farfa compilato da Gregorio di Catino.* Ed. Ignazio Giorgi and Ugo Balzani. 5 vols. Rome: Società Romana di Storia Patria, 1883–1914.

Heinrici IV diplomata. Vol. 1. Ed. Dietrich von Gladiss. *MGH Diplomata regum et imperatorum Germaniae* 6.Weimar: Böhlau, 1953. Reprint, Hannover: Hahn, 1977.

Hildemar of Corbie. *Expositio regulae ab Hildemaro tradita.* Ed. R. Mittermüller. Regensburg: Pustet, 1880.

Die Hymnen: Die mittelalterlichen Hymnenmelodien des Abendlandes. Ed. Bruno Stäblein. Monumenta Monodica Medii Aevi 1. Kassel: Bärenreiter, 1956.

Initia Consuetudines benedictinae: Consuetudines saeculi octavi et noni. Ed. Josef Semmler. *CCM* 1. Siegburg: Franz Schmitt, 1963.

Isidore of Seville. *Isidori Hispalensis episcopi etymologiarum siue originum libri XX.* Ed. W. M. Lindsay. 2 vols. Oxford: Clarendon Press, 1911.

Jaffé, Philipp, ed. *Regesta pontificum Romanorum.* Rev. ed. by Samuel Löwenfeld, Franz Kaltenbrunner, Paul Ewald, and Wilhelm Wattenbach. Leipzig: Veit, 1885.

Jerome. *Commentarii in Ezechielem.* Ed. François Glorie. *CCSL* 75. Turnhout: Brepols, 1964.

John Beleth. *Iohannis Beleth summa de ecclesiasticis officiis.* Ed. Herbert Douteil. *CCCM* 41. Turnhout: Brepols, 1976.

John of Salisbury. *Policraticus.* Ed. K. S. B. Keats-Rohan. *CCCM* 118. Turnhout: Brepols, 1993.

Jotsald of Saint-Claude. *Iotsald von Saint-Claude: Vita des Abtes Odilo von Cluny.* Ed. Johannes Staub. *MGH Scriptores rerum Germanicarum in usum scholarum separatim editi* 68. Hannover: Hahn, 1999.

Kehr, Paul Fridolin. *Italia pontificia: Roma.* Berlin: Weidmann, 1906.

Lantbert of Deutz. *Lantbert von Deutz: Vita Heriberti, Miracula Heriberti, Gedichte, Liturgische Texte.* Ed. Bernhard Vogel. *MGH Scriptores rerum Germanicarum in usum scholarum separatim editi* 73. Hannover: Hahn, 2001.

Leo I. *Sancti Leonis magni Romani pontificis tractatus septem et nonaginta.* Ed. Antoine Chavasse. *CCSL* 138A. Turnhout: Brepols, 1973.

Liber de rectoribus Christianis. Ed. Sigmund Hellmann. Quellen und
Untersuchungen zur lateinischen Philologie des Mittelalters 1.1. Munich: Beck,
1906.

Liber largitorius vel notarius monasterii Pharphensis. Ed. Giuseppe Zucchetti.
Regesta chartarum Italiae 1, 11. Rome: Istituto Storico Italiano, 1913.

Liber tramitis aeui Odilonis abbatis. Ed. Peter Dinter. *CCM* 10. Siegburg: Franz
Schmitt, 1980.

Lotharii I et Lotharii II Diplomata. Ed. Theodor Schieffer. *MGH Diplomata
Karolinorum* 3. Berlin: Weidmann, 1966.

Ludovici II diplomata. Ed. Konrad Wanner. *MGH Diplomata Karolinorum* 4.
Munich: Monumenta Germaniae Historica, 1994.

MGH Auctores antiquissimi. 15 vols. Berlin: Weidmann, 1877–1919.

MGH Diplomata Karolinorum. 4 vols. Hannover: Hahn, 1906. Reprint, Munich:
Monumenta Germaniae Historica, 1994.

MGH Leges 4, *Constitutiones* 1. Ed. Ludwig Weiland. Hannover: Hahn, 1893.

MGH Epistolae 6, *Epistolae Karolini aevi* 4. Ed. Ernest Perels. Berlin: Weidmann,
1925.

MGH Poetae Latini aeui Carolini. 6 vols. Berlin: Weidmann, 1881–1951.

The Monastic Constitutions of Lanfranc. Ed. and trans. David Knowles. Revised by
Christopher Brooke. Oxford: Clarendon Press, 2002.

*The Necrology of San Nicola della Cicogna (Montecassino, Archivio della Badia 179,
pp. 1–64).* Ed. Charles Hilken. Studies and Texts 135. Monumenta Liturgica
Beneventana 2. Toronto: Pontifical Institute of Mediaeval Studies, 2000.

Novum glossarium mediae Latinitatis. Copenhagen: Munksgaard, 1957–85.

Orthodoxa defensio imperialis. Ed. Lotharius de Heinemann. *MGH Libelli de lite
imperatorum et pontificum saeculis XI. et XII. conscripti* 2:534–42. Hanover:
Hahn, 1892. Rev. ed. 1956.

Oxford Latin Dictionary. Oxford: Oxford University Press, 1968–82.

Ottonis III diplomata. Ed. Theodor Sickel. *MGH Diplomata regum et imperatorum
Germaniae* 2/2. Hannover: Hahn, 1893.

Papsturkunden 896–1046. Vol. 2, *996–1046.* Ed. Harald Zimmermann.
Österreichische Akademie der Wissenschaften, Philosophisch-Historische
Klasse, Denkschriften 177, Veröffentlichungen der historischen Kommission 4.
Vienna: Verlag der Österreichischen Akademie der Wissenschaften, 1985.

Paschasius Radbertus. *De partu uirginis.* Ed. E. Ann Matter. *CCCM* 56C. Turnhout:
Brepols, 1985.

Patrologiae cursus completus, series Latina. Ed. Jacques-Paul Migne. 221 vols. Paris:
Migne, 1844–66.

Paul the Deacon. *Historia Langobardorum.* Ed. Ludwig Bethmann and Georg
Waitz. *MGH Scriptores rerum Langobardicarum et Italicarum saec. VI–IX.*
Hannover: Hahn, 1878.

Peter the Venerable. *The Letters of Peter the Venerable.* Ed. Giles Constable. 2 vols. Cambridge, MA: Harvard University Press, 1967.

Pippini, Carlomanni, Caroli Magni diplomata. Ed. Alfons Dopsch, Johann Lechner, Michael Tangl, and Engelbert Mühlbacher. *MGH Diplomata Karolinorum* 1. Hannover: Hahn, 1906.

Le pontifical romano-germanique du dixième siècle. Ed. Cyrille Vogel and Reinhard Elze. 3 vols. Studi e testi 226, 227, 269. Vatican City: Biblioteca Apostolica Vaticana, 1963, 1972.

Das "Pontifikale Gundekarianum": Faksimile-Ausgabe des Codex B 4 im Diözesanarchiv Eichstätt. Ed. Andreas Bauch and Ernst Reiter. 2 vols. Wiesbaden: Dr. Ludwig Reichert Verlag, 1987.

Precum libelli quattuor aeui Karolini. Ed. André Wilmart. Rome: Ephemerides liturgicae, 1940.

RB 1980: The Rule of St. Benedict in Latin and English with Notes. Ed. Timothy Fry. Collegeville, MN: Liturgical Press, 1981. (Latin text from *La règle de saint Benoît.* Ed. Jean Neufville. Sources chrétiennes 182. Paris: Cerf, 1972.)

Receuil des historiens des Croisades. 16 vols. Paris: Imprimerie impériale, 1841–1906.

Regularis concordia anglicae nationis. Ed. Thomas Symons and Sigrid Spath. *CCM* 7.3 (1984), 69–147.

Le sacramentaire grégorien. Ed. Jean Deshusses. 3rd rev. ed. 3 vols. Fribourg: Editions universitaires, 1979–92.

Strabo, Walahfrid. "Libellus de exordiis et incrementis quarundam in obseruationibus ecclesiasticis rerum." Ed. Alfred Boretius and Victor Krause. *MGH Capitularia regum Francorum* 2, 473–516. Hannover: Hahn, 1897.

Vetus disciplina monastica. Ed. Marquard Herrgott. Paris: Osmont, 1726.

William of Apulia. *Guillaume de Pouille: La geste de Robert Guiscard.* Ed. and trans. Marguerite Mathieu. Palermo: Istituto siciliano di studi bizantini e neoellenici, 1961.

William of Tyre. *Willelmi Tyrensis archiepiscopi Chronicon.* Ed. R. B. C. Huygens. *CCCM* 63, 63A. Turnhout: Brepols, 1986.

SECONDARY SOURCES

Achten, Gerard. *Die theologischen lateinischen Handschriften in Quarto der Staatsbibliothek Preussischer Kulturbesitz.* 2 vols. Berlin: Harrassowitz, 1979–84.

Agiografia e culto dei santi nel Piceno: Atti del Convegno di studio svoltosi in occasione della undicesima edizione del "Premio internazionale Ascoli Piceno," Ascoli Piceno, 2–3 maggio 1997. Ed. Enrico Menestò. Spoleto: Centro italiano di studi sull'alto medioevo, 1998.

Algazi, Gadi. "Introduction: Doing Things with Gifts." In *Negotiating the Gift,* ed. Algazi, Groebner, and Jussen, 9–24.

Analecta liturgica: Extraits des manuscrits liturgiques de la Bibliothèque Vaticane;

Contribution à l'histoire de la prière chrétienne. Ed. Pierre Salmon. Studi e testi 273. Vatican City: Biblioteca Apostolica Vaticana, 1974.

d'Andrea, Gianni, ed. *Ildefonso Schuster storico di Farfa e della Sabina.* Farfa: Biblioteca del monumento nazionale, 1994.

Andreucci, Andrea Girolamo. *Notizie storiche dei gloriosi santi Valentino prete e d'Ilario diacono martiri Viterbesi, e primi apostoli di quella città raccolte da Andrea Girolamo Andreucci della Compagnia di Gesu.* Rome: Gio. Zempel, 1740.

Arlt, Wulf. *Ein Festoffizium des Mittelalters aus Beauvais in seiner liturgischen und musikalischen Bedeutung.* 2 vols. Cologne: Arno Volk, 1970.

——. "Das Eine und die vielen Lieder: Zur historischen Stellung der neuen Liedkunst des frühen 12. Jahrhunderts." In *Festschrift Rudolf Bockholdt zum 60. Geburtstag,* ed. Norbert Dubowy and Sören Meyer-Eller, 113–27. Pfaffenhofen: Ludwig, 1990.

——. "Neues zum neuen Lied: Die Fragmente aus der Handschrift Douai 246." Forthcoming.

——. "*Nova cantica*—Grundsätzliches und Spezielles zur Interpretation musikalischer Texte des Mittelalters." *Basler Jahrbuch für historische Musikpraxis* 10 (1986): 13–62.

——. "Sequence and *Neues Lied.*" In *La sequenza medievale: Atti del Convegno internazionale, Milano, 7–8 aprile 1984,* ed. Agostino Ziino, 3–18. Lucca: Libreria musicale italiana, 1992.

Atkinson, Charles. "The *Doxa,* the *Pisteuo,* and the *Ellinici Fratres:* Some Anomalies in the Transmission of the Chants of the 'Missa Graeca.'" *Journal of Musicology* 7 (1989): 81–106.

——. "Zur Entstehung und Überlieferung der 'Missa Graeca.'" *Archiv für Musikwissenschaft* 39 (1982): 113–45.

——. "Further Thoughts on the Origin of the *Missa Graeca.*" In *De musica et cantu: Studien zur Geschichte der Kirchenmusik und der Oper,* ed. Peter Cahn and Ann-Katrin Heimer, 75–93. Musikwissenschaftliche Publikationen, Hochschule für Musik und darstellende Kunst Frankfurt/Main 2. Hildesheim: Georg Olms, 1993.

Auda, Antoine. *L'école musicale liégoise au Xe siècle: Étienne de Liège.* Brussels: Lamertin, 1923.

Avril, François, and Yolanta Załuska. *Manuscrits enluminés d'origine italienne.* Vol. 1, *VIe–XIIe siècles.* Paris: Bibliothèque nationale, 1980.

Baroffio, Giacomo. "La tradizione dei tropi e delle sequenze: Bilancio di alcune esplorazioni in Italia." *Rivista internazionale di musica sacra* 25 (2004): 11–113.

Barré, Henri. *Prières anciennes de l'occident à la mère du sauveur des origines à saint Anselme.* Paris: Lethielleux, 1963.

Barrett, Sam. "Music and Writing: On the Compilation of Paris, Bibliothèque Nationale lat. 1154." *Early Music History* 16 (1997): 55–96.

Bell, Catherine. *Ritual: Perspectives and Dimensions*. Oxford: Oxford University Press, 1997.

———. *Ritual Theory, Ritual Practice*. Oxford: Oxford University Press, 1992.

Bergman, Robert. *The Salerno Ivories: Ars Sacra from Medieval Amalfi*. Cambridge, MA: Harvard University Press, 1980.

———. "A School of Romanesque Ivory Carving in Amalfi." *Metropolitan Museum Journal* 9 (1974): 167–71.

Bernhardt, John William. *Itinerant Kingship and Royal Monasteries in Early Medieval Germany, c. 936–1075*. Cambridge: Cambridge University Press, 1993.

Berschin, Walter, and David Hiley, eds. *Die Offizien des Mittelalters: Dichtung und Musik*. Tutzing: Hans Schneider, 1999.

Bijsterveld, Arnoud-Jan A. "The Medieval Gift as Agent of Social Bonding and Political Power: A Comparative Approach." In *Medieval Transformations: Texts, Power, and Gifts in Context*, ed. Esther Cohen and Mayke De Jong, 123–56. Leiden: Brill, 2001.

Bischoff, Bernhard. "Ursprung und Geschichte eines Kreuzsegens." In Bischoff, *Mittelalterliche Studien* 2:275–84. Stuttgart: Hiersemann, 1967.

Bishko, Charles Julian. "Liturgical Intercession at Cluny for the King-Emperors of Leon." In *Spanish and Portuguese Monastic History, 600–1300*. Reprinted with an additional note from *Studia monastica* 3 (1961): 53–76. London: Variorum Reprints, 1984.

Björkvall, Gunilla, and Andreas Haug. "Text und Musik im Trinitätsoffizium Stephans von Lüttich: Beobachtungen und Überlegungen aus mittellateinischer und musikhistorischer Sicht." In *Die Offizien des Mittelalters: Dichtung und Musik*, ed. Walter Berschin und David Hiley, 1–24. Tutzing: Hans Schneider, 1999.

———. "Tropentypen in Sankt Gallen." In *Recherches nouvelles sur les tropes liturgiques*, ed. Wulf Arlt and Gunilla Björkvall, 119–74. Studia Latina Stockholmiensia 36. Stockholm: Almqvist & Wiksell, 1993.

———. "Zum Verhältnis von Verslehre und Versvertonung im lateinischen Mittelalter." In *Artes im Mittelalter*, ed. Ursula Schaefer, 309–23. Berlin: Akademie Verlag, 1999.

Black, Jonathan. "Psalm Uses in Carolingian Prayerbooks: Alcuin and the Preface to *De psalmorum usu*." *Mediaeval Studies* 64 (2002): 1–60.

Black-Veldtrup, Mechthild. *Kaiserin Agnes: Quellenkritische Studien*. Münstersche Historische Forschungen 7. Cologne: Böhlau, 1995.

Bloch, Herbert. "Monte Cassino, Byzantium, and the West in the Earlier Middle Ages." *Dumbarton Oaks Papers* 3 (1946): 163–224.

———. *Monte Cassino in the Middle Ages*. 3 vols. Cambridge, MA: Harvard University Press, 1986.

Bobeth, Gundela. "Antike Verse in mittelalterlicher Vertonung. Neumierungen in

Vergil-, Statius-, Lucan- und Terenz-Handschriften." PhD diss. University of Basel, 2004.

———. "Cantare Virgilium–Neumierte Vergilverse in karolingischen und postkarolingischen Handschriften." *Schweizer Jahrbuch für Musikwissenschaft* 23 (2003): 111–37.

Boe, John. "Chant Notation in Eleventh-Century Roman Manuscripts." In *Essays on Medieval Music in Honor of David G. Hughes,* ed. Graeme Boone, 43–57. Cambridge, MA: Harvard University Press, 1995.

———. "Music Notation in Archivio San Pietro C 105 and in the Farfa Breviary, Chigi C.VI.177." *Early Music History* 18 (1999): 1–45.

Boesch Gajano, Sofia. "Berardo." In *Dizionario biografico degli italiani* 8:767–75. Rome: Istituto della enciclopedia italiana, 1966.

Bolli, Guerriero. *Narni da Odoacre agli Ottoni.* Terni: Nuova editoriale, 1992.

Bossi, Gaetano. "I Crescenzi di Sabina: Stefaniani e Ottaviani (dal 1012 al 1106)." *Archivio della Reale Società Romana di Storia Patria* 41 (1918): 111–70.

Bouchard, Constance Brittain. "Monastic Cartularies: Organizing Eternity." In *Charters, Cartularies, and Archives: The Preservation and Transmission of Documents in the Medieval West,* ed. Adam J. Kosto and Anders Winroth, 22–32. Toronto: Pontifical Institute of Mediaeval Studies, 2002.

Bougard, François, Étienne Hubert, and Ghislaine Noyé. "Les techniques de construction en Sabine: Enquête préliminaire sur la 'chiesa nuova' de l'abbaye de Farfa." *Mélanges de l'École Française de Rome: Moyen âge* 99 (1987): 729–64.

Boynton, Susan. "The Bible and the Liturgy." In *The Bible as a Way of Life: A Casebook,* ed. Greti Dinkova-Bruun and Jennifer Harris. New York: Routledge, 2005.

———. "The Customaries of Bernard and Ulrich as Liturgical Sources." In *From Dead of Night to End of Day: The Medieval Customs of Cluny,* ed. Susan Boynton and Isabelle Cochelin. Brepols: Turnhout, 2005.

———. "The Didactic Function and Context of Eleventh-Century Glossed Hymnaries." In *Der lateinische Hymnus im Mittelalter: Überlieferung-Ästhetik-Ausstrahlung,* ed. Andreas Haug, Christoph März, and Lorenz Welker, 301–29. Monumenta Monodica Medii Aevi, Subsidia 4. Kassel: Bärenreiter, 2004.

———. "Eleventh-Century Continental Hymnaries Containing Latin Glosses." *Scriptorium* 53 (1999): 200–251.

———. "Frammenti medievali nell'Archivio dell'Abbazia di Farfa." *Benedictina* 48 (2001): 325–53.

———. "Glossed Hymns in Eleventh-Century Continental Hymnaries." PhD diss., Brandeis University, 1997.

———. "Glosses on the Office Hymns in Eleventh-Century Continental Hymnaries." *Journal of Medieval Latin* 11 (2001): 1–26.

———. "Hymn, II. Monophonic Latin." In *The New Grove Dictionary of Music and Musicians.* 6th ed. Vol. 12:19–23. London: MacMillan, 2000.

——. "Liturgy and History at the Abbey of Farfa in the Late Eleventh Century: Hymns of Peter Damian and Other Additions to BAV Chigi C.VI.177." *Sacris Erudiri* 39 (2000): 317–44.

——. "Orality, Literacy, and the Early Notation of the Office Hymns." *Journal of the American Musicological Society* 56 (2003): 99–167.

——. "Performative Exegesis in the Fleury *Interfectio puerorum*." *Viator* 29 (1998): 39–64.

——. "Prayer and Liturgical Performance in Eleventh- and Twelfth-Century Monastic Psalters." In *A History of Prayer,* ed. Roy Hammerling. Leiden: Brill, 2005.

——. "Training for the Liturgy as a Form of Monastic Education." In *Medieval Monastic Education,* ed. Carolyn Muessig and George Ferzoco, 7–20. Leicester: Leicester University Press, 2000.

——. "Work and Play in Sacred Music and Its Social Context, ca. 1050–1250." In *The Use and Abuse of Time in Christian History,* ed. Robert N. Swanson, 57–79. Studies in Church History 37. Woodbridge: Blackwell, 2002.

——. Review of Mary Stroll, *The Medieval Abbey of Farfa: Target of Papal and Imperial Ambitions. Benedictina* 46 (1999): 502–3.

Boynton, Susan, and Martina Pantarotto. "Ricerche sul breviario di Santa Giulia (Brescia, Biblioteca Queriniana, ms. H VI 21)." *Studi medievali* 42 (2001): 301–18.

Braca, Antonio. "Lavori in avorio." *Rassegna del Centro di cultura e storia amalfitana* 13 (1993): 111–28.

Bragança, Joaquim. "A adoração da cruz na espiritualidade do ocidente: 'Ordines' inéditos da França meridional." *Didaskalia* 5 (1975): 255–81.

Branciani, Luchina. "Il monte S. Martino in Sabina: Siti archeologici e storia." In *Eremetismo a Farfa: Origine e storia; Per una ricostruzione archeologico-ambientale del complesso eremitico del Monte S. Martino in Sabina,* ed. Patrizia Lombardozzi, 31–133. Quaderni della Biblioteca 3. Farfa: Biblioteca del monumento nazionale, 2000.

Brugnoli, Giorgio. "Catalogus codicum Farfensium." *Benedictina* 6 (1952): 287–303.

——. "Catalogus codicum Farfensium: Pars altera." *Benedictina* 7 (1953): 85–120.

Brunner, Lance. "Catalogo delle sequenze in manoscritti di origine italiana." *Rivista italiana di musicologia* 20 (1985): 191–276.

——. "The Sequences of Verona, Biblioteca Capitolare CVII and the Italian Sequence Tradition." PhD diss., University of North Carolina, Chapel Hill, 1977.

Buc, Philippe. *The Dangers of Ritual.* Princeton: Princeton University Press, 2001.

Bulst, Neithard. *Untersuchungen zu den Klosterreformen Wilhelms von Dijon (962–1031).* Pariser Historische Studien 11. Bonn: Ludwig Röhrscheid, 1973.

Busse Berger, Anna Maria. "Mnemotechnics and Notre Dame Polyphony." *Journal of Musicology* 14 (1996): 263–98.

Butterfield, Ardis. *Poetry and Music in Medieval France from Jean Renart to Guillaume de Machaut.* Cambridge: Cambridge University Press, 2002.

Caby, Cécile. "La mémoire des origines dans les institutions médiévales: Présentation d'un projet collectif." *Mélanges de l'École française de Rome: Moyen âge* 115 (2003): 133–40.

Cantarella, Glauco Maria. "Appunti su Rodolfo il Glabro." *Aevum* 65 (1991): 279–94.

———. "I Cluniacensi in Italia: Lineamenti di una presenza monastica." In *I rapporti tra le comunità monastiche benedittine italiane tra alto e pieno medioevo. Atti del III convegno del "Centro di studi farfensi," Santa Vittoria in Matenano 11–12–13 settembre 1992*, 247–68. Negarine di San Pietro in Cariano: Il segno, 1994.

Carruthers, Mary. *The Book of Memory: A Study of Memory in Medieval Culture.* Cambridge: Cambridge University Press, 1990.

———. *The Craft of Thought: Meditation, Rhetoric, and the Making of Images, 400–1200.* Cambridge: Cambridge University Press, 1998.

Les cartulaires. Actes de la table ronde organisée par l'École nationale des chartes et le G.D.R 121 du C.N.R.S (Paris, 5–7 septembre 1991). Ed. Olivier Guyotjeannin, Laurent Morelle, and Michel Parisse. Mémoires et documents de l'École des chartes 39. Paris: École nationale des chartes, 1993.

Di Carpegna Falconieri, Tommaso. *Il clero di Roma nel medioevo: Istituzioni e politica cittadina (secoli VIII–XIII).* Rome: Viella, 2002.

Casagrande, Carla, and Silvana Vecchio. "Clercs et jongleurs dans la société médiévale (XIIe et XIIIe siècles)." *Annales: Économies, Sociétés, Civilisations* 34 (1979): 913–28.

Chastang, Pierre. *Lire, écrire, transcrire: Le travail des rédacteurs de cartulaires en Bas-Languedoc (XIe–XIIIe siècles).* Paris: Éditions du CTHS, 2001.

Cignitti, Benedetto. "Getulio, Cereale, Amanzio e Primitivo." In *Bibliotheca sanctorum* 6 (1965): 311–12.

Citarella, Armand. *Il commercio di Amalfi nell'alto medioevo.* Salerno: Grafikart, 1977.

———. "Patterns in Medieval Trade: The Commerce of Amalfi before the Crusades." *Journal of Economic History* 28 (1968): 531–55.

———. "The Relations of Amalfi with the Arab World before the Crusades." *Speculum* 42 (1967): 299–312.

Clanchy, Michael T. *From Memory to Written Record: England, 1066–1307.* 2nd ed. Oxford: Blackwell, 1993.

Clark, Gillian. "Monastic Economies? Aspects of Production and Consumption in Early Medieval Central Italy." *Archeologia Medievale* 24 (1997): 31–54.

Cluny in Lombardia: Atti del Convegno storico celebrativo del IX centenario della fondazione del priorato cluniacense di Pontida: 22–25 aprile 1977. 2 vols. Italia benedittina 1. Cesena: Centro storico benedittino italiano, 1979–81.

Cochelin, Isabelle. "Evolution des coutumiers monastiques dessinée à partir de l'étude de Bernard." In *From Dead of Night to End of Day: The Medieval Customs of Cluny,* ed. Susan Boynton and Isabelle Cochelin. Turnhout: Brepols, 2005.

———. "Quête de liberté et récriture des origines: Odon et les portraits corrigés de

Baume, Géraud et Guillaume." In *Guerriers et moines: Conversion et sainteté aristocratiques dans l'occident médiéval,* ed. Michel Lauwers, 183–215. Collection d'études médiévales de Nice 4. Nice: Centre national de la recherche scientifique, 2003.

——. "When Monks Were the Book." In *The Bible as a Way of Life: A Casebook,* ed. Greti Dinkova-Bruun and Jennifer Harris. New York: Routledge, 2005.

Conant, Kenneth John. *Cluny: Les églises et la maison du chef d'ordre.* Medieval Academy Publications 77. Cambridge, MA: Medieval Academy of America and Mâcon: Protat Frères, 1968.

Constable, Giles. *The Reformation of the Twelfth Century.* Cambridge: Cambridge University Press, 1996.

Corbet, Patrick. "Les impératrices ottoniennes et le modèle marial: Autour de l'ivoire du château Sforza de Milan." In *Marie: Le culte de la Vierge dans la société médiévale,* ed. Iogna-Prat, Palazzo, and Russo, 109–35.

Costambeys, Marios James. "The Monastic Environment of Paul the Deacon." In *Paolo Diacono,* ed. Chiesa, 127–38.

——. "Piety, Property and Power in Eighth-Century Italy: The Rise of the Abbey of Farfa in Its Social and Political Context, c. 690–787." D.Phil. thesis. University of Cambridge, 1998.

Cottier, Jean-François. *Anima mea: Prières privées et textes de dévotion du moyen âge latin, XIe–XIIe siècles.* Recherches sur les rhétoriques religieuses 3. Turnhout: Brepols, 2001.

Cowdrey, Herbert Edward John. *The Age of Abbot Desiderius: Montecassino, the Papacy, and the Normans in the Eleventh and Early Twelfth Centuries.* Oxford: Clarendon Press, 1983.

Crippa, Luigi. "Schuster e Farfa: Motivi di una predilezione." In *Ildefonso Schuster,* ed. D'Andrea, 75–82.

Crook, John. *The Architectural Setting of the Cult of Saints in the Early Christian West c. 300–1200.* Oxford: Clarendon Press, 2000.

Crosby, Sumner. *The Royal Abbey of Saint-Denis from Its Beginnings to the Death of Suger, 475–1151.* Ed. Pamela Blum. New Haven: Yale University Press, 1987.

Davril, Anselme. "A propos d'un bréviaire manuscrit de Cluny conservé à Saint-Victor-sur-Rhins." *Revue Bénédictine* 93 (1983): 108–22.

Delaporte, Yves. "L'hymne *Salve crux sancta.*" *Revue Grégorienne* 10 (1925): 161–68.

Delogu, Paolo. "I monaci e l'origine di San Vincenzo al Volturno." In *San Vincenzo al Volturno: La nascita di una città monastica,* ed. Paolo Delogu, Richard Hodges, and John Mitchell, 45–61. Isernia: Institute of World Archeology, University of East Anglia, 1996.

The Divine Office in the Latin Middle Ages. Ed. Margot Fassler and Rebecca Baltzer. New York: Oxford University Press, 2000.

Drew, Katherine Fischer. "Land Tenure and Social Status in Medieval Italy as Demonstrated by the Cartulary of Farfa." *Rice University Studies* 58 (1972): 3–10.

Dubois, Jacques. *Les martyrologes du moyen âge latin.* Typologie des sources du moyen âge occidental 26. Turnhout: Brepols, 1978.

Dufraigne, Pierre. *Aduentus Augusti, aduentus Christi: Recherche sur l'exploitation idéologique et littéraire d'un cérémonial dans l'antiquité tardive.* Collection des études augustiniennes, série antiquité 141. Paris: Institut d'études augustiniennes, 1994.

Dyer, Joseph. "The Psalms in Monastic Prayer." In *The Place of the Psalms in the Intellectual Culture of the Middle Ages,* ed. Nancy van Deusen, 59–89. Albany: State University of New York Press, 1999.

Eberlein, Johann Konrad. "Die bildliche Austattung des 'Pontifikale Gundekarianum.'" In *Das "Pontifikale Gundekarianum":* Kommentarband, ed. Bauch and Reiter, 39–87.

Ekenberg, Anders. *Cur Cantatur? Die Funktionen des liturgischen Gesanges nach den Autoren der Karolingerzeit.* Bibliotheca Theologiae Practicae 41. Stockholm: Almqvist & Wiksell, 1987.

Ernst, Ulrich. *Carmen Figuratum: Geschichte des Figurengedichts von den antiken Ursprüngen bis zum Ausgang des Mittelalters.* Cologne: Böhlau, 1991.

Etaix, Raymond. "Le lectionnaire de l'office à Cluny." *Recherches augustiniennes* 11 (1976): 91–153.

von Falkenhausen, Vera. *Untersuchungen über die byzantinische Herrschaft in Süditalien vom 9. bis ins 11. Jahrhundert.* Wiesbaden: Otto Harassowitz, 1967.

Fallows, David. "Who Composed *Mille Regretz*?" In *Essays on Music and Culture in Honor of Herbert Kellman,* ed. Barbara Haggh, 241–52. Paris and Tours: Minerve, 2001.

Fassler, Margot. *Gothic Song: Victorine Sequences and Augustinian Reform in Twelfth-Century Paris.* Cambridge: Cambridge University Press, 1993.

——. "Mary's Nativity, Fulbert of Chartres, and the *Stirps Jesse*: Liturgical Innovation circa 1000 and Its Afterlife." *Speculum* 75 (2000): 389–434.

——. "The Meaning of Entrance: Liturgical Commentaries and the Introit Tropes." In *Reflections on the Sacred: A Musicological Perspective,* ed. Paul Brainard, 8–18. Yale Studies in Sacred Music, Worship and the Arts. New Haven: Yale Institute of Sacred Music, Worship and the Arts, 1994.

——. "The Office of the Cantor in Early Western Monastic Rules and Customaries: A Preliminary Investigation." *Early Music History* 5 (1985): 29–51.

——. "Sermons, Sacramentaries, and Early Sources for the Office in the Latin West: The Example of Advent." In *The Divine Office in the Latin Middle Ages,* ed. Fassler and Baltzer, 5–47.

Federici, Vincenzo. "L'origine del monastero di S. Vincenzo secondo il prologo di Autperto e il *Libellus constructionis farfensis.*" In *Studi di stori e diritto in onore di C. Calisse* 3:4–14. Milan: Giuffrè, 1940.

Feller, Laurent. *Les Abruzzes médiévales: Territoire, économie et société en Italie*

centrale du IXe au XIIe siècle. Bibliothèque des Écoles françaises d'Athènes et de
Rome 300. Paris: École française de Rome, 1998.

——. "Le cartulaire-chronique de San Clemente a Casauria." In *Les cartulaires:
Actes de la Table ronde organisée par l'École nationale des chartes et le G.D.R 121
du C.N.R.S Paris, 5–7 septembre 1991),* ed. Olivier Guyotjeannin, Laurent
Morelle, and Michel Parisse, 261–77. Mémoires et documents de l'École des
chartes 39. Paris: École nationale des chartes, 1993.

Felten, Franz J. "Zur Geschichte der Klöster Farfa und S. Vincenzo al Volturno im
achten Jahrhundert." *Quellen und Forschungen aus italienischen Archiven und
Bibliotheken* 62 (1982): 1–58.

Fentress, James, and Chris Wickham. *Social Memory.* Oxford: Blackwell, 1992.

Ferrari, Guy. *Early Roman Monasteries: Notes for the History of the Monastery and
Convents at Rome from the V through the X century.* Vatican City: Pontificio
istituto di archeologia cristiana, 1957.

Ferrari, Michele. "*Hrabanica:* Hrabans *de Laudibus sanctae Crucis* im Spiegel der
neueren Forschung." In *Kloster Fulda in der Welt der Karolinger und Ottonen,* ed.
Gangolf Schrimpf, 493–526. Frankfurt: Knecht, 1996.

——. *Il Liber sanctae crucis di Rabano Mauro: Testo, immagine, contesto.* Bern: Peter
Lang, 1999.

Ferreira, Manuel Pedro. "Music at Cluny: The Tradition of Gregorian Chant for the
Proper of the Mass, Melodic Variants and Microtonal Nuances." PhD diss.,
Princeton University, 1997.

Ferretti, Bernardino. "Manoscritti in notazione neumatica koiné e riforme
monastiche." *Benedictina* 45 (1998): 47–89.

——. "Molti dialetti, un'unica lingua." *Studi gregoriani* 11 (1995): 155–88.

Fiocchi Nicolai, Vincenzo, and Monica Ricciardi. *La catacomba di s. Vittoria a
Monteleone Sabino (Trebula Mutuesca).* With an appendix by Barbara Mazzei.
Scavi e restauri 2. Vatican City: Pontificia commissione di archeologia sacra,
2003.

*I fiori e' frutti santi: S. Benedetto, la Regola, la santità nelle testimonianze dei
manoscritti cassinesi.* Ed. Mariano Dell'Omo. Milan: Centro Tibaldi, 1998.

Flanigan, Clifford, Kathleen Ashley, and Pamela Sheingorn. "Liturgy as Social
Performance: Expanding the Definitions." In *The Liturgy of the Medieval
Church,* ed. Thomas Heffernan and E. Ann Matter, 695–714. Kalamazoo, MI:
Medieval Institute Publications, 2001.

Flynn, William. *Medieval Music as Medieval Exegesis.* Studies in Liturgical
Musicology 8. Lanham, MD: Scarecrow Press, 1999.

Forsyth, Ilene. "Art with History: The Role of *Spolia* in the Cumulative Work of
Art." In *Byzantine East, Latin West: Art-Historical Studies in Honor of Kurt
Weitzmann,* ed. Christopher Moss and Katherine Kiefer, 153–58. Princeton:
Department of Art and Archaeology, Princeton University, 1995.

Fournier, Paul. "La collezione canonica del *Regesto* di Farfa." *Archivio della Reale Società Romana di Storia Patria* 17 (1894): 285–301.

France, John. "Rodulfus Glaber and the Cluniacs." *Journal of Ecclesiastical History* 39 (1988): 497–508.

Fulton, Rachel. *From Judgment to Passion: Devotion to Christ and the Virgin Mary, 800–1200.* New York: Columbia University Press, 2002.

Gams, Pius Bonifacius. *Series episcoporum ecclesiae catholicae.* 3 vols. Regensburg: Josef Manz, 1873–86.

Garrison, Edward B. "Random Notes on Early Italian Manuscripts I." *La Bibliofilia* 80 (1978): 197–214.

———. "Saints Equizio, Onorato and Libertino in Eleventh- and Twelfth-Century Italian Litanies as Clues to the Attribution of Manuscripts." *Revue Bénédictine* 88 (1978): 297–315.

———. *Studies in the History of Mediaeval Italian Painting.* 4 vols. Florence: L'impronta, 1953–62.

Geary, Patrick. *Furta Sacra: Thefts of Relics in the Central Middle Ages.* Rev. ed. Princeton: Princeton University Press, 1990.

———. "Humiliation of Saints." In Geary, *Living with the Dead in the Middle Ages,* 95–115. Ithaca: Cornell University Press, 1994.

———. *Phantoms of Remembrance: Memory and Oblivion at the End of the First Millennium.* Princeton: Princeton University Press, 1994.

Gilkes, Oliver, and John Mitchell. "The Early Medieval Church at Farfa: Its Orientation and Chronology." *Archeologia Medievale* 22 (1995): 343–64.

Giorgi, Ignazio. "Il *Regesto* di Farfa e le altre opere di Gregorio di Catino." *Archivio della Reale Società Romana di Storia Patria* 2 (1879): 409–73.

Glaube und Wissen im Mittelalter. Ed. Joachim Plotzek and Ulrike Surmann. Munich: Hirmer, 1998.

Gnocchi, Claudia. "Contributo ad un'indagine sui culti farfensi nei secoli IX–XI: Festività, titolazioni di chiese e toponimi nelle opere di Gregorio di Catino." *Rivista di storia della chiesa in Italia* 54 (2000): 31–69.

———. "Un sondaggio sui documenti farfensi dei secoli XI e XII." In *Santi e culti del Lazio,* ed. Boesch Gajano and Petrucci, 83–99.

The Glory of Byzantium: Art and Culture of the Middle Byzantine Era (A.D. 843–1261). Ed. Helen Evans and William Wixom. New York: Metropolitan Museum of Art, 1997.

Gordini, G. D. "Lorenzo Illuminatore," and "Lorenzo, Vescovo di Spoleto." In *Bibliotheca sanctorum* 8 (1966): 135–36, 147.

Goudesenne, Jean-François. *Les Offices historiques ou historiae composés pour les fêtes des saints dans la province ecclésiastique de Reims, 775–1030.* Turnhout: Brepols, 2002.

Grégoire, Réginald. *Homéliaires liturgiques médiévaux: Analyse de manuscrits.* Spoleto: Centro italiano per lo studio dell'alto medioevo, 1980.

Grier, James. "*Ecce sanctum quem deus elegit Marcialem apostolum:* Adémar de Chabannes and the Tropes for the Feast of Saint Martial." In *Beyond the Moon: Festschrift Luther Dittmer,* ed. Bryan Gillingham and Paul Merkley, 28–74. Wissenschaftliche Abhandlungen 53. Ottawa: Institute of Mediaeval Music, 1990.

———. "A New Voice in the Monastery: Tropes and *Versus* from Eleventh- and Twelfth-Century Aquitaine." *Speculum* 69 (1994): 1023–69.

Grodecki, Louis, Florentine Mütherich, Jean Taralon, and Francis Wormald. *Il secolo dell'anno mille.* Milan: Rizzoli, 1974.

Gy, Pierre-Marie. "Les tropes dans l'histoire de la liturgie et de la théologie." In *Research on Tropes,* ed. Gunilla Iversen, 9–16. Stockholm: Almqvist & Wiksell, 1983.

Hack, Achim Thomas. *Das Empfangszeremoniell bei mittelalterlichen Papst-Kaiser-Treffen.* Forschungen zur Kaiser- und Papstgeschichte des Mittelalters 18. Cologne: Böhlau, 1999.

Haggh, Barbara. "Musique et rituel à l'abbaye Saint-Bavon: Structure et développement du rituel, le chant, les livres du rite et les imprimés." In *La cathédrale Saint-Bavon de Gand du moyen âge au baroque,* ed. Bruno Bouckaert, 47–85, 226, 229–31. Ghent: Ludion, 2000.

Häussling, Angelus Albert. *Mönchskonvent und Eucharistiefeier: Eine Studie über die Messe in der abendländischen Klosterliturgie des frühen Mittelalters und zur Geschichte der Messhäufigkeit.* Liturgiewissenschaftliche Quellen und Forschungen 58. Münster: Aschendorff, 1973.

Hallinger, Kassius. "Cluniacensis SS. Religionis Ordinem Elegimus: Zur Rechtslage der Anfänge des Klosters Hasungen." *Jahrbuch für das Bistum Mainz* 8 (1958–60): 224–72.

———. "Das Phänomen der liturgischen Steigerungen Klunys (10/11. Jh.)." In *Studia historico-ecclesiastica: Festgabe für Prof. Luchesius G. Spätling O.F.M.,* ed. Isaac Vázquez, 183–206. Rome: Pontificium Athenaeum Antonianum, 1977.

Hamilton, Louis. "Memory, Symbol, and Arson: Was Rome 'Sacked' in 1084?" *Speculum* 78 (2003): 378–99.

———. "The Power of Liturgy and the Liturgy of Power in Eleventh- and Twelfth-Century Italy." PhD diss., Fordham University, 2000.

Hamilton, Sarah. "'Most Illustrious King of Kings': Evidence for Ottonian Kingship in the Otto III Prayerbook (Munich, Bayerische Staatsbibliothek, Clm 30111)." *Journal of Medieval History* 27 (2001): 257–88.

———. *The Practice of Penance, 900–1050.* Woodbridge, UK: Boydell, for the Royal Historical Society, 2002.

Harting-Correa, Alice. *Walahfrid Strabo's Libellus de Exordiis et Incrementis Quarundam in Observationibus Ecclesiasticis Rerum: A Translation and Liturgical Commentary.* Mittellateinische Studien und Texte 19. Leiden: Brill, 1996.

Haug, Andreas. "Ritual and Repetition: The Ambiguities of Refrains." In *The

Appearances of Medieval Rituals: The Play of Construction and Modification, ed.
Nils Holger Petersen, Mette Birkedal Bruun, Jeremy Llewellyn, and Eyolf
Østrem, 83–96. Turnhout: Brepols, 2004.

Haug, Andreas, and Gunilla Björkvall. "Altes Lied—Neues Lied: Thesen zur
Transformation des lateinischen Lieds um 1100." In *Poesía latina medieval (siglos
v–xv),* ed. Manual C. Díaz y Díaz and José M. Díaz de Bustamante, 539–50.
Florence: Sismel: Edizioni del Galluzzo, 2005.

Heath, Robert G. *Crux imperatorum philosophia: Imperial Horizons of the Cluniac
Confraternitas, 964–1109.* Pittsburgh: Pickwick Press, 1976.

Heffernan, Thomas J. "The Liturgy and the Literature of Saints' Lives." In *The
Liturgy of the Medieval Church,* ed. Thomas J. Heffernan and E. Ann Matter, 73–
105. Kalamazoo, MI: Western Michigan University, 2001.

Heinzelmann, Karl. *Die Farfenser Streitschriften: Ein Beitrag zur Geschichte des
Investiturstreites.* Strasbourg: C. Müh, 1904.

Henriet, Patrick. *La parole et la prière au moyen âge.* Brussels: DeBoeck & Larcier,
2000.

Herman, Jószef. "The End of the History of Latin." *Romance Philology* 49 (1996):
364–82.

———. *Vulgar Latin.* College Park, PA: Penn State University Press, 2000.

Hiley, David. "Cluny, Sequences and Tropes." In *La tradizione dei tropi liturgici,* ed.
Claudio Leonardi and Enrico Menestò, 125–38. Spoleto: Centro italiano di studi
sull'alto medioevo, 1990.

———. "The Liturgical Music of Norman Sicily: A Study Centred on Mss. 288, 289,
19421 and Vitrina 20–4 of the Biblioteca Nacional, Madrid." PhD diss.,
University of London, 1981.

———. "Quanto c'è di normanno nei tropari siculo-normanni?" *Rivista italiana di
musicologia* 18 (1983): 3–28.

———. "Style and Structure in Early Offices of the Sanctorale." In *Western
Plainchant in the First Millennium: Studies in the Medieval Liturgy and its Music,*
ed. Sean Gallagher, James Haar, John Nádas, and Timothy Striplin, 157–79.
Woodbridge, UK: Ashgate, 2003.

———. *Western Plainchant: An Introduction.* Oxford: Oxford University Press,
1993.

Hodges, Richard. *Light in the Dark Ages: The Rise and Fall of San Vincenzo al
Volturno.* Ithaca: Cornell University Press, 1997.

Hoffmann, Hartmut. "Der Kirchenstaat im hohen Mittelalter." *Quellen und
Forschungen aus italienischen Archiven und Bibliotheken* 57 (1977): 1–45.

Hoffman-Brandt, Helma. "Die Tropen zu den Responsorien des Officiums." 2 vols.
PhD diss., University of Erlangen, Germany, 1971.

Hofmeister, Adolf. "Maurus von Amalfi und die Elfenbeinkassette von Farfa aus
dem 11. Jahrhundert." *Quellen und Forschungen aus italienischen Archiven und
Bibliotheken* 24 (1932–33): 287–93.

Holder, Stephen. "The Noted Cluniac Breviary-Missal of Lewes: Fitzwilliam Museum Manuscript 369." *Journal of the Plainsong and Mediaeval Music Society* 8 (1985): 25–32.

Houben, Hubert. "Il cosiddetto 'Liber Vitae' di Polirone: Problemi terminologici e metodologici." In *L'Italia nel quadro dell'espansione europea,* ed. Violante, Spicciani, and Spinelli, 187–98.

Hourlier, Jacques. "Le bréviaire de Saint-Taurin: Un livre liturgique clunisien à l'usage de l'Echelle-Saint-Taurin (Paris, B.N. lat. 12601)." *Études Grégoriennes* 3 (1959): 163–73.

———. "L'entrée de Moissac dans l'ordre de Cluny." In *Moissac et l'Occident au XIe siècle,* 25–35. Toulouse: Privat, 1964.

Huglo, Michel. "Les débuts de la polyphonie à Paris: Les premiers organa parisiens." *Aktuelle Fragen der musikbezogenen Mittelalterforschung, Forum musicologicum* 3 (1982): 93–164.

———. *Les manuscrits du processionnal.* Vol. 1. Munich: Henle, 1999.

Huyghebaert, Nicolas. *Les documents nécrologiques.* Typologie des sources du moyen âge occidental 4. Turnhout: Brepols, 1972.

Iogna-Prat, Dominique. *Agni immaculati: Recherches sur les sources hagiographiques relatives à Saint Maieul de Cluny (954–994).* Paris: Cerf, 1988.

———. "La croix, le moine, et l'empereur: Dévotion à la croix et théologie politique à Cluny autour de l'an mil." In *Haut moyen-âge: Culture, éducation et société; Études offertes à Pierre Riché,* ed. Claude Lepelley and others, 449–75. La Garenne-Colombes: Éditions européenes Erasme, 1990.

———. "The Dead in the Celestial Bookkeeping of the Cluniac Monks around the Year 1000." In *Debating the Middle Ages,* ed. Lester Little and Barbara H. Rosenwein, 340–62. Malden, MA: Blackwell, 1998. (Translation of "Les morts dans la compatibilité céleste des moines clunisiens autour de l'an mil." In *Religion et culture autour de l'an mil: Royaume capétien et Lotharingie,* ed. Dominique Iogna-Prat and Jean-Charles Picard, 55–69. Paris: Picard, 1990.)

———. "La geste des origines dans l'historiographie clunisienne des XIe–XIIe siècles." *Revue Bénédictine* 102 (1992): 125–91.

———. *Order and Exclusion: Cluny and Christendom Face Heresy, Judaism, and Islam, 1000–1150.* Trans. Graham Robert Edwards. Ithaca: Cornell University Press, 2002.

———. *Ordonner et exclure: Cluny et la société chrétienne face à l'hérésie, au Judaïsme et à l'Islam, 1000–1150.* Paris: Aubier, 1998.

———. "Panorama de l'hagiographie abbatiale clunisienne." In *Manuscrits hagiographiques et travail des hagiographes,* ed. Martin Heinzelmann, 77–118. Beihefte der Francia 24. Sigmaringen: Jan Thorbecke, 1992.

L'Italia nel quadro dell'espansione europea del monachesimo cluniacense. Ed. Cinzio Violante, Amleto Spicciani, and Giovanni Spinelli. Cesena: Badia di Santa Maria del Monte, 1985.

Jeffery, Peter. "Eastern and Western Elements in the Irish Monastic Prayer of the Hours." In *The Divine Office in the Latin Middle Ages*, ed. Fassler and Baltzer, 99–143.

——. "Monastic Reading and the Emerging Roman Chant Repertory." In *Western Plainchant in the First Millennium: Studies in the Medieval Liturgy and Its Music*, ed. Sean Gallagher, James Haar, John Nádas, and Timothy Striplin, 45–103. Woodbridge UK: Ashgate, 2003.

——. *Re-envisioning Past Musical Cultures: Ethnomusicology in the Study of Gregorian Chant*. Chicago: University of Chicago Press, 1992.

de Jong, Mayke. "Carolingian Monasticism: The Power of Prayer." In *The New Cambridge Medieval History*, vol. 2, *C. 700–c. 900*, ed. Rosamond McKitterick, 622–53. Cambridge: Cambridge University Press, 1995.

——. *In Samuel's Image: Child Oblation in the Early Medieval West*. Leiden: Brill, 1996.

Jullien, Marie-Hélène. "Les sources de la tradition ancienne des quatorze *Hymnes* attribuées à saint Ambroise de Milan." *Revue d'Histoire des Textes* 19 (1989): 57–189.

Jungmann, Joseph. *The Mass of the Roman Rite: Its Origins and Development (Missarum Sollemnia)*. Trans. Francis Brunner. 2 vols. Westminster, MD: Christian Classics, 1986.

Kahsnitz, Rainer. "Koimesis-dormitio-assumptio: Byzantinisches und Antikes in den Miniaturen der Liuthargruppe." In *Florilegium in honorem Carl Nordenfalk octogenarii contextum*, ed. Per Bjurström, Nils-Göran Hökby, and Florentine Mütherich, 91–122. Stockholm: Nationalmuseum, 1987.

Kantorowicz, Ernst. "The 'King's Advent' and the Enigmatic Panels in the Doors of Santa Sabina." *Art Bulletin* 26 (1944): 207–31.

——. *Laudes Regiae: A Study in Liturgical Acclamations and Mediaeval Ruler Worship*. Berkeley and Los Angeles: University of California Press, 1946.

——. "The Norman Finale of the *Exultet* and the Rite of Sarum." *Harvard Theological Review* 34 (1941): 129–43.

Kelly, Thomas Forrest. *The Beneventan Chant*. Cambridge: Cambridge University Press, 1989.

——. *The Exultet in Southern Italy*. New York: Oxford University Press, 1999.

——. "Melisma and Prosula: The Performance of Responsory Tropes." In *Liturgische Tropen*, ed. Gabriel Silagi, 163–80. Münchener Beiträge zur Mediävistik und Renaissance-Forschung 36. Munich: Arbeo-Gesellschaft, 1985.

——. "New Music from Old: The Structuring of Responsory Proses." *Journal of the American Musicological Society* 30 (1977): 366–90.

——. "Structure and Ornament in Chant." In *Essays on Medieval Music in Honor of David G. Hughes*, ed. Graeme Boone, 249–76. Cambridge, MA: Harvard University Press, 1995.

Kéry, Lotte. *Canonical Collections of the Early Middle Ages (ca. 400–1140): A Bibliographical Guide to the Manuscripts and Literature.* Washington, DC: Catholic University of America, 1998.

Kessler, Herbert. *Spiritual Seeing: Picturing God's Invisibility in Medieval Art.* Philadelphia: University of Pennsylvania Press, 2000.

Klopsch, Paul. *Einführung in die mittellateinische Verslehre.* Darmstadt: Wissenschaftliche Buchgesellschaft, 1972.

Kölzer, Theo. "*Codex libertatis:* Überlegungen zur Funktion des 'Regestum Farfense' und andere Klosterchartulare." In *Il ducato di Spoleto: Atti del IX Congresso internazionale di studi sull'alto medioevo, Spoleto, 27 settembre–2 ottobre 1982,* 609–35. Spoleto: Centro italiano di studi sull'alto medioevo, 1983.

——. "Die Farfenser Kanonessammlung des Cod. Vat. lat. 8487 (Collectio Farfensis)." *Bulletin of Medieval Canon Law* 7 (1977): 94–100.

——. "Mönchtum und Kirchenrecht." *Zeitschrift der Savigny-Stiftung für Rechtsgeschichte* 100 (1983): 121–42.

Kohnle, Armin. *Abt Hugo von Cluny (1049–1109).* Beihefte der Francia 32. Sigmaringen: Jan Thorbecke, 1993.

Kruckenberg, Lori. "Sequenz." In *Die Musik in Geschichte und Gegenwart,* 2nd ed., Sachteil 8, cols. 1254–86. Kassel: Bärenreiter, 1998.

Krüger, Kristina. "Architecture and Liturgical Practice: The Cluniac *Galilea.*" In *The White Mantle of Churches: Architecture, Liturgy, and Art around the Millennium,* ed. Nigel Hiscock, 138–59. International Medieval Research 10, Art History Subseries 2. Brepols: Turnhout, 2003.

——. "La fonction liturgique des *galilées* clunisiennes: Les exemples de Romainmôtier et Payerne." In *Art, cérémonial et liturgie au moyen âge,* ed. Nicolas Bock, Peter Jurmann, Serena Romano, and Jean-Michel Spieser, 169–90. Rome: Viella, 2002.

——. "Die Reichsabtei Farfa: Ein Kloster im Spannungsfeld zwischen regionaler Tradition, transalpinen Einflüssen und monastischer Reform." Forthcoming.

——. *Die romanischen Westbauten in Burgund und Cluny.* Berlin: Gebr. Mann, 2003.

——. "Tournus et la fonction des galilées en Bourgogne." In *Avant-nefs et espaces d'accueil dans l'église entre le IVe et le XIIe siècle,* ed. Christian Sapin, 414–23. Mémoires de la Section d'archéologie et d'histoire de l'art 13. Paris: CTHS, 2002.

Kurze, Wilhelm. "Zur Kopiertätigkeit Gregors von Catino." *Quellen und Forschungen aus italienischen Archiven und Bibliotheken* 53 (1973): 407–56.

LaCocque, André, and Paul Ricoeur. *Thinking Biblically: Exegetical and Hermeneutical Studies.* Trans. David Pellauer. Chicago: University of Chicago Press, 1998.

LaFontaine, Pietro. *Le traslazioni dei ss. martiri Valentino ed Ilario comprotettori della città di Viterbo.* Viterbo: Donati e Garbini, 1902.

Latinitatis Italicae medii aevi lexicon. 2 vols. In *Archivum Latinitatis medii aevi* 10

(1935), ed. Francesco Arnaldi and Maria Turriani. Brussels: Sécretariat de l'Union Academique Internationale, 1936.

Lauwers, Michel. "Mémoire des origines et idéologies monastiques: Saint-Pierre-des-Fossés et Saint-Victor de Marseille au XIe siècle." *Mélanges de l'École Française de Rome: Moyen Âge* 115 (2003): 155–80.

Leclercq, Jean. "Culte liturgique et prière intime dans le monachisme au moyen âge." *La Maison-Dieu* 69 (1965): 39–55.

Ledwon, Jacob Carl. "The Winter Office of Sant'Eutizio di Norcia: A Study of the Contents and Construction of Biblioteca Vallicelliana Manuscripts C 13 and C 5." 2 vols. PhD diss., State University of New York at Buffalo, 1986.

Leggio, Tersilio. "L'Abbazia di Farfa tra "Langobardia" e "Romania": Alcune congetture sulle origini." In *I rapporti tra le comunità monastiche benedittine italiane tra alto e pieno medioevo: Atti del III Convegno del "Centro di studi farfensi," Santa Vittoria in Matenano 11–12–13 settembre 1992*, 157–78. Negarine di San Pietro in Cariano: Il segno, 1994.

——. "I rapporti agiografici tra Farfa e il Piceno: Nuove prospettive di ricerca." In *Agiografia e culto dei santi,* ed. Menestò, 85–100.

——. "Rieti e la sua diocesi: Le stratificazioni cultuali," in *Santi e culti del Lazio,* ed. Boesch Gajano and Petrucci, 127–59.

Leisibach, Joseph. *Die liturgischen Handschriften der Kantons- und Universitätsbibliothek Freiburg,* vol. 1. Spicilegii Friburgensis Subsidia 15. Fribourg: Universitätsverlag, 1976.

Lemaître, Jean-Loup. "'Liber capituli': Le livre de chapitre, des origines aux XVIe siècle: L'exemple français." In *Memoria: Die geschichtliche Zeugniswert des liturgischen Gedenkens im Mittelalter,* ed. Schmid and Wollasch, 625–48.

——. *Mourir à Saint-Martial: La commémoration des morts et les obituaires à Saint-Martial de Limoges du XIe au XIIIe siècle.* Paris: De Boccard, 1989.

Lemarié, Joseph. "Le 'Libellus precum' du Psautier de Saint-Michel de Marturi, Florence, Bibl. Laurenz. Codd.Plut XVII.3 et Plut. XVII.6." *Studi medievali* 3rd ser., 22 (1981): 871–906.

Leroquais, Victor. *Le bréviaire-missel du prieuré clunisien de Lewes.* Paris: G. Andrieux, 1935.

Levy, Kenneth. *Gregorian Chant and the Carolingians.* Princeton: Princeton University Press, 1998.

——. "*Lux de luce:* The Origin of an Italian Sequence." *Musical Quarterly* 57 (1971): 40–61.

Leyser, Conrad. *Authority and Asceticism from Augustine to Gregory the Great.* Oxford: Oxford University Press, 2000.

Little, Lester. "Anger in Monastic Curses." In *Anger's Past: The Social Uses of an Emotion in the Middle Ages,* ed. Barbara H. Rosenwein, 9–35. Ithaca: Cornell University Press, 1998.

——. *Benedictine Maledictions: Liturgical Cursing in Romanesque France*. Ithaca: Cornell University Press, 1993.

Longo, Umberto. "Agiografia e identità monastica a Farfa tra XI e XII secolo." *Cristianesimo nella storia* 21 (2000) 311–41.

——. "Dialettiche agiografiche, influssi cultuali, pratiche liturgiche: Farfa, Sant'Eutizio, e Cluny (secoli XI–XII)." In *Santi e culti del Lazio,* ed. Boesch Gajano and Petrucci, 101–26.

——. "La funzione della memoria nella definizione dell'identità religiosa in comunità monastiche dell'Italia centrale (secoli XI e XII)." *Mélanges de l'École Française de Rome: Moyen Âge* 115 (2003): 213–33.

——. "Gregorio da Catino." In *Dizionario biografico degli italiani*, 59:254–59. Rome: Istituto della enciclopedia italiana, 2002.

——. "Riti e agiografia: L'istituzione della *commemoratio omnium fidelium defunctorum* nelle *Vitae* di Odilone di Cluny." *Bullettino dell'Istituto storico italiano per il Medio Evo e Archivio Muratoriano* 103 (2002): 163–200.

Loud, Graham. *The Age of Robert Guiscard: Southern Italy and the Norman Conquest*. Harlow: Pearson Education, 2000.

Maggi Bei, Maria Teresa. "Per un'analisi delle fonti del *Liber floriger* di Gregorio da Catino." *Bullettino dell'Istituto storico italiano per il Medio Evo e Archivio Muratoriano* 88 (1979): 317–48.

——. "I possessi dell'abbazia di Farfa in Umbria nei secoli VIII–XII." *Bollettino della Deputazione di storia patria per l'Umbria* 91 (1994): 47–86.

Magnani S.-Christen, Eliana. "Transforming Things and Persons: The Gift *Pro Anima* in the Eleventh and Twelfth Centuries." In *Negotiating the Gift,* ed. Algazi, Groebner, and Jussen, 269–84.

Magne, Catherine. "Saint Maïeul au miroir de la liturgie: Le manuscrit Paris, Bibliothèque Nationale, latin 5611." In *Saint Mayeul et son temps, Actes du Congrès international Valensole 12–14 mai 1994*, 243–58. Digne-les-Bains: Société scientifique et littéraire des Alpes de Haute-Provence, 1997.

Manoscritti cassinesi del secolo XI. Vol. 1 of *L'età dell'abate Desiderio*. Ed. Sabina Adacher and Giulia Orofino. Miscellanea cassinese 59. Montecassino: Pubblicazioni cassinesi, 1989.

Mara, Maria Grazia. "Berardo." In *Dizionario biografico degli italiani* 8:765–67. Rome: Istituto della enciclopedia italiana, 1966.

——. *I martiri della via Salaria*. Rome: Editrice studium, 1964.

Marie: Le culte de la Vierge dans la société médiévale. Ed. Dominique Iogna-Prat, Éric Palazzo, and Daniel Russo. Paris: Beauchesne, 1996.

Markthaler, Paul. "Sulle recenti scoperte nell'abbazia imperiale di Farfa." *Rivista di archeologia cristiana* 5 (1928): 39–88.

Martimort, Aimé-Georges. *Les lectures liturgiques et leurs livres*. Typologie des sources du moyen âge occidental 64. Turnhout: Brepols, 1992.

May, Florence Lewis. *Silk Textiles of Spain: Eighth to Fifteenth Century.* New York: Hispanic Society of America, 1957.

Mayr-Harting, Henry. *Ottonian Book Illumination: An Historical Study.* 2 vols. London: Harvey Miller, 1991.

McClendon, Charles. "An Early Funerary Portrait from the Medieval Abbey at Farfa." *Gesta* 22 (1983): 13–26.

——. *The Imperial Abbey of Farfa: Architectural Currents of the Early Middle Ages.* New Haven: Yale University Press, 1987.

——. "Liturgical Furniture at Farfa Abbey and Its Roman Sources in the Early and High Middle Ages." In *Mededelingen van het Nederlands Instituut te Rome/Papers of the Netherlands Institute in Rome.* Historical Studies 59 (2001 for 2000): 195–208.

——. *The Origins of Medieval Architecture: Building in Europe A.D. 600–900.* New Haven: Yale University Press, 2005.

——. "The Carolingian Abbey Church at Farfa: One Interpretation." Forthcoming in the final report on the excavations carried out at Farfa by the British School in Rome.

McKitterick, Rosamond. "Paolo Diacono e i Franchi: Il contesto storico e culturale." In *Paolo Diacono,* ed. Chiesa, 9–28.

McLaughlin, Megan. *Consorting with Saints: Prayer for the Dead in Early Medieval France.* Ithaca: Cornell University Press, 1994.

McGrade, Michael. "Modal Contrast in Chants by Hildegard of Bingen and Her Contemporaries: A New Musical Link." Forthcoming.

Memoria: Die geschichtliche Zeugniswert des liturgischen Gedenkens im Mittelalter. Ed. Karl Schmid and Joachim Wollasch. Münstersche Mittelalter-Schriften 48. Munich: Wilhelm Fink, 1984.

Valdez del Alamo, Elizabeth, and Carol Pendergast, eds. *Memory and the Medieval Tomb.* Aldershot, UK: Ashgate, 2000.

Metz, Wolfgang. "Nekrologische Quellen zum Wirkungsbereich des deutschen Königtums (919–1250)." *Historisches Jahrbuch* 107 (1987): 254–95.

Minninger, Monika. *Von Clermont zum Wormser Konkordat.* Beihefte zu J. F. Böhmer, Regesta Imperii 2. Cologne: Böhlau, 1978.

Morin, Germain. "Un bréviaire clunisien du XIIe siècle à la Bibliothèque de Fribourg." *Zeitschrift für schweizerische Kirchengeschichte/Revue d'Histoire Ecclésiastique Suisse* 38 (1944): 209–13.

Mostert, Marco. *The Library of Fleury: A Provisional List of Manuscripts.* Hilversum: Verloren, 1989.

Müssigbrod, Axel. *Die Abtei Moissac 1050–1150: Zu einem Zentrum cluniacensischen Mönchtums in Südwestfrankreich.* Münstersche Mittelalter-Schriften 58. Munich: Wilhelm Fink, 1988.

Neff, Karl. *Die Gedichte des Paulus Diaconus: Kritische und erklärende Ausgabe.* Quellen und Untersuchungen zur lateinischen Philologie des Mittelalters 3/4. Munich: Beck, 1908.

Negotiating the Gift: Pre-Modern Figurations of Exchange. Ed. Gadi Algazi, Valentin Groebner, and Bernhard Jussen. Göttingen: Vandenhoeck & Ruprecht, 2003.

Negri, Franco. "Il lezionario cluniacense a Polirone nel XII secolo." *Aevum* 70 (1996): 217–43.

Noble, Thomas F. X. *The Republic of St. Peter: The Birth of the Papal State, 680–825.* Philadelphia: University of Pennsylvania Press, 1984.

Di Nonno, Mario. "Contributo alla tradizione di Prisciano in area beneventano-cassinese: Il Vallicelliana C.9." *Revue d'Histoire des Textes* 9 (1979): 123–39.

Norberg, Dag. *Introduction à l'étude de la versification latine médiévale.* Studia Latina Stockholmiensia 5. Stockholm: Almqvist & Wiksell, 1958.

———. *An Introduction to the Study of Medieval Latin Versification.* Trans. Grant C. Roti and Jacqueline de La Chapelle Skubly. Ed. Jan Ziolkowski. Washington, DC: Catholic University of America, 2004.

———. *Les vers latins iambiques et trochaïques au moyen âge et leurs répliques rythmiques.* Filologiskt Arkiv 35. Stockholm: Almqvist & Wiksell, 1988.

North, William, and Anthony Cutler. "Ivories, Inscriptions, and Episcopal Self-Consciousness in the Ottonian Empire: Berthold of Toul and the Berlin Hodegetria." *Gesta* 42 (2003): 1–17.

Novum glossarium mediae Latinitatis, L-Nysus. Ed. Franz Blatt. Copenhagen: Munksgaard, 1957.

Odelman, Eva. "Comment a-t-on appelé les tropes? Observations sur les rubriques des tropes des Xe et XIe siècle." *Cahiers de Civilisation Médiévale* 18 (1975): 15–36.

Odilon de Mercoeur, l'Auvergne et Cluny: La "Paix de Dieu" et l'Europe de l'an mil: Actes du Colloque de Lavoûte-Chilhac. Ed. Jean Vigier and Stéphane André. Nonette: Éditions Créer, 2002.

Ortigues, Edmond, and Dominique Iogna-Prat. "Raoul Glaber et l'historiographie clunisienne." *Studi Medievali* 26 (1985): 537–72.

Ottosen, Knud. *L'antiphonaire latin au moyen-âge: Réorganisation des séries de répons de l'Avent classés par R.-J. Hesbert.* Rome: Herder, 1986.

———. *The Responsories and Versicles of the Latin Office of the Dead.* Aarhus, Denmark: Aarhus University Press, 1993.

Pacini, Delio. "I monaci di Farfa nelle valli picene del Chienti e del Potenza." In *I Benedettini nelle valli del Maceratese: Atti del II Convegno del Centro di studi storici maceratesi,* 129–74. Studi maceratesi 2. Ravenna: A. Longo, 1967.

———. "Possessi e chiese farfensi nelle valli picene del Tenna e dell'Asp (secoli VIII–XII)." In *Istituzioni e società nell'alto medioevo marchigiano.* Vol. 1, *Atti e memorie della Deputazione di storia patria per le Marche* 86 (1983 for 1981): 333–425.

Palazzo, Eric. *Le moyen âge: Des origines au XIIIe siècle; Histoire des livres liturgiques.* Paris: Beauchesne, 1993.

Paoli, Emore. *Agiografia e strategie politico-religiose: Alcuni esempi da Gregorio*

Magno al Concilio di Trento. Spoleto: Centro italiano di studi sull'alto medioevo, 1997.

Paolo Diacono: Uno scrittore fra tradizione longobarda e rinnovamento carolingio: Atti del Convegno internazionale di studi cividale del Friuli-Udine, 6–9 maggio 1999. Ed. Paolo Chiesa. Udine: Forum, 2000.

Parker McLachlan, Elizabeth. "Liturgical Vessels and Implements." In *The Liturgy of the Medieval Church,* ed. Thomas Heffernan and E. Ann Matter, 369–429. Kalamazoo, MI: Medieval Institute Publications, 2001.

Paschini, Pio. *La "Passio" delle martiri sabine Vittoria e Anatolia.* Lateranum: Pubblicazioni del Pontificio seminario romano maggiore 1. Rome: Tipografia pontificia nell'Istituto Pio IX, 1919.

Paxton, Frederick. "Death by Customary in Eleventh-Century Cluny." In *From Dead of Night to End of Day: The Medieval Customs of Cluny,* ed. Susan Boynton and Isabelle Cochelin. Turnhout: Brepols, 2005.

Pedeaux, Bryan Stephen. "The Canonical Collection of the Farfa *Register*." PhD diss., Rice University, 1976.

Penco, Gregorio. "La storiografia monastica italiana negli ultimi trent'anni." *Benedictina* 46 (1999): 445–78.

Picasso, Giorgio. "'Usus' e 'Consuetudines' cluniacensi in Italia." In *L'Italia nel quadro dell'espansione europea del monachesimo cluniacense,* ed. Violante, Spicciani, and Spinelli, 297–311.

Pirri, Pietro. *L'abbazia di Sant'Eutizio in Val Castoriana presso Norcia e le chiese dipendenti.* Studia anselmiana 45. Rome: Herder, 1960.

Poeck, Dietrich W. *"Cluniacensis Ecclesia": Der cluniacensische Klosterverband (10.– 12. Jahrhundert).* Münstersche Mittelalter-Schriften 71. Munich: Wilhelm Fink, 1998.

Pohl-Resl, Brigitte. "Legal Practice and Ethnic Identity in Lombard Italy." In *Strategies of Distinction: The Construction of Ethnic Communities, 300–800,* ed. Walter Pohl and Helmut Reimitz, 205–19. Leiden: Brill, 1998.

Poncelet, Albert. *Catalogus codicum hagiographicum Latinorum bibliothecarum Romanarum praeter quam Vaticanae.* Brussels: Société des Bollandistes, 1909.

Rampolla, Mary Lynn. "'A Pious Legend': St. Oswald and the Foundation of Worcester Cathedral Priory." In *Oral Tradition in the Middle Ages,* ed. W. F. H. Nicolaisen, 187–210. Medieval and Renaissance Texts and Studies 112. Binghamton: Center for Medieval and Early Renaissance Studies, State University of New York at Binghamton, 1995.

Remensnyder, Amy. "Croyance et communauté: La mémoire des origines des abbayes bénédictines." *Mélanges de l'École Française de Rome: Moyen Âge* 115 (2003): 141–54.

——. "Legendary Treasure at Conques: Reliquaries and Imaginative Memory." *Speculum* 71 (1996): 885–906.

——. *Remembering Kings Past: Monastic Foundation Legends in Medieval Southern France*. Ithaca: Cornell University Press, 1995.

Resnick, Irven. "Peter Damian on Cluny, Liturgy, and Penance." *Studia liturgica* 18 (1988): 170–87.

Ring, Richard. "The Lands of Farfa: Studies in Lombard and Carolingian Italy." PhD diss., University of Wisconsin, 1972–73.

Robertson, Anne Walters. "*Benedicamus Domino:* The Unwritten Tradition." *Journal of the American Musicological Society* 41 (1988): 1–62.

Robinson, Ian Stuart. *Henry IV of Germany, 1056–1106*. Cambridge: Cambridge University Press, 1999.

Römer, Gerhard. "Die Liturgie des Karfreitags." *Zeitschrift für katholische Theologie* 77 (1955): 39–93.

Rosenwein, Barbara. "Feudal War and Monastic Peace: Cluniac Liturgy as Ritual Aggression." *Viator* 2 (1971): 129–57.

——. *Negotiating Space: Power, Restraint, and Privileges of Immunity in Early Medieval Europe*. Ithaca: Cornell University Press, 1999.

——. "Perennial Prayer at Agaune." In *Monks and Nuns, Saints and Outcasts*, ed. Sharon Farmer and Barbara H. Rosenwein, 37–56. Ithaca: Cornell University Press, 2000.

——. *To Be the Neighbor of Saint Peter: The Social Meaning of Cluny's Property*. Ithaca: Cornell University Press, 1989.

Rosenwein, Barbara, Thomas Head, and Sharon Farmer. "Monks and Their Enemies: A Comparative Approach." *Speculum* 66 (1991): 764–96.

Russo, Daniel. "Les répresentations mariales dans l'art de l'Occident: Essai sur la formation d'une tradition iconographique." In *Marie: Le culte de la Vierge dans la société médiévale*, ed. Iogna-Prat, Palazzo, and Russo, 173–291.

Sackur, Ernst. *Die Cluniacenser in ihrer kirchlichen und allgemeingeschichtlichen Wirksamkeit bis zur Mitte des elften Jahrhunderts*. 2 vols. Halle: Niemeyer, 1894.

Saenger, Paul. "The Separation of Words in Italy." *Scrittura e civiltà* 17 (1993): 5–41.

Saint-Germain d'Auxerre: Intellectuels et artistes dans l'Europe carolingienne, IXe–XIe siècles. Ed. Christian Sapin. Auxerre: Musée d'art et d'histoire, 1990.

Salmon, Pierre. "La composition d'un *libellus precum* à l'époque de la réforme grégorienne." *Benedictina* 26 (1979): 285–322.

——. "*Libelli precum* du VIIIe au XIIe siècle." In *Analecta liturgica*, ed. Salmon, 123–94.

——. "Livrets de prières de l'époque carolingienne." *Revue Bénédictine* 88 (1976): 218–34.

——. "Livrets de prières de l'époque carolingienne: Nouvelle liste de manuscrits." *Revue Bénédictine* 90 (1980): 147–49.

——. *Les "tituli psalmorum" des manuscrits latins*. Collectanea biblica latina 12. Rome: Abbazia di San Girolamo, 1959.

Santi e culti del Lazio: Istituzioni, società, devozioni. Ed. Sofia Boesch Gajano and
    Enzo Petrucci. Miscellanea della Società Romana di Storia Patria 41. Rome:
    Società Romana di Storia Patria, 2000.

Sapin, Christian. "L'abbatiale de Cluny II sous saint Hugues." In *Le gouvernement
    d'Hugues de Semur à Cluny,* 435–60. Cluny: Ville de Cluny, Musée Ochier, 1990.

Saracco Previdi, Emilia. "Il patrimonio fondiario dei monaci farfensi nelle marche."
    In *Offida: Dal Monachesimo all'età comunale; Atti del II Convegno del "Centro di
    studi farfensi,"* 93–104. Negarine di San Pietro in Cariano: Il segno, 1993.

Savio, Giulio. *Monumenta onomastica romana medii aevi (X–XII sec.).* 5 vols.
    Rome: Il cigno Galileo Galilei, 1999.

Schmidt, Hermann. *Hebdomada sancta.* 2 vols. Rome: Herder, 1956–57.

Schmitz, Hermann Josef. *Die Bussbücher und die Bussdisciplin der Kirche nach
    handschriftlichen Quellen dargestellt.* 2 vols. Mainz: Franz Kirchheim, 1883.
    Reprint, Graz: Akademische Druck- und Verlagsanstalt, 1958.

Schuchert, August. "Eine unbekannte Elfenbeinkassette aus dem 11. Jahrhundert."
    Römische Quartalschrift für christliche Altertumskunde und für Kirchengeschichte
    40 (1932): 1–11.

Schupp, Volker. "Der Dichter des 'Modus Liebinc.'" *Mittellateinisches Jahrbuch* 5
    (1968): 29–41.

Schuster, Ildefonso. "L'Abbaye de Farfa et sa restauration au XIème siècle sous
    Hugues I." *Revue Bénédictine* 24 (1907): 17–35, 374–402.

——. "De fastorum agiographico ordine imperialis monasterii Pharphensis." In
    *Millenaire de Cluny: Congrès d'histoire et d'archéologie tenu à Cluny, le 10, 11, 12
    septembre 1910,* 146–76. Mâcon: Protat, 1910.

——. *L'imperiale abbazia di Farfa.* Vatican City: Tipografia poliglotta vaticana,
    1921.

——. "Martyrologium Pharphense ex apographo cardinalis Fortunati Tamburini
    OSB codicis saeculi XI." *Revue Bénédictine* 26 (1909): 433–63.

——. "Martyrologium Pharphense ex apographo cardinalis Fortunati Tamburini
    OSB codicis saeculi XI, suite." *Revue Bénédictine* 27 (1910): 75–94, 363–85.

——. "Reliquie d'arte nella badia imperiale di Farfa." *Archivio della Reale Società
    Romana di Storia Patria* 34 (1911): 269–350.

——. "Spigolature farfensi, II: Monumenti storiografici e liturgici." *Rivista storica
    benedittina* 16–17 (1909–10): 3–55.

——. "Ugo I di Farfa." In *Bollettino della Reale deputazione di storia patria per
    l'Umbria* 16 (1911): 1–212.

Schwarz, Ulrich. *Amalfi im frühen Mittelalter (9.–11. Jh.): Untersuchungen zur
    Amalfitaner Überlieferung.* Bibliothek des Deutschen Historischen Instituts in
    Rom 49. Tübingen: Niemeyer, 1978.

Schwarzmaier, Hansmartin. "Der *Liber Vitae* von Subiaco: Die Klöster Farfa und
    Subiaco in ihrer geistigen und politischen Umwelt während der letzten

Jahrzehnte des 11. Jahrhunderts." *Quellen und Forschungen aus italienischen Archiven und Bibliotheken* 48 (1968): 80–147.

Seibert, Hubertus. "Eines grossen Vaters Glückloser Sohn? Die neue Politik Ottos II." In *Ottonische Neuanfänge: Symposion zur Ausstellung "Otto der Grosse, Magdeburg und Europa,"* ed. Bernd Schneidmüller and Stefan Weinfurter, 293–320. Mainz: Philip von Zabern, 2001.

——. "Herrscher und Mönchtum im spätottonischen Reich." In *Otto III.–Heinrich II. Eine Wende?* ed. Bernd Schneidmüller and Stefan Weinfurter, 205–66. Mittelalter-Forschung 1. Sigmaringen: Jan Thorbecke, 1997.

——. "Libertas und Reichsabtei: Zur Klosterpolitik der salischen Herrscher." In *Die Salier und das Reich.* Vol. 2, *Die Reichskirche in der Salierzeit,* ed. Stefan Weinfurter with Frank Martin Siefarth, 503–69. Sigmaringen: Jan Thorbecke, 1991.

Selig, Maria. "Un exemple de normalisation linguistique dans l'Italie médiévale— Grégoire de Catino et le *Regestum Farfense.*" In *Latin vulgaire—latin tardif III: Actes du IIIème Colloque internationale sur le latin vulgaire et tardif (Innsbruck, 2–5 septembre 1991),* ed. Maria Iliescu and Werner Marxgut, 327–41. Tübingen: Max Niemeyer, 1992.

Sennis, Antonio. "Tradizione monastica e racconto delle origini in Italia centrale (secoli XI–XII)." *Mélanges de l'École Française de Rome: Moyen Âge* 115 (2003): 181–211.

Shopkow, Leah. *History and Community: Norman Historical Writing in the Eleventh and Twelfth Centuries.* Washington, DC: Catholic University of America, 1997.

Siede, Irmgard. *Zur Rezeption ottonischer Buchmalerei in Italien im 11. und 12. Jahrhundert.* Studien und Mitteilungen zur Geschichte der Benediktinerordens und seine Zweige 39. St. Ottilien: EOS, 1997.

Signorelli, Giuseppe. *Viterbo nella storia della chiesa.* 3 vols. Viterbo: Tipografia Cionfi, 1907–8.

Smith, Julia. "Old Saints, New Cults: Roman Relics in Carolingian Francia." In *Early Medieval Rome and the Christian West: Essays in Honour of Donald A. Bullough,* ed. Julia M. H. Smith, 317–39. Leiden: Brill, 2000.

Smolak, Kurt. "Poetologisches zu den Benedikthymnen in der *Historia Langobardorum* des Paulus Diaconus." In *Paolo Diacono,* ed. Chiesa, 505–26.

Steiner, Ruth. "The Music for a Cluny Office of Saint Benedict." In *Monasticism and the Arts,* ed. Timothy Gregory Verdon with John Dalley, 81–113. Syracuse, NY: Syracuse University Press, 1984.

Stella, Francesco. "La poesia di Paolo Diacono: Nuovi manoscritti e attribuzioni incerte." In *Paolo Diacono,* ed. Chiesa, 551–74.

Stotz, Peter. *Ardua spes mundi: Studien zu lateinischen Gedichten aus Sankt Gallen.* Bern: Herbert Lang, 1972.

——. *Sonderformen der sapphischen Dichtung: Ein Beitrag zur Erforschung der*

sapphischen Dichtung des lateinischen Mittelalters. Medium Aevum,
Philologische Studien 37. Munich: Wilhelm Fink, 1982.

Stratford, Neil. "Les bâtiments de l'abbaye de Cluny à l'époque médiévale: État des
questions." *Bulletin Monumental* 150 (1992): 383–411.

Stroll, Mary. *The Medieval Abbey of Farfa: Target of Papal and Imperial Ambitions.*
Leiden: Brill, 1997.

Struve, Tilman. "Die Stellung des Königtums." In *Die Salier und das Reich.* Vol. 3,
Gesellschaftlicher und ideengeschichtlicher Wandel im Reich der Salier, ed.
Stefan Weinfurter with Hubertus Seibert, 217–44. Sigmaringen: Jan Thorbecke,
1991.

Sullivan, Lawrence E. "Sound and Senses: Toward a Hermeneutics of Performance."
History of Religions 26 (1986): 1–33.

Supino Martini, Paola. "La produzione libraria negli 'scriptoria' delle abbazie di
Farfa e di S. Eutizio." In *Il ducato di Spoleto: Atti del IX Congresso internazionale
di studi sull'alto medioevo, Spoleto, 27 settembre–2 ottobre 1982,* 581–607. Spoleto:
Centro italiano per lo studio dell'alto medioevo, 1983.

——. "'Manuum mearum labore': Nota sulle 'chartae rescriptae' Farfensi."
Scrittura e civiltà 8 (1984): 83–103.

——. *Roma e l'area grafica romanesca, secoli X–XII.* Alessandria: Edizioni
dell'Orso, 1987.

Susi, Eugenio. "L'agiografia picena tra l'Oriente e Farfa." In *Agiografia e culto dei
santi,* ed. Menestò, 57–84.

——. "I culti farfensi nel secolo VIII." In *Santi e culti nel Lazio,* ed. Boesch Gajano
and Petrucci, 61–81.

——. "Strategie agiografiche altomedievali in un leggendario di Farfa."
Cristianesimo nella storia 18 (1997): 277–302.

Symons, Thomas. "A Note on *Trina Oratio.*" *Downside Review* 42 (1924): 67–83.

Taft, Robert. *The Liturgy of the Hours in East and West,* 2nd rev. ed. Collegeville,
MN: Liturgical Press, 1993.

Tambiah, Stanley. "A Performative Approach to Ritual." *Proceedings of the British
Academy* 65 (1979): 113–69.

Tappi-Cesarini, Anselmo. "Note sul reclutamento del 'conventus Pharphensis' dal
1048 al 1567." *Benedictina* 3 (1949): 307–30.

*Teaching Medieval Lyric with Modern Technology: New Windows on the Medieval
World.* A CD-ROM application supported by the National Endowment for the
Humanities and Mount Holyoke College. Margaret Switten, director. Robert
Eisenstein, production coordinator. South Hadley, MA: Mount Holyoke
College, 2001.

Toesca, Pietro. "Un cimelio amalfitano." *Bollettino d'arte* 27 (1933–34): 537–42.

Tolhurst, John Basil Lowder. *Introduction to the English Monastic Breviaries.* Henry
Bradshaw Society 80. Reprint of *The Monastic Breviary of Hyde Abbey,* vol. 6,
London: Harrison, 1942. Woodbridge, UK: Boydell, 1993.

Toubert, Hélène. *Un art dirigé: Réforme grégorienne et iconographie*. Paris: Editions du Cerf, 1990.

———. "Contribution à l'iconographie des psautiers: Le commentaire des psaumes d'Odon d'Asti, illustré à l'abbaye de Farfa." *Mélanges de l'École Française de Rome: Moyen Âge, Temps Modernes* 88 (1976): 581–619.

Toubert, Pierre. *Les structures du Latium médiéval: Le Latium méridional et la Sabine du IXe siècle à la fin du XIIe siècle*. 2 vols. Bibliothèque des Écoles françaises d'Athènes et de Rome, 221. Rome: École française de Rome, 1973.

Treitler, Leo. "The 'Unwritten' and 'Written Transmission' of Medieval Chant and the Start-up of Musical Notation." *Journal of Musicology* 10 (1992): 131–91.

Tutsch, Burkhardt. "Die Rezeptionsgeschichte der Consuetudines Bernhards und Ulrichs von Cluny im Spiegel ihrer handschriftlichen Überlieferung." *Frühmittelalterliche Studien* 30 (1996): 248–93.

———. *Studien zur Rezeptionsgechichte der Consuetudines Ulrichs von Cluny*. Vita Regularis 6. Münster: LIT, 1998.

———. "Texttradition und Praxis von *consuetudines* und *statuta* in der Cluniacensis ecclesia (10.–12. Jahrhundert)." In *Vom Kloster zum Klosterverband: Das Werkzeug der Schriftlichkeit*, ed. Hagen Keller and Franz Neiske, 173–205. Münstersche Mittelalter-Schriften 74. Munich: Wilhelm Fink, 1997.

———. "Zur Rezeptionsgeschichte der Consuetudines Bernards und Ulrichs von Cluny." In *Schriftlichkeit und Lebenspraxis im Mittelalter: Erfassen, Bewahren, Verändern*, ed. Hagen Keller, Christel Meier, and Thomas Scharff, 79–94. Münstersche Mittelalter-Schriften 76. Munich: Wilhelm Fink, 1999.

Uhlirz, Mathilde. "Die italienische Kirchenpolitik der Ottonen." *Mitteilungen des Österreichischen Instituts für Geschichtforschung* 48 (1934): 246–52.

Van Dijk, Stephen Joseph Peter. "Saint Bernard and the *Instituta Patrum* of Saint Gall." *Musica Disciplina* 4 (1950): 99–109.

Vogtherr, Thomas. *Die Reichsabteien der Benediktiner und das Königtum im hohen Mittelalter (900–1125)*. Stuttgart: Thorbecke, 2000.

Waddell, Chrysogonus, ed. *The Twelfth-Century Cistercian Hymnal*. Trappist, KY: Gethsemani Abbey, 1984.

Wälli, Siliva. *Melodien aus mittelalterlichen Horaz-Handschriften: Edition und Interpretation der Quellen*. Monumenta Monodica Medii Aevi, Subsidia 3. Kassel: Bärenreiter, 2002.

Ward, John. "The Monastic Historiographical Impulse, c. 1000–1260: A Re-assessment." In *Historia: The Concept and Genres in the Middle Ages*, ed. Tuomas M. S. Lehtonen and Päivi Mehtonen, 71–100. Commentationes humanarum litterarum 116. Helsinki: Societas Scientiarum Fennica, 2000.

Warner, David. "Ideals and Action in the Reign of Otto III." *Journal of Medieval History* 25 (1999): 1–18.

———. "Ritual and Memory in the Ottonian *Reich*: The Ceremony of Adventus." *Speculum* 76 (2001): 255–83.

——. "Thietmar of Merseburg on Rituals of Kingship." *Viator* 26 (1995): 53–76.

Weinfurter, Stefan. *Heinrich II (1002–1014): Herrscher am Ende der Zeiten.* Regensburg: Pustet, 1999.

——. *The Salian Century: Main Currents in an Age of Transition.* Trans. Barbara M. Bowlus. Philadelphia: University of Pennsylvania Press, 1999.

White, Stephen D. *Custom, Kinship, and Gifts to Saints: The Laudatio Parentum in Western France, 1050–1150.* Chapel Hill: University of North Carolina Press, 1988.

Wickham, Chris. *Il problema dell'incastellamento nell'Italia centrale: L'esempio di San Vincenzo al Volturno.* Florence: all'Insegno del Giglio, 1985.

——."A che serve l'incastellamento?" In *Incastellamento: Actes des Rencontres de Gérone (26–27 novembre 1992) et de Rome (5–7 mai 1994),* ed. Miquel Barceló and Pierre Toubert, 31–41. Rome: École française de Rome and Escuela española de historia y arqueología en Roma, 1998.

——. "The *Terra* of San Vincenzo al Volturno in the 8th to 12th centuries: The historical framework." In *San Vincenzo al Volturno: The Archaeology, Art and Territory of an Early Medieval Monastery,* ed. Richard Hodges and John Mitchell, 227–58. BAR International Series 252. Oxford: British Archaeological Reports, 1985.

Willmes, Peter. *Der Herrscher-'Adventus' in Kloster des Frühmittelalters.* Münstersche Mittelalter-Schriften 22. Munich: Wilhelm Fink, 1976.

Wilmart, André. "Cluny (Manuscrits liturgiques de)." In *Dictionnaire d'archéologie chrétienne et de liturgie* IV.2:2074–92. Paris: Letouzey et Ané, 1914.

——. "Prières médiévales pour l'adoration de la Croix." *Ephemerides liturgicae* 48 (1932): 22–65.

——. "Le recueil des poèmes et des prières de saint Pierre Damien." *Revue Bénédictine* 41 (1929): 342–57.

Wirth, Jean. "La représentation de l'image dans l'art du haut moyen âge." *Revue de l'Art* 79 (1988): 9–21.

Wollasch, Joachim. "Zur Datierung des *Liber tramitis* aus Farfa anhand von Personen und Personengruppen." In *Person und Gemeinschaft im Mittelalter: Karl Schmid zum fünfundsechzigsten Geburtstag,* ed. Gerd Althoff and others, 237–55. Sigmaringen: Jan Thorbecke, 1988.

Yates, Frances. *The Art of Memory.* Chicago: University of Chicago Press, 1966.

Zelzer, Klaus. "Von Benedikt zu Hildemar: Zu Textgestalt und Textgeschichte der Regula Benedicti auf ihrem Weg zur Alleingeltung." *Frühmittelalterliche Studien* 23 (1989): 112–30.

Zielinski, Wilhelm. "Gregor von Catino und das *Regestum* Farfense." *Quellen und Forschungen aus italienischen Archiven und Bibliotheken* 55–56 (1976): 361–404.

——. *Studien zu den spoletinischen Privaturkunden des 8. Jahrhunderts und ihrer Überlieferung im Regestum Farfense.* Tubingen: Niemeyer, 1972.

Ziolkowski, Jan. "*Nota Bene:* Why the Classics Were Neumed in the Middle Ages." *Journal of Medieval Latin* 10 (2000): 74–114.

———. *Nota Bene: Reading Classics and Writing Songs in the Early Middle Ages.* Publications of the Journal of Medieval Latin. Turnhout: Brepols, forthcoming.

———. "Women's Lament and the Neuming of the Classics." In *Music and Medieval Manuscripts: Paleography and Performance; Essays Dedicated to Andrew Hughes,* ed. John Haines and Randall Rosenfeld, 128–50. Aldershot, UK: Ashgate, 2004.

GENERAL INDEX

Page numbers in italics indicate illustrations; figure numbers in italics indicate illustrations that appear in the color insert within Chapter 4.

Consuetudines antiquiores of Cluny, 90, 118, 122 n75

Corbet, Patrick, 149

S. Cosimato, Rome, 10 n45, 134

Crescenzio family, 13, 135

S. Crisogono, Rome, 159 n66

Cross
  Adoration of, 65, 89, 98–101
  and Henry II, 105, 162–66, 231
  hymn to, 162–66
  prayers to, 98–104, 163, 231
  relics, 102–3, 165
  theology of, 102, 105

crosses
  pectoral, 101–2
  processional, 104–5, 166
  reliquary, 102–3

crucifixes, 102

crypt, Farfa, abbey church, 197–98, 202

Cum sederit Filius hominis, 128–29, 242

customaries, 16, 90–91, 107, 109, 121–22.
    See also Liber tramitis; Bernard of
    Cluny; Ulrich of Zell

Damian, Peter. *See* Peter Damian

dead, commemoration of, 5, 17, 25, 87,
    108–9, 114, 122, 144–48, 150, 165–68

death ritual, 135–43

dedication of a church, 17, 36–39, 196–97

Delogu, Paolo, 212

dependencies. *See* priories

Desiderius, abbot of Montecassino, 172

Desiderius, Lombard king, 6

Destructio farfensis, 8 n31, 9, 195, 199, 231

Dinter, Peter, 119, 121, 124–25

Dodo, bishop of Rieti, 196–97

donations, 5, 31, 144–48

Dormition of the Virgin, 155–56, *169,*
    170–71, 173

doxa, 181–83

dreams, 26–28, 30–31, 207, 209, 211, 213

Dyer, Joseph, 86

Ecce mitto angelum meum, 127–28, 131

Ecclesia cluniacensis, 107, 112

election of abbots, 10, 14, 23, 25, 119–21,
    215–16, 228

emunitas see immunity

Entry into Jerusalem, 156–57

Epiphany, 160

S. Eustachio, Rome, 10 n45, 134

Euticius, Saint, 159 n134, 209

S. Eutizio, Norcia, 59, 208–9

evangelistary, 153–54

Exaltation of the Cross, 13, 105 n123, 135

exegesis, 36, 64–70, 80–86

exemption, 106

Exultet, 174–81, 231

familiar psalms. *See Psalmi familiares*

Faroald II, Lombard Duke of Spoleto, 6

Fassler, Margot, 53

Feller, Laurent, 33

foundation legends, monastic, 214
  of Farfa, 35–41
  of S. Vincenzo al Volturno, 209–14

Frederick Barbarossa, 14, 229

frescoes *see* church, Farfa Abbey (paint-
    ing, wall)

Fruttuaria, 10 n43, 109

Fulbert of Chartres, 53, 74

Galilea, 114, 123

S. Gall, 48, 153

Garrison, Edward B., 153

Geary, Patrick, 16, 195

Getulius, Saint, 159, 205–6

Ghent, S. Bavo, 114

gifts, 144–48

Giorgi, Ignazio, 40

Gisulf I, Lombard Duke of Benevento,
    207, 211–13

S. Giulia, Brescia, 192 n24

Glaber, Radulfus, 27–28, 107–9, 112

Gloria, 181–83

MANUSCRIPTS CITED